Frédéric Godet

Commentary on St. Paul's First Epistle to the Corinthians

Vol. 01

Frédéric Godet

Commentary on St. Paul's First Epistle to the Corinthians
Vol. 01

ISBN/EAN: 9783337728885

Printed in Europe, USA, Canada, Australia, Japan

Cover: Foto ©Lupo / pixelio.de

More available books at **www.hansebooks.com**

CLARK'S

FOREIGN

THEOLOGICAL LIBRARY.

NEW SERIES.
VOL. XXVII.

Godet on St. Paul's First Epistle to the Corinthians.
VOL. I.

EDINBURGH:
T. & T. CLARK, 38 GEORGE STREET.

COMMENTARY

ON

ST. PAUL'S

FIRST EPISTLE TO THE CORINTHIANS.

BY

F. GODET,

DOCTOR OF THEOLOGY, PROFESSOR OF THE FACULTY OF THE INDEPENDENT
CHURCH OF NEUCHATEL.

Translated from the French

BY REV. A. CUSIN, M.A., EDINBURGH.

VOLUME FIRST.

EDINBURGH:
T. & T. CLARK, 38 GEORGE STREET.
1889

[*This Translation is copyright, by arrangement with the Author.*]

PREFACE.

In publishing this new Commentary, I do not feel altogether free from anxiety. The welcome given to its elder brothers encourages me, it is true; but the apostolic book explained in these pages is so practical in its nature, and consequently touches on so many existing religious phenomena, that it is difficult to avoid drawing certain parallels which may injure the objectivity of the work. Then the commentator's responsibility increases the more the results which he obtains are fitted to exercise a direct influence on the solution of questions which are now occupying the Church. And so I am specially constrained to ask God to avert every hurtful consequence that might flow from errors I may have committed in interpreting this important book, and to say to my readers, like the apostle himself, but in a sense slightly different from his: "Judge yourselves what I say."

I shall only add a word of explanation in regard to the fixing of the text. I have been charged more than once in England with my *defective criticism* on this point, which, if I am not mistaken, means at bottom that I am wrong in not fully adhering to the critical theory and practice of Westcott and Hort. I respect and admire as much as any one the immense labour of these two critics; but it is impossible for me to accept without reserve the result at which they have arrived. Exegesis has too often convinced me of the mistakes of the *Sinaïticus* and *Vaticanus*, taken separately or even together, to allow me to give myself up with eyes bandaged to these manuscripts, as the esteemed authors whom I have just named think themselves bound to do. I shall call the attention of my readers to three passages only in our Epistle, where the faultiness of the text of the documents, which are called neuter or Alexandrine or both, seems to me manifest; they are: iv. 1, ix. 10, and xiii. 3. In these cases, as in many others, it seems to me that healthy criticism dares not sacrifice exegetical sound sense to the transcription of two copyists of the fourth century, who are so often found in the wrong. Besides, I cannot possibly believe that a man like Chrysostom could, by adopting in full and without scruple the Syrian or Byzantine text, blindly give the preference to a work of quite recent compilation, and the authority of which found no support in earlier documents.

I hope that the second volume may appear in a few months. May this work contribute somewhat to the glory of the Lord and to the good of His Church!

F. GODET.

NEUCHATEL.

CONTENTS.

	PAGE
INTRODUCTION,	1–35
CHAP. I. The Founding of the Church of Corinth,	4
CHAP. II. The External Circumstances in which the Epistle was composed,	11
CHAP. III. The Events which took place at Corinth in the Interval between the Founding of the Church and the Composition of the Epistle,	17
CHAP. IV. Plan of the Epistle,	27

COMMENTARY.

PREFACE (I. 1–9)—The Address (i. 1–3),	37–60

BODY OF THE EPISTLE (I. 10–XV. 58).

I. The Parties in the Church of Corinth (i. 10–iv. 21),	61–238
1. Statement of the Fact and its Summary Condemnation (i. 10–17),	61
2. Nature of the Gospel (i. 18–iii. 4),	89
3. The True Nature of the Christian Ministry (iii. 5–iv. 5),	171
4. Pride the First Cause of the Evil (iv. 6–21),	214
II. Discipline (chap. v.),	239
III. Lawsuits (vi. 1–11),	283
IV. Impurity (vi. 12–20),	302
V. Marriage and Celibacy (chap. vii.),	315
VI. The Use of Meats offered to Idols, and Participation in the Sacrificial Feasts (Chaps. viii.–x.),	401

INTRODUCTION.

A QUITE peculiar interest attaches to the correspondence of St. Paul with the Church of Corinth. Having founded the Church himself and lived in the heart of it for nearly two years, he had not to expound *his gospel* to it in writing, as to the Church of Rome. But he was called by particular circumstances to complete his teaching on various points, and especially to combat certain corruptions which had arisen or which threatened to force their way into the life of the Church. Our two Epistles to the Corinthians were thus the product of special circumstances, local and temporary. This is the reason why an eminent critic, Weizsäcker, has called them: "A fragment of ecclesiastical history like no other."

It might be concluded from the purely occasional character of these two Epistles that they belong to a past which no more concerns us, and consequently have no longer for us a present religious value. Even if it were so, would it not be something to be transported by them into the full ecclesiastical life of the earliest times, and to stand by, as it were, and witness the crises through which the new converts of eighteen centuries ago had to pass? But the interest excited by these Epistles goes much further and deeper. The heart of man remains the same throughout all ages. The experiences of the apostolic Christians do not differ essentially from those through which we pass ourselves. This observation is especially true in regard to the Church of Corinth. For it is not here, as in Galatia, against Jewish prejudices that the apostle has mainly to contend, at least in the First Epistle. In Achaia we witness the first contact of the gospel with Hellenic life, so richly endowed and brilliant, but, on the other hand, so frivolous and fickle, and in so many respects resembling our modern life. In particular, the tendency to make religious truths the subjects of intellectual study rather than a work of conscience and of heart-acceptance, the disposition resulting therefrom, not always to place the moral conduct under the influence of religious conviction, and to give scope to the latter rather in oratorical discourse than in vigour of holiness,—these are defects which more than one modern nation shares in common with the Greek people. And the question is whether the apostle, after having drawn from the gospel, as the Lord had revealed it to him (Gal. i. 11, 12), the word of emancipation fitted to free the conscience from the Mosaic yoke, will find in it also the power necessary to check Gentile licence and lead the will captive to the law of holiness, without relapsing into the use of legal forms.

But what gives the liveliest interest to the questions raised by the state of the Church of Corinth, is the manner in which the apostle discusses and resolves them. In treating each particular matter submitted to his judgment, the apostle does not stop at the surface; he endeavours to penetrate to the very root of those various manifestations. Instead of summarily settling the questions as by the article of a code, he searches the depths of the gospel for the permanent principle which applies to the passing phenomenon, so that to judge of the analogous manifestations and tendencies of our day, we have only ourselves to fall back from the practical rule with which he closes each of those discussions on the evangelical principle from which he drew it, that in our turn we may apply this principle to the contemporary phenomenon with which we have to do. There is no exercise at once more stimulating to the understanding and more fitted to form the Christian conscience than this. By the Epistle to the Romans, we know St. Paul as a teacher; in that to the Galatians he appears as the consummate polemic and dialectician; we learn to know him in the First Epistle to the Corinthians in his character of apostolical pastor and casuist, taking the latter word in its best sense.

Finally, another kind of interest is awakened in us by the study of this letter. M. Renan says of St. Paul: "He had not the patience needed for writing; he was incapable of method." These summary judgments are law with many, and are eagerly repeated by superficial writers. We shall have occasion very particularly, in the study of this Epistle, to put this judgment to the proof. The question of method presented itself in this case in a more difficult way than in any other. When the apostle had to develop a side of Christian truth, his course was marked out for him by the subject itself and by the logical form of his thought. Here there is nothing of the kind. St. Paul finds himself face to face with a certain number of particular practical questions, without any direct relation to one another. The matters in question include divisions, scandals, trials at law, marriage and celibacy, meats offered in sacrifice, the behaviour of women in public worship, love feasts, the resurrection, and we ask, not without curiosity, whether his mind will succeed in commanding this multiplicity of subjects and arranging them rationally, so that here, as well as elsewhere, he will leave the impression of order and unity.

In the introduction to the Epistle to the Romans, I have treated of the life of St. Paul in general; I shall not return to it here. Four subjects will occupy us :

1. The founding of the Church of Corinth.

2. The external circumstances in which our first canonical Epistle was addressed to it.

3. The events which had supervened since the founding of the Church and which gave occasion to this letter

4. The arrangement adopted by the apostle in the order and grouping of the subjects to be treated.

CHAPTER I.

THE FOUNDING OF THE CHURCH.

It was, if we are not mistaken, about the autumn of the year 52, shortly after the assembly called the Council of Jerusalem, that Paul set out from Antioch with Silas to make a second missionary journey. They first visited the Churches of Lycaonia and Pisidia, founded by Paul and Barnabas, in the course of their first journey. Then, according to all probability, they proclaimed the gospel in the province of Galatia, situated more to the north, and, crossing Asia Minor from east to west without being permitted by the Spirit to preach in it, they reached the shore of the Egean Sea, at Troas, and there, with the young Timothy, whom they had associated with them in Lycaonia, and the physician Luke, already no doubt a Christian, whom they met in this city, they embarked for Macedonia. After founding the Church in the two principal cities of that province, Philippi and Thessalonica, Paul set out alone for southern Greece, and repaired first to Athens, then to Corinth, the capital of the province of Achaia. He was soon afterwards rejoined in the latter city by his two fellow-labourers, Silas and Timothy, and he remained there with them for about two years.

Destroyed by the Romans in 146 B.C., it was nearly a century since Corinth had risen from its ruins. In the year 44 Julius Cæsar had rebuilt it and peopled it with numerous colonists, mostly Roman freedmen; these had been joined by a certain population of Greeks, and shortly afterwards by a Jewish colony. At the time when the apostle arrived in it, the city counted from six to seven hundred thousand inhabitants, of whom two hundred thousand were freemen and four hundred thousand slaves. It had a circuit of a league and a half. This immense and rapid growth, which compares with that of certain cities in the United States of America, was due above all to its situation on the isthmus which bears its name, and which, connecting the Peloponnesus with the continent, separated the Egean and Ionian seas. Corinth possessed two principal ports, that of Cenchrea, opening to the east, and that of Lechæum, to the west. It had quickly become the great emporium of commerce between Asia and the west. So speedily had this city, which was formerly called "the light and ornament of Greece," recovered its ancient splendour. On the summit of its Acropolis shone the temple of Venus, of incomparable magnificence. Corinth possessed all the means of culture then enjoyed by the capitals of the civilized world, workshops and studios, halls of rhetoric and schools of philosophy. An ancient historian says that one could not take a step in the streets of Corinth without meeting a sage.

But here, as elsewhere and still more, corruption of morals had proceeded step by step with the development of culture and riches. The mixture of heterogeneous elements composing the population of new Corinth had no doubt contributed to produce this state of things. One word tells all. By the term κορινθιάζειν, *to live as a Corinthian*, men designated a kind of life which was absolutely dissolute. The phrases *Corinthian banquet*, *Corinthian drinker*, were proverbial.

It was in the midst of this society, in a state of full outward prosperity, but also of complete moral dissolution, that the quickening salt of the gospel was now to fall with the arrival of St. Paul, twenty-four years after the Ascension of the Lord Jesus.

If Paul, at the time of his conversion, about the year 37, was thirty years old at least, he must have been approaching the fifties on the day when he entered Corinth. Let us imagine the apostle, making his solitary entry as a simple workman, into the great city. His profession was that either of a tent-weaver or tent-carpenter; the term tent-maker (Acts xviii. 3) admits of both significations. The second, however, seems the more probable. The apostle was not long in discovering a Jewish family who followed the same trade as himself; they had just arrived from Rome, in consequence of an edict of the Emperor Claudius banishing the Jews from the capital. He joined them, and while sharing their work, gained them for his faith. Some have held that Aquila and Priscilla were already believers on their arrival. This supposition is contrary to the terms of the narrative ("a certain *Jew* named Aquila"); it has no other object than to furnish support to the idea of the existence of a Judeo-Christian Church at that period among the Jews of Rome.

The narrative of the Acts shows us the apostle beginning his work at Corinth in the midst of the Jewish colony. This narrative has been recently relegated to the domain of fable.[1] For what reasons? Paul, says Heinrici, would never have been so imprudent, as by his preaching of the gospel, needlessly to brave the anger of the synagogue, whose insurmountable prejudices he knew. But, though Paul certainly did not flatter himself that he would convert all the members of the synagogue, he could hope to gain at least some of the better disposed, and

---

[1] Heinrici, *Erklärung der Corintherbriefe*, 1880, i. p. 7 seq.; Holsten, *das Evangelium des Paulus*, 1881, i. p. 186.

to find in them the solid nucleus of the society of believers which he desired to form at Corinth. He knew well it was not in vain that God had paved the way for the preaching of the gospel in the Gentile world by the dispersion of the people of Israel, and that this was the door providentially opened for the proclamation of the good news in the midst of heathendom. The manner in which the foundation of the Church in general had taken place by the preaching of the apostles among the Jewish people, prior to any mission to the Gentiles, was a guide to him as to the method to be followed in founding the Church in every heathen city in particular. It was on this principle that Paul had proceeded with Barnabas on his first mission in Asia Minor (Acts xiii. 14 seq., xiv. 1 seq.); it was thus he had continued with Silas in his second, at Philippi (Acts xvi. 13 seq.), at Thessalonica (xvii. 1 seq.), at Berea (v. 10 seq.). He himself positively declares (Rom. i. 16: "to the Jews *first*, then to the Greeks") that this procedure was not accidental, but rested on a deliberate conviction. Why should he not have remained faithful to it at Corinth? The narrative of the Acts is therefore not in the least open to suspicion on this point, and if this initial preaching in the synagogue were not expressly recorded, we should have to suppose it. Holsten raises another objection. If Paul had begun among the Jews of the synagogue, why should he have been intimidated even to trembling, according to his own description, ii. 1–5? Was he not accustomed to this kind of hearers? But when the apostle arrived at Corinth, he knew well that if he came there with the intention of addressing the

Jews first, he did not come solely or even mainly for them. He had before him the spectacle of that great Greek capital, and felt himself charged alone, at least in those first days, with the responsibility of the Divine message which he carried. He was not unaware that even in the synagogue he would meet a select body of proselytes belonging to every class of Corinthian society, and that the time was not far off when it would be among these latter especially, and the entire Greek population, that he would have to deliver his message. It was the first time he found himself in such a situation, if we except the case of his preaching at Athens, the result of which was not fitted to encourage him. Face to face with such audiences, he had no longer the support which was afforded him before Jews by the law and the prophets; and, on the other hand, he was resolved not to have recourse to the modes of action generally used in public conferences, brilliance of oratorical art, dialectic skill, profound speculation. There remained to him only one force— and his grandest act of faith was to wish no other— the simple testimony rendered to Christ and His Cross; the Divine fact itself expounded without art, and, if one may so speak, in its nakedness. If we put ourselves in the apostle's place at this point of his career, we can understand the feeling of powerlessness and anxiety which overwhelmed him at the outset of his ministry in this city. Far from our finding therein anything fitted to raise a doubt of the circumspection with which he proceeded in addressing himself first to the Jews, it may be said that this prudent step was imposed on him by the very anxiety which he felt.

Paul then preached for some weeks in the synagogue. But soon, seeing the exasperation of his Jewish adversaries increase to such a degree that it was no longer possible to labour usefully in this sphere, he established himself with the believers, Jews and proselytes, in a neighbouring house belonging to one of his Jewish converts, and from that time he preached especially to Gentiles, not clothing the salvation of Christ either with the charms of eloquence, or with the attraction of human wisdom, so that if his preaching exercised a powerful influence, it was solely through the Divine working which accompanied it, and, as the apostle says, by the demonstration of Spirit and of power. Hearts seriously disposed were laid hold of in their depths, really gained. A church formed of a certain number of Jews, and "of a great multitude of Gentiles," rose in the midst of this city of business and debauchery. The majority of its members did not belong to the upper, rich, cultivated classes (1 Cor. i. 26–28); they were for the most part poor, slaves, people despised for their ignorance and their low social condition. But the work was only the more solid; it was not mingled with human alloy. There were only so many wounded consciences which the power of God had healed and restored.

For nearly two years (Acts xviii. 11, 18), Paul continued to sow this fruitful soil, living by the labour of his hands, sometimes also on the help which was sent him by the churches recently founded in Macedonia (2 Cor. xi. 7–9, xii. 13–15). The proconsul of Achaia resided at Corinth; at that time Gallio, the brother of the philosopher Seneca. He is known by his correspondence with his brother; he was an equitable man, and full of urbanity. He showed himself such toward St. Paul, when the latter was dragged by the Jews before his tribunal. Thus this first sojourn of Paul at Corinth closed in peace. Paul left this city about Pentecost of the year 54 to go to Jerusalem, and thence to Antioch, where he thought of making only a short stay. His plans for the future were formed. Between the two domains where he had broken ground in his two first journeys lay the western portion of Asia Minor, the rich and interesting country of ancient Ionia, then called the province of Asia, with Ephesus for its capital; there it was that he now felt himself called to labour. On his departure from Corinth, he was accompanied by Aquila and Priscilla, who were to await him at Ephesus, and to prepare the way for him in this new field of labour.

CHAPTER II.

THE EXTERNAL CIRCUMSTANCES IN WHICH THE EPISTLE WAS COMPOSED.

WE have not to discuss at length the authenticity of the First Epistle to the Corinthians, against which no serious objection has ever been raised. Its composition by St. Paul appears with great evidence from the letter itself; and first from the testimony of its author (i. 1), as well as from the manner in which he speaks of himself as founder of the Church (iv. 15 *et al.*). In confirmation of this testimony, Schleiermacher has brought out the relation between the historical details of our Epistle and those contained in the book of Acts. "When we compare," says this theologian,[1] "many passages of the Acts (chaps. xviii.–xx.) with the personal details which begin and close the two Epistles to the Corinthians, everything fits in, all is perfectly complete, and that nevertheless in such a way that each of the documents follows its own course, and the facts contained in the one cannot be borrowed from those of the other." But these coincidences of detail are a still less striking proof than is the picture, so living and real, which the letters give us of the state of a primitive Christian Church. The following is Baur's[2] impression on this point: Our First Epistle carries the seal of its authenticity in itself; for, "more than any other writing of the New Testament, it transports us into the living centre of a Christian Church in formation, and procures for us a view of the circumstances through which the development of the new life evoked by Christianity had to pass." Beet (*Commentary*) also brings out forcibly the proof of authenticity contained in the very severe and humiliating rebukes addressed to the Church of Corinth in these two letters. No Church would so easily and without a rigorous investigation have accepted and preserved "the monument of its degradation."

These internal evidences are confirmed by the testimony of *tradition*. So early as about the end of the first century, Clement of Rome, in his letter to the Corinthians, quotes our Epistle several times. The

---

[1] *Einleitung in das N. T.*, p. 148.
[2] Baur, *Der Apostel Paulus*, 1st edit. p. 260.

passage of chap. xlvii. is particularly remarkable : " Take up again the Epistle of the blessed Apostle Paul : what did he write to you in the outset, at the beginning of the preaching of the gospel? Verily, he gave you spiritual directions as well about himself as about Cephas and Apollos, because even then ye were giving yourselves up to preferences." It does not seem to us to admit of question that when Ignatius, in his Epistle to the Ephesians, chap. xviii., calls the cross " a stumbling-block to unbelievers," and exclaims, " Where is the wise, where is the disputer ? " he is reproducing the terms of our Epistle. The same is the case with Polycarp, in his Epistle to the Philippians, chap. v., the enumeration which he makes of the vicious is exactly parallel to that of 1 Cor. vi. 9, 10, and he closes it also by declaring that such believers " shall not inherit the kingdom of God." In the homily commonly called *the Second Epistle of Clement*, and which must have been written in Greece between 120 and 140, we find these words taken from the first chapter of our Epistle : " It pleased Him to make us to be of that which is not." It would be useless to pursue this list of testimonies in detail. We should have to mention, probably, Justin Martyr, *Dialogue*, chap. xiv. (" the old leaven " and " the unleavened bread "; comp. 1 Cor. v. 8) and chap. iii. (" Christ our Passover ") ; more certainly the *Epistle to Diognetus*, filled with thoughts drawn from our Epistle ; probably also the *Doctrine of the Twelve Apostles* (between 120 and 160), where there are thought to be some allusions to 1 Cor. (Gebhardt, Edwards) ; very certainly the *Fragment of Muratori*; Athenagoras, Theophilus ; finally, Irenæus,

Clement of Alexandria, and Tertullian. I refer readers who desire to be more exactly informed on this point to Charteris, *Canonicity*, 222–229.

What really concerns us is to fix the time and place in the apostle's life at which he composed this letter; and the task is not difficult.

The *place* of composition can be no other than Ephesus. "I will tarry," says the apostle, "at Ephesus till Pentecost; for a great door is opened unto me" (xvi. 8, 9). It is not clear at the first glance how, in view of so positive a text, the subscription of the Epistle in a certain number of manuscripts, as well as in many of our translations, can be thus stated: "The First Epistle to the Corinthians was written from Philippi." It is probable that this account arises from the ignorant or superficial reading of xvi. 5: "For I do pass through Macedonia." It was not understood that the present *I do pass* referred, not to a present fact, but to the journey as planned by the apostle. It was obvious, however, that if Paul was already in Macedonia, he must have sent salutations from the Churches of this province, and not from those of Asia, as he does in ver. 19. In this same verse there is likewise found the salutation of Aquila and Priscilla, who, as we have seen, had gone with Paul to settle at Ephesus. The subscription in the *Vaticanus* is accurate: "*was written from Ephesus.*"

The entire stay of Paul at Ephesus lasted about three years (Acts xx. 31). Our concern is to know at what time of this sojourn we must place the composition of our letter. On this point we have several clear enough indications:

1st. The words we have just quoted prove that Paul's stay in Asia was drawing to a close.

2nd. At the time when Paul was composing this letter, he had Apollos beside him, who had returned from Corinth (xvi. 12). Now, this Alexandrine teacher, converted at Ephesus by Aquila and Priscilla shortly after their arrival in that city, and before that of Paul (Acts xviii. 24, 26), had gone thence to Achaia with a recommendation from Aquila to continue the work of Paul there, and had exercised a very influential ministry, after which he had returned to Ephesus. This all supposes a considerable time to have elapsed since Paul's arrival at Ephesus, and so brings us to an advanced period of his sojourn in that city.

3rd. We read Acts xix. 21, that after labouring two years and three months at Ephesus (vers. 8, 10), Paul formed in his mind vast designs. He meditated bidding a final adieu to the East and consecrating the remainder of his life to the West. But before proceeding to Rome he felt bound to visit Jerusalem once more, and to offer the Church of that city a solemn testimony of love and spiritual fellowship from all the Churches founded by him among the Gentiles. He therefore determined, according to Acts xix. 22, to send Timothy and Erastus from Ephesus to make preparation in Macedonia and Achaia for the execution of his project. Now this sending of Timothy to Corinth coincides perfectly with that which is twice mentioned in our First Epistle (iv. 17; xvi. 10). It took place at the time when the apostle was composing it, and shortly before his setting out, for in it Paul announces the sending of his young fellow-labourer as an already accomplished fact.

4th. This great collection for which Timothy was to prepare, and which is expressly mentioned, xvi. 1, and 2 Cor. viii. and ix., can only be that with which the apostle closed his ministry in the East, and of which he speaks in the two passages, Rom. xv. 24, 33, and Acts xxiv. 17. Here is a new indication which again brings us to the same date.

As it is impossible for all these reasons to suppose a date previous to the circumstances mentioned, it is no less so to suppose a later one. In fact, at the time when the apostle writes, he is yet freely disposing of his person. But it is well known that shortly after, when he had delivered the sum collected into the hands of the leaders of the flock at Jerusalem, he was thrown into prison, and from that time remained a prisoner for a long course of years.

If the sojourn of Paul in Asia, by the time when our letter was written, had lasted about two years and three months (Acts xix. 8, 10), dating from the end of the year 54 when Paul arrived at Ephesus, it was composed in the spring of the year 57, before the Pentecost of that year, probably at the time of the feast of Passover to which there seems to be an allusion in the passage v. 7, 8. We shall afterwards see how the indication of Acts xx. 31 is to be explained, according to which the stay at Ephesus lasted three entire years.

CHAPTER III.

THE EVENTS WHICH TOOK PLACE AT CORINTH IN THE INTERVAL BETWEEN THE FOUNDING OF THE CHURCH AND THE COMPOSITION OF THE EPISTLE.

WE have here to enumerate a series of facts which it is indispensable to know if we are to understand our Epistle, but in regard to which we have almost no information except from the Epistle itself. It is one of the most striking examples of the legitimate influence which exegesis and criticism have to exercise on one another.

1. The first fact known to us which modified the state of the Church of Corinth after the departure of its founder, was the ministry of the Alexandrine teacher Apollos. We possess two testimonies of the influence exercised at Corinth by this eloquent preacher,—the one, the first four chapters of our Epistle, the other, the end of chap. xviii. of Acts. "He helped much through grace," it is said in the latter passage, "them which had believed: for he disputed powerfully with the Jews, and that publicly, showing by the Scriptures that Jesus was the Christ." From this passage it follows that the ministry of Apollos must have brought about a double change in the state of the Church. Powerful in the interpretation of the Scriptures, Apollos gained to the gospel a very large number of Jews, evidently of those who had withstood the ministry of St. Paul. The propoition between the two elements of which the young Church was composed was thus modified to the

B

advantage of the Jewish element. It is probable, moreover, that while the Jewish minority was increased through the labours of Apollos, a certain number of Gentiles belonging to the lettered class were attracted by the oratorical talent and brilliant gifts of the young teacher. Only it is natural to suppose that the conversion of these newcomers did not proceed from such profound conscience-work as that which had led the most of the former converts to baptism. The wants of the understanding and imagination had, in many cases, more to do with their adherence than those of the heart and conscience.

2. Besides the visit of Apollos, must we hold the arrival at Corinth of a still more important personage, the Apostle Peter? In the passage chap. i. 12 mention is made of a party of Cephas, which is placed after that of Apollos. Are we to regard this as an indication of a stay made by this apostle in Achaia at this period? Such a fact seems far from probable. In the year 54 we find Peter at Antioch (Gal. ii.). No doubt, in the course of the three years which followed down to the spring of the year 57, he might have gone from Syria to Achaia. But there is no reason to suppose that Peter turned so early toward the west; and it would be difficult to understand how our Epistle, which bears such evident traces of Apollos' sojourn at Corinth, did not present some still more marked traces of Peter's visit. Still, while abstracting wholly from a personal visit of Peter to Corinth, we cannot mistake in the phrase to which we have just pointed, the evidence of a serious fact in the development of the young Church, a sensible influence from Palestinian Christianity must

certainly have been exercised at that period in the Church of Corinth. In what direction? This is a point we shall consider afterwards.

3. We are forced to hold at the same time a vexatious recrudescence of the old pagan habits, with which the new converts had at first completely broken. The powerful earnestness of St. Paul's preaching had at first ruled the Church and repressed the vicious tendencies under the dominion of which the most of the new Christians had formerly lived (1 Cor. vi. 11). But in proportion as the first impressions grew weak, and the community received new members less profoundly stirred and transformed, Greek lightness revived again and threatened the Divine work. We have proofs even of the abuse made by many of the principle of spiritual liberty which St. Paul proclaimed (vi. 12, x. 23). The truly sanctified members of the Church were obliged then to ask what they had to do respecting those who thus fell back into their old way of living. The question was put to the apostle. He replied in a letter anterior to our two canonical Epistles (comp. 1 Cor. v. 9). He asked "that they should not mingle with such men," that is to say, that by breaking off every private relation with the vicious members, the Church should protest against that false profession of the Christian faith, and should show conspicuously that they did not recognise it as earnest.

4. This letter from Paul was followed by a reply from the Corinthians to the apostle. They objected that if they were to break thus with all the vicious, there was nothing left them but to go out of the world (v. 10). They questioned him also on some new

subjects, such as the preference to be given to celibacy over marriage, and the free use of meats which had figured on the altars of idols. As to the former of those subjects, Paul introduces it expressly with the words: "Concerning the things *whereof ye wrote unto me*" (vii. 1). And it is probable that when he introduces the latter by saying (viii. 1): "Concerning meats offered to idols," he passes to another point also treated in their letter. As we again find the same form (xii. 1) when the apostle comes to deal with the questions relating to the use of spiritual gifts, it is equally probable that here again he takes up a subject about which they had consulted him. There had therefore been since the founding of the Church a somewhat active correspondence between it and the apostle.[1]

5. Besides this reply of the Corinthians to Paul, three delegates from the Church had reached the apostle. They are designated by their names and characterized in the most honourable way (xvi. 15-18). Were they the bearers of the Church's letter? or did they arrive later under the stress of new and more delicate circumstances? We cannot tell. But such a step proves in any case the gravity of the situation, even then. We do not think that, as the subscription of our Epistle has it, and as is frequently repeated, it

[1] The two letters found in the Armenian Church, and the authenticity of which has been defended by Rinck, could not, even if they were Paul's, be those the loss of which we are here asserting. Rinck acknowledges this himself, for they treat of quite different subjects from those which are supposed by our Epistle. And in those letters it is the Corinthians who write first and Paul who replies. But their authenticity is moreover wholly untenable. They are simple collections of Pauline sayings, without logical connection; and their citation by Gregory the Illuminator, in the fourth century, cannot evidently guarantee their apostolic composition.

was those deputies who, on their return, were the bearers of the First Epistle to the Corinthians. The passage xvi. 11 : " I expect him (Timothy) with the brethren," seems to me to prove that they were yet at Ephesus with the apostle, when this letter, which was to arrive in time to recommend Timothy to a cordial welcome from the Corinthians, was sent off.

6. In fact Timothy was then on his way first to Macedonia, then to Corinth, charged with an important mission from Paul. He was to support by his personal influence the effect which Paul desired to produce by our First Epistle (iv. 17), and then no doubt to prepare for the carrying out of the projected collection in favour of the Church of Jerusalem (1 Cor. xvi. 1). Though Timothy had set out before the letter, it was to arrive before him, because it was sent directly by sea, while Timothy made the tour through Macedonia.

7. To these various circumstances there must be added another, purely accidental, but which had perhaps the most considerable influence on the letter we are to study. A lady, named Chloe, arrived at Ephesus from Corinth, where she had lived (i. 12). We do not know whether, being herself of Corinth, she had made a journey to Ephesus, or whether, being an Ephesian by birth, she was returning from a visit to Corinth. Those of her household, either her children or slaves, informed Paul of a circumstance which must have touched him deeply. The Church was divided into parties which came into conflict in the general gatherings. Cries such as these were raised : *"As for me, I am of Paul;"*—thus no doubt spake the oldest converts, those who had felt most deeply the holy efficacy

of the gospel;—or, "*But as for me, I am of Apollos;*"—this was the watchword of those who had been gained by the eloquent and able demonstrations of this teacher;—then again, "*But as for me, I am of Cephas;*"—these were no doubt chiefly Christians of Jewish origin who had heard tell of Peter, or who had met him in their journeys to Jerusalem at the feasts. They naturally enough concluded that the first place in the Church belonged to the head of the apostolic college chosen by Jesus, and that if there was any difference between Paul and him, it was the latter who should be followed. Lastly, others, daringly casting off all apostolic authority,—Peter's, as it seems, no less than Paul's,—replied to all the others: "*But as for me, I am of Christ,*" as if to say: "I recognise no one intermediate between the Lord and me; I claim to depend directly on Him and on Him alone."

It is asked, Who could these last be, and how could such a party have arisen at Corinth? Were they Christians of Gentile origin, who, admiring Christ's teachings, thought that these should be disentangled from the Jewish forms in which the apostles, and even to a certain extent Paul himself, clothed them? Or were they Christians of Jewish origin and tendency, who, rejecting Paul's gospel, condemned the concessions which the Twelve thought it right to make to this apostle, and that by alleging against them the example and sayings of Christ? This is a question which we cannot examine here, and which we shall treat in the commentary in connection with i. 12. St. Paul has said somewhere, "Is any offended, and I burn not?" If it was so when the offence of a simple believer was in question, what must he have felt on learning that one of the most flourishing Churches which it had been given him to found, was almost threatened with dissolution?

We have now before us the whole of the circumstances which had filled the time since St. Paul had left Corinth, and we can form an idea of the manifold concerns which filled his heart as he set himself to dictate our First, or strictly speaking, his Second Epistle to this Church.

It remains to examine here in few words a question much discussed of late, and on which the most recent investigations are not at one. From several passages of the Second Epistle to the Corinthians, it seems to follow that the apostle had been twice at Corinth before the time when he wrote this letter. These passages are mainly the four following: ii. 1, xii. 14, xii. 21, xiii. 1 and 2. Indeed, in the last three Paul seems to say that his next visit to Corinth will be the third, and from the first it seems to follow that the second had been so painful to him that he had shrunk from exposing himself till now from visiting them anew in similar circumstances. Now, nothing in all we have seen can lead us to suppose that Paul had returned to Corinth after his first sojourn, during which he had founded the Church.

There are three ways of treating these passages. Either they may be regarded, as is done by Baur, Hilgenfeld, Renan,[1] and others, not as indicating real visits so much as *projects* which the apostle had formed, but had not been able to execute. But it is impossible

---

[1] *Saint Paul*, p. 451, note; comp. also Farrar, *Life and Work of St. Paul*, ii. p. 101, note 2; Edwards, p. xiv.

on this view to account for the two passages xii. 14 and ii. 1. The former is thus translated: "Lo, this is the third time I am ready to come to you," instead of: "Lo, I am ready to come to you for the third time." But it is forgotten that the apostle is here declaring his firm resolution not to allow himself to be supported by the Church during his next sojourn, for he adds: "and I shall not be chargeable to you." Now it follows that the *"for the third time"* implies two previous sojourns, not only announced, but *real.* For a projected sojourn costs nothing. The passage ii. 1 confirms this conclusion. The words: "I determined that I would not come again to you with sorrow," are explained in this sense: "I have determined that my second sojourn, which I am about to make among you, shall not be a painful and sorrowful one." This meaning is compatible with the form of the received text; but the latter has against it the authority of all the Majuscules. According to the true position of the words "*with sorrow,*" this regimen refers not only to the idea of *coming,* but to the whole phrase, "*coming again to you.*" It follows, therefore, from these words, that Paul had already made a *sorrowful* sojourn among them, which cannot refer to the sojourn during which he had founded the Church, and consequently implies a second visit which had taken place since then.[1]

If, then, the apostle had certainly stayed twice at Corinth before writing our Second Epistle to this

---

[1] Farrar thinks with Chrysostom that the phrase thus understood might also refer to a purely hypothetical sojourn, a sojourn which, if it had taken place, *would have had* a sorrowful character (ii. p. 101, note 3). But the authority of Chrysostom does not suffice to render so forced an interpretation possible.

Church, the question is, Whether this stay ought to be placed before or after our First Epistle to the Corinthians? Following Bleek, who first treated this question thoroughly,[1] a large number of writers have placed the second journey before our First Epistle. Some, like Anger, have taken it to be simply the second part of the sojourn occupied in founding the Church, which was divided into two by an excursion to the north of Greece. Others, like Reuss, suppose that during his long stay at Ephesus, Paul made a rapid visit to Greece, and specially to Corinth. But the former of these explanations does not correspond with the expression *come*, which indicates an arrival strictly so called, and not a return after a simple excursion. As to the latter, Hilgenfeld rightly asks, How could Paul's adversaries at Corinth have said that he was always putting off his arrival because he dared not return to this Church (1 Cor. iv. 18), if he had visited it quite recently? Reuss rests on 1 Cor. xvi. 7 : "I will not see you now by the way;" words which, according to him, imply that he had recently made a short stay with them. But this conclusion, drawn from the word *now*, is unfounded. Paul simply means : "The circumstances are such at this moment that I do not wish to see you simply by the way," which does not at all suppose that a short visit had preceded. By this observation Paul would explain a change in the plan of his journey which he had previously announced, according to which he had proposed to make a rapid visit to Corinth, on his way to Macedonia, and then to return for a longer time from

[1] *Studien und Kritiken*, 1830.

Macedonia to Corinth. He now gives up the thought of doing so; he first visits Macedonia, and thence he will proceed to them to stay. — There is one fact above all which prevents our placing Paul's second visit to Corinth before the First Epistle to the Corinthians. In this letter Paul does not make a single allusion to a second stay in the midst of this Church, while he frequently refers to the circumstances of his stay at its founding (i. 14–17, 26 seq., ii. 1 seq., iii. 1 seq., 10, 11, iv. 15, xv. 1, 2). That would be impossible, if he had visited the Corinthians again in the time which preceded this Epistle. On the other hand, it is in the Second Epistle that all the allusions occur to the stay of which we are speaking. It must therefore be placed, as has been thought by Ewald and Eylau, in a remarkable programme,[1] between the composition of our two canonical Epistles. In general, I think with the latter, that the interval between the First and Second Epistles to the Corinthians must have been much more considerable and more full of incidents than is generally held. Bleek has proved, in the article quoted above, that many passages of the Second Epistle suppose not only a second stay of Paul at Corinth, but even an Epistle now lost which should be placed between our First and Second Epistles to the Corinthians. If this second fact is admitted,—as I think it ought to be,—the history of the relations between Paul and the Church at this period necessarily becomes complicated, and must have been completed by important and numerous facts, into the exposition

[1] *Programm des Gymnasiums zu Landsberg*, a. d. W. 1873; *Zur Chronologie der Corintherbriefe*, v. Dr. Gustav Otto Eylau.

of which we cannot enter here, and which explain the strange expression *three years*, which the apostle uses (Acts xx. 31) to denote the duration of his stay at Ephesus.

We hold, then, a second visit of Paul to Corinth, before the stay which he made in this city during the three months of winter, in the years 58-59. But we must not rank this stay among the factors which told on the composition of the First Epistle, because in our view it is posterior to this letter, and should be placed between our two Epistles.

CHAPTER IV.

PLAN OF THE EPISTLE.

TEN subjects, more or less extended and very heterogeneous, were present to the apostle's mind, when he set himself to compose this letter; and the question which arises is this: Will he confine himself to passing from the one to the other by way of juxtaposition, or will he find the means of binding them to one another by a logical or moral gradation, so as to leave an impression of order and unity on the mind of the reader. In other words, will the First Epistle to the Corinthians be a heap or a building? In this very letter St. Paul compares himself to an architect who has wisely laid the foundation of the Church. We shall immediately see that, whatever Renan may think, he has shown himself such also in the composition of the letter which he has addressed to it.

What must have concerned him above all, was to put an end to the divisions which reigned in the Church. To be listened to by all on the different subjects which he had to treat, he must first have reconquered his position of authority with the entire congregation. Hence the subject to which he assigns the first place is that of the parties which have been formed at Corinth. He begins by examining the real nature of the gospel; then he expounds that of the ministry; finally, he states the true relation between the Church and its teachers, and thus saps the evil at the root.

This question belongs to the ecclesiastical domain; thence he passes to the subjects which enter into the moral domain, and that by beginning with a question which belongs still in a way to the organization of the Church, that of the action which the community should exercise on those of its members who, by scandalous conduct, dishonour the Christian profession. There follow four questions of a purely moral order: first, these two which are easily settled by the very spirit of the gospel, that of lawsuits between Christians, carried before heathen tribunals, and that of the vice of impurity; then two others, the treatment of which is more difficult, because it is complicated by the part which the fact of Christian liberty plays in such matters: they are that of the preference to be given to celibacy over marriage, and that of the use of meats which have been offered to idols. Accordingly the solution of these two last questions gives rise to long discussions and very delicate distinctions.

After these matters of a moral nature, the apostle places those which refer to the religious life and to the celebration of worship. Here he meets with three subjects,—the first, in which the element of Christian liberty still plays a certain part, is the behaviour of women in the assemblies. The apostle afterwards deals with the way in which believers ought to conduct themselves at the love-feast preceding the observance of the Supper. Finally, he treats with particular care the most difficult and delicate of all the subjects: the best way of using spiritual gifts, gifts bestowed at Corinth with remarkable abundance, especially the gifts of tongues and of prophecy.

Thus far we observe in the course followed by the letter a tendency to go from the external to the internal: Paul in closing reaches what is most profound, most decisive, and most vital for the Church, the domain of doctrine. For, as the plant is only the embodied sap, the Church and the Christian are only evangelical doctrine realized. The apostle here treats of the resurrection of the body, which some at Corinth denied, and he shows the relation of this point of doctrine, apparently so secondary, to the Christian salvation viewed as a whole, and to the victory gained by Christ over evil in the midst of humanity.

The subjects treated are thus classified, notwithstanding their profound diversity, in four natural groups, and these groups show a rational gradation:

I. An *ecclesiastical* question: chaps. i. 10–iv. end.

II. Five *moral* questions; foremost that of discipline, which still touches the ecclesiastical side: chaps. v.–x.

III. Three questions which are *liturgical* or relative to public worship: chaps. xi.–xiv.

IV. A *doctrinal* question : chap. xv.

The passage i. 1-9 forms the preface ; as usual it comprehends the address and a thanksgiving. Chap. xvi. is a conclusion like that with which Paul closes each of his Epistles, containing commissions, news, and greetings.

Are we to think with Renan that St. Paul "was incapable of method," and "that he did not possess the patience necessary to make a book"? Never, as it seems to us, was an intellectual edifice more admirably conceived and carried out than the First Epistle to the Corinthians, though with the most varied materials.

It has been asked whence the apostle drew the means of resolving all those doctrinal and practical problems which were put to him at that time by the state of the Church, and the answer has been given: "From the conception which forms the pivot of his whole theology, the *mystical union* between Christ and the believer" (Edwards, p. xxii.). We think this answer would rather satisfy certain of Paul's modern commentators than Paul himself. The apostle's clear and positive mind is averse to all that is vague and cloudy. As the basis of every judgment of his, there is always a precise idea, and this idea is always the inner representation of a positive fact. The Christ crucified, whom the apostle makes the foundation of our Epistle (chap. i.), and the risen Christ, whom he makes the consummation of his letter (chap. xv.), these are the twofold treasure from which he draws the solutions he needs throughout the whole course of his work. It is by analyzing the historical Christ that he resolves the question of the ministry (i. 13, iii. 23); it is to the power of the glorified Christ that he appeals to resolve that of discipline (v. 4); and so successively on to that magnificent chapter in which the study of the risen Christ furnishes him with the solution of all eschatological problems.

It is therefore not the mystical union, that cloud-land whence every one brings whatever pleases him, it is the historical, ever-living Christ, who is the foundation on which Paul rests the edifice raised in his letter.

APPENDIX.

IT remains to say a few words regarding the most important *documents* of the text, and also on the most recent *works* on our Epistle.

Of the nineteen manuscripts or fragments of manuscripts written in uncial letters, in which the Epistles of St. Paul have been preserved, there are fifteen which contain the First Epistle to the Corinthians in whole or in part.

These are,—

א (*Sinaïticus*) and B (*Vaticanus*), of the 4th century.

A (*Alexandrinus*) and C (*C. of Ephrem*), of the 5th century.

D (*Claromontanus*), H (*Coislinianus*), I (fragment, at St. Petersburg), of the 6th century.

F^a (two verses quoted as marginal notes in H), of the 7th century.

E (*Sangermanensis*), F (*Augiensis*), G (*Börnerianus*), K (*Mosquensis*), L (*Angelicus*), M (fragment, in London), P (*Porfirianus*), of the 9th century.

We do not speak here either of minuscules, or versions, or quotations of the Fathers, referring for such apparatus of criticism to the works of general introduction to the New Testament.

As to commentaries, it is needless to speak of the most ancient and of those among the moderns which are universally known, the more so as we can refer on this head to the truly masterly exposition of the history of interpretation from its beginning to our day in Edwards' introduction to his commentary (pp. 25-35). Of the most recent works, we shall mention only the following as in our estimation the most important:—

Hofmann (1874): sagacious, exact, profound, but often fanciful in the extreme.

Reuss (*Les épîtres pauliniennes*, 1878): the spirit and manner of this author are well known.

Lang (in the 2nd vol. of the *Protestanten-Bibel*): short notes interpreting our Epistle according to the views of Baur's school.

Heinrici (1880). Two features distinguish this commentary: the great abundance of interesting parallels taken from classical writers, and the attempt to deduce the forms of Church organization, established in Greece by St. Paul, from the constitution of the religious associations which then flourished in the country with a view to protect the individual against the sufferings of isolation and indigence (θίασοι, θιασῶται); comp. in the commentary, pp. 20-29, and moreover the author's profound treatise : *Die christliche Gemeinde und die religiösen Gemeinschaften der Griechen (Zeitschr. für wissensch. Theol.*, 1876, iv.). Nevertheless this latter opinion has not hitherto found a very favourable reception among the critics who have discussed it (Weizsäcker, Hilgenfeld, Holsten, Schürer). The formation of the Christian ecclesiastical constitution might rather be explained by the importation of synagogal forms. But it is evidently the product of the Christian mind itself, and in its development it has followed its own course. In any case, as Holsten observes, the apostle would not have been the man to borrow the forms of the Church of God from religious brotherhoods celebrating a worship which he regarded as that of demons. It is at Jerusalem we see the first elements of organization appear : elders and deacons. It is in the Churches of Asia Minor, founded long before Paul's arrival in Greece, that we meet with the first election of elders under his direction (Acts xiv. 23). Baptism, the love feast, the Holy Supper go back much further than the first contact of the gospel with the Greek world, even to our Lord Himself. That the Greek consciousness made a close relationship between the Church and those Hellenic brotherhoods is possible, even probable; and this seems to follow from the term θιασῶται, which Celsus applies to Christ's disciples (Orig. *Cont. Cels.* iii. 22), and from the title θιασάρχης (Christian), which Lucian gives to his *Peregrinus*. Comp. Neumann : θιασῶται Ἰησοῦ, in *Jahrbücher für protestantische Theologie*, 1885, i. But this close relationship, which the Pagans naturally made, has nothing in common with the influence which Heinrici attributes to the forms of the Hellenic associations on the constitution of the Christian Church.

Holsten (*Das Evangelium des Paulus*, Theil. i., 1880): penetrating, brief, original, bold, but swayed by the premisses of the Tübingen school. In imitation of the Dutch theologian Straatmann, who has recently discovered a whole series of interpolations, more or less grave, in chaps. xi.-xv. of our Epistle, but with more moderation and less fancifulness, Holsten thinks he can eliminate from the text a host of alleged glosses: as if the apostolic documents had not been preserved in the Churches with the greatest care, but had been abandoned to the mercy of the first comer!

Beet (1883). This English commentator is known by his work on the Epistle to the Romans. He seems to me to possess in a high degree the gift of expounding the course of the apostle's ideas in a simple, clear, and judicious way.

Edwards (1885). The author of this, the most recent commentary, is Principal of a University College in Wales; he possesses high philological culture. The spirit and value of his exegesis will appear from the quotations which we shall not fail to make from his important work.

THE TITLE.

THE title comes to us in its simplest form in the documents dating from the 4th, 5th and 6th cents. (א B A C D): πρὸς Κορινθίους ἡ πρώτη, *the First to the Corinthians*. Later it is gradually amplified till it takes the form found in L (9th cent.) : *the First Epistle to the Corinthians of the holy and illustrious Apostle Paul.*

The original title must have been quite simply πρὸς Κορινθίους ; for this letter was not *the first* which the apostle addressed to this Church (Introduction, p. 26), and had it been, he could not have foreseen that he would afterwards write a second. The title, as we find it in the oldest MSS., has been edited by those who formed the collection of St. Paul's letters.

This letter presents the same general framework as all the others of the same apostle :

1. The *preface,* comprehending the address and a thanksgiving : i. 1–9.

2. The *body of the letter,* where the subjects are treated which gave rise to its composition : i. 10–xv. end.

3. The *conclusion,* containing commissions, news, and greetings : chap. xvi.

COMMENTARY.

PREFACE (I. 1-9).

The Address (I. 1-3).

Ver. 1. " Paul, an apostle of Christ Jesus[1] by call,[2] through the will of God, and Sosthenes the brother."— The addresses of Paul's letters are generally drawn on the type of the ancient address : N. to N., greeting ! Comp. Acts xxiii. 26. Paul does not confine himself to translating this received form into Christian language ; he modifies it each time according to the interests which occupy his heart, and with a view to the state of the Church to which he writes. To his name he adds the title in virtue of which he is now addressing his readers ; it is as an *apostle* that he writes them. The special mark of this office is the call directly received from Christ Himself. Paul puts this mark in relief by the epithet κλητός, *called;* a qualifying adjective, and not a participle (κληθείς), as if the apostle had meant, called *to be* an apostle. The meaning is, " an apostle in virtue of a call." He means that he has not taken this office at his own

---

[1] B D E F G It. place Χριστου (*Christ*) after Ιησου.
[2] A D E omit κλητος; (*called*).

hand, but that he has received it by a Divine act. I do not think that there is here a polemical intention against parties who might deny his apostleship : what would this assertion prove? He means rather to place the whole contents of the letter which is to follow under the warrant of Him who confided to him his mission. We must read, according to several ancient Mjj. : *of Christ Jesus*, that is to say, " of the Messiah who is Jesus ; " and not *of Jesus Christ* (Jesus who is the Messiah), according to the received text. The technical form has been mechanically substituted for the less ordinary by the copyists. By this complement, Paul may designate Christ as the *Author* of the call, or perhaps as the Master whose *property* he became by that call. As the regimen following ascribes the call to God, the second meaning is to be preferred. The words, *through the will of God*, refer to all the providential circumstances of Paul's birth and education, whereby his apostolic mission had been prepared for ; and especially the extraordinary act which completed this preparation, and triumphed over his resistance ; all which Paul sums up in those expressions of the Epistle to the Galatians (i. 15) : " But when it pleased God who separated me from my mother's womb, and called me by His grace. . . ."[1] It is with a feeling of profound humiliation that he emphasizes so expressly this idea of the will of God ; for he feels that it needed unfathomable mercy to snatch him from the obstinate rebellion to which he was giving himself up. But at the same time he is powerfully strengthened in relation

---

[1] See the development of this idea in my *Commentary on the Epistle to the Romans*, vol. i. pp. 3–6. [Trans. T. & T. Clark, Edin.].

to himself and to the Church, by the assurance that what he is, he is by the will of God. But at the same time he is powerfully strengthened, as regards himself and the Church, by the assurance that it is God who has willed that he should be what he is.

Paul joins with his name that of a Christian, the *brother Sosthenes*. Reuss regards this man merely as an obscure person who no doubt acted as secretary to the apostle. I believe that there are here two errors; the place in our verse ascribed to Sosthenes is wholly different from that which the apostle gives to a simple secretary, as, for example, Tertius (Rom. xvi. 22). Paul uses particular delicacy in his way of mentioning those whom he associates with him in the composition of his letters. In his two Epistles addressed to the Church of Thessalonica, of which Silas and Timothy had been the founders along with him, he mentions them absolutely as his equals, except in so far as he puts himself in the first place; and the first person plural, which he frequently uses, again and again applies, as in ver. 2, to the three taken together. It is nearly the same in Phil. i. 1, where Timothy's name is closely associated in the address with that of Paul, no doubt because Timothy had laboured with him in founding that Church. There is a marked difference between this form and that of the Epistle to the Colossians, where Timothy's name is certainly associated with Paul's, but where it is more profoundly distinguished from it by an appendix added to the latter, in the first place, then by the title of *apostle* given to Paul and the name *brother* to Timothy. This difference arises from the fact that neither the one nor the other having founded the Church, Paul writes here in his character of apostle to the Gentiles, which Timothy does not share. In the letters to the Romans and Ephesians, whom Paul addresses more expressly still as the apostle of the Gentile world, he associates no name with his own. The position given to Sosthenes in our address is therefore somewhat like the place of Timothy in the Epistles to the Philippians and Colossians. Paul makes this brother share to a certain extent in the composition and responsibility of the letter. Sosthenes is perhaps his secretary; but he is more than that: he must be a man enjoying high consideration among the Corinthians, a fellow-labourer with the apostle who, as well as Timothy (2 Cor. i. 1), co-operated in the evangelization of Corinth and Achaia. If it is so, it is probable that we here find the same person who, as chief of the synagogue of Corinth, had played a part in the scene of Paul's appearance before Gallio (Acts xviii. 17). It was he who, after Paul's liberation, as the account of the Acts says, "was beaten by *all*" (the words—*the Greeks* are a gloss), consequently by Jews and Greeks, without Gallio's taking any concern. He took probably a doubtful attitude in this affair, later his position was more decided (see Hofmann). The place assigned him here is consequently, as Heinrici says, a place of honour; it reminds us of that ascribed by Paul to those mentioned in the address of the Epistle to the Galatians (i. 2): "and all the brethren who are with me." Assuredly those brethren were not all his secretaries, but all, in name of the Christian brotherhood, exhorted the Galatians to take to heart the warnings which Paul addressed to them as their spiritual father; so it is that the credit which Sosthenes has with the Church must be added to the superior authority of the apostle. Clement of Alexandria, according to the account of Eusebius (*H. E.* i. 12), made Sosthenes one of the seventy disciples: the statement is without value.

From the author, Paul passes to the readers:

Ver. 2. "To the Church of God, the sanctified in Christ Jesus,[1] which is at Corinth, saints by call, with all that in every place call upon the name of our Lord Jesus Christ, who is[2] theirs and ours."—The term ἐκκλησία, *Church*, formed of the two words, ἐκ, *out of*, and καλεῖν, *to call*, denotes in ordinary Greek language an assembly of citizens called out of their dwellings by an official summons; comp. Acts. xix. 41. Applied to the religious domain in the New Testament, the word preserves essentially the same meaning. Here too there is a summoner: God, who calls sinners to salvation by the preaching of the gospel (Gal. i. 6). There are the summoned: sinners, called to faith thenceforth to form the new society of which Christ is the head. The complement *of God* indicates at once Him who has summoned the assembly, and Him to whom it belongs. The term, *the Church of God*, thus corresponds to the ordinary Old Testament phrase: *Kehal Jehova, the assembly* (congregation) *of the Lord;* but there is this difference, that the latter was recruited by way of filiation, while in the new covenant the Church

---

[1] B D E F G It. place after θεου (*of God*) the words ηγιασμενοις εν Χριστω Ιησου (*sanctified in Christ Jesus*); T. R. places them, with א A L P Syr., after τη ουση εν Κορινθω (*which is at Corinth*).

[2] א A B D F G omit the τε before και, which is the reading of T. R. with E L P.

is formed and recruited by the personal adherence of faith.

According to the reading of several Mjj. (*Vatic.*, *Clarom.*, etc.), the apostle immediately adds to the words: *the Church of God*, the apposition ἡγιασμένοις ἐν Χριστῷ Ἰησοῦ, *the sanctified in Christ Jesus*. As the Church is composed of a plurality of individuals, the apostle may certainly, by a construction *ad sensum*, join to the singular substantive this apposition in the plural. The received reading separates this substantive from its apposition by placing between the two the words τῇ οὔσῃ ἐν Κορίνθῳ, *which is at Corinth*. This arrangement seems at first sight more natural; but for that very reason it has the character of a correction. It seems to me probable that, thinking already of the moral disorders which stained this Church, the apostle felt himself constrained to characterize the community he is addressing rather morally than geographically. God is holy, and the Church of God ought to be holy like Him to whom it belongs. The perfect participle ἡγιασμένοις indicates not an obligation to be fulfilled, but a state which already exists in them, and that in virtue of a previously accomplished fact. That fact is faith in Christ, which implicitly contains the act of total consecration to God. To embrace Christ by faith is to accept the holiness which He realized in His person; it is to be transplanted from the soil of our natural and profane life into that of His *Divine* holiness. The regimen, *in Christ Jesus*, expresses this idea,—that our holiness is only participation in His in virtue of the union of faith with Him: " For their sakes I sanctify myself," says Jesus (John xvii. 19), " that they also might be sanctified in truth." Several Fathers have applied the expression, *sanctified in Jesus Christ*, to the fact of baptism; their error has been confounding the sign of faith with faith itself.

After having thus characterized the assembly of God as composed of consecrated ones, the apostle adds the local definition: *which is* (which really exists, οὔσῃ) *at Corinth.* He had passed from the unity of the Church to the plurality of its members; he returns from this plurality to the unity which should continue. One feels that his mind is already taken up with the divisions which threatened to break this unity. When we think of the frightful corruption which reigned in this city (Introd. p. 6), we can understand with what inward satisfaction the apostle must have written the words, "the Church of God . . . at Corinth"! Bengel has well rendered this feeling in the short annotation: *Ecclesia in Corintho, lætum et ingens paradoxon.*

Immediately after the words: *sanctified in Christ Jesus,* it is surprising to find: *saints by call,* which seem after the preceding to form a pleonasm. The solution of this difficulty is involved in the explanation of the regimen which follows: *with all those who call upon* . . . This regimen has been connected with the dative τῇ ἐκκλησίᾳ, as if the apostle meant: I address my letter, or I address this salutation, to the Church which is at Corinth, and not only to it, but also to the Christians of the whole world (Chrysostom, Theodoret, Calvin, Osiander, Reuss). But, on the contrary, no apostolical letter has a destination so particular and local as the First Epistle to the Corinthians. Meyer limits the application of the words: *with all who call upon*, like the similar address of 2 Cor. i. 1 : "with all the saints who are in all Achaia," and thinks that those referred to here are simply all the Christians scattered throughout the province of Achaia, and who are grouped round the Church of the metropolis; so, after him, Beet, Edwards, and others. But the passage quoted proves exactly the contrary of the conclusion drawn from it. For it shows how Paul would have written here also, if such had been his meaning. Holsten, feeling the impossibility of importing such a restriction, imagines another less arbitrary. He refers the words to the Christians of other Churches, who might be at present staying at Corinth, especially to the emissaries who had come from Jerusalem (*those of Christ*), of whose presence Paul was well aware. But the phrase used is far too general to admit of so limited an application. Mosheim, Ewald think that Paul means by it expressly to include in his salutation all the parties which were formed. But the preposition σύν, *with*, would imply that one of the parties was already separated from the Church itself, while the whole letter proves that they still formed part of it. We must therefore give up the attempt to make the regimen "*with all them who . . .*" dependent on the term: *the Church of God*, and connect it, as is in itself more natural, with the preceding words: "*saints by call.*" The meaning is: "saints in virtue of the Divine call, and that in communion with all them who invoke the name of the Lord in every place." Thus the tautology disappears which is implied in the words: "saints by call," with the preceding: "sanctified in Christ Jesus." There is not here a new synonymous epithet needlessly added to the preceding. The sainthood of the faithful is expressed a second time to connect this new feature with it: that sainthood is the common seal of the members of the Church universal. The words κλητοῖς ἁγίοις are there solely as the point of support for the following regimen: σὺν πᾶσι, *with all them who* . . . This construction also explains quite naturally the two adjectives, πᾶσι, *all*, and παντί, *every* (*place*), which follow. More than once in this letter the apostle will have to censure the Corinthians for isolating their course from that of the rest of the Church, and for acting as if they were the only Church in the world (comp. especially xiv. 36); and therefore in the very outset he associates them with a larger whole, of which they are only one of the members, and with which they ought to move in harmony. Heinrici, while explaining the σύν exactly as we do, thinks he can separate κλητοῖς from ἁγίοις by a comma, and connect the σύν with κλητοῖς alone: "saints, called with all them who . . ." This translation is grammatically forced, and besides it leaves the pleonasm of "saints" and "sanctified" as it was.

Holiness is the normal character *of all them that call on the name of the Lord*, says the apostle. This expression is evidently in his view the paraphrase of the term "believers." A Christian is therefore, according to him, a man who calls on the name of Jesus as his Lord. The term ἐπικαλεῖσθαι is applied in the Old Testament (by the LXX.) only to the invocation of Jehovah (Isa. xliii. 7; Joel ii. 32; Zech. xiii. 9). Immediately after Pentecost, the name for believers was, "they who call on the name of the Lord" (Acts ix. 14, 21; Rom. x. 12, 13); the name of Jesus was substituted in this formula for that of Jehovah in the Old Testament. The very word NAME, applied, as it is in these passages, to Jesus, includes the idea of a Divine Being; so when the Lord says of His angel, Ex. xxiii. 21, "My name is in him," that is to say, He makes this being His perfect revelation. The title *Lord* characterizes Jesus as the one to whom God has committed the universal sovereignty belonging to Himself; and the Church is, in the apostle's eyes, the community of those who recognise and adore Him as such. It is therefore on an act of adoration, and not on a profession of faith of an intellectual nature, that he makes the Christian character to rest. The words: ἐν παντὶ τόπῳ, *in every place*, designate the universality of the Christian Church in point of right (and already, in part, of fact, when St. Paul wrote); comp. 1 Tim. ii. 8. This idea accords with the πᾶσι, *all*, which precedes, and, as we have seen, it agrees with the context. But a large number of commentators endeavour to limit the sense of this expression, by assigning to it as its complement the words following: αὐτῶν καὶ ἡμῶν, "*of them and of us*," or "*theirs and ours.*" But what would the expression signify: "*their* and *our* place"? De Wette, Osiander, Rückert understand thereby Corinth and Ephesus; Paul would mean: all them that call upon the Lord on your side of the sea, as well as on ours. But to what purpose is this distinction? Besides, the Church of Corinth had already been sufficiently described at the beginning of the verse. Mosheim and Ewald think that by "our place" the apostle means to denote the place of worship of his own partisans, and by "their place" the rooms where the other parties assembled. This explanation is already refuted by our foregoing remarks (p. 44). And Paul would have carefully avoided legalizing in any way the separation which he blamed so severely. Meyer's explanation, followed by Beet and Edwards, seems to me still more forced; the expression, *our* place, denotes the Christian communities of Achaia, in so far as morally the property *of the apostles;* here of Paul and Sosthenes, who preached the gospel in them; and the expression, *their* place, refers to those same communities, in so far as they depended on the Church of Corinth, their metropolis. Does such an exegetical monstrosity deserve refutation? Yet it is surpassed still, if that be possible, by Hofmann's explanation, according to which Paul means that Christians (*them*), more especially the preachers of the gospel (*us*), are found everywhere among those by whom Christ is invoked! We must, with Chrysostom, Calvin, Olshausen, etc., simply give up the attempt to make the complements *of them* and *of us* depend on the word *place;* and leave the phrase, *in every place*, in its absolute and general sense. As to the two pronouns, αὐτῶν and ἡμῶν, *of them* and *of us*, they depend on the word *Lord*, and are the more detailed repetition of the pronoun ἡμῶν (*our* Lord), which preceded: "Our Lord, who is not only *yours*, our readers, but also *ours*, your preachers." There is here, as it were, a protest beforehand against those who, forgetting that there is in the Church only one Lord, say: "As for me, I am of Paul; I, of Apollos; I, of Peter!" "Who is Paul, who is

Apollos, other than *servants* by whom ye believed, by each of them according as *the Lord* gave to him?" (iii. 5, 22, 23). So thoroughly is this the prevailing concern in the apostle's mind, from the very beginning of this letter, that six times, between vers. 1 and 10, he repeats the expression: *of our Lord Jesus Christ*. The received reading, τε καί, instead of the simple καί, may certainly be maintained, though it has against it several important manuscripts; it dwells a little more strongly on the fact that believers have Jesus Christ for *their only* Lord, as well as preachers, and thus better justifies the repetition of the preceding ἡμῶν in these two pronouns.

Ver. 3. " Grace and peace be unto you, from God our Father, and from the Lord Jesus Christ!"—This prayer is the Christian paraphrase of two salutations, the Greek (χαίρειν, Acts xxiii. 26) and the Hebrew ("Peace be to thee").—*Grace* is the Divine good will, bending compassionately toward the sinner to pardon him; toward the reconciled child, to bless him. *Peace* is the profound tranquillity with which faith in this Divine love fills the believer's heart.—Paul does not say: "be to you from God *by* Jesus Christ," but "from God *and from* Jesus Christ," for Jesus is not in his eyes the impersonal channel of the Divine love; He loves with His own peculiar love as brother, as God loves with His love as Father.—By this prayer, the apostle invites the Corinthians to take their place ever anew under the influence of this double source of salvation, the love of the Father and the love of the Son.

We have said that in the address of Paul's letters

there are already betrayed the concerns with which his mind is preoccupied at the time of writing; this is easy to establish in the Epistles to the Romans and to the Galatians, and we have seen the proof of it also in the address we have just studied. Holiness is the characteristic of the members of the Church; the relation of a common life between the particular Church and the Church universal; the dignity of Lord, as competent to Jesus only: such are the traits which distinguish this address from every other; and is it not manifest that they are dictated to the apostle by the particular circumstances of the Church of Corinth, at the time when he wrote?

THE THANKSGIVING (I. 4-9).

The Epistle to the Galatians is the only one in which the apostle passes directly from the address to the handling of his subject, without interposing a thanksgiving. This is due to the tone of abrupt and severe rebuke which characterizes the beginning of the letter. In his other Epistles, before speaking to the Church of what it lacks, of what he would teach or correct in it, the apostle begins by expressing his gratitude for the work already accomplished, and the desires he cherishes for fresh progress to be made. This is what he does here in vers. 4-9. But, as in the addresses, there is in these thanksgivings a great variety, according to the state of each Church. If we compare that which follows with those of the two Epistles to the Thessalonians, the wide difference will be immediately perceived: there, he congratulates the Thessalonians on the work of their *faith*, the labour of their *love*, the patience of their *hope* (1 Thess. i. 3; 2 Thess. i. 3 seq.). Here, there is nothing of the kind: the apostle blesses God for the spiritual gifts, both of *knowledge* and of *speech*, which He bestows abundantly at Corinth. We shall have no difficulty in understanding the reason of this difference.

Vers. 4–6. "I thank my[1] God always on your behalf, for the grace of God which is given you in Jesus Christ; 5. That in everything ye were enriched in Him, in every kind of utterance, and in every kind of knowledge; 6. Even as the testimony of Christ[2] was confirmed in you."—On account of the severity of the rebukes to be found in this letter, some commentators have detected in this thanksgiving a touch of flattery or even of irony. But the whole Epistle shows that the apostle is no flatterer, and irony is excluded by the expression, "I thank my God." Though many things were wanting in the Church of Corinth, the gratitude which the apostle expresses to his God for what He has done in its behalf is nevertheless sincere and earnest; as appears besides from the very measuredness of his commendations shown in the terms he uses.

He addresses his thanks to *his* God: thereby he describes God as the Being in close communion with whom he lives and labours; who, in particular, stood by him in his work at Corinth, and there gave him the most personal proofs of His help and love (Acts xviii. 9, 10); if he uses the word *my* instead of *our* (Sosthenes and I), it is because the matter involves his

---

[1] ℵ B omit the word μου (*of me*).
[2] B F G read θεου (*of God*) instead of του Χριστου (*of Christ*).

personal relation to God, in which he can associate none of those who labour with him. It is undoubtedly by mistake that the *Sinaït.* and the *Vatic.* have omitted this pronoun μου. The first corrector of the *Sinaït.*, who is almost contemporary with the copyist, has supplied it (Edwards).—The word *always* might seem exaggerated; but the apostle's constant concern was the Church in general, and that of Corinth was one of its most important members.—The general term: *on your behalf,* is defined by the more precise phrase, *for the grace of God which* . . ., intended to express the more special subject of the thanksgiving. This grace comprehends the whole state of salvation, with the new life which has been displayed in the Church. It is a mistake, as it seems to me, in many interpreters to limit the application of the word *grace* to the spiritual gifts about to be spoken of: the term is more general.

Ver. 5. With the meaning of the word *grace,* which we have rejected, ὅτι would require to be translated by *in that.* But if we take the word *grace* in the most general sense, ὅτι should be translated by "*seeing that,*" or "*because.*" Indeed, there is here a new fact proving the reality of the preceding. Only from the state of grace could the abundance of gifts arise which distinguishes the Church of Corinth, and which more especially gives occasion to the apostle's gratitude.— The *in everything* is qualified by the two following terms, *knowledge* and *utterance.* The sequel of the Epistle leaves no doubt as to the meaning of these two terms. Chaps. xii.–xiv. will show what a wealth of gifts, both of Christian knowledge and of manifestations in utterance (tongues, prophecies, doctrine), had been bestowed on this Church. We see from viii. 1 and 10, xiii. 2, 8, and 9, that the word γνῶσις, *knowledge*, denotes the understanding of the facts of salvation and of their manifold applications to Christian life. Here it includes the idea of σοφία, *wisdom*, which is sometimes distinguished from it; comp. xii. 8.—The term *utterance* has been applied by de Wette to the rich Christian instruction which the Corinthians had received from Paul's mouth and from which they had derived their knowledge of the gospel. But the term *utterance* must denote a spiritual gift bestowed on the Corinthians, and in connection with the term knowledge. What the apostle has in view, therefore, is those different forms of the new tongue which the Holy Spirit had developed in the Church. The verb ἐπλουτίσθητε denotes their abundance; the word παντί, *every*, their variety; comp. xiv. 26: "When ye come together, each of you hath a psalm, a teaching, a tongue, a revelation, an interpretation." Edwards sees in this aorist an allusion to the present loss of those former riches, as if it should be translated, "Ye *had been* enriched." This is certainly a mistake; the riches remained still, as is shown by chaps. xii.-xiv. The aorist simply relates to the point of time at which the spiritual endowment of the Church took place, when its faith was sealed by the communication of the Spirit. It is not by accident that the apostle only mentions here the speculative and oratorical powers, and not the moral virtues; the *gifts* of the Spirit and not the *fruits* of the Spirit, as at Thessalonica. His intention is not doubtful; for in chap. xiii. 8–13 he himself contrasts the two principal gifts of utterance, tongues, and prophecy, and then knowledge, as things which pass away, with the three things which abide: faith, hope, and love. Here then, side by side with the riches for which the apostle gives thanks, we already discover the defect which afflicts him, but of which he does not speak, because it would be contrary to the object of the passage as one sacred to thanksgiving. This defect stood in relation to the character of the Greek mind, which was distinguished rather by intellectual and oratorical gifts than by seriousness of heart and conscience.

Ver. 6. This verse may be understood in two ways: some (Meyer, Edwards, etc.) regard it as indicating the *cause* of that abundance of gifts which has just been mentioned. They then apply the term ἐβεβαιώθη, *was confirmed*, or rather *affirmed*, to an internal fact: "in consequence of the depth and firmness of faith with which the gospel impressed (affirmed) itself in you." To support this meaning, they rely on the βεβαιώσει of ver. 8; but we shall see that this ground proves nothing, because there the idea of confirmation applies, not to the gospel, but to the persons of the Corinthians. This explanation is not in keeping with the natural meaning of καθώς, *according as*, which indicates rather a mode than a cause. The sense seems to me quite different: the apostle means, not that the wealth of their gifts is due to the depth and solidity of their faith, which would be contrary to the spirit of the whole passage, but that these gifts have been the *mode* of confirming the gospel specially granted to the Church of Corinth. Elsewhere, God could confirm the apostolic preaching otherwise; by miracles, for example, or by moral virtues, fruits of the Spirit; comp. Heb. ii. 3: "The salvation which, having at the first been spoken by the Lord, was *confirmed* unto us by them that heard Him, God Himself bearing witness with them by signs and wonders and by distribution of the powers of the Spirit;" also, 1 and 2 Thess. i. 3 and Gal. iii. 2. The conj. καθώς agrees perfectly with this meaning: "Thus, and not otherwise, did the Divine confirmation of the testimony rendered to Christ take place among you."—The term *testimony* is here used to denote preaching, because this is essentially the attestation of a historical fact (vers. 23, 24). The gen. Χριστοῦ denotes the subject of the testimony, and not its author. It would be otherwise with the gen. θεοῦ, *of God*, if this reading were adopted with the *Vatic.*

Ver. 7. "So that ye come behind in no gift, waiting for the revelation of our Lord Jesus Christ."—In the explanation of the preceding verse, which we have rejected, the ὥστε, *so that*, is made to refer to the verb ἐβεβαιώθη of ver. 6: "Your faith was confirmed in such a way, that in consequence no gift was lacking to you . . ." But in the sense of ver. 6, which we have adopted, this verse being rather an observation thrown in by the way, it is natural to refer the ὥστε to the ἐπλουτίσθητε of ver. 5, which gives a simpler and clearer meaning: "Ye were so enriched, that in point of gifts ye lacked nothing." There is indeed an evident contrast between the two ideas of *being enriched* and *lacking.*—The word ὑστερεῖσθαι, *to lack*, denotes a deficiency either relatively to the normal level which a Church should attain (xvi. 17; Col. i. 24; 1 Thess.

iii. 10), or comparatively to other Churches more richly endowed (2 Cor. xi. 5, xii. 11). The first of these two meanings is evidently the more suitable here. The Corinthians realize, in respect of gifts, χαρίσματα, all that can be desired for a Church on the earth. The ἐν μηδενί corresponds to the ἐν παντί of ver. 5.

The word χάρισμα, *gift*, will play a large part in this Epistle. As the form of the Greek term indicates, it denotes in general every concrete product in which grace is embodied. Several commentators (Calvin, de Wette, Meyer) apply the word here to the blessings of salvation in general, as in Rom. i. 11; but the evident relation to ver. 5 (comp. the reference of ὑστερεῖσθαι to πλουτισθῆναι, and that of μηδενί to παντί) leads us to give a more definite sense to the word χάρισμα. According to the two expressions, *knowledge* and *utterance*, it must be applied here to the new spiritual powers with which the Spirit had endowed the members of the Church at Corinth. These various powers, which so often in Paul's writings bear the name of χαρίσματα, *gifts of grace*, are certainly the effects of the supernatural life due to faith in Christ; but they fit in notwithstanding to pre-existing natural aptitudes in individuals and peoples. The Holy Spirit does not substitute Himself for the human soul; He sanctifies it and consecrates its innate talents to the service of the work of salvation. By this new direction, He purifies and exalts them, and enables them to reach their perfect development. This was what had taken place at Corinth, and it was thus especially that the apostolic testimony had been divinely confirmed in this Church. We see how Paul still carefully avoids (as in ver. 5) speaking of the moral fruits of the gospel, for this was the very respect in which there was a deficiency, and a grave deficiency, at Corinth.

The following words, *waiting for the revelation* . . ., have been very variously understood. Grotius and Rückert have seen in them an indirect reproof to those of the members of the Church who, according to chap. xv., denied the resurrection. But the apostle speaks of waiting for the Lord's *return*, and not of faith in the resurrection. Chrysostom supposes that he wishes to alarm them by thus glancing at the approach of the judgment; but this would not be very suitable to a thanksgiving. Calvin, Hofmann, Meyer suppose, on the contrary, that he wishes to encourage them: "Ye can go to meet the Lord's advent with confidence, for ye possess all the graces that suffice for that time;" or, as Meyer says: "The blessings which ye have received fit you to see the Lord come without fear." But would the apostle thus reassure people whom he saw filled with the most presumptuous self-satisfaction, and given over to a deceitful security? Comp. iv. 6–8, x. 1–22. Reuss supposes that Paul wishes to lead them to put to good account the spiritual aids which they now enjoy. But Paul would have declared this intention more clearly. Mosheim seems to me to have come nearer the true sense, when he finds irony here: "Ye lack nothing, waiting however the great revelation!" Without going the length of finding a sarcasm which would be out of place here, I think that there is really in this appendix, "waiting the revelation . . .," the purpose of bringing this too self-satisfied Church to a more modest estimate. Rich as they are, they ought not to forget that as yet it is only a waiting state: they lack nothing . . . waiting for the moment which will give them everything. As is said, indeed (xiii. 11), all our present gifts of utterance and knowledge have still the character of the imperfect state of childhood, in comparison with that which the perfect state will bring about. There was a tendency among the Corinthians to anticipate this latter state; they already imagined that they were swimming in the full enjoyment of the perfected kingdom of God (iv. 8). The apostle reminds them that real knowledge is yet to come; and this no doubt is the reason why he here uses the term, *the revelation of Jesus Christ*, to denote His advent. He means thereby less to characterize His visible presence ($παρουσία$), than the full revelation both of Him and of all things in Him, which will accompany that time. In that light what will become of your knowledge, your present prophesyings and ecstasies? Comp. 2 Thess. i. 7; 1 Pet. i. 7, where the use of this term is also occasioned by the context.—The term $ἀπεκδέχεσθαι$, compounded of the three words, $ἀπό$, *far from* (here, *from far*), $ἐκ$, *from the hands of*, and $δέχεσθαι$, *to receive*, admirably depicts the attitude of waiting.

After expressing his gratitude for what God has already done for his readers, the apostle, as in Eph. i. 17 seq., and Phil. i. 6 seq., adds the hope that God will yet accomplish in them all that is lacking, that they may be able to stand in that great day; such is the idea of the two following verses.

Ver. 8. "Who shall also confirm you unto[1] the end,

[1] D E F G: $ἄχρι τέλους$, instead of $ἕως τέλους$.

that ye may be blameless in the day¹ of our Lord Jesus Christ. 9. God is faithful, by whom² ye were called unto the fellowship of His Son Jesus Christ our Lord." — The pron. ὅς, *who*, refers of course to the person of *Jesus Christ* (ver. 7). But this name being expressly repeated at the end of the verse, many commentators have been led to refer the pronoun ὅς to θεός, *God* (ver. 4). But this reference would reduce the whole passage, vers. 5–7, to a simple parenthesis; it has besides against it the repetition of the word θεός in ver. 9. If the expression *our Lord Jesus Christ* appears again at the end of the verse, instead of the pronoun, this arises from the fact that the term "the day of Christ" is a sort of technical phrase in the New Testament; it corresponds to the "day of the Lord" in the Old Testament.—The καί, *also*, implies that the work to be yet accomplished will only be the legitimate continuation of that which is already wrought in them. There is undoubtedly an intentional correlation between the βεβαιώσει, *will confirm*, of ver. 8, and the ἐβεβαιώθη, *was confirmed*, of ver. 6. Since God confirmed Paul's preaching at Corinth by the gifts which His Spirit produced there, He will certainly confirm believers in their faith in the gospel to the end.—This end is the Lord's coming again, for which the Church should constantly watch, for the very reason that it knows not the time of it; comp. Luke xii. 35 and 36; Mark xiii. 32. If this event does not happen during the life of this or that generation, death takes its place for each, till that generation for which it will be

---

[1] D E F G It.: παρουσια, instead of ημερα.
[2] D F G: ὑφ' ου, instead of δι' ου.

realized externally. The phrase, *in the day of Christ*, does not depend on the verb *will confirm*, but on the epithet ἀνεγκλήτους, *unblameable*. We must understand between the verb and the adjective the words εἰς τὸ εἶναι, as in Rom. viii. 29 ; 1 Thess. iii. 13 ; Phil. iii. 21 (where the words εἰς τὸ γενέσθαι are a gloss) : the end is directly connected with the means. —Ἀνέγκλητος signifies *exempt from accusation*, and many apply the word to the act of justification which will cover the infirmities and stains of believers in that supreme hour, so that, as Meyer says, the epithet is not equivalent to ἀναμάρτητος, *exempt from sin*. It does not seem to me that this meaning suits the parallels 2 Cor. vii. 1, 1 Thess. v. 23 ; for these passages represent believers as completely sanctified at that time. If then they are no longer subject to any accusation, it will not be only, as during their earthly career, in virtue of their justification by faith, it will be in virtue of their thenceforth perfected sanctification. The Greek - Latin reading παρουσία, *advent*, instead of ἡμέρα, *day*, has no probability.

Ver. 9. The asyndeton between the preceding verse and this arises from the fact that the latter is only the emphasized reaffirmation, in another form, of the same idea : the faithfulness of God, as the pledge of the confirmation of believers in their attachment to the gospel. The assurance here expressed by the apostle is doubtless not a certainty of a mathematical order ; for the entire close of chap. ix. and the first half of chap. x. are intended to show the Corinthians that they may, through lack of watchfulness and obedience, make shipwreck of the Divine work in them; the certainty in question is of a moral nature, implying the acquiescence of the human will. As the *ye were called* assumes the free acceptance of faith, so continuance in the state of salvation supposes perseverance in that acceptance. But the apostle sets forth here only the Divine factor, because it is that which contains the solid assurance of this hope.

The words, *by whom ye were called,* sum up the work already accomplished at Corinth by Paul's ministry; comp. Phil. i. 6. We need not with Meyer apply the phrase, *the fellowship of His Son Jesus Christ,* to the state of glory in the heavenly kingdom. The term κοινωνία, *fellowship,* implies something inward and present. Paul means to speak of the participation of believers in the life of Christ, of their close union to His person even here below. The form, *Jesus Christ our Lord,* recurs so to speak in every phrase of this preface; it reappears again in the following verse. It is obvious that it is the thought which is filling the apostle's mind; for he is about to enumerate the human names which they dare at Corinth to put side by side with that of this one Lord.

This thanksgiving has therefore, like the foregoing address, a character very peculiarly appropriate to the state of the Church. While frankly commending the graces which had been bestowed on them, the apostle gives them clearly to understand what they lack and what they must yet seek, to be ready to receive their Lord. He now passes to the treatment of the various subjects of which he has to speak with them.

BODY OF THE EPISTLE.

I. 10 – XV. 58.

I.

The Parties in the Church of Corinth

(I. 10 – IV. 21).

Ewald has well stated the reason why the apostle puts this subject first, of all those he has to treat in his Epistle. He must assert his apostolical position in view of the whole Church, before giving them the necessary explanations on the subjects which are to follow.

1. *Statement of the fact and its summary condemnation* (i. 10-17).

Ver. 10. "Now I beseech you, brethren, by the name of our Lord Jesus Christ, that ye all speak the same thing, and that there be no divisions among you, but that ye be perfectly joined together in the same mind and in the same judgment." — The δέ is not adversative: it is the transition particle by which Paul passes from thanksgiving to rebuke. — By the address ἀδελφοί, *brethren*, he puts himself by the side of his readers, and appeals to their affection in view of the serious censure which he has to pass on them.

He rests his exhortation on the revelation made to him and the knowledge which they have of the person and work of the Lord Jesus Christ ; such is the meaning of the term ὄνομα, *the name.* The word *Lord* implies His authority ; the name *Jesus Christ* calls up the memory of all the tender proofs of Divine love displayed in Him who bore the name. It is the eleventh time that the name Jesus Christ appears, and we are at the tenth verse !—The following exhortation bears on three points. The first, τὸ αὐτὸ λέγειν, *to speak the same thing,* is the most external. The phrase includes an allusion to the different formulas enumerated ver. 12. —The two other points relate to the inward conditions of community of language ; the first is negative : that there be no schisms, divisions into different camps, bringing with them opposing watchwords. What a view is here of a Church divided into distinct parties ! The other condition is of a positive nature : it is the perfect *incorporation* of all the members of the Church in a single spiritual organism. The term καταρτίζειν denotes, in the first place, the act of adjusting the pieces of a machine with a view to its normal action ; hence the equipment of a workman for his work (Eph. iv. 12) ; then, in the second place, the rectification of a disorganized state of things, such as the re-establishment of social order after a revolution, or the repairing of an instrument (Mark i. 19 : fishing-nets). Order being disturbed at Corinth, we might here apply the latter meaning. But in this case Paul would rather have used the aor. κατηρτίσθητε δέ than the perfect which denotes the stable condition. The first signification is also somewhat more delicate. Paul does not mean, " that ye be reconstituted," as if he thought them already disorganized, but, " that ye may be in the state of a well-ordered assembly." How so ? He indicates this in the two following terms : by the agreement of the νοῦς and that of the γνώμη. These two words are often distinguished by making the first apply to knowledge, the second to practical life. This distinction, without being false, is not however sufficiently precise ; the νοῦς, as is shown in ii. 16, denotes the Christian way of thinking in general, the conception of the gospel in its entirety ; the γνώμη, according to vii. 25, refers rather to the manner of deciding a particular point, what we call opinion, judgment. The apostle therefore desires that there should be among them, in the first place, full harmony of view in regard to Christian truth, and then perfect agreement in the way of resolving particular questions. The conjunction ἵνα shows that in his mind the matter in question is rather an object to be attained than a duty which he expects to be immediately realized ; it is the state to be aspired after, for the honour of the name of Jesus Christ, whatever may be the sacrifices of self-love and of interest which such an aim may demand of each. After this introduction the apostle comes to the fact which gives rise to this exhortation.

Vers. 11, 12. "For it hath been signified unto me concerning you, my brethren, by them which are of the household of Chloe, that there are contentions among you. 12. Now this I mean, that each one of you saith, I am of Paul; and I of Apollos ; and I of Cephas ; and I of Christ."—At the moment of enumerating these different parties, the apostle once again unites all the members of the Church under the one common and affectionate address, *my brethren.*—Perhaps the markedly express indication of the source to which he owes this news is intended to exclude in this matter the delegates of the Church who are at this time with Paul. Those of Chloe's household may be the children or slaves of that Ephesian or Corinthian lady (see Introd. p. 21).—The word ἔριδες, *contentions,* denotes bitter discussions which would easily degenerate into *schisms,* σχίσματα (ver. 10).

Ver. 12. Calvin has translated, " I say this *because* . . . ;" but it is more natural to make the τοῦτο, *this,* refer to the following ὅτι : " When I speak of contentions, *I mean this that* . . . " The phrase, *Every one of you saith,* is of course inexact ; for every member of the Church did not pronounce the four watchwords. Paul thus expresses himself to indicate that the sin is general, that there is not one among them, so to speak, who has not in his mouth *one* of these formulas. The four are presented dramatically and in the form of direct speech ; we hear them, as it were, bandied from one to another in the congregation. Their painful character appears first from the ἐγώ, *I,* put foremost,—there is a preponderance of personal feeling,—then from the δέ, which is evidently adversative : *but,*—there is the spirit of opposition,—finally and chiefly, from the names of the party leaders. Some ancient commentators supposed that the apostle had here substituted the names of eminent men for the obscure names of the real party leaders, to show so much the better how unjustifiable such rivalries are. The passage iv. 6 is that which induced Chrysostom, and others after him, to make so unnatural a supposition. But we shall see that this verse gives it no countenance.

The apostle puts in the forefront the party which takes name from himself; he thereby gives proof of great tact, for by first of all disapproving of his own partisans, he puts his impartiality beyond attack. It has been supposed that in the enumeration of the four parties he followed the historical order in which they were formed; but from the fact that Paul was the founder of the Church, and that Apollos came after him, it does not follow that Paul's party was formed first and that of Apollos second; we must rather suppose the contrary. Paul's partisans had only had occasion to pronounce themselves as such, by way of reaction, against the exclusive partiality inspired by the other preachers who came after him. We have indicated in the Introduction, p. 22 seq., how we understand these opposite groups to have been formed. We cannot concede the least probability to the suppositions of Heinrici, who ascribes to Apollos a Gnostic and mystic tendency, and particularly views on baptism of the strangest kind. From the fact that he arrived at Ephesus as a disciple of John the Baptist, we have no right to conclude, with this theologian, that Apollos established a special bond of solidarity between the baptized and their baptizer like that which, in the Greek mysteries, united initiated and initiator! Heinrici goes the length of supposing that to Apollos and his party is to be ascribed the practice alluded to xv. 29, of baptizing a living Christian in place of a believer who died without baptism! Is it possible to push arbitrariness further ? This has been well shown by Hilgenfeld (*Zeitschrift für wissenschaftliche Theologie*, 1880, p. 362 seq.). What distinguished Paul from Apollos, according to iii. 5 seq. and iv. 6, could not be an essential difference, bearing on the substance of the gospel; it could only be a difference of form such as that indicated by the words, " I have planted, Apollos watered, and God gave the increase." By his exegetical and literary culture, acquired at Alexandria, Apollos had gained for Christ many who had resisted Paul's influence; perhaps Sosthenes, the ruler of the synagogue during Paul's stay, was of the number. If it is so, we can better understand how the apostle was induced to associate this person's name with his own in the address of the letter.

We have already said that the existence of a Cephas-party does not necessarily imply a visit of Peter to Corinth. Personal disciples of this apostle might have arrived in the city, or Jewish Christians from Corinth might have met Peter at Jerusalem, and on their return to Achaia they might have reported that this apostle differed from Paul in continuing personally to keep the law, though without wishing to impose it on Gentile converts. The Aramaic name Cephas is perhaps a proof of the Palestinian origin of the party.

As to the last watchword, the Greek Fathers, and Calvin, Mosheim, Eichhorn, Bleek among the moderns, think that it, according to the apostle, gives the true formula by which Paul would designate those whom he approves. Mayerhoff and Ebrard go even the length of thinking that by the word *I*, Paul means to designate himself: "But as for me, Paul, this is my watchword: I am of Christ, and of Christ only!" The symmetry of the four formulas evidently excludes these interpretations. The fourth comes under the censure which falls on the three preceding, "Every one of you saith . . . ," and it is this one above all which gives rise to the following question,—"Is Christ divided?" There was really then a fourth party which claimed to spring directly from Christ, and Christ alone, without having need of any human intermediary. As Paul adds not a single detail regarding this party, either in this passage or in the rest of the Epistle, the field of hypothesis is open, and we shall consecrate to the much discussed question the appendix to be immediately subjoined.

Some commentators seem to us to have exaggerated the character of the division, by supposing that the different parties no longer met in common assemblies, and that the rending of the Church into four distinct communities was an accomplished fact. The contrary appears from the passage xiv. 23, where Paul speaks of the assembling together of the whole Church in one and the same place, and even from the term ἔριδες, *contentions*, which would be too weak in that case. On the other hand, Hofmann has far too much attenuated the importance of the fact mentioned when he reduces it to hostile pleadings in the meetings of the Church, arising from the personal preference of each group for that servant of Christ who had contributed most to its edification. Undoubtedly the external unity of the Church was not broken, but its moral unity was at an end, and we shall see that the disagreement went much deeper into the way of understanding the gospel than this commentator thinks.

Otherwise, would the apostle have spent on it four whole chapters? It has often been attempted to distribute the numerous subjects treated by the apostle in our Epistle among these different parties, as if they had been furnished to him, one by one party, another by another. These attempts have not issued in any solid result. And we must say the same of the most recent attempt, that of Farrar. This critic sees in the Apollos-party the precursors of Marcion and of the Antinomian Gnosticism of the second century; in the Peter-party, the beginning of the anti-Pauline Ebionism of the Clementine *Homilies*. Finally, in the Christ-party, an invasion of Essenism into Christianity, which continued later. The division which Farrar makes of the questions treated by Paul among those different tendencies is ingenious, but lacks foundation in the text of the Epistle.

The party called "those of Christ."

We have already set aside the opinions of those who take the fourth formula to be the true Christian profession approved by the apostle, or the legitimate declaration of a group of believers, offended by the absorbing partiality of the other groups for this or that teacher.

I.

The opinion which comes nearest this second shade is that developed by Rückert, Hofmann, Meyer, Heinrici, and to a certain extent by Renan, according to whom the fourth party, pushed by the exclusive preferences of the others, was carried to the opposite extreme, and declared itself independent of the apostolate in general, putting itself relatively to Christ in a position absolutely equal to that of Paul or Peter. "Some," says Renan, " wishing to pose as spirits superior to those contentions, created a watchword sufficiently spiritual. To designate themselves they invented the name 'Christ's party.' When discussion grew hot . . . , they intervened with the name of Him who was being forgotten: I am for Christ, said they" (*Saint Paul*, p. 378). It is for them, it is held, that Paul calls to mind, iii. 22, that if the Church does not belong to the teachers who instruct it, the latter are nevertheless precious gifts bestowed on it by the Lord. Nothing simpler in appearance than this view. An extreme had led to the contrary extreme; partiality had produced disparagement. It was the rejection of apostolical authority as the answer to false human dependence. We should not hesitate to adopt this explanation, if certain passages of Second Corinthians, which we shall afterwards examine, did not force us to assign graver causes and a much graver importance to the formation of this party; comp. especially 2 Cor. x. 7, and xi. 22 and 23.

II.

Have we to do, as Neander[1] once thought, with Corinthians of a more or less rationalistic character, with cultivated Greeks who, carried away by enthusiasm for the admirable teachings of Christ, and especially for His sublime moral instructions, conceived the idea of freeing this pure gospel from the Jewish wrapping which still veiled it in the apostolic preaching? In order to make faith easy for their countrymen, they tried to make Jesus a Socrates of the highest power, which raised Him far above the Jesus taught by the Twelve, and by Paul himself. It is against this attempt to transform the gospel into a pure moral philosophy, that it is said the apostle conducts the polemic i. 18-24, and iii. 18-20. This hypothesis is seductive, but the passages quoted can be explained without it, and the Second Epistle proves that the party *those of*

---

[1] In the first editions of the *Apostolic Age*; later, he adhered to the opinion of Bleek (see above).

Christ had not its partisans at Corinth among converted Gentiles, but in Palestine, among Christians of Jewish origin and tendency.

III.

This is recognised by some commentators, such as Dähne [1] and Goldhorn; these seek the distinctive character of this fourth party in the elements of Alexandrine wisdom, which certain Jewish doctors mingled with the apostolic teaching. We shall no doubt discover the great corruptions introduced by the Judaizing heads of the Christ-party into the evangelical doctrine. But it is impossible to establish, by any solid proof whatever, the Alexandrine origin of these new elements.

IV.

So Schenkel,[2] de Wette, Grimm have pronounced for a more natural notion. According to them, the heads of this party founded their rejection of the apostolic teaching and the authority of their own on supernatural communications which they received from the glorified Christ, by means of direct visions and revelations. Similar claims were put forth a little later, as we know, among the Judaizing teachers of Colosse; why should they not have existed previously in Asia Minor, and thence invaded the Churches of Greece ? To support this opinion, there has been alleged chiefly the way in which Paul dwells on that transport even to the third heaven, which had been granted to himself (2 Cor. xii. 1 seq.); and it is thought that he meant thereby to say : "If these men pretend to have had revelations, I have also had them, and still more astonishing." But this would be a mode of argument far from conclusive and far from worthy of the apostle; and we shall see that those teachers probably did not come from the land of mysticism, Asia Minor, but from that of legal Pharisaism, Palestine.

---

[1] *Die Christus-Partei in der apostol. K. zu Kor.*, 1842.
[2] *De eccl. Cor. primæva faction. turbata*, 1838.

V.

This is now recognised by most critics. No doubt we do not see the Judaizing teachers who are concerned here presenting themselves at Corinth, exactly as they did formerly at Antioch and in Galatia. They understood that to gain such men as the Greeks of Corinth, they must avoid putting forward circumcision and gross material rites. But they are nevertheless servants of the legal party as formed at Jerusalem. To be convinced of this, it is enough to compare the two following passages of 2 Cor. x. 7: "If any one trust to himself that he belongs to Christ ($X\rho\iota\sigma\tau o\hat{v}$ $\epsilon\hat{i}\nu a\iota$, lit. 'to be Christ's'), let him of himself think this again, that as he is Christ's, so are we Christ's." To whom is this challenge addressed? Evidently to persons who claim to be Christ's by a juster title than the apostle and his partisans, precisely like the men who specially call themselves *those of Christ* in the First Epistle. And who are they? The second passage, xi. 22 and 23, informs us: "Are they Hebrews? so am I. Are they Israelites? so am I. Are they the seed of Abraham? so am I. Are they ministers of Christ? (I speak as a fool); I am more." They were then Jewish believers who boasted of their theocratic origin, and who sought to impose, by means of their relations to the mother Church, on the young Churches founded by Paul in the Gentile world, no doubt with the intention of bringing them gradually under the yoke of the Mosaic law.

But in what sense did such men designate themselves as *those of Christ?*

1. Storr, Hug, Bertholdt, Weizsäcker suppose that they took this title as coming from James, the head of the flock at Jerusalem, known under the name "the Lord's brother;" and that it was because of this relationship between James and Jesus, that they boasted of being in a particular sense men of Christ. But this substitution of Christ's name for that of James is rather improbable, and this explanation could in any case only apply to the few foreign emissaries who came from Palestine, and not to the mass of the Corinthian party which was grouped around them.

2. According to Billroth, Baur, Renan, these people were

the same as "those of Cephas." They designated themselves as *those of Peter* when they wished to denote their human head; as *those of Christ* when they wished to declare the conformity of their conduct with that of the Lord, who had constantly observed the law, and had never authorized the abolition of it, which Paul preached. In reality, the third and fourth party were thus only one; its double name signified, " disciples of Peter, and, as such, true disciples of Christ."

In favour of this identification, it is alleged that in a dogmatic point of view the two first parties, that of Paul and that of Apollos, also formed only one. But we have proved without difficulty the shade which distinguished the partisans of Apollos from those of Paul, and though it did not bear on dogmatic questions, we cannot confound these two parties in one, nor consequently can we identify the last two parties so clearly distinguished by the apostle. Besides, nothing authorizes us to ascribe to Peter a conception of the gospel opposed to that of Paul. We know, from Gal. ii., that they were agreed at Jerusalem on these two points: that believers from among the Gentiles should not be subjected to the Mosaic rites, and that believers from among the Jews might continue to observe them. But we know also from the same passage, that there was a whole party at Jerusalem which did not approve of this concession made to Paul by the apostles. Paul distinguishes them thoroughly from the apostles and from James himself, for he declares that if he had had to do only with the latter, he might have yielded in the matter of the circumcision of Titus; but it was because of the former, to whom he gives the name of "false brethren, brought in," that he was obliged to show himelf inflexible in his refusal. There was therefore a profound difference in the way in which the circumcision of Titus was asked of him by the apostles on the one hand, and by the false brethren on the other. The former asked it of him as a voluntary concession, and in this sense he could have granted it; but the latter demanded it as a thing obligatory; in this sense the apostle could not yield without compromising for ever the liberty of the Gentiles. Consequently, beside Peter's followers, who, while observing the law themselves, conceded liberty to the Gentiles, there was room for another party, which, along with the maintenance of the law for the Jews, demanded the subjection of the Gentiles to the Mosaic system. What more natural than to find here, in *those of Christ*, the representatives of this extreme party? We can understand in this case why Paul places *those of Christ* after those of Peter, and thus makes them the antipodes of his own party.

Far, then, from finding in our passage, as Baur and Renan will have it, a proof of Peter's narrow Judaism, we must see in it the proof of the opposite, and conclude for the existence of two classes of Jew-Christians, represented at Corinth, the one by Peter's party, the other by Christ's.

3. Schmidt has thought that the Judaizers, who called themselves *those of Christ*, were those who allowed the dignity of being members of the kingdom of *Christ*, the Messiah-King, only to the Jews and to those of the Gentiles who became Jews by accepting circumcision. In this explanation the strict meaning of the term $X\rho\iota\sigma\tau\acute{o}\varsigma$, *Messiah*, must be emphasized. But it seems evident from our two Epistles that the Judaizing emissaries at Corinth were wise enough not to demand circumcision and the Mosaic ritual from the believers there, as from the ignorant Galatians.

4. Reuss, Osiander, Klöpper think those emissaries took the name of *those of Christ*, because they relied on the personal example of Jesus, who had always observed the law, and on certain declarations given forth by Him, such as these, "I am not come to destroy the law, . . . but to fulfil it;" and "Ye have one Master, Christ." Starting from this, they not only protested against Paul's work, but also against the concessions made to Paul by the Twelve. They declared themselves to be the only Christians who were faithful to the mind of the Church's Supreme Head, and on that account they took the exclusive title, *those of Christ*. This explanation is very plausible; but, as we shall see, certain passages of the Second Epistle to the Corinthians lead us to ascribe a quite special dogmatic character to the teaching of *those of Christ;* and it would be difficult to understand how, while wishing to impose on the Corinthians Christ's mode of acting during His earthly life, they could have freed them, even provisionally, from circumcision and the other Mosaic rites.

5. Holsten and Hilgenfeld suppose that the title, *those of*

Christ, originated in the fact that these emissaries had been in personal connection with Jesus during His earthly life. They were old disciples, perhaps of the number of the *Seventy* formerly sent out by Christ, or even His own brothers; for we know from 1 Cor. ix. 5 that these filled the office of evangelist-preachers. Persons who had thus lived within the Lord's immediate circle might disparage Paul as a man who had never been in personal connection with Him, and had never seen Him, except in a vision of a somewhat suspicious kind. There is mention, 2 Cor. iii. 1, of letters of recommendation with which those strangers had arrived at Corinth. By whom had those letters been given them, if not by James, at once the Lord's brother and head of the Church of Jerusalem?

In answer to this view, we have to say that if James acted thus, he would have openly broken the solemn contract of which Paul speaks (Gal. ii. 5–10), and taken back in fact the hand of fellowship which he had given to this apostle. Holsten answers, indeed, that it was Paul who had broken the contract in his conflict with Peter at Antioch; and that after that scene James felt himself free to act openly against him. But supposing—what we do not believe—that Paul went too far in upbraiding Peter for his return to the observance of the law in the Church of Antioch, there would have been no good reason in that why James should retract the principle recognised and proclaimed by himself, that of the liberty of the Gentiles in regard to the law. What has been recognised as true does not become false through the faults of a third.

6. As none of these explanations fully satisfy us, we proceed to expound the view to which we have been led. We shall find ourselves at one partly, but only partly, with the result of Beyschlag's studies, published by him in the *Studien und Kritiken*, 1865, ii., and 1871, iv. We have seen, while refuting Baur's opinion, that there existed even at Jerusalem a party opposed to the Twelve, that of the "false brethren, brought in," whom Paul clearly distinguishes from the apostles (Gal. ii. 4, 6). They claimed to impose the Mosaic law on Gentile converts, while the Twelve maintained it only for Christians of Jewish origin, and the further

question, whether these might not be released from this obligation in Churches of Gentile origin, remained open. We think that this ultra-party was guided by former members of the priesthood and of Jewish Pharisaism (Acts vi. 7, xv. 5), who, in virtue of their learning and high social position, regarded themselves as infinitely superior to the apostles. It is not therefore surprising that once become Christians, they should claim to take out of the hands of the Twelve, of whom they made small account, the direction of the (Christian) Messianic work, with the view of making this subservient to the extension of the legal dispensation in the Gentile world. Such were the secret heads of the counter mission organized against Paul which we meet with everywhere at this period. It had now pushed its work as far as Corinth, and it is easy to understand why the portion of the Church which was given up to its agents, distinguished itself not only from the parties of Paul and Apollos, but also from that of Peter. They designated themselves as *those of Christ*, not because their leaders had personally known Jesus, and could better than others instruct the Churches in His life and teaching,— who in these two respects would have dared to compare himself to Peter or put himself above him?—but as being the only ones who had well understood His mind and who preserved more firmly than the apostles the true tradition from Him in regard to the questions raised by Paul. They were too prudent to speak at once of circumcision and Mosaic rites. They rather took the position in regard to converted Gentiles which the Jews had long adopted in regard to the so-called proselytes *of the gate*. And moreover—and here is where I differ from Beyschlag—when they arrived on Greek soil, they certainly added theosophic elements to the gospel preached by the apostles, whereby they sought to recommend their teaching to the speculative mind of the cultivated Christians of Greece. It is not without cause, that in the Second Epistle to the Corinthians, Paul speaks, x. 5, of "reasonings exalted like strongholds against the knowledge of God," and of "thoughts to be brought into captivity to the obedience of Christ," and that, xi. 3, he expresses the fear that the Corinthians are allowing themselves to be turned away from the simplicity which is in Christ, as Eve let herself be seduced by the cunning of the serpent. Paul even goes the length of rebuking the Corinthians, in the following verse, for the facility with which they receive strange teachers who bring to them *another Jesus* than the one he has proclaimed to them, *a Spirit* and *a gospel* different from those they have already received.[1] Such expressions forbid us to suppose that the doctrine of those emissaries was not greatly different from his own and that of the Twelve, especially from the Christological standpoint (*another Jesus*). There is certainly here something more than the simple legal teaching previously imported into Galatia. It was sought to allure the Corinthians by unsound speculations, and Paul's teaching was disparaged as poor and elementary. Hence his justification of himself, even in the First Epistle, for having given them only " milk and not meat " (iii. 1, 2). Hence also his lively polemic against the mixing of human wisdom with the gospel (iii. 17–20). All this applied to the preaching of *those of Christ*, and not in the least to that of Apollos. We do not know what exactly was the nature of their particular doctrines. It did violence to the person and work of Jesus. Thus is explained perhaps Paul's strange saying, 1 Cor. xii. 3, "No man speaking by the Spirit of God saith: Jesus is accursed!" The apostle is speaking of spiritual manifestations which made themselves heard even in the Church. There were different kinds of them, and their origin required to be carefully distinguished. The truly Divine addresses might be summed up in the invocation, "Jesus, Lord!" While the inspirations that were not Divine terminated—though one can hardly believe it—in declaring Jesus accursed! Such a fact may however be explained when we call to mind a doctrine like that professed by the Judaizing Christian Cerinthus, according to which the true Christ was a celestial virtue which had united itself to a pious Jew called Jesus, on the occasion of His baptism by John the Baptist, which had communicated to Him the power of working miracles, the light from which His doctrines emanated, but which had abandoned Him to return to heaven, before the time of the Passion; so that Jesus had

---

[1] This seems to me the only possible meaning, whatever Beyschlag may say. The καλῶς ἠνείχεσθε signifies, "Ye took it very well" (when that happened); "it did not revolt you in the least."

suffered alone and abandoned by the Divine Being. From this point of view what was to prevent one pretending to inspiration from exclaiming: "What matters to us this crucified One? This Jesus, accursed on the cross, is not our Christ: He is in heaven!" It is known that Cerinthus was the adversary of the Apostle John at Ephesus; Epiphanius—on what authority we know not—asserts that the First Epistle to the Corinthians was written to combat his heresy. It is remarkable that this false teacher was Judaizing in practice, like our false teachers at Corinth. But it is by no means necessary to suppose that it was exactly this system which Paul had in view. At this epoch many other similar Christological theories might be in circulation fitted to justify those striking expressions of Paul: "another Jesus, another Spirit." Thus the name of Christ, in the title which these persons took, *those of Christ*, would be formulated, not only in opposition to the name of the apostles, but even to that of Jesus.[1] Let us mention, by way of completing this file concerning *those of Christ*, the apostle's last word, 1 Cor. xvi. 22, a word certainly written with his own hand after the personal salutation which precedes: "If any man love not the Lord, let him be anathema!" It is the answer to the "Jesus anathema!" of xii. 3.—We adopt fully, therefore, the words of Kniewel (*Eccl. Cor. vetustiss. dissentiones*, 1842), who has designated *those of Christ* as "the Gnostics before Gnosticism."

There remains only one question to be examined in regard to *those of Christ*. In the Second Epistle to the Corinthians Paul twice speaks of persons whom he designates as οἱ ὑπερλίαν ἀπόστολοι, that is to say, "the apostles transcendentally" or "archapostles" (xi. 5 and xii. 11), and whom he puts in close connection with the *Christ-party*. Baur alleges that he meant thereby to designate the Twelve ironically as authors of the mission carried out against his work by their emissaries

[1] Origen relates, *Cont. Cels.* vi. 2, of the sect of the Ophites, that no one was received into their order until he had cursed Jesus; and of the Gnostic Carpocrates (about the year 135), that he taught that when the question was put to Christians in times of persecution: "Believest thou in the crucified One?" it was allowable to answer: "No;" for it was Simon of Cyrene who was crucified, and not Jesus, and we needed to adhere only to the spiritual Christ. Comp. Volkmar, *Ursprung der vier Evangelien*, p. 45.

arrived at Corinth. We have here, according to him, the most striking testimony of the directly hostile relation between Paul and the original apostles; it was they, and James in particular, who furnished those disturbers with letters of recommendation. On this interpretation rests Baur's whole theory regarding the history of primitive Christianity. But this application is inadmissible for the following reasons:—

1. The Twelve had recognised in principle Paul's preaching of the gospel among the Gentiles, and had found nothing to add to it; they had moreover declared his apostleship to have the same Divine origin as Peter's; this is narrated by Paul, Gal. ii. 1–10. How should they have sent persons to combat such a work?

2. If the expression "archapostles," which Paul evidently borrows from the emphatic language of the party recruited by those persons at Corinth, referred to the Twelve, who in that case must have been considered as being an *apostle* in the simple sense of the word? Obviously it could only be Paul himself. His adversaries would thus unskilfully have declared an apostle the very man whose apostleship they were contesting!

3. In the passage, 2 Cor. xi. 5, Paul says, "he supposes he is not a whit behind the archapostles, for though he be rude in speech ($ἰδιώτης$), he is not so in knowledge." Now it cannot be held that the Twelve were ever regarded at Corinth as superior to Paul in the gift of speech, first because they had never been heard there, and next because they were themselves expressly characterized as $ἀγράμματοι$ and $ἰδιῶται$ (Acts iv. 13).

4. The apostle gives it to be understood ironically (xii. 11 seq.) that there is a point undoubtedly in which he acknowledges his inferiority as compared with the archapostles, to wit, that he has not, like them, been supported by the Church. Now it is certainly of the Church of Corinth that he is speaking when he thus expresses himself; this appears from xi. 20, where he describes the shameless conduct of those intruders toward his readers. As yet the Twelve had not been at Corinth; it is not they, but the newcomers whom Paul designates by this ironical name.

5. How could St. Paul, justly asks Beyschlag, in this same

letter in which he recommends a collection for the Church *of the saints* (that of Jerusalem), designate men sent by that Church and by the apostles, as "servants of Satan whose end will be worthy of their works" (xi. 14, 15)?

Hilgenfeld and Holsten have themselves given up applying the expression archapostles to the Twelve. Agreeably to their explanation of the term, *those of Christ*, they apply it to those immediate disciples of Christ, such as the Seventy or the brothers of Jesus, from whom the party had taken its name, and whom the apostles had recommended to the Corinthians. But this comes nearly to the same, for the brothers of Jesus were at one with the apostles (1 Cor. ix. 5). And besides, how would *those of Christ* have contrasted their leaders as archapostles with Peter himself?

There remains only one explanation. These archapostles are no other than the emissaries of the ultra-Judaizing party, of whom we have spoken. Their partisans at Corinth honoured them with this title, to exalt them not only above Paul, but above the Twelve. We have already explained how this was possible: their object was to break the agreement which was established between the Twelve and Paul; and the letters of recommendation which they had brought were the work of some one of those high personages at Jerusalem who sought to possess themselves of the direction of the Church.

In the following verses, the apostle summarily condemns the state of things he has just described, and defends himself from having given occasion to it in any way. Edwards thinks he can divide the discussion which follows, thus: condemnation of the parties by the relation of Christianity: 1, to Christ, i. 13–ii. 5; 2, to the Holy Spirit, ii. 6–iii. 4; 3, to God, iii. 5–20; 4, to believers, iii. 21–23. But such tabulation is foreign to the apostle's mind. His discussion has nothing scholastic in it. The real course of the discussion will unfold of itself gradually.

Ver. 13. "Is the Christ divided? was Paul crucified

for you,[1] or were ye baptized in the name of Paul?" Several editors (Lachmann, Westcott, and Hort) and commentators (Meyer, Beet) make the first proposition an indignant affirmation: "Christ then among you is rent, lacerated!" But the transition to the following questions does not in that case seem very natural. It is more simple to see here a question parallel to the two following, these being intended to show the impossibility of the supposition expressed by the first. The term *the Christ* denotes the Messiah in the abstract sense, that is to say, the Messianic function, rather than the person who filled the office. The latter would certainly be designated by the name of Jesus or by the word *Christ* without article. How, besides, could we suppose the person of Christ divided into four? Paul means,—is the function of Christ, of Saviour, and founder of the kingdom of God divided between several individuals, so that one possesses one piece of it, another, another? Taken in this sense, the question does not refer only to the fourth party, but to the other three. "Are things then such that the work of salvation is distributed among several agents, of whom Jesus is one, I another?" and so on. Edwards explains thus: "Is not that which is manifested of the Christ in Paul at one with that which is manifested of Him in Apollos, etc. . . . ? Do not these elements form all one and the same Christ?" The meaning is good, but one does not see how in this case the censure applies to the fourth party, which the question, thus understood, seems on the contrary to justify. It is evident the word, Christ, cannot be applied with Olshausen to the

---

[1] B D read περι υμων, instead of υπερ υμων.

Church, nor with Grotius to the doctrine of Christ.— The form of the first question admitted of a reply in the affirmative or negative; that of the two following (with μή) anticipates a negative answer, serving as a proof to the understood negative answer which is evidently given to the first: "Paul was not, however, crucified for you, was he, as would be the case if a part belonged to him in the work of salvation?" He might have put the same question in regard to Apollos and Cephas; but by thus designating himself he naturally disarms the other parties.—The first question relates to the function of Saviour, the second to that of Lord, which flows from it. Edwards well indicates the relation between the two. The cross has made Christ the head of the body. By baptism every believer becomes a member of that body. The reading of the *Vatic.*, περὶ ὑμῶν, cannot be preferred to that of all the other documents: ὑπὲρ ὑμῶν. This ὑπέρ signifies *in behalf of.* The idea, *in the place of*, which would be expressed by ἀντί, is included in it only indirectly. It is by substitution that the benefit expressed by ὑπέρ has been realized. *To be baptized in the name of*... signifies: to be plunged in water while engaging henceforth to belong to Him in whose name the external rite is performed. In the *name* there is summed up all that is revealed regarding him who bears it, consequently all the titles of his legitimate authority. Baptism is therefore a taking possession of the baptized on the part of the person whose name is invoked over him. Never did Paul dream for an instant of arrogating to himself such a position in relation to those who were converted by his preaching.

Yet this would be implied by such a saying as, *I am of Paul.*—And not only could it not be so in fact, but the apostle is conscious of not having done anything which could have given rise to such a supposition.

Vers. 14–16. "I thank God[1] that I baptized none of you but Crispus and Gaius, 15. lest any should say that ye were baptized[2] in my name. 16. I baptized also the household of Stephanas; besides, I know not whether I baptized any other."—Paul's thanksgiving proves that there had been no calculation on his part, when, as a rule, he had abstained from baptizing. The real motive for the course he followed will be given in ver. 17. This is why he is thankful for the way in which God has ordered things. Rückert objects to this reasoning, that if Paul had wished to form a party of his own, he might have done so by getting one of his friends to baptize in his name, as well as by baptizing himself. True; but would he easily have found any one to lend himself to such a procedure? What seems to me more difficult to explain is the supposition itself, on which this passage rests, of a baptism administered in another name than that of Jesus. This idea, which now seems to us absurd, might seem more admissible in the first times of the Church, especially in Greece. In the midst of the religious ferment which characterized that epoch, new systems and new worships were springing up everywhere; and in these circumstances the distance was not great between an eminent preacher like Paul, and the head of a school, teaching and labour-

---

[1] ℵ B omit τω θεω (*to God*), which T. R. reads with the other Mjj.
[2] ℵ A B C read εβαπτισθητε (*ye were baptized*); T. R. with all the other documents, εβαπτισα (*I baptized*).

ing on his own account. The apostle of the Gentiles, no doubt, passed in the eyes of many as the true founder of the religion which he propagated; and the supposition which he here combats might thus have a certain degree of likelihood. There is no need, therefore, in accounting for this passage, either of Hofmann's hypothesis, according to which there were people at Corinth who boasted of having received baptism at Jerusalem from Peter's own hand,—Paul would thus congratulate himself on not having given occasion to such a superstition,—or for that of Keim and Heinrici, who ascribe a similar superstition to the Apollos-party (see above, p. 65).—The regimen τῷ θεῷ, *to God*, omitted by the *Sinaït.* and *Vatic.*, is unnecessary; it has rather been interpolated than omitted.—Crispus, the ruler of the synagogue at the time of Paul's arrival, had been one of his first converts (Acts xviii. 8); Gaius, his host during one of the stays which followed (Rom. xvi. 23), was also probably one of the first believers. Thus, probably, is explained why Paul had baptized them himself; his two assistants, Silas and Timothy, had not yet arrived from Macedonia, when they were received into the Church. It cannot be held with Beet that Paul deliberately made an exception in these two cases because of their importance: this idea would contradict the very drift of the whole passage. It matters little that in the account given in the Acts the order of events does not agree with what we say here.

Ver. 15. The ἵνα, *that*, refers to the intention of God, who has so ordered the course of things.—It is possible to defend both readings, that of the Alexandrine and that of T. R. The first, *ye were baptized*, might be taken from ver. 15, or be intended to avoid the monotonous repetition of the word ἐβάπτισα, *I baptized*. On the other hand, as Edwards observes, Paul was less afraid of their ascribing a bad motive to him personally, than of their misunderstanding the real meaning of baptism itself; in this sense, the Alexandrine reading suits better.

Ver. 16. The apostle all of a sudden recollects a third exception. Stephanas was one of the three deputies from Corinth who were with Paul precisely at that time.—By the words, *besides I know not* . . . , Paul guards against any omission arising from a new slip of memory. Those who make the inspiration of the Holy Spirit go directly to the pen of the sacred writer, without making it pass through the medium of his heart and brain, should reflect on these words.

Ver. 17. "For Christ sent me not to baptize, but to preach the gospel[1]; not with wisdom of words, lest the cross of Christ should be made of none effect." —Between vers. 16 and 17 the logical connection is this, "If I baptized, it was only exceptionally; for this function was not the object of my commission." The essential difference between the act of baptizing and that of *preaching the gospel*, is that the latter of these acts is a wholly spiritual work, belonging to the higher field of producing faith and giving new birth to souls; while the former rests in the lower domain of the earthly organization of the Church. To preach the gospel is to cast the net; it is apostolic work. To baptize is to gather the fish now taken and put

---

[1] B reads εὐαγγελίσασθαι instead of εὐαγγελίζεσθαι.

them into vessels. The preacher gains souls from the world; the baptizer, putting his hand on them, acts as the simple assistant of the former, who is the true head of the mission. So Jesus Himself used the apostles to baptize (John iv. 1, 2); Peter acted in the same way with his assistants; comp. Acts x. 48. Paul certainly does not mean that he was forbidden to baptize; but the terms of his apostolic commission had not even mentioned this secondary function (Acts ix. 15, and xxii. 14, 15). Though he might occasionally discharge it, the object of his mission was different. To the aorist εὐαγγελίσασθαι, the reading of the *Vatic.*, the present εὐαγγελίζεσθαι is to be preferred, which better suits the habitual function.

The connection of the last proposition of ver. 17 with what precedes is not obvious at the first glance. But the study of the following passage shows that we have here the transition to the new development which is about to begin. This transition is made very skilfully: it resembles that of Rom. i. 16, by which the apostle passes from the preface to the exposition of his subject. There might be a more subtle way of appropriating souls to himself than that of baptizing them in his name, even that of preaching in such a way as to attract their admiration to himself by diverting their attention from the very object of preaching: Christ and His cross; now this is excluded by the term *evangelizing* (preaching the gospel), taken in its true sense. Paul means, "I remained faithful to my commission, not only by evangelizing without baptizing, but also by confining myself to evangelizing in the strict sense of the word, that is to say, by delivering my message without adding to it anything of my own." The term *evangelizing* signifies, in fact, to announce good news; it denotes therefore the simplest mode of preaching. It is the enunciation of the *fact*, to the exclusion of all elaboration of reason or oratorical amplification, so that the negative characteristic, *without wisdom of words,* far from being a strange and accidental characteristic added to the term evangelize, is taken from the very nature of the act indicated by the verb. Thus Paul has not only continued steadily in his function as an evangelist; he has at the same time remained faithful to the spirit of his function. He has therefore done absolutely nothing which could have given rise to the formation of a Paul-party at Corinth.—The objective negative οὐ is used because the regimen refers, not to ἀπέστειλε, *sent me,*—in that case the negative would depend on the Divine *intention* in the sending, and the subjective negative, μή, would be required,—but to εὐαγγελίζεσθαι, which denotes the fact of preaching itself.

This second part of the verse contains the theme of the whole development which now follows. The formation of parties at Corinth evidently rested on a false conception of the gospel, which converted it into the wisdom of a school. Paul restores the true notion of Christianity, according to which this religion is above all a fact, and its preaching the simple testimony rendered to the fact: the announcement of the blessed news of salvation (εὐαγγελίζεσθαι). It is thus clear how the second part of the verse is logically connected with the first, the idea of *wisdom of words* being excluded by the very meaning of the term *evangelize.*—The phrase σοφία λόγου, *wisdom of words*, is not synonymous with σοφία τοῦ λέγειν, *the art of speaking well*. The emphasis is rather on the word *wisdom* than on *words*. The former term applies to the matter of discourse; it denotes a well-conceived system, a religious philosophy in which the new religion is set forth as furnishing a satisfactory explanation of God, man, and the universe. The latter bears on the form, and denotes the logical or brilliant exposition of such a system. Most critics think that by this phrase Paul means to allude "to the teaching of Apollos, at once profound and highly flavoured." "The orator preferred to Paul," says Reuss, "was no other than his friend and successor Apollos." We know few commentators who have been able, like Hilgenfeld, to rise above this prejudice, which has become in a manner conventional. As for me, this application seems to be directly contrary to all that Paul himself will afterwards say of Apollos, and to the way in which his teaching is described in the Acts. Paul, in this very Epistle, iv. 4–8, testifies to the closest relation between his own work and that of Apollos. Far from there having been conflict between the two works, that of Paul is represented, iii. 6, under the figure of *planting*, and that of Apollos under that of *watering*. Paul adds, ver. 8: "He that planteth and he that watereth *are one*." The apostle, on the contrary, characterizes in the following verses the mode of teaching which he would here combat, as belonging to that *wisdom of the world* (ver. 20) which the gospel comes to destroy; he applies to it (iii. 20) these words of a Psalm: "The thoughts of the wise are only vanity;" he accuses it of "destroying the temple of God," and threatens its propagators "with being destroyed" in their turn "by God" Himself (iii. 17, 18); and it is of the teaching of his friend and disciple Apollos that he meant to speak! According to Acts xviii. 27, 28, the whole preaching of Apollos was founded *on the Scriptures*, and not at all on a human speculation which he had brought from Alexandria, as is alleged by those who make him a disciple of Philo. It is even said that "*by the grace* of God he was *very profitable* to those who had believed." The person of Apollos must therefore be put out of the question here: it is impossible even to suppose that all which follows applies to his partisans. We have much more reason to think that those referred to here are the teachers who, under the name *those of Christ*, were propagating strange doctrines at Corinth regarding the person of Christ, and whom Paul accuses, 2 Cor. xi. 2-4, "of corrupting minds from the simplicity which is in Christ," and of beguiling them "as the serpent beguiled Eve."

The systematic and brilliant exposition of the fact of the cross would have the effect, according to Paul's phrase, of κενοῦν, literally *emptying* it. Those who, like Meyer and so many others, apply the foregoing expressions to Apollos, attenuate the meaning of this term as much as possible; according to them, it merely signifies that in consequence of this mode of preaching, the salutary effects of preaching will be ascribed rather to the brilliant qualities of the orator than to the matter of the doctrine, the cross. But this meaning is obviously far from coming up to the idea expressed by the word κενοῦν, *to make void.* Kling comes nearer to the energy of the expression when he refers to the fact that a dialectic and oratorical mode of preaching may indeed produce an intellectual or æsthetical effect, but not transform the egoistical *self*. But if Paul had meant nothing more than this, he would rather have used the word which is familiar to him, καταργεῖν, *to deprive of efficacy*. The term κενοῦν denotes an act which does violence to the object itself, and deprives it of its essence and virtue. Salvation by the cross is a Divine act which the conscience must appropriate as such. If one begins with presenting it to the understanding in the form of a series of well-linked ideas, as the result of a theory concerning man and God, it may happen that the mind will be nourished by it, but as by a system of wisdom, and not a way of salvation. It is as if we should substitute a theory of gravitation for gravitation itself (Edwards). The fact evaporates in ideas, and no longer acts on the conscience with the powerful reality which determines conversion. The sequel will be precisely the development of this thought.

2. *The nature of the gospel* (i. 18-iii. 4).

The gospel in its essence is not a *wisdom*, a philosophical system; it is a salvation. It is this thesis, summarily formulated in the second part of ver. 17, which the apostle proceeds to develop in the following passage. We have already pointed out, p. 86, the close relation in which it stands to the question that is the subject of this part of the Epistle, that of the parties formed in the Church.

The thesis itself is treated from two points of

view which complete one another : in a first passage, i. 18–ii. 5, the apostle demonstrates it directly ; in the second, ii. 6–iii. 4, he prudently limits its application. Undoubtedly the gospel *is* not essentially wisdom ; but it nevertheless *contains* a wisdom which is unveiled to the believer in proportion as the new life is developed in him, and which is really the only true wisdom.

The gospel is not a wisdom: i. 18–ii. 5.

Such, strictly speaking, is the truth which Paul is called to expound to the Corinthians. He demonstrates it to them :

1. By the irrational character of the central fact of the gospel, the cross : vers. 18–25.

2. By the mode of gaining members to, and the composition of their Church : vers. 26–31.

3. By the attitude taken in the midst of them by the preacher of the gospel : ii. 1–15.

Vers. 18-25.

Ver. 18. "For the preaching of the cross is to them that perish foolishness ; but unto us which are saved it is the power of God."—The *for* announces the proof of the assertion (ver. 17) : that to preach the gospel as a word of wisdom would be to destroy its very essence.—The antithesis of the words *foolishness* and *power* is regarded by Rückert and Meyer as inexact, because the opposite of foolishness is wisdom, not force. But these commentators have failed to see that the term wisdom would here have expressed too much or too little : too much for those who reject the gospel, and in whose eyes it can be nothing else than folly; too little for those who are disposed to receive it, and who need to find in it something better than a wisdom enlightening them. As sin is a fact, salvation must be laid hold of above all as a fact, not as a system. It is an act wrought by the arm of God, telling with power on the conscience and on the heart of the sinner: this alone can rescue from ruin a world which is perishing under the curse and in the corruption of sin.—The two datives: τοῖς ἀπολλυμένοις, *to them that perish*, and τοῖς σωζομένοις, *for those who are saved*, have not an exactly similar meaning; the former indicating a simple subjective appreciation, the latter including besides an effective relation, the idea of an effect produced. The participles are in the present, not as anticipating a final, eternal result (Meyer), or as containing the idea of a Divine predestination (Rückert), but as expressing two acts which are passing into fulfilment at the very time when Paul mentions them. In fact, perdition and salvation gradually come to their consummation in man simultaneously with the knowledge which he receives of the gospel.—The addition of the pronoun ἡμῖν, *to us*, is due to the fact that the letter is intended to be read to the believers in full assembly.

This way of treating human wisdom taken by God in the gospel is the fulfilment of threatenings already pronounced against it in the prophetic writings:

Ver. 19. "For it is written: I will destroy the wisdom of the wise, and will set aside the understanding of the prudent."—Isaiah, xxix. 14, had declared at the time when Sennacherib was threatening Judah, that the deliverance granted by Jehovah to His people would be His work, not that of the able politicians who directed the affairs of the kingdom. Was it not they on the contrary who, by counselling alliance with Egypt, had provoked the Assyrian intervention and thus paved the way for the destruction of Judah? It is on the same principle, says the apostle, that God now proceeds in saving the world. He snatches it from perdition by an act of His own love, and without deigning in the least to conjoin with Him human wisdom, which on the contrary He sweeps away as folly.—The verbs in the future, *I will destroy . . . I will set aside*, express a general maxim of the Divine government, which applies to every particular case and finds its full accomplishment in salvation by the cross. Paul quotes according to the LXX., who directly ascribe to God ("I will destroy . . ." etc.) what Isaiah had represented as the result of the Divine act: "Wisdom will perish," etc.—'Ἀθετεῖν, *to set aside*, as useless or worth nothing. Not only has God in His plan not asked counsel of human wisdom, and not only in the execution of it does He deliberately dispense with its aid, but He even deals its demands a direct contradiction. The following verse forcibly brings out this treatment to which it is subjected in the gospel.

Ver. 20. "Where is the wise? Where is the scribe? Where is the disputer of this age? Hath not God made foolish the wisdom of the[1] world?"—This exclamatory form has the same triumphant tone as in the words of Isaiah of which our passage seems to be an imitation (Isa. xix. 12, xxxiii. 18); comp. in

[1] Τούτου (*of this*) in T. R. is omitted by א A B C D P.

Paul himself xv. 55, and Rom. iii. 27. At the Divine breath the enemy has disappeared from the scene ; he is sought for in vain.—Rückert thinks that we should not seek rigorously to distinguish the meaning of the three substantives, that there is here rather a simple rhetorical accumulation. He refers all three to Greek wisdom, with a slight shade of difference in meaning. The emotional tone of the passage might justify this view in any other writer than Paul. But in this apostle every word is always the presentation of a precise idea. The ancient Greek commentators apply the first term, σοφός, *wise*, to Gentile philosophers ; the second, γραμματεύς, *scribe*, to Jewish doctors ; the third, συνζητητής, *disputer*, to Greek sophists ; but, in this sense, the last would be already embraced in the first term. It would therefore be better, with Meyer, to give to the word σοφός a general meaning : the representatives of human wisdom, and to the two last, the more particular sense of Jewish scribe and Greek philosopher. But the term *wisdom*, applying throughout this whole passage to human wisdom represented by the Greeks (ver. 22), I think it more in keeping with the apostle's thought to apply the first term to Greek philosophers, the second to Jewish scribes,—its ordinary meaning in the New Testament ; for that of *secretary*, Acts xix. 35, belongs to an altogether special case,—then to unite these two classes in the third term : "those in general who love to dispute," who seek truth in the way of intellectual discussion, by means either of Greek dialectic or Scripture erudition. — The complement, *of this world*, refers undoubtedly to the three substantives, and not only to the last.—The word αἰών, *age*, derived either from ἄω, *to breathe*, or from ἄει, *always*, denotes a period. The Jews divided history into a period anterior to the Messiah—this was what they called ὁ αἰὼν οὗτος, *this present age*—and the period of the Messianic kingdom, which they named ὁ αἰὼν μέλλων, *the age to come*. But, from the Christian point of view, these two periods are not merely successive ; they are partly simultaneous. For the present age still lasts even when the Messiah has appeared, His coming only transforming the actual state of things slowly and gradually. Hence it follows that for believers the two periods are superimposed, as it were, the one above the other, till at length, in consequence of the second and glorious advent of the Messiah, the old gives place entirely to the new.

The second question explains the first. How have the wise of the world thus disappeared ? By the way of salvation which God gives to be preached and which has the effect of bringing human wisdom to despair.— The verb ἐμώρανεν is usually taken in a declarative sense : "By putting wisdom aside in the most important affair of human life, God has *ipso facto declared* it foolish." But this verb has a more active sense, Rom. i. 22 ; it would require, therefore, at the least to be explained thus : "He has *treated* it as foolish, by taking no account of its demands." But should there not be given to it a more effective meaning still ? " He has, as it were, *befooled* wisdom. By presenting to it a wholly irrational salvation, He has put it into the condition of revolting against the means chosen by Him, and by declaring them absurd, becoming itself foolish." The complement, *of the world*, is not absolutely synonymous with the preceding term, *of this age:* the latter referred rather to the *time*,—the wisdom of the epoch anterior to the Messiah ; the term *world* bears rather on the *nature* of this wisdom,—that which proceeds from humanity apart from God.

But it is asked why God chose to treat human wisdom so rudely. Did He wish to extinguish the torch of reason which He had Himself lighted ? Ver. 21 answers this question; it explains the ground of the judgment which God visits on human reason, by the irrational nature of the gospel; to wit, that in the period anterior to the coming of Christ, reason had been unfaithful to its mission.

Ver. 21. "For after that in the wisdom of God the world by wisdom knew not God, it pleased God by the foolishness of preaching to save them that believe."— The γάρ, *for*, does not signify, as Edwards thinks, that the apostle is proceeding to expound the manner in which God has punished wisdom ; it introduces the indication of the *ground* why He thought good to deal so severely with it.—'Επειδή, *after that* (ἐπεί), as any one can attest (δή). The δή is added to show that Paul is speaking of a patent fact, on which one may in a manner put his finger. This fact is that of the aberrations to which human reason gave itself up during the times of heathenism, during those ages which the apostle calls, Acts xvii. 30, *the times of ignorance*.

The first proposition describes the sin of reason, and the second—the principal—its chastisement. These two ideas are so developed that the exact correspondence between the sin and the punishment appears from each of the terms of the two propositions. The phrase, *in the wisdom of God*, is not synonymous with the following, *by (means of) wisdom*. The absence of the complement, *of God*, in the second, of itself shows that the idea of wisdom is taken in the second instance more generally and indefinitely. The matter in question is not a manifestation of the Divine wisdom, but the mode of action followed by human reason, what we should call the exercise of the understanding, the way of reasoning. Hence, also, in this second expression the apostle uses the prep. διά, *by means of*, while in the former, where he is speaking of the wisdom *of God*, he makes use of the prep. ἐν, *in*, which indicates a domain *in which* Divine wisdom has been manifested. It is not difficult to understand what the theatre is of which Paul means to speak, on which God had displayed His wisdom in the eyes of men before the coming of Christ. In the passage Rom. i. 20, the apostle speaks of God's works "in which are visible, as it were, to the eye, from the creation of the world, His invisible perfections, His eternal power and Godhead." In his discourse at Lystra (Acts xiv. 17), he declares that God "has not left Himself without witness before the eyes of men, sending rain from heaven and fruitful seasons, and filling the hearts of men with abundance and joy." In the midst of the Areopagus (Acts xvii. 27), he declares that the end God had in view in distributing men over the face of the earth, was to make them "seek the Lord that they might touch Him as with the hand, and find Him." This universe is indeed, as Calvin says, "a brilliant specimen of the Divine wisdom." In the immense organism of nature, every detail is related to the whole, and the whole to every detail. There we find a perceptible, though unfathomable, system of hidden causes and sensible effects, of efficacious means and beneficent ends, of laws that are constant and yet pliant and capable of modification, which fills the observer with admiration and reveals to his understanding the intelligent thought which has presided over the constitution of this great whole. Man, therefore, only needed to apply to such a work the rational processes, the principles of substance, of causality, and finality, with which his mind is equipped, to rise to the view of the wise, good, and powerful Author from whom the universe proceeds. There was in the work a revelation of the Worker, a revelation constituting what the apostle calls, Rom. i. 19, τὸ γνωστὸν τοῦ θεοῦ, "that which is naturally knowable of the Divine person." To welcome the rays of this revelation, and to reconstruct the image of Him from whom it proceeded, such was the noble mission of the reason with which God had endowed man : it should have come by this normal exercise of His gift (*by means of wisdom*) *to know God in His wisdom.* But as Paul expounds, Rom. i. 21, human reason was unfaithful to this mission; man's heart would neither *glorify* God as such, nor even *give thanks to Him*, and reason, thus interrupted in its exercise, instead of rising to the knowledge of the Worker by contemplating the work, deified the work itself. Unable to overlook altogether the traces of the Divine in the universe, and yet unwilling to assert God frankly *as God*, it resorted to an evasion ; it gave birth to heathenism and its chimeras.

G

Some sages, indeed, conceived the idea of a God one and good, but they did not succeed in carrying this vague and abstract notion beyond their schools; the popular deities continued to stand, dominating and falsifying the human conscience. In Israel alone there shone the knowledge of a God, one, living, and holy; but this light was due to a special revelation. We must therefore take care not to include the Jewish revelation, as Meyer and Holsten do, in the meaning of the expression : ἐν τῇ σοφίᾳ τοῦ θεοῦ, *in the wisdom of God*. Not till afterwards, vers. 22–24, will the apostle deal with the Jews, and that in a way absolutely subsidiary, and applying to them a quite different term to that of *wisdom*. As little must we give to the words, *in the wisdom of God*, as is done by Rückert and Reuss, the meaning of our modern phrase, "*In His unfathomable design*, it pleased God. . . ." This interpretation would make the wandering of human wisdom the effect of a Divine decree. Men thus find the doctrine of absolute predestination which they ascribe to the apostle. But how can we fail to see that this would be to exculpate reason at the very moment when the apostle is engaged in condemning it ? Finally, it is not in accordance with the thought of the apostle to see in the expression διὰ τῆς σοφίας, *by means of wisdom*, with Billroth and Holsten, the indication of the obstacle which hindered man from arriving at the knowledge of God : "After that, *through an effect of its wisdom*, the world knew not God in . . ." Very far from condemning the exercise of the natural understanding, the apostle on the contrary charges this faculty with turning aside from its legitimate use.

After the ground of the punishment, the punishment itself. The term εὐδόκησεν indicates an act, not of arbitrariness, but of freewill: "He judged good," evidently because it was good in fact. Reason had used its light so ill that the time was come for God to appeal to a quite different faculty.—He therefore presents Himself to man with a means of salvation which has no longer, like creation, the character of wisdom, and which is no more to be apprehended by the understanding, but which seems to it, on the contrary, stamped with folly: a Crucified One! The gen. τοῦ κηρύγματος, *of the preaching*, designates the apostolic testimony as a known fact (art. τοῦ, *the*).—This term includes the notion of authority: God lays down His salvation; He offers it such as it has pleased Him to realize it. There is nothing in it to be modified. It is to be accepted or rejected as it is. It need not be thought with Hofmann and others, because of the prep. διά, *by means of*, that this regimen is the counterpart of διὰ τῆς σοφίας, *by means of wisdom*, in the preceding proposition. It corresponds rather to the regimen ἐν τῇ σοφίᾳ τοῦ θεοῦ, *in the wisdom of God*, in His original revelation which had the character of wisdom. Man not having recognised God in this form by the healthy use of his understanding, God manifests Himself to him in another revelation which has the appearance of folly. The reason why Paul here uses the prep. *by*, to correspond to the *in* of the first proposition, is easily understood. *In* His revelation in the heart of nature, God waits for man; He would see if man, by the exercise of his understanding, will be able to discover Him: " to see whether they will put their hand on Him," as it runs, Acts xvii. 27. It is this expectant attitude which is expressed by the ἐν, *in*. Not having been found thus, God now takes the initiative; He Himself seeks man by the proclamation of salvation. Hence Paul in this case employs the διά, *by means of*, which denotes the prevenient activity.

The term which in the second proposition is the true counterpart of the phrase διὰ τῆς σοφίας, *by means of wisdom* (in the first), is found at the end of the sentence; it is the word τοὺς πιστεύοντας, *them that believe*. The faculty to which God appeals in this new revelation is no longer reason, which had so badly performed its task in reference to the former; it is *faith*. To an advance of love like that which forms the essence of this supreme manifestation, the answer is to be given, no longer by an act of intelligence, but by a movement of confidence. What God asks is no longer that man should investigate, but that he should give himself up with a broken conscience and a believing heart.—Finally, to the two contrasts: *in the wisdom of God and by the foolishness of preaching; by wisdom*, and, *them that believe*, the apostle adds a third: that of the two verbs *know* and *save*. Man ought originally to have known God, and by this knowledge have been united to Him; it was for this end that God revealed Himself to his understanding in an intelligible way. Man not having done so, God now comes to *save* him, and that by means absolutely irrational. Man, first of all, will have to let himself be snatched from perdition and reconciled to God by a fact which passes beyond his understanding. Thereafter he will be able to think of knowing. It would seem to follow from these words of the apostle, that if reason had performed its task of *knowing* God, it would not have been necessary for God to *save* man; a sound philosophy would have raised him up to God. The apostle gives no explanation on this head; but his thought was probably this: if man had risen by his wisdom to the true knowledge and worship of God, this legitimate use of his reason would have been crowned by a mode of salvation appropriate to the laws of this faculty. In the second revelation the Divine wisdom would have rayed forth with more brilliance still than in the first. Thus the character, so offensive to reason, under which the salvation offered to man presents itself in the preaching of the cross, is the consequence of the abuse which reason made of its faculty of knowing. If it had developed itself as an organ of light, the mode and revelation of salvation would have been adapted to its wants. Obviously we cannot know what salvation and the preaching of salvation would have been in such different conditions.

The verse which we have just explained contains in three lines a whole philosophy of history, the substance of entire volumes. As from the standpoint of Judaism the apostle divides history into two principal periods, that of law and that of grace, so from the standpoint of Hellenism he also distinguishes two great phases, that of the revelation of God in wisdom, and that of His revelation in the form of foolishness. In the first, God lets Himself be sought by man; in the second, He seeks man Himself. Such is the masterly survey which the apostle casts over the course of universal history. There was singular adroitness on his part in throwing such a morsel as this development to those Corinthians, connoisseurs in wisdom as they affected to be, and apt to overlook the apostle's superiority. Paul says to them, as it were, "You will have speculation, and you think me incapable of it; here is a specimen, and true also! It is the judgment of God on your past." But at the same time, with what marvellous subtlety of style does he succeed in putting and cramming, as it were, into the two propositions of this verse, all that wealth of antitheses which presented themselves at once to his mind! To construct such a period there needed to be joined to the thought of Paul the language of Plato.

Vers. 22–25 state the historical fact which demonstrates the judgment enunciated in ver. 21: The salvation of all, Gentiles and Jews, has really been accomplished by that which is folly in the eyes of the one, and which scandalizes the other.

Vers. 22 and 23. "*For indeed*[1] the Jews require signs,[2] and the Greeks seek after wisdom; 23. but we preach Christ crucified, unto the Jews a stumbling-block, and unto the Gentiles[3] foolishness."—This second ἐπειδή, *for indeed*, should, according to Meyer and Kling, begin a new sentence, the main proposition of which is found in ver. 23: *But as for us, we preach*. The δέ, *but*, would not be irreconcilable with this construction. The δέ is often found in the classics as the sign of the apodosis when this expresses a strong contrast to the preceding proposition (see Meyer); comp. in the New Testament, Col. i. 22. But two reasons are opposed to

---

[1] All the documents except F G Syr^sch read καί before Ιουδαιοι (*both Jews*).

[2] T. R. with L and Mnn. reads σημειον (*a miracle*).

[3] T. R. reads Ελλησι (*to the Greeks*); but all the Mjj. read εθνεσι (*to the Gentiles*).

this construction : first, the absence of a proper particle to connect this new sentence with the preceding ; then the simple logic ; for the idea of ver. 22, that Greeks and Jews ask for wisdom and miracles, cannot form a ground for that of ver. 23 : that preaching presents a Christ who is to them an offence and folly. The *object* of God, in this mode of preaching, could not have been to scandalize the hearers ; in ver. 24 the apostle even expressly adds the opposite thought : to wit, that Christ is to the believers of both peoples power and wisdom. The ἐπειδή of ver. 22 does not therefore begin a new sentence, like that which began ver. 21, and which related to εὐδόκησεν, *it pleased God.* Yet it is not on this account a repetition and amplification of that sentence. The first ἐπειδή (ver. 21) served to explain the rejection visited by God on human wisdom ; the second (ver. 22) simply affirms the *reality* of this judgment : " for in reality, as experience may convince you, while men demand wisdom and miracles, we preach to them a Saviour who is quite the contrary, but who nevertheless is to them who receive Him miracle and wisdom." We have not to see, then, in these three verses the development of the words, *them that believe . . .* (Hofmann), nor that of the term, "*foolishness* of preaching" (Rückert, de Wette) ; they give the proof of the fact of the decree expressed in ver. 21 : "It pleased God to save . . ." (Billroth, Osiander, Beet, Edwards). What a strange dispensation ! The world presents itself with its various demands : prodigies, wisdom ! The cross answers, and the apparent meaning of the answer is : weakness, foolishness ! But to faith its real meaning is : power, wisdom ! Thus in the gospel God rejects the demands of the world so far as they are false, but only to satisfy them fully so far as they are legitimate.

The apostle divides the ancient world into two classes of men; those whom God has taken under His direction and enlightened by a special revelation, *the Jews;* the others whom He "has left to walk in their own ways" (Acts xiv. 16), the Gentiles, designated here by the name of their most distinguished representatives, *the Greeks.* The two subjects are named without an article: *Jews, Greeks;* it is the category which the apostle would designate.—The particle καί . . . καί, *both . . . and,* indicates that each of those groups has its demand, but that the demands are different. For the Jew it is *miracles,* the Divine materialized in external prodigies, in sensible manifestations of omnipotence. The plural σημεῖα, *miracles,* ought certainly to be read with almost all the Mjj.; the received text reads the singular σημεῖον, *a sign,* with L only. This last reading is undoubtedly a correction occasioned by Matt. xii. 38 and xvi. 1, where the Jews ask from Jesus *a sign* in heaven. Paul's object is not to refer to a particular fact, but to characterize a tendency; this is indicated by the plural, signs, and yet more signs! For it is of the nature of this desire to rise higher and higher in proportion as it is satisfied. "On the morrow after the multiplication of the loaves," says Riggenbach, "the multitudes ask: What signs doest thou then?" Every stroke of power must be surpassed by a following one yet more marvellous.—The Greek ideal is quite different; it is a masterpiece of *wisdom:* the Divine intellectualized in a system eloquently giving account of the nature of the gods, the origin, course, and end of the universe. This people, with their inquisitive and subtle mind, would get at the essence of things. The man who will satisfy Greek expectation will be, not a thaumaturge, making the Divine appear grossly in matter, but a Pythagoras or a Socrates of double power.—Thus we have the two great figures of the ancient world ineffaceably engraved. Let us remark, finally, with what delicacy the apostle chooses the two verbs used to characterize the two tendencies: for the Jew, αἰτεῖν, *ask;* the miracle comes from God—it is received; for the Greek, ζητεῖν, *seek;* system is the result of labour—it is discovered. It is obvious that in this description of the ancient world, from the religious standpoint, the figure of the Jew is placed only for the sake of contrast; the Greeks are and remain, according to the context, the principal figure. It is always wisdom contrasted with the *fact* of salvation.

Ver. 23. As ver. 22 went back on the first proposition of ver. 21, "The world by wisdom knew not God in His wisdom," so ver. 23 (with ver. 24) goes back on the second, "It pleased God to save by . . ." The δέ is strongly adversative. By the ἡμεῖς, *we,* the subject of these verses is also contrasted with that of the previous verse. I mean the preachers of the crucified Christ with the unbelieving Jews and Greeks. Instead of a series of acts of omnipotence transforming the world, or of a perfect light cast on the universe of being, what does the apostolic preaching offer to the world? A Crucified One, a compact mass of weakness, suffering, ignominy, and incomprehensible absurdity! There is enough there absolutely to bewilder Jewish expectation; in the first place, it is a stone against which it is broken. Σκάνδαλον: what arrests the foot suddenly in walking and causes a fall. And the Greek? The term *Christ* seems at first sight not to apply to the expectation of this people. But all humanity, as is seen in Greek mythology, aspired after a celestial appearance similar to that which the Jew designated by the name of *Christ*, after a communication from above capable of binding man to God. So Schelling did not hesitate to say, when paraphrasing ver. 5 of the prologue of John: " Christ was the light, Christ was the consolation of the Gentiles."[1] The apostle can therefore speak also of the Christ in relation to the Greeks. But here again, what a contrast between the desired manifestation and the reality! Must not salvation by the Crucified One be to the Greek, instead of the solution of all enigmas, the most sombre of mysteries?—The participle ἐσταυρωμένον is an attribute, *as crucified*, otherwise it would be preceded by the article; the two substantives, σκάνδαλον and μωρίαν, are appositions.

It might be asked, no doubt, in connection with this verse, whether Jesus, by His numerous miracles, did not satisfy the Jewish demand? But His acts of miraculous power had been annulled, so to speak, in the eyes of the Jews by the final catastrophe of the cross, which seemed to have fully justified His adversaries, and did not suffer them to see in Him any other than an impostor or an agent of diabolical power.

And yet as to this preaching which so deeply shocks the aspirations of men, Jews and Gentiles, so far as

[1] " *Christus war der Heiden Licht; Christus war der Heiden Trost.*"

these are false, it turns out—and daily experience demonstrates the fact—that received with faith, it contains both for the one and the other the full satisfaction of those same aspirations so far as they are true :

Ver. 24. "But unto those [*of them*] which are called, both Jews and Greeks, Christ the power of God, and the wisdom of God."—The αὐτοῖς δέ forcibly separates the called, Jews and Gentiles, from the mass of their fellow-countrymen, while identifying them with it so far as their past life was concerned : "But unto them, those same Jews and Gentiles, once become believers . . ." Those Jews and Greeks themselves who saw in the preaching of the cross only the contrary of what they sought, — weakness, foolishness, — no sooner become believers than they find in it what they asked : power and wisdom.—The term κλητοί, *called*, here includes the notion of *believers*. Sometimes calling is put in contrast to the acceptance of faith; thus in the maxim, Matt. xxii. 14 : "Many called, few chosen." But often also the designation called implies that of accepter; comp. i. 1, 2, and Rom. viii. 30; and it is certainly the case here, where the term τοῖς κλητοῖς, *the called*, stands for τοὺς πιστεύοντας, *them that believe* (ver. 21). The apostle exalts the Divine act in salvation; he sees God's arm laying hold of certain individuals, drawing them from the midst of those nationalities, Jewish and Gentile, by the call of preaching; then, when they have believed, he sees the Christ preached and received, unveiling Himself to them as containing exactly all that their countrymen are seeking, but the opposite of which they think they see in Him.—The accusative Χριστόν might be regarded as in apposition to the Χριστόν of ver. 23 (Hofmann); but the phrase, "to preach Christ as Christ," is unnatural; Χριστόν should therefore be regarded as the direct object of κηρύσσομεν, *we preach* (ver. 23), and the two substantives, *power* and *wisdom*, are not attributes (*as* power, *as* wisdom), but cases of simple apposition, in the same category as σκάνδαλον and μωρίαν. The apostle here omits the ἐσταυρωμένον not without purpose. For the two terms, *power of God* and *wisdom of God*, embrace not only the Christ of the cross, but also the glorified Christ.—The complement, *of God*, contrasts with the power and wisdom of the world, that wisdom and power of a wholly different nature, which on that account the world does not recognise. The *power of God* is the force from above, manifested in those spiritual wonders which transform the heart of the believer; expiation which restores God to him, the renewal of will which restores him to God, and in perspective the final renovation, which is to crown these two miracles of reconciliation and sanctification (ver. 30). The *wisdom of God* is the light which breaks on the believer's inward eye, when in the person of Christ he beholds the Divine plan which unites as in a single work of love, creation, incarnation, redemption, the gathering together of all things under one head, the final glorification of the universe. The believer thus finds himself, as Edwards says, in possession of " a salvation which is at once the mightiest miracle in the guise of weakness [this for the Jew], and the highest wisdom in the guise of folly [this for the Greek]." [1]

[1] Edwards, p. 31.

But how can that which is apparently most feeble and foolish thus contain all that man can legitimately desire of power and light in point of fact? The apostle answers this question by the axiom stated in ver. 25.

Ver. 25. "Because the foolishness of God is wiser than men; and the weakness of God is stronger than men."—The neuter adjectives, τὸ μωρόν, τὸ ἀσθενές, do not denote qualities belonging to the being of God Himself, but certain categories of Divine manifestations having the two characters mentioned. If one dared translate thus,—the weak, foolish product of Divine action. And God's masterpiece in these two respects is the cross. The gen. τοῦ θεοῦ, *of God*, is at once that of origin and property. The second member of comparison is sometimes completed by paraphrasing,— "wiser than *the wisdom* of men; stronger than *the strength* of men;" but this supposed ellipsis weakens the thought. The apostle means: wiser than men with all their wisdom; stronger than men with all their strength. When God has the appearance of acting irrationally or weakly, that is the time when He triumphs most certainly over human wisdom and power.

What God makes of human wisdom has been clearly manifested by the character of folly which He has stamped on the salvation offered by Christ; it is equally so in the choice God makes of those in whom this salvation is realized by faith in the preaching of it. Such is the idea of vers. 26-31, a passage in which the apostle shows us the most honoured classes of society remaining outside the Church, while God raises up from the very depths of Gentile society a new people of saved and glorified ones who hold everything from Him.

Vers. 26–31.

Ver. 26. "For[1] see your calling, brethren, there are among you not many wise men after the flesh, not many mighty, not many noble."—This mode of recruiting the Church confirms the conclusion drawn above from the nature of the gospel. Hence the γάρ, *in fact*, which is certainly the true reading. It was not the leading classes of Corinthian society which had furnished the largest number of the members of the Church. The majority were poor, ignorant, slaves. God shows thereby that He has no need of human wisdom and power to support His work.—The verb βλέπετε should be taken as imperative and not as indicative: "Open your eyes, and see that..." This meaning is not incompatible with the γάρ. Meyer rightly quotes Sophocles, *Phil.* v. 1043: ἄφετε γὰρ αὐτόν.—Paul has come near to his readers in reminding them of this fact which touches them so closely; hence the address, — *brethren!* — The word κλῆσις, *calling*, has sometimes been taken in the sense wrongly given to the word *vocation*, as denoting social position. But this meaning is foreign to the New Testament. Paul would describe by it the manner in which God has proceeded in drawing this Church by the preaching of the gospel from the midst of the Corinthian population. Jesus had already indicated a similar dispensation in Israel, and had rendered homage to it: "Father, I thank Thee because Thou hast hid these things from the

---

[1] Instead of γαρ (*for*), D E F G read ουν (*therefore*).

wise and prudent, and hast revealed them unto babes. Even so, Father, for so it seemed good in Thy sight" (Matt. xi. 25, 26). The fact was not therefore accidental; it belonged to the Divine plan. God did not wish that human wisdom should mix its alloy with His: the latter was to carry off victory alone. Meyer makes πολλοί, *many*, the subject, and σοφοί, *wise*, the attribute : "There are not many who are wise . . . mighty . . ." But in this sense the πολλοί must have been completed by the genitive ὑμῶν, *of you*. It is better simply to understand the verb ἔστε, "*Ye are not many wise.*"—In the adjunct κατὰ σάρκα, *according to the flesh*, the word *flesh* denotes, as it often does, human nature considered in itself, and apart from its relation to God. This adjunct has not been added to the two following terms, *mighty . . . noble*, because, as de Wette says, these latter obviously denote advantages of an earthly nature.—Οἱ δυνατοί, *mighty*, denotes persons in office ; εὐγενεῖς, *the noble*, persons of high birth, descendants of ancient families.[1]

Vers. 27–29. "But God hath chosen the foolish things of the world to confound the wise, and God hath chosen the weak things of the world to confound the things which are mighty ; 28. and base things of the world, and things which are despised, and

---

[1] Hasenklever (*Jahrb. f. prot. Theol.*, 1882, i.) states that, as is proved by the inscriptions in the Catacombs, most of the members of the Primitive Church, at Rome also, belonged to the lower or middle classes (bakers, gardeners, tavern-keepers, freedmen, a few advocates); he observes that the Christians are characterized in *Minutius Felix* (vii. 12) as *indocti, impoliti, rudes, agrestes ;* and he rightly regards this fact as the most eloquent testimony in favour of Christianity, which has gained victory over hostile powers, without any external aid, by the sole force of its internal virtue.

things[1] which are not, to bring to nought things that are; 29. that no flesh should glory before God."[2]—The emotion with which the apostle signalizes this providential fact is betrayed by the threefold repetition of the words *God has chosen*, by the thrice expressed contrast between the two opposite terms, *God* and *the world*, and by the emphatic position of the object (thrice repeated) at the beginning of the proposition. The neuter form of the three adjectives, *foolish, weak*, and *vile*, contrasted as it is with the masculines preceding, the *wise*, the *mighty*, the *noble*, is not used accidentally; these neuters indicate a mass in which the individuals have so little value that they are not counted as distinct personalities. So the word τὸ ἀνδράποδον, *the domestic* [thing], is used for slaves. The term ἐκλέγεσθαι does not here denote a decree of eternal predestination, but the energetic action whereby God has taken to Him (the Middle λέγεσθαι) from the midst of the world (ἐκ) those individuals whom no one judged worthy of attention, and made them the bearers of His kingdom. The strong, the wise, etc., are thus covered with shame, because the weak, etc., are not only equal to them, but preferred. In the phrase, *things which are despised*, is concentrated all that disdain with which the ignorant and weak and poor were overwhelmed in the society of heathendom; and the final term, *things which are not*, expresses the last step of that scale of abasement on which those beings vegetated. The subjective negative μή before ὄντα does not deny real

---

[1] T. R. with B E L P Syr. reads καί here (*also* or *even*); this word is omitted by the other Mjj.

[2] T. R. with C Syr. reads αυτου (*Him*) instead of θεου (*God*).

existence, as would be done by οὐ, but the recognition of any value whatever in public opinion; all those beings were to it *as non-existent*. The καί, which in the received text precedes the last participle, is omitted by most of the Mjj. The meaning *even* would be the only suitable. But how could we explain this καί, if it were authentic, otherwise than the previous ones? It is better therefore to reject it. The asyndeton is perfectly in place; it makes this last word the summary, and, so to speak, the accumulation of all the preceding. There is a corresponding gradation in the verb καταργεῖν, *to annul* (bring to nought), to reduce to absolute powerlessness, which takes the place of the preceding and less strong term καταισχύνειν, *to cover with confusion*. Already the wise and mighty were humiliated by the call addressed to their social inferiors; now they disappear from the scene. And for what end does God act thus? The apostle answers in the following sentence:

Ver. 29. Ὅπως, *that thus*. This conjunction denotes the *final* end with a view to which all the preceding ἵνα, *that*, indicated only means. The negative μή, according to a well-known Hebraism, applies to the verb only, and not at the same time to the subject *all flesh;* for Paul does not mean to say that *some* flesh at least should be able to glory. The word *flesh* is taken in the sense pointed out, ver. 26. No man, considered in himself and in what he is by his own nature, can glory before God, who knows so well the nothingness of His creature. The words, *all flesh*, seem to go beyond the idea of the preceding propositions, where the question was merely of the humiliation of the wise and mighty. But is it not enough that these last be stripped of the right of glorying that the whole world may be so along with them, the weak and ignorant being already abased by their natural condition? As Hofmann says: The one party are humiliated because with all their wisdom and might, they have not obtained what it concerned them to reach, salvation; the other, because if they have obtained it, it is impossible for them to imagine that it is by their own natural resources that they have come to it.

The mode of the *Divine calling*, to which the apostle pointed the attention of his readers, ver. 26, had two aspects: the first, the rejection of things wise and mighty; the second, the choice which had been made of things foolish and weak. The first of these two sides has been expounded, vers. 26-29; the apostle now presents the second.

Vers. 30, 31. "But of Him are ye in Christ Jesus, who, on the part of God,[1] has been made unto us wisdom, as also[2] righteousness and sanctification and redemption; 31. that, according as it is written, He that glorieth, let him glory in the Lord."—Rückert, with his usual precision, asks whether the thought expressed in these two verses is logically connected with the passage as a whole; he answers in the negative, and sees in those two verses only an appendix. We think, as we have just pointed out, that they are on the contrary the indispensable complement of the passage. Vers. 26-29: " See what your calling is not,

---

[1] T. R. with L Syr. places ημιν (*us*) before σοφια (*wisdom*), while the nine other Mjj. It. place it after that word

[2] F G read: και δικαιοσυνή, instead of δικαιοσυνη τε και.

and understand why!" Vers. 30–31: "See what it is, and again understand why!" The δέ is therefore adversative to the vain boasting of the things that are wise, etc., henceforth reduced to silence; there is opposed the cry of triumph and praise on the side of the things foolish and weak; for ver. 31 evidently forms the counterpart of ver. 29.—'Εξ αὐτοῦ, *of Him* (*God*), expresses the essential idea of this conclusion: If things that were not have now become something, it is due to God alone; ἐκ therefore indicates the origin of this spiritual creation; comp. Eph. ii. 9. 'Υμεῖς, *ye*: the things formerly weak, powerless, despised. This pronoun resumes the address of ver. 26.—Calvin, Rückert, Hofmann see in the word ἐστέ, *ye are*, a contrast to the preceding expression: things *which are not*. "It is of God that your transition from nothingness to being proceeds." The words, *in Christ*, would thus express, secondarily, the means whereby God has accomplished this miracle. Others strictly connect ἐξ αὐτοῦ with ἐστέ in the sense of the Johannine phrase: to be of God, to be born of God. But these two explanations have the awkwardness of separating the words ἐν Χριστῷ 'Ιησοῦ from ἐστέ; whereas we know well how frequently Paul uses the form εἶναι ἐν Χριστῷ. It is better therefore, as it seems to me, to translate thus: "It is of Him that ye *are in Christ*;" that is to say: "It is to God alone that you owe the privilege of having been called to the communion of Christ, and of having thereby become the wise and mighty and noble of the new era which is now opening on the world." The following proposition will explain, by what Christ Himself *was*, these glorious effects of communion with Him. — The phrase εἶναι ἐν, *to be in*, denotes two moral facts : first, the act of faith whereby man lays hold of Christ ; second, the community of life with Him contracted by means of this act of faith. In this relation the believer can appropriate all that Christ was, and thus become what he was not and what he could not become of himself.—In the proposition which follows, the apostle substitutes for ὑμεῖς, *ye*, the pronoun ἡμῖν, *to us;* and this because the matter in question now is, what Christ is objectively to men, and not the subjective appropriation of Him by believers.—The aor. Passive, ἐγενήθη, is generally regarded (Meyer, Edwards) as equivalent in meaning to the aor. Middle, ἐγένετο, *was, became.* It is, indeed, a form springing up from the dialects, and which was only introduced latterly into Attic Greek. But that does not, we think, prevent there being a difference in the use of the two forms. The passive form occurs in the New Testament only some fifty times, compared with about 550 times that the aor. Middle is used ; and it is easy in each of those instances to see the meaning of being made, which is naturally that of the *Passive*. I think, therefore, that we must translate, not, "has been" or "has become," but, *has been made*. This is confirmed by the adjunct ἀπὸ θεοῦ, *on the part of God*. Yet it should be remarked that the apostle has not written ὑπὸ θεοῦ, "*by* God." The ἀπό, *on the part of*, weakens the passivity contained in the ἐγενήθη, and leaves space for the free action of Christ. In using the words ὃς ἐγενήθη, *who has been made* (historically), the apostle seems to have in mind the principal phases of Christ's being : *wisdom*, by His life and teaching;

righteousness, by His death and resurrection; *sanctification*, by His elevation to glory; *redemption*, by His future return.

The received text places the pronoun ἡμῖν, *to us*, before σοφία, *wisdom*. This reading would have the effect of bringing this substantive into proximity with the three following, from which it would only be separated by the adjunct ἀπὸ θεοῦ; and this adjunct again can be made to depend, not on the verb ἐγενήθη, but on the substantive σοφία itself: "wisdom coming from God." In this case there would be nothing to separate it from the three following substantives. But the authority of the mss. speaks strongly in favour of the position of ἡμῖν after σοφία; and the adjunct ἀπὸ θεοῦ depends more naturally on the verb ἐγενήθη; it serves to bring out the idea of the ἐξ αὐτοῦ at the beginning of the verse. It must thus be held that the apostle's intention was clearly to separate the first substantive from the other three, and this has led him to interpose between σοφία and the other substantives the two adjuncts: ἡμῖν and ἀπὸ θεοῦ.—If it is so, it is impossible to maintain the relation which Meyer establishes between the four substantives, according to which they express three co-ordinate notions: 1, that of knowledge of the Divine plan revealed in Christ (*wisdom*); 2, that of salvation, regarded on the positive side, of the blessings which it brings (*righteousness* and *holiness*); 3, that of salvation from the negative view-point, deliverance from condemnation and sin (*redemption*). Meyer rests his view on the fact that the particle τε καί binds the second and third terms closely together, isolating them at the same time from the first and fourth. But regard to philological exactness may have misled this excellent critic here, as in so many instances. Why, in that case, interpose the two adjuncts between the first term and the second? And is it not obvious at a glance that the three last terms are in the closest relation to one another, so that it is impossible to separate them into two distinct groups, co-ordinate with the first? This is what has led a large number of commentators (Rückert, Neander, Heinrici, Edwards, etc.) to see in the three last terms the explanation and development of the first: Christ has become our *wisdom*, and that inasmuch as He has brought us the most necessary of blessings, salvation, consisting of *righteousness, sanctification,* and *redemption*. It is easy in this case to understand why the first term, which states the general notion, has been separated from the other three which are subordinate to it. Only this explanation is not in harmony with the special sense of religious *knowledge*, in which the word *wisdom* is taken in the passage. *Wisdom*, as a plan of salvation, is contrasted, ver. 24, with salvation itself as a Divine *act* (δύναμις, *power*). How does it come to be identified here with salvation itself? The word, therefore, cannot denote anything else here than the *understanding* of the Divine plan communicated to man by Jesus Christ. The parallel ver. 24 leads us, I think, to the true explanation which Osiander has developed. According to him, the last three terms are the unfolding of the notion of δύναμις, *power*, as the counterpart to that of *wisdom*. In Christ there has been given first the knowledge of the Divine plan, whereby the believer is rendered wise; then to the revelation there has been added the carrying out of this salvation, by the acquisition of which we become strong. This effective salvation includes the three gifts: *righteousness, holiness, redemption*. The only objection to this view is that the τε καί would require to be placed so as to connect together σοφία on the one hand, and the following three terms on the other, whereas by its position this copula rather connects δικαιοσύνη and ἁγιασμός (*righteousness* and *holiness*), as the second καί connects the third substantive with the fourth. But the omission of a copula fitted to connect the first substantive with the other three may have been occasioned by two circumstances: 1, the two adjuncts which separate the word wisdom from the following three; 2, the difficulty of adding to the copula τε καί, which joins the word *righteousness* with the following, a new copula intended to connect it with the preceding (see Osiander). Then, if it is remembered that the *salvation* described in the last three substantives is only the realization of the Divine *plan* designated by the first (*wisdom*), it will be seen that these may be placed there as a sort of grammatical apposition to the first.

The idea of δικαιοσύνη, *righteousness*, is that developed by Paul in the first part of the Epistle to the Romans, chaps. i.–v. It is the act of grace whereby God removes the condemnation pronounced on the sinner, and places him relatively to Himself, as a believer, in the position of a righteous man. The possibility of such a Divine act is due to the death and resurrection of Christ.—The term ἁγιασμός, *holiness* or *sanctification*, is the Divine act which succeeds the preceding, and whereby there is created in the believer a state in harmony with his position as righteous. It is the destruction of sin by the gift of a will which the Holy Spirit has consecrated to God. This act is that described by the apostle in the succeeding passage of the Epistle to the Romans, vi. 1–viii. 17. I have sought to show in my Commentary on that Epistle, at vi. 19, that the term ἁγιασμός denotes sanctification, not in the sense in which we usually take the word, as a progressive human work, but as the state of holiness divinely wrought in believers. Justification is generally regarded as a gift of God; but sanctification as the work by which man ought to respond to the gift of righteousness. St. Paul, on the contrary, sees in holiness a Divine work no less than in righteousness: Christ Himself is the holiness of the believer as well as his righteousness. This new work is due to His exaltation to glory, whence He sends the Holy Spirit; and by Him He communicates His own life to the justified believer (John vii. 39, xvi. 14). If, then, our righteousness is Christ *for* us, our sanctification is Christ *in* us, Christ *is* our holiness as well as our righteousness.[1] — He is finally our *redemption*, our complete and final deliverance. Such is the meaning of the word ἀπολύτρωσις. The development of this third idea is found, Rom. viii. 18–30. This deliverance, which consists of entrance into glory, is the consummation of the two preceding acts of grace. It is by His glorious advent that Jesus will thus eman-

---

[1] How evident it is, from this so well-marked distinction between *righteousness* and *sanctification*, that in the eyes of the apostle *righteousness* had the declarative sense, and *sanctification* alone contained the sense of an effectual communication !

cipate justified and sanctified believers from all the miseries of their present state, and give them an external condition corresponding to their spiritual state. Meyer asserts that this meaning of ἀπολύτρωσις would demand the complement τοῦ σώματος, *of the body*, as in Rom. viii. 23. But the term *redemption* embraces much more than the simple fact of the resurrection of the body. It has the wide sense in which we find it, Luke xxi. 28; Eph. i. 14, and iv. 30; Heb. xi. 35. As to the view of Meyer, who sees in this word only the negative side of moral redemption, deliverance from guilt and sin, it is certainly too weak, and besides this blessing was already implied in the two foregoing terms.—If we so obviously find in the Epistle to the Romans the development of the three last terms, in which the notion of salvation is summed up, we cannot forget that the development of the first, σοφία, occurs immediately afterwards in the same Epistle, in chaps. ix.-xi., which so admirably expound the whole plan of God.—Calvin rightly observes that it would be hard to find in the whole of Scripture a saying which more clearly expresses the different phases of Christ's work.

Ver. 31. In ver. 29 all human glorying has been declared to be excluded; in this, the apostle invites the new people, the wise and mighty whom God has raised up by preaching, to strike up a song of praise, but of praise relating to God alone.—The term κύριος, *Lord*, in the passage of Jer. ix. 23, 24, quoted by the apostle, denotes Jehovah; but it could hardly fail in the mind of Paul to be applied at the same time to Christ, by whom the Lord has done this work, and

who has so often received the title in this chapter.—
Here is no commonplace exhortation to glorify the
Lord. What we have to see in these words is a hidden
antithesis, which is sufficiently explained by the
passage, iii. 21-22: "Therefore let no man glory in
men; for all things are yours, whether Paul, or
Apollos, or Cephas; and ye are Christ's, and Christ
is God's." What they have become by the gospel,
they owe to the Lord alone, and not to His instruments. For as to what they have been able to do,
it is He who has done it by them; therefore it is He
only who is to be glorified. The imperative καυχάσθω
does not correspond grammatically to the conjunction
ἵνα, *in order that*. But the apostle directly transforms
the logical conclusion into the moral exhortation contained in the prophetic saying.

This last word sums up the dominant idea of the
whole passage from ver. 13 : viz. Christ's unique place
in relation to the Church. Let others be teachers,
He alone is κύριος; for He alone has paid the ransom.
To Him alone be the praise!

As God in the salvation of humanity has set aside
human wisdom, first of all by the mode of salvation
which He has chosen, then by the mode of propaga-
tion which He has adopted for the Church, the apostle
has also set it aside in his mode of preaching; such is
the idea which he develops in closing this passage,
ii. 1-5. Thus all is harmonious in the Divine work:
the gospel, the work, the preacher.

II. 1-5.

St. Paul applies to his own ministry at Corinth the principle which he has just laid down, and shows that he has been faithful to it. This is the conclusion of the whole passage.

Vers. 1, 2. "And I also, brethren, when I came to you, came not with excellency of speech or of wisdom, declaring unto you the testimony[1] of God; 2. For I determined not to know[2] anything[3] among you, save Jesus Christ, and Him crucified."—In the first word, κἀγώ, *and I also*, there is contained the connection between this conclusion and the passage as a whole. It does not signify, as de Wette thought: "I, as well as the other apostles," but: "I also, like the gospel itself." Paul has abstained, in harmony with the nature of the gospel, from seeking his strength in the help of human eloquence or wisdom: like Evangel, like evangelist.—The form ἐλθὼν ἦλθον is a frequent expression in Greek (see examples in Edwards), the object of which is to emphasize the verbal notion. The idea the apostle would bring out is that it was with this full-drawn plan that he arrived among them. This method was not the result of a passing state of mind, or of painful experiences he might have made at Corinth in a different way; from his first step in their city, his resolution was taken.—The adjunct καθ' ὑπεροχήν does not bear on the verb ἦλθον, *I came*; it rather explains the mode of preaching than that of

---

[1] ℵ A C Syr^sch Cop. read μυστηριον (*the mystery* of God). T. R. with the seven other Mjj. lt.: μαρτυριον (*the testimony*).

[2] T. R. reads του before ειδεναι (*for* knowing), with L only.

[3] B C P place τι before ειδεναι; the others after.

arriving (Meyer). It therefore qualifies the complex phrase ἦλθον καταγγέλλων, *I came declaring*. The word ὑπεροχή denotes strictly the act of overhanging, or the thing which overhangs; hence superiority, preeminence. By Byzantine writers it is used in the sense, "Your Excellency." There is a slight touch of irony in the use of this sonorous and emphatic word. —This exhibition of superiority which he disdained might have been that of philosophic depth (σοφίας), or that of dialectic and oratorical form (λόγου). He would no more have the one than the other.—The term καταγγέλλειν is here chosen deliberately to denote preaching. He came as a man who simply *announces* (καταγγέλλων) a fact. And this is what is expressed by the use of the word τὸ μαρτύριον, *the testimony*, to designate the gospel. The matter in question is not a system of ideas to be exhibited, but merely a testimony rendered to a fact. The genitive θεοῦ is that of the author and not of the object. The idea: the testimony which has God for its subject, would be much too general and would have little ground in the passage. Paul means that he has simply reproduced the testimony which goes forth from God, inasmuch as it is God who, after having effected salvation, has charged him to proclaim it. The reading of the *Sinait.*, μυστήριον, followed by Westcott and Hort, Edwards, etc., is absolutely misplaced in this context, though Edwards tries to account for it by reference to σοφία. This word μυστήριον has been imported here from ver. 7.—We must note well the two adjuncts, πρὸς ὑμᾶς, *among you*, and ὑμῖν, *to you;* the more that we shall again meet in ver. 2 with the same idea in the ἐν ὑμῖν, *among you*. On another theatre the apostle would not perhaps have guarded himself with so much care against the danger of lending to the gospel another force than that which properly belongs to it. But arriving at a city like Corinth, where he knew that philosophical and literary curiosity reigned, the apostle had said to himself that, to prevent the Divine work from being corrupted in its essence, preaching must from the first have the simplest character and address itself solely to the conscience. Origen, and in our day Neander, have thought that this resolution was the consequence of the failure which Paul had experienced at Athens when using a more philosophical procedure in his preaching. But the apostle here represents this method as connected with the very essence of the gospel; and it must be remembered that his discourse at Athens was not preaching strictly so called. He had first of all to explain himself in reference to the accusation raised against him, and only after that could he come to the proclamation of salvation; this is what he was about to do at the moment when he was interrupted.

Ver. 2. This verse confirms the preceding (γάρ), supporting it by the idea that this mode of acting was the result of a plan fixed beforehand. The term ἔκρινα, *I judged good*, is well explained by Heinrici by means of Cicero's phrase: *Mihi judicatum est.* Comp. vii. 37; 2 Cor. ii. 1. The apostle does not say, "*I determined* (judged good) not to know . . .*" but, "*I did not judge good to know . . .*" He intentionally set aside the different elements of human knowledge by which he might have been tempted to prop up the preaching of salvation. He deemed that he ought not to go in quest of such means. The word τοῦ, *for* or *to the end of*, which the received text reads before the infinitive εἰδέναι, *to know*, emphasizes, a little too much perhaps, the idea of a resolution taken after reflection.—Paul might have used the word *say* instead of *know*. But the latter implies a renunciation, not only outward but inward, of the use of those foreign elements.—By *Jesus Christ*, the apostle understands His manifestation in general, His life, death, and Messianic dignity. Yet, while confining himself to this elementary theme of preaching, he might still have found means to recommend Jesus to the attention and admiration of the wise; in Jesus Himself he believed that he should exhibit only the side that was least attractive to human wisdom, but alone able to save,—*Jesus Christ crucified*,—so much did he dread giving rise to cases of adherence which would have rested only on an intellectual or æsthetical, and consequently superficial, attraction. The ἐν ὑμῖν, *among you*, however, leaves room for the idea that, where he has not to reckon with this danger, he will allow himself to go beyond this limit; comp. ver. 6. But the true servant of Christ thinks of converting before giving himself up to the pleasure of instructing.

In ver. 3, before finishing the development of this idea, the apostle reminds the Corinthians how his *personal attitude* at Corinth corresponded to this humble form which he determined to give to His teaching.

Ver. 3. "And I was with you in weakness, in fear, and in much trembling."—The words καὶ ἐγώ, *and I*, are not the repetition of the κἀγώ of ver. 1; they announce a new feature subordinate to the preceding and in agreement with it. As he did not seek to render his preaching brilliant in matter or form, so in his personal demeanour he did not affect the airs of one assured of success. He felt and showed only one feeling, that of his own weakness. Addressing himself to this Gentile community, he had not, as among Jews, the point of support supplied by the prophecies. On the other hand, he surrendered what might have been his help in his new surroundings — depth of thought and charm of language. What remained to him? Humanly speaking, he felt like one disarmed; hence the ἐν ἀσθενείᾳ, *in weakness* And this feeling of weakness went the length of *fear*, when he weighed the gravity of a work like his, and the responsibility it laid on him. By repeating the prep. ἐν before τρόμῳ, " and *in* trembling," which Paul does not do in the other instances when he joins these two substantives (2 Cor. vii. 15; Eph. vi. 5; Phil. ii. 12), he distinguishes the second from the first more precisely; fear even produced in him a sort of physical tremor. Perhaps he also felt himself humbled by the weakness of his outward appearance (2 Cor. x. 10). All this sufficiently explains the terms of this verse, without the necessity of having recourse to fear of persecutions, of which Chrysostom thinks, or even to the supposition of ill-health, according to Rückert. It is interesting to compare the picture which Paul here traces of his inward frames with the narrative of the external facts of his ministry in Acts xviii. The first of these pictures remarkably completes the second, and explains why the Lord found it necessary to grant to His servant the vision, related Acts xviii. 9, and to say to him, like a friend encouraging his friend : " Fear not ; speak and be not silent."—The words *I was with you* embrace not only his public teachings, but his private conversations and all his personal relations.—What a contrast between this humble, even timid, attitude of the apostle, and the bold confidence of the Greek rhetorician stepping before his auditory as a man sure of the success of his person and piece !

Vers. 4, 5. "And my speech and my preaching were not with persuasive[1] words of wisdom,[2] but in demonstration of the Spirit and of power ; 5. that your faith should not stand in the wisdom of men, but in the power of God."—The apostle returns from his person to his preaching. Λόγος, *speech*, and κήρυγμα, *preaching*, have been distinguished in many ways : " My discourses in general, and especially my preaching" (Meyer) ; or, " My private conversations and my public discourses" (Neander, Rückert, etc.). I rather think that λόγος applies to the matter, and κήρυγμα to the form ; the λόγος is the gospel itself ; the κήρυγμα is the testimony the apostle renders to it. Neither the one nor the other has been corrupted in his work by the infiltration of human elements or by self-seeking. — The adj. πειθός is not known in classic Greek, in which the word πιθανός is used for *persuasive*. But it is nevertheless regularly formed from the verb πείθω ; comp.

---

[1] Πειθοις (*persuasive*) is read in א A B C D E L P Vulg. Or. Eus., etc. Macar. Chrys. read πιθανοις. Some Mnn. It. Syr^sch Or. (twice) Eus. (twice) and others read πειθοι (*persuasion*). This reading requires us to read λογων or λογου, instead of λογοις, with some Fathers and Versions.— Λογοις is omitted by F G.

[2] Ανθρωπινης (*human*) is added here by T. R., after A C L P and some Fathers.

φειδός, from φείδομαι; and it is possible that in the apostle's day πειθός belonged only to the spoken language. Some documents have substituted for this adjective the dative πειθοῖ of the substantive πειθώ, *persuasion* (*Itala:* "in *persuasione* sapientiæ verbi"). Heinrici adopts this reading, though it is almost entirely destitute of authorities, because of the fine contrast between this word πειθώ and the following term, ἀπόδειξις. But in that case we should have to read λόγου or λόγων, which are only found in very few authorities, and which are evidently corrections. The adj. ἀνθρωπίνης, *human,* found in the received text, is insufficiently supported.—Instead of endeavouring to satisfy the understanding by means of a system (*wisdom*) ably presented (*persuasive discourses*), the apostle has sought his strength in action of a wholly different nature, in what he calls "the *demonstration of Spirit and of power.*" The word ἀπόδειξις indicates a clearness which is produced in the hearer's mind, as by the sudden lifting of a veil; a conviction mastering him with the sovereign force of moral evidence; comp. xiv. 24, 25.— The gen. πνεύματος, *of Spirit,* is the complement of cause; it is the Divine Spirit alone who thus reveals the truth of salvation; comp. Eph. i. 17, 18. We have to represent this Spirit to ourselves acting at once in him who speaks and in him who hears, in such a way as to make the light pass, through the intervention of the spoken word, from the mind of the one into the mind of the other. The second gen. δυνάμεως, *of power,* is the complement of quality: it denotes the mode of the Spirit's action; it is, so to speak, a taking possession of the human soul, of its understanding and will, by the inward ascendency of the truth. Chrysostom, and in our day, Beet, apply these expressions to the outward miracles which St. Paul sometimes wrought by the power of the Holy Spirit (2 Cor. xi. 12; Rom. xv. 19). Such an interpretation, allowable in the infancy of exegesis, should now be no longer possible. The apostle has just been stigmatizing the going after miracles on the part of the Jews, and we are to suppose him saying here that he sought to render the faith of the Corinthians immovable by the evidence of miracles!

Ver. 5. *"Ἵνα, in order that,* indicates the apostle's object in the course he has followed. He was not ignorant that a faith, founded on logical arguments, could be shaken by other arguments of the same nature. To be solid, it must be the work of the power of God, and in order to be that, proceed from a conviction of sin and a personal appropriation of salvation, which the Spirit of God alone can produce in the human soul. The preacher's task in this work lies, not in wishing to act in the place and stead of the Spirit with the resources of his own eloquence and genius, but in opening up the way for Him by simple testimony rendered to Christ.

By these last words, we are brought back to the point of departure of the whole passage, i. 18: the gospel is not a wisdom, but a power; not a philosophy, but a salvation. If the Corinthians were divided into parties, it was because they had failed to know this truth. By making the gospel a system, they had changed the Church into a school, and its ministers into teachers and rhetoricians. Hence it is that St. Paul begins by re-establishing in the mind of the Corinthians the true notion of the gospel. But some of his expressions might lead us to suppose that wisdom was banished from the domain of the gospel. Now this was not what the apostle had meant; and it is this possible misunderstanding which he sets aside in the following passage, where he shows that if the gospel is not essentially wisdom, it nevertheless *contains* a wisdom, and that the true wisdom, superior to all that the human understanding could have discovered.

The gospel contains a wisdom : ii. 6–iii. 4.

The apostle had already declared in passing, i. 23, 24, that for Jews and Gentiles Christ crucified, received by faith, becomes not only the *power of God*, but also the *wisdom of God*. This is the thought which he develops in the passage, which forms in a sense the antithesis, and thereby the complement of the preceding. The first proposition of ver. 6 states its theme, just as the second part of i. 17 contained the summary of the passage i. 18–ii. 5.

Ver. 6. "Howbeit we speak wisdom among them that are perfect, yet not the wisdom of this world, nor of the princes of this world, that come to nought."— The δέ is rather restrictive than adversative. It is intended to limit the idea previously developed, that the cross is not a wisdom. In the case of him who has once experienced the salvation it brings to man, it does not fail to become a light which illumines his understanding and directs his whole life. It is obvious in this sense why the term σοφία, *wisdom*, heads the sentence in the original : it is the essential word, and in a manner the summary, of the passage.

This first proposition has been understood in two very different ways. Some (Chrysostom, Luther, Calvin, Beza, Grotius, Olshausen, Heinrici, etc.) think that Paul, when speaking of οἱ τέλειοι, *the perfect*, means all believers, and that σοφία, *wisdom*, denotes the gospel in the ordinary sense of the word. "But," the apostle says, it is held, "this preaching of the cross, which seems folly to unbelievers, is wisdom in the eyes of believers." This meaning seems to us inadmissible. The term οἱ τέλειοι, *the perfect*, is too special to be taken as the simple equivalent of οἱ πιστοί, *believers*. In ver. 1 of chap. iii. the word τέλειος is replaced by πνευματικός, *spiritual*, and the latter is opposed to νήπιος, the infant, which cannot speak yet. The same contrast reappears in τέλειος γίνεσθαι and νηπιάζειν, xiv. 20 ; comp. also Eph. iv. 13, 14 ; Heb. v. 13, 14. Now in all these passages νήπιος denotes, not the unconverted, but believers, believers, however, who are only at the first steps of the new life, and whose conversion needs yet to be confirmed. "Ye are yet carnal," says the apostle to the Corinthians, iii. 3, to explain this state of infancy. The word *perfect* has therefore a meaning much narrower than *believer*. It denotes the state of the *mature man*, in opposition to that of the infant. Paul thereby denotes believers who have reached, not absolute perfection (comp. Phil. iii. 12–17), but the full maturity of Christian faith and life. Heinrici objects that in Christianity there is no aristocracy, and Holsten that according to Paul every believer has received the Spirit, and that the Spirit cannot make progress. To the first objection Rückert has already made answer, that every believer being called to that state of maturity, all aristocratic distinctions are *ipso facto* banished. And as to the second, if the Spirit is not open to progress, the believer's life may be gradually penetrated by this perfect principle. Does not the apostle say to the Galatians (iv. 19): "My little children, of whom I travail in birth again until Christ be formed in you." The perfect are therefore in his eyes the most confirmed Christians in whom the new life has attained the normal stature of Christ (Eph. iv. 13, 14).—The form λαλεῖν ἐν is equally incompatible with the interpretation before us. The ἐν, *in*, would in that case mean : *in the eyes of, in the judgment of.* This preposition may sometimes have this meaning with verbs containing the idea of being or appearing ; comp. xiv. 11. But with the verb λαλεῖν this sense is inadmissible. The *in* cannot be taken otherwise than in the local sense : *among, in the midst of.* Paul means that when he is in the midst of confirmed believers, mature Christians, he feels himself free to set forth the treasures of wisdom contained in the gospel; comp. Col. ii. 3 : " Christ, in whom are hid all the treasures of wisdom and knowledge." For then the question is no longer one of conversion to be wrought or confirmed. He can therefore, as he says, iii. 1, present the gospel, not as the *milk* of babes, but as the *meat* of the strong. This is the meaning which has been recognised by Erasmus, Bengel, de Wette, Rückert, Reuss (" as to philosophy, I preach it to mature men"), Osiander, Neander, Hofmann, Edwards, etc. It is mistaken or obscured in Oltramare's version : " Nevertheless it is wisdom which we teach among the perfect."

To the wisdom which Paul reserved for exposition to

full-grown men in Christ there doubtless belonged what he expounds in passages such as Rom. ix.-xi. (God's plan in regard to the salvation of Jews and Gentiles), in the Epistles to the Ephesians and to the Colossians (the cross as the centre of the history of the universe, as the bond of union between the first and the second creation, as the means of first uniting Jews and Gentiles, and then men and angels, under the sovereignty of Christ, their common head); finally, also in chap. xv. of our Epistle (the Christian eschatology). These admirable designs of God, which have guided and still guide all His dispensations toward men, and whose gradual realization is being effected by the Christian economy, were things which Paul expounded as a teacher, not as a missionary. For they can indeed promote the growth of believers in knowledge and love; but they are not what is needed to convert sinners. It is not the light which rays from the cross which changes the heart, it is the cross itself.

The subject of the verb λαλοῦμεν might be: "I and the other apostles;" but the first verses of chap. iii. show that it is of himself—including, perhaps, his fellow-labourers—that Paul is thinking. His object, indeed, is not to set forth a theory regarding the preaching of the gospel in general, but to justify the manner in which he himself exercised this ministry at Corinth.— The term λαλεῖν is purposely chosen; it denotes communications which are not, like the καταγγέλλειν or the κηρύσσειν, preachings properly so called.—It has been asked whether the apostle meant by the term τέλειος to allude to the position of those *initiated* into the Greek mysteries (τελεταί), and there has been alleged in favour of this supposition the word μυστήριον, *mystery*, which he uses in ver. 7. But in the Epistle to the Hebrews the term τέλειος is used in the same sense as here, and yet nothing is less probable than an allusion to the Greek mysteries in that letter. And as to the word μυστήριον, it refers, in the language of St. Paul, not to a fact into which one man initiates another, but to a plan hidden in God, and which He alone unveils. The word, besides, frequently drops from the pen of the apostle, and that where all allusion to the mysteries would be out of place (Rom. xi. 25, xvi. 25 ; Eph. iii. 4 ; Col. i. 27, etc.).

In the following passage the apostle successively develops the three terms embraced in the theme which is stated, ver. 6ᵃ :—

Σοφίαν, *wisdom*, vers. 6ᵇ–9.

Λαλοῦμεν, *we speak*, vers. 10–13.

'Εν τοῖς τελείοις, *among the perfect*, vers. 14–16.

Thereafter he concludes by applying all he has just said to his own teaching, iii. 1–4.

Vers. 6ᵇ–9.

The apostle describes wisdom, of which he speaks from the viewpoint of its superhuman origin (vers. 6ᵇ and 7), then from that of its impenetrable obscurity to the natural understanding (vers. 8 and 9).—And first, its origin, what it is not (ver. 6ᵇ), and what it is (ver. 7).

This wisdom is not a conception due to the mind of the world, nor even to the genius of its most illustrious representatives. The δέ indicates the resumption of the idea of σοφία, which is about to be developed ; comp.

the δικαιοσύνη δέ, Rom. vi. 22.—On αἰών, see on i. 20.— The ἄρχοντες, *princes of this world,* are not, as has been thought by Origen, Ambrosiaster, Bertholdt, the demons. Some have alleged the Johannine expression ὁ ἄρχων τοῦ κόσμου and Eph. vi. 12. But how could Paul say of the demons, in ver. 8, that if they had known Jesus Christ, they would not have crucified Him? Precisely the opposite would be the case. It is equally mistaken to think with others, of the Greek philosophers, who could not be accused of having crucified the Lord (ver. 8). Paul rather means those who in his time directed the national mind of Israel, those who were the authorities in the Sanhedrim, and perhaps, also, of the Jewish and Gentile representatives of political power in Israel, such as Herod and Pilate. These representatives of human intelligence and politics took part directly or remotely in the execution of the Divine plan, without even suspecting it. And so its growing accomplishment goes to make them disappear. The present participle τῶν καταργουμένων, *who are abolished,* is connected by Meyer with the near date of the Parousia, and by Rückert with God's unchangeable decree. It seems to me that it is simpler to regard it as indicating the actual fact: in proportion as the power of the gospel increases on the earth, the representatives of human wisdom lose their dominion, which will end by escaping from their hands altogether.—In the following verse the apostle indicates the true origin of evangelical wisdom.

Ver. 7. "But we speak the wisdom of God,[1] which is a mystery, the hidden wisdom, which God pre-

---

[1] T. R. with L reads σοφιαν θεου; the others, θεου σοφιαν.

ordained before the ages, unto our glory;"—This verse is the antithesis of the foregoing one (ἀλλά, *but*). The term λαλοῦμεν, *we speak*, is repeated because of the remoteness of this verb in ver. 6.—The gen. θεοῦ, *of God*, is that of origin and possession. The workshop whence this plan has proceeded, where it remains shut up till its revelation, is the mind of God Himself. The ἐν μυστηρίῳ, *in mystery*, or *in the form of mystery*, is naturally joined with the principal term σοφία, *wisdom*, which the apostle aims to distinguish positively, in opposition to the negative definitions of the former verse. The word *mystery* has taken in theological language a meaning which it has not in the New Testament, to wit, a truth which human reason cannot fathom. In Paul's writings it simply signifies a truth or a fact which the human understanding cannot of itself discover, but which it apprehends as soon as God gives the revelation of it. Thus Jesus says, Luke viii. 10 : " It is given to you to know the mysteries of the kingdom," and Paul applies the word mystery to things which we perfectly comprehend; for example, Rom. xvi. 25, to the general plan of salvation; Eph. iii. 4, to the calling of the Gentiles; Rom. xi. 25, to the restoration of the Jews; in our Epistle, xv. 51, to the transformation of the faithful at the moment of the Parousia. The term is here contrasted with a system having the spirit of man for its author (ver. 6), and which consequently does not need to be revealed. Many commentators, Erasmus, Rückert, de Wette, Osiander, Meyer, Hofmann, Edwards, Beet, make the adjunct ἐν μυστηρίῳ depend on the verb λαλοῦμεν : " We speak of this wisdom in the form of a mystery ;" or, as

Beet says, "in words containing a secret of infinite value, and which only they understand to whom God reveals it, the τέλειοι." But this idea of a speaking on the part of the apostle taking place mysteriously, and, as it were, in secret, is foreign to all we know of his procedure. The sense equally contradicts the use of the term μυστήριον by Paul; for the word refers, not to the relation of one man to another, but to that of God to man.[1] Meyer attempts to meet this last objection; he translates: "We speak this wisdom as being a Divine mystery;" but the phrase λαλεῖν ἐν cannot have this meaning. Other commentators, such as Theodoret and Thomas Aquinas, connect ἐν μυστηρίῳ with τὴν ἀποκεκρυμμένην: "the wisdom hidden in the form of a mystery." But what would this adjunct add to the idea of the participle? And besides, the article τήν would have its natural place *before* the adjunct. The simplest connection is that which we have followed in beginning; it is that which the position of the words itself indicates. The absence of the article τήν before ἐν μυστηρίῳ has been objected; but when the adjunct is closely united in one and the same idea with the substantive on which it depends, the omission of the article is legitimate; comp. the phrase ἡ δωρεὰ ἐν χάριτι (Rom. v. 15).—The epithet τὴν ἀποκεκρυμμένην, *the hidden*, that is to say, which has remained hidden (perfect participle), is not a repetition. It adds to the idea of the *mode*, contained in ἐν μυστηρίῳ, the notion of *time*. This plan, while a secret conceived by God and known to Him alone, might have been revealed much earlier, from the beginning of the existence of humanity; but

---

[1] See the exegesis on xiv. 2.

it pleased Him to keep silence about it for long ages (μυστηρίου χρόνοις αἰωνίοις σεσιγημένου, Rom. xvi. 25; "which was not revealed to other generations as it is now," Eph. iii. 5). It might even be thought that by the article τήν, *the*, this long-concealed wisdom is contrasted with another which God had unveiled long before, that of which Paul has spoken, i. 21, which was displayed from the creation of the world in the works of nature (Rom. i. 20).

To these two features which distinguish the wisdom revealed in the gospel from all the products of the human understanding, its higher origin and its non-revelation up to that hour, the apostle adds a third · its saving end in behalf of man, the eternal object of Divine concern.—Some have thought that the term ὁρίζειν, *to mark out by limit, to decree*, did not suit the idea of wisdom, and have thought we should understand an infinitive like γνωρίζειν, *to make known*: "which God had determined . . . to make known." If this wisdom were only a system or a theory, the verb ὁρίζειν might really be applied to it without difficulty. But it should be remembered that the subject in question is a plan to be realized in history, and to which consequently the term *decree* is perfectly suitable. The preposition πρό, added to the verb, is afterwards developed in the words, *before the ages*. It is therefore an eternal decree. No doubt eternity is not a *prius* in relation to time; to hold this would be to bring it into time. The πρό, *before*, therefore expresses in the inadequate form of temporal priority a superiority of *dignity*, in relation to the decree of creation. The universe exists with a view to man, and man exists with a view to glory. This object, δόξα, was the logical *prius* of all that is, of the existence of man himself. These words, *for our glory*, find their explanation in other sayings of the apostle, particularly Rom. viii. 29 : "He hath predestinated us to be conformed to the image of His Son, that He might be the firstborn among many brethren;" ver. 17 : "Heirs of God and joint-heirs with Christ;" 1 Cor. xv. 28 : "That God may be all in all." A society of intelligent and free beings, of men perfectly holy, made capable of reflecting God's glory, and of serving as instruments for His holy action, in filial communion with the Father and in fraternal union with the Son : such was the end which God set before Him in creating the human race. All His particular plans are subordinate to this end. To understand all things from this viewpoint, is the wisdom of which Paul speaks; it is this Divine wisdom which, long kept hidden, is at length unveiled to mankind by the gospel of the cross.

In the two following verses St. Paul *demonstrates* the superhuman and consequently mysterious nature of this wisdom, such as he has just described it negatively and positively in vers. 6, 7. He gives two proofs of it : first, a known fact, ver. 8 ; next, a prophetic saying, ver. 9.

Ver. 8 : "which none of the princes of this world knew; for had they known it, they would not have crucified the Lord of glory;"—The idea of wisdom being that which dominates the entire passage, the pronoun ἥν, *which*, should not be made relative to the word δόξαν, *glory*, which expresses only a secondary idea, but to the phrase σοφίαν θεοῦ, *wisdom of God*.

What proves this wisdom to be a conception superior to all human thought, is the fact that when it was realized in an individual person, the princes of human thought did not discern it; these princes are those spoken of in ver. 6. They had no perception of the glorious destination which God has assigned to humanity, and hence they rejected and crucified Him, who first realized it in His person. The apostle characterizes Jesus Christ as the *Lord of glory*. This title is in keeping with the term δόξα, *glory*, by which he has defined the end of the Divine decree. Glory is the lustre shed by the Divine perfections. This lustre is one day to shine in man, and Jesus Christ, as the first, has realized in Himself that splendour which He is to communicate to all believers. If the representatives of Jewish wisdom and Roman power had understood the higher glory which Jesus was bringing to them, they would undoubtedly have sacrificed that which they possessed. But as they did not discern the former, they chose at any price to maintain their earthly power, and they sought to destroy Him at whose feet they should have abdicated; comp. the parable of the husbandman and the deliberation of the Sanhedrim, John xi. 47. There is an intentional antithesis between the term *crucified*, which indicates the lowest degree of humiliation and suffering, and the title *Lord of glory*. To this proof from fact, the apostle adds the Scriptural demonstration, ver. 9.

Ver. 9: "but as it is written: things which the eye hath not seen, and which the ear hath not heard, and which have not entered into the heart of man, which [1]

---

[1] A B C read ὅσα instead of ἅ (*which*), as read by all the rest.

God hath prepared for them that love Him."—The grammatical connection of this verse has been variously understood. Erasmus, Estius, Meyer (last ed.), Heinrici, Edwards make ἅ, *things which*, the object of λαλοῦμεν, *we speak*, ver. 7, and consequently in apposition to *the wisdom of God*. But this relation is grammatically forced and logically inadmissible: the apostle does not mean to point out what he speaks among the perfect, but to prove the nature of that wisdom to be sublime and inaccessible to man. Hofmann thinks we should begin a new sentence with ver. 9; the verb on which the ἅ depends would then be ἀπεκάλυψεν, *He revealed*, ver. 10: "What eye hath not seen . . . God hath revealed to us . . ." The δέ of ver. 10 would not be absolutely opposed to this explanation (see on i. 23). But the καθὼς γέγραπται, *as it is written*, would be strangely placed at the beginning of this subordinate sentence. And then, instead of beginning ver. 10 with ἡμῖν δέ, *but unto us*, the apostle ought rather to have written ἀπεκάλυψεν δὲ ἡμῖν ὁ θεός; for the antithesis between the idea of keeping concealed and that of revealing would alone account for the δέ placed at the beginning of the principal sentence. De Wette and Osiander prefer to hold an anacolouthon; the phrase, "things which no eye hath seen," is thrown in, they say, as a description which remains grammatically suspended, "being lost," as de Wette says, "in a mysterious remoteness." It seems to us more natural simply to understand the notion of the verb *to be* in this sense: "It is indeed this very wisdom which is described in the words: Things which the eye hath not seen, etc."—The ἀλλά, *but*, signifies,

"But it could not be otherwise, for Scripture had spoken in these terms." It is difficult to know to what passage of our holy books this quotation refers. Nowhere in the Old Testament are these words literally found. Chrysostom and Theophylact did not know whether they belonged to a prophecy now lost, or if they were taken from Isa. lii. 15 : "They to whom it had not been told shall see, and they who had not heard it shall understand." Origen thought they were taken from an apocryphal writing entitled the Apocalypse of Elias.[1] But nowhere do we find the apostle making similar quotations from uncanonical books, and it cannot be supposed that he would have applied to such books the formula *as it is written*, which would evidently imply the idea of Divine authority. Meyer acknowledges this; only he holds that, by a slip of memory, the apostle, while quoting this apocryphal book, thought he was quoting Isaiah; so also Weiss (*Bibl. Theol.*, p. 274). I cannot see the necessity of so strange a supposition. Jerome already pointed out the true source of this quotation : it is the passage Isa. lxiv. 4 combined with lxv. 17 : "Men have not heard nor perceived, neither hath the eye seen a God beside Thee which worketh for him that waiteth for Him . . ."; and, "The former things shall not be remembered, nor come into mind." Clement of Rome, who, in chap.

---

[1] We must correct an error which may be caused by the expressions used by Meyer regarding the testimony of Zacharias Chrysopolitanus (of the twelfth century) relative to this declaration of Origen. This author does not say a word to make us suppose "*that he had himself read*" the passage in the apocryphal book of which Origen speaks. Referring simply to that Father, he says : "In nullo enim regulari libro hoc positum invenitur nisi in secretis Eliæ prophetæ" (*Maxima Bibliotheca Veterum Patrum*, t. xix. p. 937).

xxxiv. of his Epistle to the Corinthians, quotes this passage from Paul (with the combination of the two sayings of Isaiah), so well understands it is from the book of this prophet that Paul draws, that he substitutes for the last words of our verse: τοῖς ἀγαπῶσιν αὐτόν, *for them that love Him*, the exact expression of Isaiah (in the LXX.: τοῖς ὑπομενοῦσιν αὐτόν, *for them that wait for Him*. Similar combinations of several prophetic quotations are not rare in Paul's writings; comp. Rom. ix. 33, where are united Isa. xxviii. 16 and viii. 14; and Rom. xi. 26, 27, where Isa. lix. 20 and xxvii. 9 are blended in one). — In the first passage, the prophet, speaking of the work which God will accomplish in favour of His exiled people when He will restore them, says to God: "We can wait until such a God as Thou, like whom is no other, do for us things which surpass all that has been seen and told until now, and all that can be imagined." Or indeed we may suppose that Isaiah transfers himself to the time when all will be accomplished, and that he means: "Never will there have been seen or heard or imagined such things as those which Thou shalt have done for us." No doubt the expression, *come into the mind of man*, taken from Isa. lxv. 17, refers in the context to the memory of things already accomplished, but accomplished merely in prophetic intuition. By combining the three terms *seeing, hearing*, and *entering into the heart*, the apostle wishes to designate the three means of natural knowledge: sight, or immediate experience; hearing, or knowledge by way of tradition; finally, the inspirations of the heart, the discoveries of the understanding proper. By none of these means can man reach the conception of the blessings which God has destined for him. From Irenaeus to Meyer, a host of commentators have applied the ἅ, *things which*, in Paul's sense, to the felicities and glories of heaven. But we have seen, ver. 6ª, that the Divine wisdom of which Paul speaks embraces the kingdom of God in its present form; and the words of ver. 12: "That we might know the things that are freely given to us of God," clearly show that Paul is thinking of the knowledge the believer receives of all the riches of the Divine plans toward him and toward the Church, of what he himself calls, Eph. iii. 18, "their breadth and length, and depth and height." The blessings to come are of course comprehended in such phrases.

The reading ὅσα of A B C has been admitted by Lachmann, Tischendorf, Westcott and Hort, and rightly, as it seems to me, for there is somewhat of enthusiasm in the saying: "those great things which God has prepared." For the *will do*, ποιήσει (LXX.), Paul substitutes the word ἡτοίμασεν, *has prepared*, used also by Clement. The idea is the same, for what God *will do* in the future is precisely what He *has prepared* in the past. The term ἑτοιμάζειν, *to prepare*, recalls the words of Jesus: "the kingdom prepared for you from the foundation of the world" (Matt. xxv. 34), Instead of τοῖς ὑπομενοῦσιν αὐτόν, "for them that wait for Him with perseverance," the apostle substitutes τοῖς ἀγαπῶσιν αὐτόν, *for them that love Him*. This change arises from the fact that the Christian now enjoys the salvation which the Israelite was still waiting for, and is grateful for it to its Author. Thus is exhausted the development of the idea of wisdom (ver. 6ª).

K

Vers. 10-13.

With ver. 10 the apostle passes to the development of the second term of his theme: λαλοῦμεν, *we speak*. This wisdom, being God's conception, and inaccessible to the mind of man, how can Paul expound it to his brethren? Vers. 10-12 indicate the means by which he received the knowledge of it; and ver. 13 describes the manner, in keeping with those means, in which he declares it.

Ver. 10. "But[1] God[2] hath revealed them unto us by His Spirit; for the Spirit[3] searcheth all things, yea, the deep things of God."—The δέ is strongly adversative: "This wisdom was hidden, *but* it has been revealed to us." The *for*, which the *Vatic.* reads here, could only refer to the, *we speak*, of ver. 7; but the distance between these two words is too great for this connection to be natural.—The dat. *to us* heads the proposition, to contrast strongly those denoted by this pronoun with the world and its princes to whom the Divine wisdom is veiled. This pronoun neither refers to Christians in general, nor, as Edwards thinks, to the perfect in particular; for the ἡμεῖς, *we*, to whom the revelation is granted, are evidently identical with the *we*, the subject of λαλοῦμεν, *we speak*, in vers. 6, 13. For it is that they may be able to speak that they receive the revelation. Now, in ver. 16, they are expressly contrasted with the τέλειοι, *the perfect*, and

---

[1] B some Mnn. read γαρ (*for*) instead of δε (*but*).

[2] T. R. with L and Mnn. place ο θεος before απεκαλυψεν; the rest, after.

[3] א A B C here omit αυτου (*of Him*), which is read by T. R. with the rest.

à *fortiori* with the members of the Church in general. The *we* can therefore only designate the apostles collectively, or Paul himself, with his fellow-labourers. But Paul has no reason to speak here of the other apostles; it is his teaching at Corinth which he wishes to justify (iii. 1–4). It is therefore of himself, and no doubt also of Silas and Timothy (comp. 2 Cor. i. 19), that he is here speaking.—It is natural to place the verb ἀπεκάλυψε, *has revealed*, immediately after ἡμῖν, as is done by almost all the Mjj., and not after the subject ὁ θεός, *God* (T. R.); this is the decisive act from which follows that of the λαλεῖν, *to speak*, ver. 13. —'Ἀποκαλύπτειν, *to remove the veil*. The text runs, *has revealed to us*, without an object; it is not the thing revealed, it is the act of revelation which Paul would emphasize. By the aorist, he goes back to a determinate point of time, which for him can only be that which he describes, Gal. i. 12, 16. There is undoubtedly a revelation also for the simple believer; comp. Eph. i. 17: "That God may give you the Spirit of wisdom and revelation." But this revelation is only secondary. It is solely the reproduction of the primordial revelation granted to the first interpreters of the Divine thought, and it takes place only through the intervention of the latter. Between the two there is therefore a difference, not only of degree, but of nature and quality. The former, contained originally in the apostolic *declaration*, is now found in the *writings* wherein that declaration is deposited, which are thus the permanent means of which God makes use to effect the latter (John xvii. 20).

The agent by whom God wrought this unveiling in

the mind of the apostle is the Spirit. The pronoun αὐτοῦ, *of Him*, is probably a gloss. The following proposition serves to explain how the Spirit can fill this revealing function: *He searcheth all things.* Instead of ἐρευνᾷ, א A B C read ἐραυνᾷ; an Alexandrine form. Was it the apostle who used it, or the Alexandrine copyists who introduced it? We read—ραυ John v. 39 in א B; vii. 52 in א B T; Rom. viii. 27 in א; xi. 33 in א A B; 1 Pet. i. 11 in א B, and Rev. ii. 23 in A C.—There is no reason for restricting the πάντα, *all things*, to Divine things; on the contrary, the following proposition would in that case be a mere tautology. The Divine Spirit is the luminous principle which possesses and from which proceeds all knowledge; it is in His light alone that everything comes to the light where there are consciousness and intelligence.— The *deep things of God* designate God's essence, then His attributes, volitions, and plans. The operation of *searching*, here ascribed to the Spirit, has been applied by De Wette to the believer who has received the Spirit, or, what comes to the same thing, to the Spirit as dwelling in the Church and acting through believers. The sense would thus be, that through possession of the Spirit, man can penetrate all things, even the deepest purposes of God; comp. ver. 16. But (1) this sense does not accord with the contrast between the verbs *reveal* and *search;* the first is in the past and aorist, and consequently indicates a determinate Divine act, wrought once for all; the second, which is in the present, denotes, on the contrary, a permanent act, which, once the act of revelation is effected, would no longer have any reason for its existence if it was really man's. On the contrary, it is clear that this permanent act of searching, applied to the unceasing activity of the Spirit in God, serves to explain (γάρ, *for*) the revealing function of that Spirit. (2) If Paul meant to speak in ver. 10 of the working of the Divine Spirit dwelling in man to penetrate the Divine decrees, how would he compare this working in ver. 11 with that of man's spirit searching what passes within himself? The two compared relations would be incommensurate. Finally (3), in the passage, xiii. 10-12, Paul declares that here below we know only fragmentarily and as in a dim mirror; how could he say here that the Christian's knowledge extends to all things and penetrates even what is deepest in God? Our passage, therefore, certainly relates to the intra-Divine activity of the Holy Spirit.

Ver. 11. "For what man knoweth the things of man, save the spirit of man[1] which is in him? Even so the things of God hath no man known,[2] but the Spirit of God."—To make intelligible to his readers this inward activity of the Divine Spirit, the apostle invites them to contemplate the working of man's spirit in man himself. For man is made in the image of God, and that precisely in virtue of his spiritual nature. There is in every man a life hidden from all eyes, a world of impressions, anxieties, aspirations, and struggles, of which he alone, in so far as he is a spirit, that is to say, a conscious and personal being, gives account to himself. This inner world is unknown to

---

[1] F G Orig. omit του ανθρωπου (*of man*).
[2] All the Mjj., with the exception of L, read εγνωκεν instead of οιδεν, the reading of T. R.

others, except in so far as he reveals it to them by speech. Such is the likeness of what passes in the phenomenon of revelation between God and man.—In thus appealing to what we call in philosophical language the fact of consciousness, Paul knows well that he is teaching nothing new. Hence the interrogative form: "What man knoweth . . . ?" He adds, when speaking of the spirit of man, τὸ ἐν αὐτῷ, *which is in him*. He did not express himself so when speaking of the Spirit of God. No doubt because he would not have it supposed that in his eyes the analogy was complete. The Spirit is not *in* God, as if God were for him a place.—In the second proposition we must read, with almost all the Mjj., ἔγνωκεν, not οἶδεν, which has undoubtedly been imported from the first sentence. The difference is, as Edwards well puts it, that the latter denotes the knowledge of a fact, the former the knowledge of the inner nature of the thing. The latter is well rendered in Latin by *cognitum habet*. After this short explanation (ver. 11), the apostle, in ver. 12, connects with the principal idea that of the ἀπεκάλυψε, ver. 10: "There was in our favour an act of revelation." And as, in vers. 6, 7, he had contrasted worldly wisdom with Divine wisdom, he contrasts, in ver. 13, the revelation of the Spirit from above with all earthly knowledge.

Ver. 12. "Now we have received, not the spirit of the world,[1] but the Spirit which is of God, that we might know the things that are freely given to us of God:"—This verse is the development of the word *by the Spirit* (ver. 10).—The Divine Spirit is contrasted

[1] D E F G add τούτου (*of this*).

with another, which also has the power of making revelations of another nature, that of *the world*. Beet understands thereby, "the spirit which worketh in the children of disobedience" (Eph. ii. 2); Meyer: the spirit which animates unbelieving mankind, the diabolical spirit. Does the expression used authorize us to go so far? Man, at the time of his creation, received a πνεῦμα; for he participates in the spiritual nature and power which are the essence of God (Gen. ii. 7; John iv. 24). With the Fall, this endowment was not withdrawn from humanity. By its separation from God, the spirit of man became profane, worldly; but it remained in man, as a collective being, as a principle of knowledge and invention, enthusiasm and exaltation. This it is which Pagans called the Muse, and which is concentrated in philosophical and artistic geniuses, communicating to them marvellous insight and words of wondrous power, by which they give tone to their age. And hence the apostle does not scruple himself to quote sayings of the Greek poets, and to designate one of them by the name of *prophet* (Acts xvii. 28; Tit. i. 12). But to whatever degree of power this spirit of the world may rise, it cannot give man the knowledge of the Divine plans, nor make an apostle even of the greatest genius. The expression οὐκ ἐλάβομεν, *we have not received*, signifies, "The spiritual power which has made us what we are, is not that." Comp. an analogous form, Rom. viii. 15.

With this spirit which rises, so to speak, from the heart of the κόσμος, the apostle contrasts the Divine Spirit, literally, *the Spirit which proceeds* (ἐκ) *from God*. This form emphasizes the transcendent character of His inspiring breath. He was in God, and He proceeds from Him to enter into man; comp. Rom. v. 5. This is something different from human inspiration, even when raised to its highest power.—The art. τό, after πνεῦμα, was not strictly necessary (see on ver. 7). But it is put here to remind us of the contrast to the other spirit, the cosmical spirit: "We are certainly neither Platos, nor Demostheneses, nor Homers; but if you would learn what are the thoughts of God toward you, listen to us! The Spirit proceeding from God Himself is He who has revealed them to us."—There is a very marked contrast between the two terms, εἰδῶμεν, *that we might know*, and τὰ χαρισθέντα, *the things which have been* (freely) *given to us*. By this second term Paul understands the gracious blessings of salvation, the gift of the Son, the expiation accomplished by Him, and all the benefits flowing from them: justification, sanctification, final redemption (i. 30). These blessings one may enjoy by simple faith, but without yet measuring all their greatness, because the εἰδέναι, *knowing*, is yet wanting in a certain degree. And hence the apostle asked for the Ephesians (iii. 18) that they might be able "to understand with all saints what is the breadth and length, the depth and height," and for the Colossians (ii. 2, 3), "that they might be brought unto all riches of the full assurance of understanding, to the acknowledgment of the mystery of God and of Christ; in whom are hid all the treasures of wisdom and knowledge." Here, therefore, the εἰδέναι, *knowing*, denotes the account which the believer renders to himself of all that is contained in the τὰ χαρισθέντα, the facts of salvation wrought out for him. It is those higher lights the domain of which we have sought briefly to indicate (see on ii. 6). Between faith in the simple facts of salvation and these more elevated views of the Divine work, there is all the distance which separates the preaching of the *evangelist* from the doctrine of the Christian *teacher*, or, if you will, all the difference which exists between the contents of the gospel history and the teaching of the Epistles.

To this teaching of Divine wisdom, the end of this whole deduction, Paul comes in ver. 13.

Ver. 13. " Which things also we speak, not in the words which man's wisdom teacheth, but which the Spirit[1] teacheth, appropriating spiritual things to spiritual[2] men." — Here is the resuming of the λαλοῦμεν, *we speak*, of ver. 6 ; it has been prepared for by vers. 10-12 : " This hidden wisdom God has revealed to us by His Spirit, and we speak it with words formed in us by this same Spirit. He gives us the form, after having given us the matter." Καί, *also*, prominently brings out precisely this relation between the two operations of the Spirit, *revelation* and *inspiration*. As Paul has contrasted wisdom with wisdom (vers. 6-9), revelation with revelation (vers. 10-12), he now contrasts Divine inspiration with earthly inspiration. By revelation God communicates Himself to man ; inspiration bears on the relation of man to man. — The genitives, σοφίας and πνεύματος, *wisdom* and *Spirit*, may, according to Greek usage,

---

[1] T. R. with E L P adds αγιον (*holy*).
[2] B reads πνευματικως (*spiritually*), instead of πνευματικοις (*to the spiritual*).

depend, not on the subst. λόγοις, *words*, but on the verbal notion expressed by the adjective διδακτοῖς (John vi. 45): " Words taught, not by wisdom, but by the Spirit," and this connection is also that which agrees best with the context. To teach things which the Spirit has revealed, terms are not made use of which man's own understanding and ability have discovered. The same Divine breath which lifted the veil *to reveal*, takes possession also of the mouth of its interpreter when it is *to speak*. Inspiration is, as it were, the language of revelation. Such is the secret of the peculiar and unique style of the Scriptures.— Meyer justly remarks that the term διδακτός, *taught*, while it positively includes the idea of inspiration, nevertheless excludes all mechanical representation of the fact, and implies in the person inspired a living assimilation of the truth expressed.

Very various meanings have been given to the last clause of this verse, according to the different senses in which the word συγκρίνειν may be taken, and according to the two genders, masculine or neuter, which may be ascribed to the adj. πνευματικοῖς, *spiritual*. The rarely used verb συγκρίνειν strictly denotes the act of bringing two things together to compare them and fix their relative value. This is certainly its meaning in the only other passage in the New Testament where it occurs, 2 Cor. x. 12. But in the LXX. this verb frequently takes the meaning of *interpreting*, especially in speaking of dreams (Gen. xl. 8, 16, 22 ; Dan. v. 15–17), because the interpretation of a dream consists in comparing the image with the idea discovered in it. Several commentators have proceeded on this second meaning;—

Chrysostom : *explaining* Christian doctrines by comparing them with the types of the Old Testament (πνευματικοῖς, neuter) ; Grotius, on the contrary : *explaining* the prophecies of the Old Testament by comparing them with the doctrines of Christ; Bengel, Rückert, Hofmann : *explaining* the things of the Spirit to spiritual men (πνευματικοῖς, masculine). This third explanation would in the context be the only admissible one. But this meaning of *interpreting* given to συγκρίνειν is at once foreign to the New Testament and to classical Greek.—Erasmus, Calvin, de Wette, Meyer, Osiander seek to come nearer to the real sense of the verb by explaining thus : *joining*, adapting spiritual words to spiritual things (πνευματικοῖς, neuter). It is on this view the justification of the procedure which the apostle has just described in the first part of the verse. To a spiritual body (the wisdom revealed by the Spirit) no other is suitable than a spiritual dress (a language taught by the Spirit). The meaning is excellent ; but the last clause would really add nothing to the contents of the previous proposition, and neither in this way is the meaning of the verb συγκρίνειν exactly reproduced. Should not these words form the transition to the development of the third word of the theme (6ᵃ). *among the perfect*, which will form the subject of the following verses ? We must, if it is so, take πνευματικοῖς as a masculine and see in it the equivalent of τέλειοι, *the perfect ;* comp. ver. 15 and iii. 1. The word συγκρίνειν has exactly in that case the meaning given it by Passow in his dictionary, a meaning which differs only by a slight shade from the first which we have indicated :

mit Auswahl verbinden, to adapt two things to one another with discernment; which leads us to this explanation: " adapting, applying, appropriating with discernment spiritual teachings to spiritual men." This is precisely the idea which is developed in vers. 14-16, and which will be applied in the final passage iii. 1-4.

This passage has a peculiar importance. It shows that what in Paul's view was the object of the revelation of which he speaks at this point, was not the historical facts from which salvation flows, nor the simple meaning in which they are presented by the preaching used in evangelization; but that it was the Divine plan which is realized through them, their relation to the history of humanity and of the universe, all that we find expounded in the passages quoted above (Eph. and Col., Rom. ix.-xi., 1 Cor. xv.). There we find unveiled the plan of God in all its dimensions (*its length, breadth, depth, height*); all that system of Divine thoughts eternally conceived with a view to *our glory*, of which ver. 7 spoke; the cross, as the centre from which there rays forth in all the directions of time and space the splendour of Divine love. This Christian speculation we have not to make or to seek. It is given: God is its author; His Spirit, the revealer; St. Paul and each of the apostles, in his measure, the inspired interpreter. But this wisdom, revealed to those who are to be its organs, is to be spoken by them only to those who are fit to receive it (vers. 14-16).

VERS. 14-16.

We come to the development of the third term: *among the perfect.*

Ver. 14. "But the natural man receiveth not the things of the Spirit of God, for they are foolishness unto him, neither can he know them, because they are spiritually discerned."—It seems at first sight that γάρ, *for*, would have been more suitable than δέ: "We appropriate spiritual things to spiritual men; *for* others would not understand them." But the thought is different. The δέ signifies: "*But*, as to the non-spiritual, we give them nothing of the kind, for we should thereby be doing them more ill than good." Paul here designates the non-spiritual man by the term ψυχικός, *psychical*. This word denotes a being animated with that breath of natural or earthly life (ψυχή) which man possesses in common with all the living beings of creation. It implies here the absence of that breath of higher life which puts moral beings in communication with God, and which Scripture calls τὸ πνεῦμα, *the spirit*. Thus xv. 44, the terrestrial body is called a *psychical* body, inasmuch as it is organized to serve as the dwelling-place and organ of a simple ψυχή, while the future body is called *pneumatical*, spiritual, inasmuch as it is destined to be the organ of a *spirit*. Holsten concludes from this expression of Paul that he denied all possession of the πνεῦμα, *the spirit*, to the natural man. It seems to me that 1 Thess. v. 23 proves the contrary. By putting *body*, *soul*, and *spirit*, parallel to one another, as the three constant objects of Christian sanctification, he shows that in his view these are the three essential elements of the whole human person. Only, before the coming of the Divine Spirit, the spirit in man is rather an aspiration, or, as de Wette says, a *receptivity*, than a power and life. It is simply the organ with which the human soul is endowed for the Divine, the sense destined to perceive and receive it; it is a capacity which the Divine Spirit will change into a real power and a new principle of life when He comes to take possession of it. No doubt *soul*, which is the principle of life common to man and the animals, is in the former endowed with faculties superior to that of all other animated beings. But *spirit* alone puts man into relation with God, and thus forms his really distinctive character among all the animals. The term *psychical* man, which we render by *natural* man, does not therefore exclude the presence of spirit in such a man; it only implies the latent and inactive state of this element, so long as the Divine Spirit has not awakened it to enter into union with Himself and to become through it master of the soul and thereby of the body. In this state man possesses only the natural intelligence with which his soul is endowed, and by means of which he judges things of the present life and is guided in this sphere; it is in this sense that Paul calls him psychical. Meyer thinks that the epithet has not an essentially different sense from the word *carnal*, iii. 1. But in this last passage it is Christians who are spoken of, though weak Christians, *babes in Christ*. Paul would not apply to true believers such strong expressions as those of our verse: "The things of the Spirit are foolishness unto them." Meyer's mistake arises from his not understanding that between ver. 14 and iii. 1 there is by no means a relation of equality. "This wisdom cannot be explained to the psychical man, who has only his natural reason to apprehend it; and as for myself when I was with you, carnal as you still were, though believing, I could not enter on this domain." See also on iii. 16.

The term οὐ δέχεται, *he does not receive*, indicates that in his inner man there is nothing corresponding to this light; it does not penetrate into him. What ravishes advanced believers with joy and admiration leaves him cold, and even produces in him, with all his intelligence in other domains, the impression of something foolish. Why so? Are there two logics: one for the converted, the other for the unconverted? Certainly not. The laws of the syllogism are valid for every sane mind. The difference arises from the fact that the experience of salvation establishes in the believer new premisses, foreign to the natural man's experience. As the egoist cannot believe in the heroism of devotion, and treats it as an impossibility,—not because he has another logic than the man of heart, but because a necessary moral premiss is wanting to him to appreciate the moral fact,—so the purely psychical man, not having made experience of the Divine love, does not possess the premiss necessary for understanding the Divine plan, and with the same understanding as the believer, he calls that *foolishness* which is heaven to the latter.

The apostle adds, *neither can he know them*, as if to say: " If he does not understand them, it is not so much his fault as that of the ill-advised teacher who expounds a Christian philosophy to the man who needs first to have salvation declared to him; who expatiates in the high regions of knowledge, when he should have laboured at the renewing of the heart." Here we see clearly how Paul distinguishes between the simple preaching of salvation and the *wisdom* of which he speaks throughout this whole passage. For certainly he never thought that to the unregenerate there is no need of preaching salvation by the cross, and that it is not their own fault if they do not understand, and so reject it. The use of the adverb πνευματικῶς, *spiritually*, has nothing in common with the Alexandrine system of interpretation, according to which those were called *spiritual* who could distinguish in Scripture the profound (allegorical) sense from the grammatical. The word simply means here, " in virtue of spiritual premisses." And the verb ἀνακρίνειν, to make an examination, analyze, discern, denotes the analysis made by the νοῦς (the understanding) of things transmitted to it, and the judgment resulting from it.

From this Paul could pass directly to the application which he has in view (iii. 1–4). But, as Rückert has well observed, he here interposes a short episode, vers. 15, 16, fitted to pave the way for this application, and to give it its full gravity.

Vers. 15, 16. "But he that is spiritual judgeth[1] all things,[2] yet he himself is judged of no man; 16. for who hath known the mind of the Lord, that he may instruct Him? But we have the mind of the Lord."[3]— Ver. 6 supposed in a preacher the faculty of discerning in each case whether he had to do with a psychical or a spiritual man. This is the faculty which the apostle affirms, ver. 15, and the possession and free exercise of which he claims for himself, ver. 16. The link between vers. 15 and 14 is in the term and idea ἀνακρίνειν, to

---

[1] T. R. here reads with B E L P, μεν, which is omitted by A C D F G It. Syrsch. This ver. is wanting in ℵ.

[2] A C D P read τα before παντα.

[3] Instead of κυριου (*of the Lord*), which is read by B D F G, T. R. reads Χριστου (*of Christ*) with ℵ A C E L P Syr.

judge. In virtue of the sway exercised by the πνεῦμα, *the Spirit*, over the psychical faculties of the regenerated man, he is endowed with a superior tact which gives him the power of estimating men and things with certainty. As Edwards says, " If the profane man cannot understand holiness, the holy man can understand the depths of evil." From the higher stage one can look into the lower, but not inversely.— The μέν, which T. R. reads with some Mjj., seems to me to throw rather too much emphasis on the antitheses of the two propositions. I am inclined to suppress it. — Instead of πάντα, some Mjj. read τὰ πάντα, which would here designate the totality of things, absolutely speaking. It is more natural to read πάντα without the article : " All things, each as it presents itself." Several commentators make this πάντα a masculine : *each man.* This sense would be perfectly justified, first by the context, according to which Paul claims for the spiritual man the faculty of discerning in each case with what kind of hearer he has to do, next by the οὐδενός, *none*, which follows, and which is evidently a masculine. But it is nevertheless true that the neuter sense is that which presents itself most naturally to the reader, and it is wide enough to include the other : *all things*, that is to say, every circumstance, every situation, and consequently, also, every person with whom one meets. St. Paul therefore had the right to estimate the spiritual state of the Corinthians, and to judge what suited or did not suit their state.—But, on the other hand, this spiritual man is subject to the scrutiny and sentences *of none.* The masculine sense of the pronoun οὐδενός is evident, since

L

it is only intelligent beings who are capable of judging. From this principle flowed the application which Paul proposed to make to the Corinthians (iii. 1-4); he can judge them, but they are not in a position to judge him.

Ver. 16. "With the humble, more humble; with the proud, more proud," says some one. Never did any one practise this maxim better than the Apostle Paul. Face to face with those who disparage him, he rises to an incomparable height. Jehovah, in Isaiah, addressing ignorant man, threw out this challenge: "Who hath measured the Spirit of the Lord? Who being His counsellor hath taught Him?" Such is the position which the apostle takes up as against his detractors. He quotes this saying after the LXX. (omitting the words of the middle clause, whereas he preserves them, Rom. xi. 34, while omitting the end), and says with them, *who hath known?* instead of, *who hath measured?* Just as the natural man is incapable of judging by his simple reason the ways of God in creation and the government of the world, so is he in no position to appreciate the procedure of the spiritual man. Why so? Because the latter, having the mind of the Lord, stands over against him in the same position as the Lord Himself.—The word συμβιβάζειν signifies strictly, to cause to walk together, and hence, to adjust, combine, conclude (Acts xvi. 10), to demonstrate (Acts ix. 22); it is used in the classics only with the *thing* as object (to demonstrate a thing), while in the LXX. it is used with the *person* as object; and so in them it takes the sense of *instructing*, which it has here.—In the ἡμεῖς, *we,* there is a well-marked contrast to the ὑμεῖς, *ye*, of iii. 1-3. It is obvious how profoundly, in virtue of the revelation he has received, the apostle distinguishes himself from the Church. — The term νοῦς, properly, *understanding*, and hence *mind*, is not synonymous with Spirit. It denotes the mind of God as to the destination of humanity and the best means of realizing it. The Spirit is the agent by whom this mind of God is communicated to the spiritual man.— Of the two readings, *of the Lord* and *of Christ*, the second seems to us preferable; the copyists have been naturally led to substitute Κυρίου (*of the Lord*) for Χριστοῦ (*of Christ*), to give this passage the form of a regular syllogism : " Who hath known the mind of God ? But we know it ; therefore no one can judge our mode of acting." But Paul has substituted for, the mind *of the Lord* (of God), the mind *of Christ*, which he tacitly identifies with that of God, because the former is only the reflection of the latter in a human intelligence. By the ἔχομεν, *we hold, we possess*, the mind of Christ is identified in its turn with that of Paul, who knows it by the revelation of the Spirit. Thus the minister of a sovereign could say, after an intimate conversation with his king, I am in full possession of my master's mind. From this moment, therefore, to criticize the servant is to criticize the master.

III. 1-4.

After demonstrating that though the gospel is not a wisdom, yet it contains one, but one which cannot be expounded except to those who by their spiritual maturity are in a condition to understand it, the apostle applies this truth to his relation to the Church of Corinth. The passage iii. 1-4 is the pendant of ii. 1-5. Edwards well says: I preached to you the gospel as a power (ii. 1-5); I could not preach it to you as wisdom (iii. 1-4).

Vers. 1, 2. "And I also, brethren, could not speak unto you as unto spiritual, but as unto carnal,[1] as unto babes in Christ. 2. I have fed you with milk,[2] not with meat: for hitherto ye were not strong enough, and not[3] even yet are ye."—The apostle, after rising to the height assigned him by the revelation which he has received, severely humbles the presumption of the Corinthians.—The κἀγώ (T. R. καὶ ἐγώ) surprises; it seems as if it should be, "But I," instead of, *And I also*. "This wisdom we have, *but* I could not declare it to you." Yet the *And I also* is easily explained. Paul does nothing more than apply to himself, in his relation to the Corinthians, what he has just said of the relation of the spiritual man to purely natural men. "And I also, as a spiritual man, judged and acted accordingly; comp. the κἀγώ absolutely parallel, ii. 1.—The word ἀδελφοί, *brethren,* serves to soften this personal application.—The *I could not* is an implicit answer to the disdainful charge of his enemies: "He knew not." It was in themselves the obstacle was; his *not being able* was caused by theirs; comp. the "*he cannot* understand," in speaking of the natural man, ii. 14.—Paul no longer uses here ψυχικός, the

---

[1] ℵ A B C D read σαρκίνοις instead of σαρκικοῖς, the reading of E F G L P.

[2] ℵ A B C P reject the καὶ (*and*), which T. R. reads with the rest.

[3] T. R. with L reads οὔτε (*neither*); all the rest read οὐδὲ (*and no more* or *and not even*).

natural man, which would have been too strong. For he did not mean that the Corinthians were entirely destitute of the Divine breath; how could they have been in possession of the χαρίσματα (*gifts*), the presence of which he had recognised in them (i. 5, 7)? Hence it is he uses the term *carnal*, which does not exclude the possession, to a certain degree, of the new life. The Spirit is there, but He has not yet taken a decided preponderance over the instincts of the flesh, the unregenerate nature. By these, indeed, must not be understood merely sensual inclinations. This is plain from ver. 3. For what was there sensual in the divisions which were produced at Corinth? The word *flesh*, which denotes strictly the soft and sensitive parts of the body, denotes also by extension natural sensibility, quick, even purely moral receptivity, for agreeable or disagreeable impressions in general. Thus the man who prefers the intoxicating pleasures of *speaking in tongues* to the holy austerity of prophesying, or the noble simplicity of teaching, is in Paul's eyes like a yet carnal babe; comp. xiv. 20. Consequently those who have found in the different forms in which the preaching of the gospel has appeared in Corinth an occasion for inflating themselves or disparaging others, and thereby tearing the Church into factions, while satisfying their personal vanity, have shown how the flesh, self-complacency, still ruled the new life, and the action of the Spirit in them. Paul would not, however, have called such men *psychical*, as if the Spirit of God were not within them in any sense. Indeed, the psychical man may also be called *carnal*. But there is this difference,—that if in the regenerate man the flesh hinders the action of the Spirit, in the unregenerate man, who possesses only the breath of natural life (the ψυχή), it reigns as lord (Rom. vii. 14–18). The T. R. with some Byz. and Greco-Lats. reads σαρκίκοις, while the Alex. with D read σαρκίνοις. The two adjectives signify *carnal*. But the latter refers to the substance and nature of the being so qualified (2 Cor. iii. 3; Heb. vii. 16), the former to his tendency and activity. The word σάρκινος is rare in the New Testament, while σαρκικός is pretty frequently used. Thus we are not allowed to think that the first has been substituted for the second by the copyists, the more that σαρκικός reappears in ver. 3 almost without a variant. The copyists had therefore no great inclination to substitute for it σάρκινος; while the relation between vers. 1 and 3 could easily lead in ver. 1 to the substitution of σαρκικοῖς for σαρκίνοις. We must therefore read σαρκίνοις in ver. 1, and see in this term, which indicates the hurtful persistence of the state of nature, not so much a reproach as the statement of a fact fitted to explain Paul's conduct when he was among them. This is confirmed by the expression, *babes in Christ*, which he adds as an equivalent term. The word characterizes a state of transition in a sense natural in the development of the believer. Time is needed to become a πνευματικός, as in the natural life there is need of growth to pass from the infant state to that of the mature man. It is obvious how much better than the other the term σάρκινος, carnal in nature, suited the ideas expressed in ver. 1; and how far Meyer is mistaken in regarding it as conveying a more emphatic rebuke than the term σαρκικός in ver. 3.

Ver. 2. The figures used by the apostle relate to the term *babes*. *Milk*, according to ii. 2, denotes the preaching of Jesus crucified, with its simplest contents and its most immediate consequences, expiation, justification by faith, the sanctification of the justified believer by the Holy Spirit, what saves by converting and regenerating. *Meat* represents what Paul has just called *wisdom*, the contemplation of the Divine plan in its entirety from its eternal predestination to its final consummation. The same figure occurs Heb. v. 12 and vi. 2, but with this difference, that there the persons in question are former Hebrews, and that the rudiments of religious knowledge (milk) are not exactly the same for those who were formerly Jews as for those who were formerly heathen.—The apostle says (literally), *I have given you to drink*, and that in relation to the two substantives, though the figure only corresponds to the first. It is a usual inaccuracy; comp. Luke i. 64.—The words, *Ye could not yet*, naturally refer to the time of Paul's first stay. Meyer, Edwards think that it is unnecessary to understand an infinitive (to bear meat); perhaps they are right; it is in this sense that I have translated, "Ye were not strong enough."—Paul adds (what is still more humiliating) that this weakness characterizes even their present condition. The οὐδέ, *and no more* or *not even*, which is the reading of almost all the Mjj., is harder than the οὔτε, *neither*, of the T. R. This second reading is more delicate. I should not be surprised if the οὐδέ had been substituted for the οὔτε, because the τε wanted its correlative particle.—Billroth was the first to ask how this saying agrees with chap.

xv. of our Epistle, where the apostle enters into such profound details respecting Christian eschatology. I think that the *Ye are not able* did not exclude an excursion into the domain of wisdom, when positive negations demanded it. And perhaps, as Rückert supposes, the apostle thought good to seize this opportunity to show his detractors how far he could rise when it pleased him to spread his wings.

Vers. 3, 4. "For ye are yet carnal :[1] for whereas there is among you envying and strifes,[2] are ye not carnal, and walk as men ? 4. For while one saith, I am of Paul; and another, I of Apollos, are ye not men ?"[3]—The apostle here uses, according to the great majority of the documents, the term σαρκικοί, carnal by acts. The matter in question is no more a simple state of weakness which continues in spite of regeneration, but a course of conduct which attacks the new life and tells actively against it. — The form ὅπου, *there where*, borrowed from the notion of place, is used here, as often, in a logical sense.—Ζῆλος has most frequently in the New Testament an unfavourable sense : heat, jealousy ; thence springs ἔρις, *strife*, which is only the manifestation of the ζῆλος in words.—The third term in the T. R., *divisions*, seems to be unauthentic ; perhaps the enumeration of the works of the flesh, Gal. v. 20, gave rise to this interpolation.—Such a state can only arise from self-complacency, either on the part of the leaders or their adherents ; and that is *the flesh*. What completes the proof that such a state is a fruit

---

[1] D F G, σαρκινοι ; all the rest σαρκικοι.

[2] T. R. adds here, with D E F G L It. Syr. Ir. Chrys. etc. : και διχοστασιαι (*and divisions*).

[3] T. R. with L P Syr.: σαρκικοι (*carnal*), instead of ανθρωποι (*men*).

of man's natural heart, is the analogy presented by the Church thus divided with the spectacle offered in the midst of the Greek people by the rival schools of philosophy. And doubtless that is what the apostle means by the expression : *walking according to man*, that is to say, following a conduct after the manner of man left to himself. No doubt a wholly different meaning could be given to the term, *walking according to man*, did we explain it by the following verse. It would signify : to make oneself dependent on a man, a party leader. But this meaning would depart somewhat from the idea which rules in this passage : the influence of the carnal mind on the conduct of the believer.

Ver. 4. The two examples the apostle gives in this verse are intended to prove that what he blames in the divisions which have been formed, is not any hostility they may have to his person, but the fact of those divisions themselves. And hence he puts forward his own party and the nearest to his own, that of Apollos. It follows that Paul starts from the fact of the most intimate harmony between him and Apollos, and that every attempt to apply to the ministry and party of this evangelist the foregoing polemic against worldly wisdom should be abandoned.—Instead of the received reading, *Are ye not carnal?* which is a surprise, as simply repeating the question of ver. 3, there is read in most of the Mjj., *Are ye not men*, or rather, *Are ye not* (human) *beings?* A question which seems stranger still. We must undoubtedly explain it by the preceding expression : *walking according to man*. " Are ye not falling back from the higher state to which faith had raised you, into the state of the natural man? Are ye not becoming again what ye were before being in Christ?" Meyer quotes as an analogous form the word of the *Anabasis*: ἄνθρωπός εἰμι, "I am a man," meaning: I am only a weak and fallible man. It is in the same sense that it is said, Gen. vi. 3, "They are but flesh." Hofmann rather sees in this question an appeal to the feeling of their dignity as men. But the question thus understood, to have a logical connection with the preceding proposition: "While one saith . . . ," would require to be put thus, "Are ye men?" The οὐκ or οὐχί is superfluous in this sense.—The placing of the μέν would lead us to suppose that he who pronounces the first watchword is the same person as pronounces the second (δέ); there is here an inaccuracy common in the classic style (see Meyer). This μέν must be logically put to the account of Paul in explaining the fact, not to the account of the interlocutor whom he brings on the stage.

Ver. 4 expresses the result of the whole foregoing development, and forms the transition to the following passage. In order to attack the spirit of rivalry with effect, and the divisions which had invaded the life of the Church, Paul had gone to the very root of the evil: the false way of regarding the gospel itself. He had shown that the preaching of the gospel was, not the exposition of a new religious speculation, but the good news of a fact, and that a fact absurd in the eyes of reason: the salvation of humanity by a Crucified One; and now he deduces therefrom the true notion of the Christian ministry and of the part it has to play within the Church.—Holsten and others think that the apostle turns at this point to the partisans of Apollos to upbraid their infatuation for this teacher. This we think is an error arising from a misunderstanding of vers. 4 and 5. We shall see that this special intention is foreign to the true sense of the following passage.

3. *The true nature of the Christian ministry* (iii. 5–iv. 5).

In this passage, Paul expounds :

1. The place of preachers, in relation to the Church (vers. 5–20).
2. The place of the Church, in relation to preachers (vers. 21–23).
3. He closes, as at the end of the two previous passages (ii. 1–5 and iii. 1–4), by applying the truth expounded to his own relation to the Corinthians (iv. 1–5).

VERS. 5–20.

In order to show what, in a religious organization like that which the gospel creates, is the place of preachers, the apostle takes two examples : Apollos and himself ; and he develops what he means to expound regarding the true place of Christian preachers, by applying it more specially to those two principal agents of the Divine work at Corinth.

Ver. 5. " What[1] then is Apollos ?[2] And what is[3] Paul ? Ministers[4] by whom ye believed, and that, as

---

[1] T. R. reads τις with C D E F G L P Syr. Cop. ; א A B It. read τι.

[2] T. R. with L Syr. puts the question relating to Paul before that relating to Apollos.

[3] א A B C P here read εστιν, which T. R. omits with D E F G L It.

[4] T. R. reads αλλ' η (before διακονοι) with L P Syr.

the Lord gave to each."—There is no difficulty, whatever Hofmann may object, in connecting the *then* with the previous verse, provided we see in this verse the conclusion and consequently the summary of all that goes before from i. 17 and even from i. 12 : "Now if, in virtue of the very nature of the gospel (which is a salvation, not a system), its preachers are not what you make them when you say : I am of Paul or of Apollos, what are they *then ?* " Rückert regards this question as an objection raised by an interlocutor of the apostle. But it belongs to the train of his argument; it is the theme of the whole following passage. Besides, Paul indicates such interruptions more precisely (xv. 35). — The Greco-Lat. and Byz. mss. read τίς : *who* are they (as individuals) ? The Alex. read τί : *what* are they (as to their office) ? The second reading is more in keeping with the context. It is no doubt, as Meyer thinks, the personal names which have led to the substitution of the masculine for the neuter.—T. R. places the question relating to Paul *before* that which concerns Apollos, probably under the influence of the preceding verse and of i. 13. But the apostle has not here the same reason as formerly for putting himself first. For he is no longer dealing with a personal preference to be condemned; here he begins a matter of doctrine.—The ἀλλ' ἤ, *other than*, in T. R. is probably a gloss; the answer is more direct : *ministers*. Such is the great word, that which without any roundabout states the nature of the position : not heads of schools, not founders of religious societies, as having a work of their own, but simple *employés* labouring on the work of another. This situation of ministers is characterized by two features : "*By whom* ye have believed." As Bengel well says : "*By* whom, and not *in* whom ; " simple agents (διά). The *ye believed* applies also to Apollos, though the Church was already founded when he arrived at Corinth ; for he had increased the number of believers and contributed to sustain the faith of those whom Paul had led to believe.—Καί, *and that ;* and moreover : Neither do those agents who labour on another's account do anything at their own hand. This is the second feature and, in a sense, the second form of their dependence : *as the Lord gave to each.* The following verse shows that Paul is here thinking of the kind of work which the Master commits to each labourer, while rendering him fit for it by personal gifts which He confers on him and by the special commission which He gives him.—The ἑκάστῳ, *to each,* is placed by inversion, as in vii. 17 and elsewhere, before the conjunction, to bring out clearly the *distinction* between those different tasks. For hereby is completed the idea of dependence : All *for* a master, as all *by* this master ! This master is denoted by the term ὁ Κύριος, *the Lord,* in opposition to the preachers who are only διάκονοι, *servants.* This Lord, according to Chrysostom, de Wette, Meyer, is God ; comp. ver. 6. But in general in the New Testament, when the term Κύριος does not belong to an Old Testament quotation, it denotes Jesus Christ. This is particularly the case in the first chapter of this Epistle. And ver. 6 proves nothing in favour of the opposite sense, for the action of Jesus and that of God, though distinct, are not separate. Comp. xii. 5, where the functions of ministers are also put in relation to Christ, as Lord of the Church, and their efficacy in relation to God, as the last source of all power.

Vers. 6, 7. "I planted, Apollos watered, but God gave the increase; 7. So then neither is he that planteth anything, neither¹ he that watereth, but God that giveth the increase."— The asyndeton between ver. 6 and the preceding one arises from the fact that the verse reaffirms in a new form the last proposition of ver. 5, of which it is only the development. In the two functions of *planting* and *watering*, there reappears in specialized form the idea of distribution contained in the "*as* the Lord gave *to each*." In respect of Corinth Paul had received the mission of planting, that is to say, of founding the Church; Apollos, that of watering, that is to say, of developing the Church already founded. And if the labour of the one and the other had had some true success, it was due solely to the concurrence of God. As Edwards says: "God is the source of life in the physical as in the moral world. Man can indeed put the seed in contact with the soil; but life alone makes it spring and grow; and this life is not only beyond the power but even beyond the knowledge of man." The imperfect ηὔξανεν denotes a Divine operation, which was in process at the very time when Paul and Apollos were labouring.—The apostle wishes decidedly to take away all individual and independent worth from the labour of the two workers whom he has chosen as examples, in view of a Church which tends to falsify the position of its ministers. This choice then has a

¹ א C: ουδε instead of ουτε.

perfectly natural explanation : was it not by speaking of himself and his friend that he could, with least scruple, remind them of the humble position of Christ's ministers, by leaving it to the Church itself to make application of the truth to the other workers whom it exalted ?

Ver. 7. What harvest would have sprung up from the labour of the two workers without the life which God alone could give ? What then are those workers ? —There is ordinarily understood as the predicate of the last proposition : *is everything*. But why not simply retain the preceding predicate : *is anything?* If in this work God alone is anything, is not this equivalent to saying that He is *everything?* The reading οὐδέ, *nor any more*, in two Alex., insists perhaps too specially on applying the idea of nothingness to Apollos.—This first development, vers. 5-7, is directed against the folly of raising servants to the rank of masters. The following combats the opposition which it is sought to establish between them by comparing them with one another, and taking the liberty of rating their respective merits.

Ver. 8. "Now he that planteth and he that watereth are one, but every man shall receive his own reward according to his own labour."—The δέ is here a particle of transition, but with a shade of contrast : "*Now*, despite this difference of functions (pointed out, vers. 5-7), these ministers are one." This unity is not that of their common nothingness (Bengel : "Neuter æque *quidquam* est "), nor that of the part of simple servants (de Wette, Meyer, Heinrici, etc.); it is that of the work on which they labour together. To understand what Paul means by this unity, it is enough to consider the foregoing figures (vers. 6, 7). Between two gardeners, one of whom plants and the other waters one and the same garden, who would think of setting up any rivalry? Would not the labour of the one become useless without that of the other? What folly, then, to disparage the one and exalt the other!

But yet there will one day be—the second δέ is adversative—a difference established between them: the difference of the reward they will receive, which will depend on the degree of their fidelity in their respective labours. This idea, expressed in the second part of the verse, is that which Paul proceeds to develop in the passage, vers. 10-15. Of course it is the Master who will pass this estimate; it will take place at the day of judgment. And so what folly it is to anticipate it by comparisons made beforehand! The terms ἴδιος μισθός, *his own reward*, and ἴδιος κόπος, *his own labour*, recall the saying, Gal. vi. 5: "Every man will bear his own burden." The estimate of the fidelity of each servant will not rest on the comparison of it with another's, but on the labour of each compared with his own task and his own gift. Now who else than God could pronounce such a sentence? And not only has He alone the power, but He alone has the right. This is what is brought out in ver. 9.

Ver. 9. "For we are labourers together with God; ye are God's husbandry, God's building."—It is not without reason that in the original the word θεοῦ, *God's*, heads the three propositions of this verse. God alone is Judge, for He is the proprietor in whose service all this work is done. It is therefore a mistake in

Holsten and others to refer the *for* to the idea of the unity of the workers (ver. 8ᵃ). It bears on what immediately precedes (ver. 8ᵇ). The worker's responsibility in this labour is presented in two aspects; and first from the standpoint of the servant's own position: συνεργοὶ θεοῦ, *labourers together with God*. It is grammatically inexact to apply the preposition σύν, in the word συνεργοί, to the community of labour existing among the workers themselves: "fellow-labourers in God's service" (Bengel, Olshausen, Heinrici). This sense is connected with the false explanation which regards *for* as a confirmation of the unity of the workers among themselves (ver. 8ᵃ). According to Greek usage, the regimen of σύν, in the composite συνεργός, is expressed by the following complement: comp. Rom. xvi. 3, and Phil. i. 24, συνεργὸς ἡμῶν (*the fellow-worker with us*). The meaning therefore is: "We are at work with God Himself." Some have shrunk from this bold idea of making Christ's minister in the Church the fellow-labourer of God. And yet what else is said by ver. 6? In every sermon, in every instance of religious instruction, in every pastoral visit, is not the pastor the agent by means of whom God works in souls? But, perhaps, with a complement like θεοῦ, *of God*, there must be added to the idea of joint labour that of dependence. The meaning would then be: "*God's* day-labourers, working *with* Him." Consequently it is His to pay the workmen, and to value their labour! Is it not His goods that are in question? To Him belongs the Church, *His* field, *His* house. The word γεώργιον is not fully rendered by the term *field;* this would rather be

M

expressed by ἀγρός (Matt. xiii. 24; Luke xiv. 18) The term γεώργιον embraces the idea of cultivation along with that of the field; and therefore we translate "God's *husbandry.*" It is nearly the same with the term οἰκοδομή, which is unknown to classic Greek down to Aristotle (Edwards). It is taken here rather in the sense of a building *in course of construction* (οἰκοδόμησις) than in the sense of a building finished (οἰκοδόμημα); for, according to the context, the workmen are still at work. It is therefore to a Divine possession that the workers put their hand! We feel that the apostle has passed to a new idea, that of the responsibility of the workers. What gravity attaches to such labour! To cultivate a field the harvest of which is *God's!* To build the house which *God* Himself is to inhabit! God alone can estimate such labour, and He will not fail to do so. Vers. 10–15 describe this responsibility and the inevitable judgment which will hallow it. It is less to the Church than to preachers themselves that the immediate sequel is addressed. For several of them at Corinth were certainly not innocent of what had happened. The use of a second figure, that of *building* after that of a *field* (used in vers. 6-8), is due to the feeling of the apostle that the latter does not suffice to depict what he is about to express. He needs one which lends itself better to the dramatic exposition of the *two opposite results* which human labour may have.

But before indicating this difference between the two kinds of building, the apostle thinks good to put his own work out of the question. For it is ended, and—as the result has proved—well ended.

Ver. 10. "According to the grace of God which is given unto me, as a wise master builder, I laid¹ the foundation, and another buildeth thereon; but let every man take heed how he buildeth thereupon!"— The apostle first looks backwards (*I laid*), in order to put himself out of the question; hence the asyndeton. —*The grace given him* is that of founding the Church among the Gentiles, particularly at Corinth, with the totality of gifts which he received for this mission, and the use of them which he has been enabled to make. The phrase, *according to the grace* . . ., softens the eulogy which he seems to award himself in speaking, as he does here, of his work at Corinth.—One might see in the words, *as a wise master builder*, nothing more than an idea analogous to that expressed in Matt. vii. 24–27. Paul would then simply mean: "I did not build on ground without laying a foundation; as a good architect, I provided a foundation for the building." But the idea of prudence, or better still, of ability, contained in the term σοφός, seems rather to relate to the *manner* in which he laboured in laying the foundation, than to the simple act itself of laying it. He took care to avoid factitious modes of procedure, means borrowed from human eloquence and speculation; he deliberately confined himself to bearing testimony to the fact of salvation, leaving the Holy Spirit to act, and refraining from entering before the time into the domain of Christian speculation; his wisdom, as a founder, was to make no account of wisdom; comp. ii. 1–5, and iii. 1–4.—The *master*

---

¹ ℵ A B C read ἔθηκα, instead of τέθεικα, the reading of T. R. with D E L P.

builder is not only he who draws the plan of the building,—in this sense the title would revert to God,—but also the man who directs its execution.—The perfect τέθεικα, which is read in the received text, might appear preferable to the aorist ἔθηκα of the Alexandrines; for the foundation, once laid, remains. But the aorist, which denotes the act done once for all, better contrasts Paul's work with the subsequent labours which are still going on.—These labours are denoted by the term ἐποικοδομεῖν, "*building on* (the foundation laid)." The ἄλλος, *another*, is referred specially to Apollos. Two things should serve to set aside this idea: first, the present ἐποικοδομεῖ, *builds upon;* for, at the time when Paul wrote, Apollos was no longer at Corinth; then the word *each* which follows, and which shows that the ἄλλος, *another*, is a collective term. The word, in fact, denotes the whole body of individuals who, as prophets, teachers, or speaking in tongues, had laboured, since Paul's departure, in developing the Church founded by him. Apollos was one of them, and he certainly belongs, in Paul's view, to the number of those who had built with materials of good quality, ver. 14; comp. vers. 6, 7. The end of the verse is an admonition addressed to all these workers, and prepared for by all that precedes from ver. 8[b]. The πῶς, *how* (that is to say: with what sort of materials), is the theme of the whole following development.

Ver. 11. "For other foundation can no man lay than that is laid, which is Jesus[1] Christ."—The γάρ, *for*, announces an explanation of the warning contained in

---

[1] T. R with some Mnn. reads ὁ before Χριστός (*the* Christ).

the βλεπέτω, *let him consider well.* The γάρ refers, not to ver. 11 taken separately,—this verse is only a reservation, and, so to speak, a μέν relatively to the following δέ,—but to the whole passage, vers. 12–15. The apostle means that his work, all that has been his, has been relatively simple. He has had nothing else to do than take the foundation laid by God Himself in the person of the living Christ, dead and risen again, and lay it in the heart by preaching, as the foundation of Christian faith and salvation. The participle κείμενον, *which is laid,* refers to God's work, and the verb θεῖναι to the labour of the preacher who founds the Church by testifying of this work. If the preacher would lay another foundation, it would be the beginning of a new religion and a new Church, but not the continuation of the Christian work. Now Paul is speaking here of preachers assumed to be Christians.—But the work of those who have to construct the building on the foundation laid is not so simple; and hence they should take good care as to the way in which they do it.

Vers. 12, 13. "But if any man build upon this foundation[1] gold,[2] silver,[3] precious stones, wood, hay, stubble; 13. every man's work shall be made manifest; for the day shall declare it, because it shall be revealed by fire, and the fire[4] shall try every man's work of what sort it is."—The δέ is adversative: "My work, the part assigned to me, is done, and well done. *But* let those who labour now take heed what they

[1] ℵ A B C omit τουτον (*this*), the reading of T. R. with D E L P It. Syr.
[2] ℵ B : χρυσιον instead of χρυσον.
[3] ℵ B C : αργυριον instead of αργυρον.
[4] A B C P read αυτο (after το πυρ), which is omitted by ℵ D E I. It.

do!" The εἰ might be taken interrogatively: Is it that? as sometimes. But it is simpler to translate it in its ordinary sense of *if*, and to find the principal proposition at the beginning of ver. 13.—The guidance of converted souls is a much more delicate work than the labour bestowed on their conversion; in fact, it is easy to employ materials in the work of their spiritual development which shall be more hurtful than useful. Now the Church is God's house, God's habitation, and into such a building no materials should enter save such as are worthy of its sublime destination. Oriental palaces and temples presented to the eye only the most precious materials: marble, jasper, alabaster (*precious stones*), besides gold and silver in profusion. This is what is still seen at the present day when one penetrates into the interior of the dwellings of rich Oriental merchants. The houses of the poor, on the contrary, are built of wood and of earth hardened with straw, and covered with thatch. — The diminutives χρυσίον and ἀργύριον differ from χρυσός and ἄργυρος (in T. R.) only in this that they denote specially either an ingot, or a piece of gold or silver.

God, the owner of the Church which is to become His dwelling, is represented here as a Lord who has contracted with numerous builders each charged with a part of the building. They are of course held bound to employ only materials appropriate to such an edifice, and to the dignity of him who means to make it His habitation. Most modern commentators think that the three kinds, whether of good or of bad materials, represent the *doctrines* taught by preachers, the didactic developments added by them to the fundamental truth of the gospel, that of salvation. This, with shades of difference, is the opinion of Clement of Alexandria, Erasmus, Luther, Beza, Calvin, Grotius, Neander, de Wette, Meyer, etc. But is not this to forget that the edifice to be built is not a book of dogmatics, but the Church itself, composed of living personalities? Other commentators have been led by this reflection to apply the figure of the various materials to the different classes in the membership of the Church: so Pelagius, Bengel, Hofmann; preachers, according to this view, are regarded as responsible for the good or bad composition of the churches which they instruct and guide. But if Paul could censure those preachers for having tolerated unworthy members or allowed them to make their way into the Church, could he have accused them of having voluntarily introduced them into it, as would be implied by the figure of the bad materials employed in the work? And could preachers of this kind end with being saved (ver. 15)? The good or bad materials can therefore neither represent the doctrines preached, true or false, nor the members of the Church, worthy or unworthy. There remains only one interpretation, which is to a certain extent that of Origen, Chrysostom, Augustine, and, in our day, of Osiander. The apostle means to speak of the religious and moral fruits produced in the Church by preaching. The spiritual life of the members of the flock is, in a certain measure, the teaching itself received, assimilated, and realized in practice. Either the pastor, by his preaching, his conversation, his example, the daily acts of his ministry, succeeds in developing among his flock a healthy religious life, drawn from communion with

Christ, abounding in the fruits of sanctification and love; and it is this strong and normal life which St. Paul describes under the figure of precious materials; or the pastor, by his pathetic discourses, his ingenious explanations, succeeds indeed in attracting a great concourse of hearers, in producing enthusiastic admiration and lively emotions; but all this stir is only external and superficial; with it all there is no real consecration to the Saviour. This faith without energy, this love without the spirit of sacrifice, this hope without joy or elasticity, this Christianity saturated with egoism and vanity: such are the wood, hay, stubble. The apostle himself sets us on the way of this explanation when in chap. xiii. he calls faith, hope, and love "the three things *which remain;*" these then are the materials which will survive intact the trial by fire.—It was for the successors of Paul and Apollos to judge whether they had continued in the spirit which had animated the authors of the work. Chaps. xii.-xiv. show plainly enough that it was not so.—It would be a mistake to think that the gold, silver, precious stones represent three different stages of the Christian life. As, in the figure, these three kinds of materials have their normal place side by side with one another in the temple or palace, they must be taken to represent the different forms of spiritual life which are produced in souls by healthy evangelical preaching.

The apostle had declared, ver. 8, that each would be appraised and recompensed according to the nature of his work. He now points out when and how this discrimination will take place.

Ver. 13. The same figure continues. The edifice before being inhabited by the Master must pass through the proof of fire, in which the materials of bad quality will be reduced to ashes, but from which the good materials will come forth intact.—Commentators are mostly at one in our time in applying the *day* of which the apostle speaks to the epoch of the Lord's advent. Grotius thought of the meaning of the Latin *dies* in the phrase *dies docebit*: "time will show." Neander also held that the history of the Church is the grand means of putting to the proof the doctrines of teachers. Calvin, adopting a similar interpretation, understands by *the day* the time when true Christian knowledge comes out in its clearness; as happened, for example, at the epoch of the Reformation. But it is impossible to prove that this meaning, with its different shades, can be that of the term *the day*. Others have applied it to the date of the destruction of Jerusalem, because this event was particularly suited to dissipate in the Church the Jewish opinions which Paul was combating; but what Paul combats in this whole passage is worldly wisdom rather than theocratic prejudices. St. Augustine thought of the day of affliction which puts to the proof the reality of the inner life; and Hofmann, of Antichrist's great persecution, which will bring victory to the good, defeat to the bad. It seems that such was the meaning already given to our passage by the author of the Διδαχὴ τῶν δώδεκα ἀποστόλων (*the doctrine of the twelve apostles*) in the second century; for in chap. xvi. the warning, "Watch," is first founded on the calamities of the last days, and next the author adds: "Then will appear, like a Son of God, the seducer of the world, and the race of men will come εἰς τὴν πύρωσιν τῆς δοκιμασίας (*into the burning of trial*)," words which can only be taken from our passage. But, when that day is referred to in Scripture, it is more distinctly qualified; comp. Eph. vi. 13 (*the evil day*); Heb. iii. 8 (*the day of temptation*); 1 Pet. ii. 12 (*the day of visitation*); Rev. iii. 10 (*the hour of trial*), etc. It is therefore more natural to abide by the first meaning: the day of Christ, when the separation will be made between believers themselves; comp. i. 8, iv. 5.—The manifestation which will take place at that time will be effected by means of *fire*. Many, and Meyer himself, seem to take this word in its literal sense, quoting as parallel 2 Thess. i. 8, where the Lord is represented as coming from heaven with flames of fire. But it must not be forgotten that the building to be proved exists only figuratively, and that consequently the fire which is to put it to the proof can only be also a figurative fire. The term therefore can only denote here the incorruptible judgment pronounced by the omniscience and consuming holiness of the Judge who appears. His Spirit will thoroughly explore the fruit due to the ministry of every preacher. When, in the Apocalypse, the judgment is described which the Lord passes on the Seven Churches, it is said in connection with that of Thyatira (ii. 18): "These things saith the Son of God, who hath eyes like unto a flame of fire." The look of a holy man may become an insupportable fire to the wicked, how much more that of the Lord! This penetrating look will then separate between what is real, solid, indestructible, and what is only transient, apparent, factitious. The subject ordinarily assigned the verb ἀποκαλύπτεται, *is manifested*, is that of the preceding proposition, *the day*: "The day of Christ is manifested with fire or by fire. But then it seems no more possible to take the term fire in the figurative sense. Others take as subject that of the first proposition of the verse, the *work*: "The work is manifested by means of fire." But this sense leads to an intolerable tautology with the following proposition; the apostle does not so repeat himself. Bengel and Osiander understand as subject, *the Lord;* but to reach this subject we must go back to ver. 11; then it is difficult to suppose that Paul would have said: "The Lord is manifested with fire." Is it not better to take ἀποκαλύπτεται in the impersonal sense? "For it is by fire that manifestation takes place," that is to say, that things are manifested as what they really are. This proposition enunciates not a fact, but a principle; hence the verb in the present ἀποκαλύπτεται, which contrasts with the two futures the preceding (δηλώσει) and the following (δοκιμάσει).—The ὅτι, *because,* supposes the principle recognised, that judgment, of which fire is the emblem, accompanies the day of the Lord.

From this principle flows the consequence enunciated in the last proposition. — If the pronoun αὐτό is authentic, which is read after πῦρ by the *Vatic.* and three other Mjj., it may be taken as relating to the fire: "the fire *itself,*" that is to say: the fire in virtue of its own proper nature; or what seems simpler, it should be taken in relation to the work, ἔργον, and made the object of δοκιμάσει: "the fire will attest it, the work, so as to bring out what it is" (ὁποῖόν ἐστι).

—The double result of this putting to the proof is described in vers. 14, 15.

Vers. 14, 15. "If any man's work shall abide which he hath built thereupon, he shall receive the reward; 15. if any man's work shall be burned, he shall suffer loss [of reward]; but he himself shall be saved, yet so as through fire."—Μένει is generally taken as a future (μενεῖ, *shall abide*), because of the future which follows κατακαήσεται, *shall be burned*. But there is no force in this reason; the act of burning is instantaneous; hence the future, which refers to a definite time, while that which abides, abides always: the thought expressed by the present μένει. The μισθὸν λήψεται, *shall receive the reward*, might be rendered in this everyday form: When it shall have been recognised that the work was of good quality, his cheque will be paid to him. This reward cannot be salvation; for the faithful workman was already in possession of this supreme blessing when he was labouring. We have to think then of more particular privileges, such as the joy of being the object of the Master's satisfaction: "Good and faithful servant!" then the happiness of seeing invested with glory the souls whom a faithful ministry has contributed to sanctify; finally, the possession of a glorious position in the new state of things established by the Lord at His Parousia: "Thou hast gained ten pounds; receive power over ten cities" (Luke xix. 17).

Ver. 15. To understand the picture which the apostle draws of the opposite result, we must undoubtedly suppose the workmen occupying the portion of the building which has been committed to them, and to which they are putting the last touch. In proportion as the fire, set to the building, consumes the combustible materials of which the bad workman has made use, the latter of course finds himself in danger of perishing along with his work; if he is saved, it can only be by escaping through the flames, and thanks to the solidity of the foundation.—The second future κατακαήσεται, *shall be burned*, is an ancient form (Homer, Hesiod) which had been replaced by the first future καυθήσομαι, and which reappears in the later Greek writers. By the perishable *work* of this labourer, Paul understands the Christian life without seriousness, humility, self-denial, personal communion with Christ, which has been produced among the members of the Church by the ministry of a preacher solely concerned to move sensibility, to charm the mind and please his audience.—The *loss*, ζημία, with which he is threatened, consists above all in the proved uselessness of his labour and in its destruction, which will take place under his own eyes. With what pain will he contemplate the merely external fruits of his brilliant or profound preaching passing away in smoke! Then he will see himself refused the reward of the faithful servant, the honourable position in Christ's kingdom, to which he imagined himself entitled: the payment of his cheque will be refused him.

But the apostle adds that this worker *shall be saved.* Chrysostom and the old Greek commentators understood the word *save* here in the sense of keep: "kept in Gehenna to suffer for ever." But the pronoun αὐτός establishes an evident contrast between the reward lost and the person saved; then the verb σώζειν, *to save*, is always taken in a favourable sense; Paul would have required to say in the sense indicated τηρηθήσεται, *shall be kept;* finally, the διὰ πυρός, *through fire*, is not identical with ἐν πυρί, *in fire*. The apostle certainly means, that though this workman has put bad materials into the building, yet because he built on the foundation he will not be given over to condemnation. But if he reaches salvation, it will only be through the furnace, like one who is obliged, in order to save his life, to pass through the flames. This furnace comprehends all the terrors of this judgment: the shame of this revelation, the horror caused by the look of the offended Judge, the grief of seeing the work on which he congratulated himself reduced to nothingness, and the souls whom he thought he had built up incapable of undergoing the last trial, and lost partly through his fault . . . ! " I have searched myself and I have found myself," said a dying pastor; "this is all the punishment God reserves for me." Were not these the first kindlings of the fire of which the apostle here speaks?

Some Catholic commentators have thought to find in the words, *as through fire*, a proof in favour of the doctrine of purgatory, and the Council of Florence, in 1439, based the dogma on this passage (Edwards). This is to forget,—1. that the fire is allegorical like the building; 2. that it is only teachers who are in question; 3. that the trial indicated is a means of valuation, not of purification; 4. that this fire is lighted at Christ's coming, and consequently does not yet burn in the interval between the death of Christians and that advent; 5. that the salvation of the worker, of which Paul speaks, takes place not *by*, but *in spite of* the fire.

There is something more serious than to build badly, and that is to do violence to what is already built. Such is the relation between the following passage, vers. 16-20, and the preceding. Hofmann well states this transition: "Paul passes from those who took upon them, without serious reflection, to continue his work at Corinth, to those who did not fear to destroy the fruit of his labour." Only it need not be said: of *his* labour; for he has not given himself out as one of the ἐποικοδομοῦντες, of those who have raised the building on the foundation laid. We must therefore speak of the work done, and successfully done, after Paul's ministry. To whom are we to ascribe such labour if not to Apollos, who had watered what the apostle had planted? As, then, it was impossible to apply to this teacher the figure of the bad workman in the previous picture, it is still more impossible to apply to him the figure of the destroyers in the following representation. And since the labour of demolition, about to be spoken of, is attributed to that same human wisdom spoken of in chap. i., we find the opinion confirmed which we had expressed in explaining the chapter, viz. that it had no reference whatever to the ministry of Apollos.

Vers. 16, 17. "Know ye not that ye are a temple of God, and that the Spirit of God dwelleth in you? 17. If any man destroy the temple of God, him[1] will God destroy;[2] for the temple of God is holy, which temple ye are."—The asyndeton between vers. 15 and

[1] A D E F G Syr^{sch} read αυτον, instead of τουτον, the reading of T. R. with א B C L P.

[2] D E F G L P read φθειρει (*destroys*), instead of φθειρει (*shall destroy*), the reading of T. R. with א A B C.

16 is to be remarked; it is as if, on occasion of what the apostle has just said about bad workers, a sudden view took possession of his heart, that of the gravity of the act of those workmen who not only build badly, but who destroy what is already constructed. Everything in this abrupt transition betrays emotion; the interrogative form: Know ye not . . . ? which appeals to the conscience of the Church and to the livelier feeling which it should have of its own dignity; the phrase, *temple of God*, forming a step higher than the simple *building* (ver. 9); finally, the two analogous gradations, that of the first $\phi\theta\epsilon\iota\rho\epsilon\iota\nu$, *destroy*, rising above the act of bad *building thereon*, and that of the second $\phi\theta\epsilon\iota\rho\epsilon\iota\nu$, denoting the punishment, rising above the simple fact of $\zeta\eta\mu\iota o\hat{\upsilon}\sigma\theta\alpha\iota$, *suffering loss* (of reward). —We must avoid translating, "*the* temple of God." The Church of Corinth is not the universal Church. The absence of the article before $\nu\alpha\acute{o}s$, *temple*, makes this word the indication of a simple quality: "Ye are a temple of God; ye partake of the sacred character of such a building!" This applies to every believer at Corinth, and at the same time to the Church as a whole. And how do they all possess such a dignity? The following proposition explains: God dwells in Christ, and Christ by the Holy Spirit dwells in the believer. The Father and the Son, according to the promise of Jesus, thus make, by the Spirit, "their abode in him" (John xiv. 23). The same figure: Eph. ii. 19–22; 1 Pet. ii. 4, 5.—The adjunct $\dot{\epsilon}\nu\ \dot{\upsilon}\mu\hat{\iota}\nu$, *in you*, may signify within you or in the midst of you. The context speaks rather in favour of the second meaning, since Paul is addressing the Church as such. But as

God dwells *among* believers only on condition of dwelling *in* them, the second meaning implies the first. Is the apostle thinking of the temple of Jerusalem, for which henceforth the Church, the true spiritual temple, is to be substituted? Possibly. Now if it was a sacrilege to profane the shadow, what will it be to do violence to the body (Col. ii. 17)!

Ver. 17. Again an asyndeton. Ver. 16 was the minor of the syllogism of which ver. 17 is the major: "Ye are a temple . . .; he is destroyed who destroys a temple . . ., therefore . . ." The conclusion which is self evident is understood.—The future $\phi\theta\epsilon\rho\epsilon\hat{\iota}$, *shall destroy*, is no doubt the true reading, though the present $\phi\theta\epsilon\acute{\iota}\rho\epsilon\iota$ might also be defended as the present of the idea, and consequently of certain realization. In ver. 15, notwithstanding the loss of the reward (the $\zeta\eta\mu\iota o\hat{\upsilon}\sigma\theta\alpha\iota$), the salvation of the workman was reserved; here, it is excluded. The punishment increases with the guilt: "As thou has treated the house of God, thou shalt be treated." The Greco-Lat. reading, $\alpha\mathring{\upsilon}\tau\acute{o}\nu$, *him*, emphasizes the *identity* of the man who has destroyed and who is destroyed. But the Alex. and Byz. reading, $\tau o\hat{\upsilon}\tau o\nu$, *him, this man*, is at once better supported and more forcible.—The following proposition gives us to know the wherefore of this severe treatment; the dignity of the building to which this sacrilegious workman does violence. The force of the proof rests on the attribute $\mathring{\alpha}\gamma\iota o\varsigma$, *holy*. What is holy, that is to say, consecrated to God, partakes of the inviolability of God Himself.—The apostle finding it superfluous to enunciate the conclusion in full, contents himself with suggesting it by the last words:

"a holy temple, which ye are." The plural pronoun οἵτινες is a case of attraction from the following ὑμεῖς. This relative pronoun of quality is to be connected not with ναός only, nor with ἅγιος only, but with the entire phrase, ναὸς ἅγιος, *holy temple*.

To what persons did this warning and threatening apply? Evidently to those who had laboured at Corinth in such a way that they had ended with disorganizing the Church, poisoning its religious and moral life, and compromising the Divine work so happily begun and carried forward in that great city. Here it is, as it seems to me, that we find the full explanation of the end of chap. ii., where Paul spoke of the *psychical* or natural man, distinguishing him from the yet carnal Christian (iii. 1–4). The majority of the Church of Corinth belonged to the second category; but there was certainly a minority in it whom the apostle ranked in the first. It was they whom he had in view in the last two so severe verses of chap. ii.: the man who has only his natural understanding; and it is to them he returns in the verses immediately following, where he again, as in chap. i., puts worldly wisdom on its trial. We have already said: these various passages, as it seems to us, can only concern *those of Christ*, as they are unmasked in the Second Epistle. But why does the apostle address this warning not to the guilty themselves, but to the Church: "Know ye not that *ye are* a temple of God," and all that follows? It is because he wishes to excite the whole Church to a holy indignation, and to call forth within it a vigorous reaction against the authors of these troubles; comp.

the appeal to the vigilance of believers, Phil. iii. 2 : "Beware of evil workers." In the following verses, Paul shows the source of the evil, as he had already pointed it out in chap. i., in order to open the eyes of both.

Ver. 18. "Let no man deceive himself; if any man thinketh that he is wise among you, let him become a fool in this world, that he may become wise."—Again an asyndeton, testifying to the emotion which fills the apostle's heart.—The illusion, to which he points in the first words of the verse, according to some, is the security in which those teachers live, not suspecting the danger which they run (vers. 16, 17). But the words εἴ τις δοκεῖ, *if any man thinketh*, imagines, claims, lead us rather to connect the idea of *self-deceiving* with what follows. There are people who have claims to wisdom, and who display their eloquence within the Church. Edwards concludes from the ἐν ὑμῖν, *among you*, that if they were among them, they were not of them; otherwise Paul would have said, τίς ὑμῶν. The fact that those people were strangers may be true, but the term used does not necessarily say so. Its meaning is rather this : "If any individual whatever, Corinthian or other, while preaching the gospel *in your assemblies*, assumes the part of the wise man and the reputation of a profound thinker (iv. 10), let him assure himself that he will not attain to true wisdom till he has passed through a crisis in which that wisdom of his with which he is puffed up will perish, and after which only he will receive the wisdom which is from above." This crisis of death to false wisdom is what the apostle characterizes by the words: *let him become a fool!*

To renounce this imaginary wisdom, which is only a human conception, to own his ignorance in what concerns the great matter of salvation, and, after taking hold of Christ crucified, who is foolishness to the wise of this world, to draw from Him the Divine wisdom which He has revealed to the world, such is the only way of realizing the claim expressed in the words, "thinketh he is wise."—Does the phrase, ἐν τῷ αἰῶνι τούτῳ, *in this world*, belong to the preceding or the succeeding proposition? in other words, does this adjunct qualify the idea of being wise in the Church, or that of becoming a fool? In the former case the words would characterize a preacher who tries to gain the reputation of wisdom among Christians by putting himself forward in the midst of them as the *representative of the wisdom of the world*. In the latter case Paul would say: "If thou claimest to be a wise man in the Church, well! But in that case begin with humbling thy reason, accepting the foolishness of the cross, and with thus becoming a fool *in the eyes of the wise of the world*, and then thou shalt be able to become really the organ of Divine wisdom in the Church." Notwithstanding the able pleading of Rückert in favour of the former meaning, we think, with Hofmann, that the second deserves the preference. The antithesis between the *among you* and the *in this world* stands out more precisely, and the sense is simpler. — The following verses justify the necessity of dying to the wisdom of the world. Of old has not God, the only wise, charged it with foolishness? Two scriptural declarations are alleged in proof.

Vers. 19, 20. "For the wisdom of this world is

foolishness with God. For it is written, 'He that taketh the wise in their craftiness.' 20. And again, 'The Lord knoweth the reasonings of the wise, that they are vain.'"—The first passage declares the powerlessness of the wisdom of the world to reach the ends at which it aims, consequently its vanity from the standpoint of utility. It is taken from Job v. 13. The devices of the wise themselves become the net in which God takes them, so that they are forced in the end to confess that the more subtle, the more foolish they have been. The verb δράσσειν, *to close the fist upon* (from δράξ, *the fist*), is much more expressive than the word καταλαμβάνειν used by the LXX. to render the Hebrew term. The apostle likewise improves the translation of the LXX. by substituting for φρόνησις, *prudence*, the word πανουργία, from πᾶν and ἔργον, the capacity for doing everything, not in good, but in evil, to attain the end in view.

Ver. 20. This passage is taken from Ps. xciv. 11. It proclaims the emptiness of human wisdom, not now as to its result, but as to its very essence. The Hebrew and the LXX. say, " the thoughts of *man.*" The apostle says, *of the wise*, because it is through them that mankind exercise their understanding.—The verb *knowing* has two objects in the original texts (Hebrew and Greek), as is often the case; first, the object known, the thought; then what God knows of those thoughts: that they are vain. We cannot render this forcible turn of expression in French.[1]—The apostle here judges human wisdom only from the point of view

[1] [Our Authorized English Version imitates the Hebrew and Greek. —Tr.]

of the discovery and attainment of salvation. He certainly respects every sincere effort to discover the truth (Phil. iv. 8); but salvation is a thought of God superior to all the discoveries of human wisdom (ii. 6-8).

Though he had addressed the whole Church (ver. 17: *Ye are* . . .), it was those who encouraged disorders whom the apostle had indirectly threatened in the foregoing verses. The three following verses contain the direction which it remains to him to give to the Church itself as to its conduct toward Christ's true ministers. They are therefore the conclusion of the passage begun ii. 5.

VERS. 21-23.

Ver. 21. "So then, let no man glory in men, for all things are yours."—The apostle began by reminding the Corinthians of what preachers are in relation to the Church: *servants* (ministers) of the one Lord; then, in a passage which may be regarded as an episode, he put before the eyes of the Church and of ministers themselves the grave responsibility incurred by the latter (vers. 10-20). Now he concludes; this is shown by the particle of transition ὥστε, *so that;* we can only translate it here by *so then,* because of the following imperative. We shall see that this same conjunction is ordinarily used in this Epistle to announce the practical conclusion to be drawn from a foregoing statement of doctrine; comp. vii. 38, xi. 33, xiv. 39, xv. 58.—On the imperative after ὥστε, see on i. 31.—*To glory in a person* can only mean: to boast of one's relation to him, to take honour from belonging to him, as a servant or a disciple takes glory from the name of an illustrious master. It is an allusion to the formulas: "I am of Paul, ... Apollos, ..." etc. Far from its being believers who belong to their teachers, it is much rather these who belong to them; and not only their teachers, but *all things*. Stoic wisdom had said: *Omnia sapientis sunt*, because the wise man can make use of everything, even of what is adverse to him. The believer can say so with a yet loftier and surer title, because he belongs to God, who puts all things at the service of His own. It is in this sense that Paul says, Rom. viii. 28: "All things work together for good to them that love God." As he develops it in the same passage, God, in His eternal plan, has disposed all things with a view to the salvation and glory of those who He knew beforehand would believe on His Son. The contents of this πάντα, *all things*, are detailed in the following enumeration, which has been called, not without reason, "the inventory of the possessions of the child of God," and in which death itself figures.

Vers. 22, 23. "Whether Paul, or Apollos, or Cephas, or the world, or life, or death, or things present, or things to come, all are yours; 23. and ye are Christ's, and Christ is God's."—In the front are placed the names of the three teachers who had been made party chiefs, and in connection with whom all this instruction is given. To express his conclusion, Paul has only to give back the three formulas. Instead of saying, "I am Paul's," the Corinthian should say, "Paul is mine." The Church is the end; the ministers are the means. Peter, with his personal memories of the life of Jesus, Apollos, with his knowledge of the Scriptures and the irresistible charm of his eloquence, Paul, with his superior knowledge of God's plan for the salvation of the world and his incomparable apostolic activity, are not masters to whom the Church should bow as a vassal, but gifts bestowed on it, and which it is bound to turn to advantage, without despising one or going into raptures over another. Paul cannot, of course, give back the watchword of the fourth party in the same way; for in itself this formula exactly expressed the truth. We shall see, by and by, how he brings it back to its true meaning.

These three gifts represent one and the same idea, that of the ministry, that is to say, in general, gifts of a spiritual order. In contrast to them Paul names *the world*, the totality of beings who, outside the Church, may tell on the lot of believers, or of the Church itself. Animate or inanimate, the creatures obey Christ who has received power over all things, and, through Him, the Church, which is His body (Eph. i. 22).—Of the powers acting in the world there are two, of formidable and mysterious greatness, which seem to decide the course of the universe, *life* and *death*. The first comprehends all phenomena which are characterized by force, health, productiveness; the second, all those which betray weakness, sickness, decay. From the one or other of these two forces proceed all the hostile influences of which the believer feels himself the object. But he knows also that he is not their puppet; for it is Christ his Lord who guides and tempers their action. Chrysostom, Grotius, and others have restricted the application of these two terms, *life* and *death*, to the teachers of the Church. But the apostle, on the contrary, would have them taken in their widest generality.—To these two pairs, that of the spiritual order and the terrestrial order, and that of life and death, the apostle adds a third in relation to time, *things present*, and *things to come*. The participle τὰ ἐνεστῶτα, strictly: what is imminent, here, as often, in contrast to "things future," takes the sense of *things present*. It comprehends all that can happen us in the present state of things, and as long as we form part of it; while *the things to come* denote the great expected transformation, with its eternal consequences. Then the apostle sums up his enumeration by reproducing the bold paradox with which he had begun: "Yea, I tell you, *all is yours.*" It is easy to see what the apostle wishes: to exalt the consciousness of this Church, which is degrading itself by dependence on weak human instruments (ἀνθρώποις, ver. 21), to the height of its glorious position in Christ. He strives to restore it to self-respect. It is the same intention which comes out in the following words.

Ver. 23. We might be tempted to give the words, *and ye are Christ's*, a restrictive meaning: "Ye are His alone, not your teachers'." But in the two analogous propositions, that which precedes and that which follows, Paul certainly does not mean: "All things are only yours," and "Christ is only God's." It is not restrictions we have here, but strong affirmations; the thought is not limited, it rises. "All things are the Church's, because it belongs itself to Christ, and depends on Him." It is in this saying, *and ye are Christ's*, that allusion is found to the fourth party. It is not merely a few presumptuous people, puffed up with conceit of their own wisdom, who can say: *And as for me, I am Christ's;* this is the privilege of the whole Church.—And, as if to put the last stroke to the annihilation of all human glory, Paul denies it even in the person of that Lord in whom all mankind might legitimately glory: *and Christ is God's.* As the Church possesses all things because it depends on Christ, Christ possesses all things because He depends on God; comp. xi. 3. God in Christ, such then for man is the one subject of glorying (i. 31). It has been asked, from the first ages of the Church, whether these words referred to Christ as man, or as a Divine Being. The old commentators and several of the Fathers, even Athanasius (see Edwards), applied them to the eternal relation between the Son and the Father. This is done also by Meyer, Kling, etc. Hence would follow the subordination of the Son to the Father, even within the Trinity. Others, Augustine, Calvin, Olshausen, de Wette, Edwards, apply them to Christ only in His humanity, in order to maintain the essential equality of the Father and the Son. It must be remembered, above all, that they refer to the Lord in His present state of glory, for it is as glorified that He is the Head of the Church. But this itself proves that the first explanation is not less true than the second; they are as inseparable from one another as the two states, the human and Divine, in the person of the exalted Christ. That is to say, we apply the notion of dependence contained in Paul's expression, not only to the Lord's humanity, but also to His Divinity. Is not this implied besides in the names of *Son* and *Word* used to denote His Divine being? And is not Beet right in affirming that only this notion of the essential subordination of the Son to the Father enables us to conceive the unity in the Divine Trinity? The meaning therefore is, that as to His one and indivisible person as Son of God and Son of man, Jesus receives all from the Father, and consequently belongs to Him wholly. It is on this absolute dependence that His universal sovereignty rests.

As soon as the Church of Corinth rises to the view of these relations, what will become of the miserable desire among its members to magnify themselves and to turn what may be wanting to others into a ground of self-satisfaction? How will it be possible for one, when he contemplates the absolute dependence in which the Son abides relatively to the Father, still to glory in himself or in another? Each believer will possess everything, even the eminent teachers who enable him to make progress, as gifts from His hand.

After thus making the Corinthians ashamed of their guilty infatuations, it only remains to the apostle to check the rash judgments in which some indulge respecting him : this is what he does in the following passage, which closes this section.

IV. 1–5.

Ver. 1. "Let a man so account of us as of ministers of Christ and stewards of the mysteries of God."—After explaining what preachers *are not*, to show that no man should make himself dependent on them, the apostle declares *what they are*, to withdraw them from the rash judgments of the members of the Church. He does so first by continuing to speak of himself and

Apollos (*us*; comp. vi. 6), then he speaks singly of himself (*me*, v. 3).—The word οὕτως, *thus*, which begins this passage, has been understood in the sense of *so then*. Thus taken, it would connect this passage with the preceding, announcing a consequence drawn from it. But vers. 21-23 had already drawn the consequence (ὥστε, ver. 21) from the preceding exposition. And the logical relation between what follows and what precedes would rather be that of contrast. The end of ver. 23 had raised the readers to such a height, that the apostle does not care to connect with it what follows by any particle whatever, and continues by an asyndeton. It seems to me indeed, as to Rückert, that the οὕτως is nothing else than the antecedent of of the ὡς, *as*, which follows; comp. John vii. 46; Eph. v. 33; James ii. 12, etc. The meaning is: "*See how you ought to regard us.*"—The word ἄνθρωπος might be translated by the French pronoun *on*; perhaps it is better rendered by *each*;[1] comp. xi. 28. Edwards sees in the use of the word an imitation of the Hebrew *Isch*. Bengel thinks that the term is intended to contrast man's judgment with that of God. I think the apostle wishes it to be felt that he is addressing the Church in the person of *each* of its members, and recalling to their minds the notion of ignorance and weakness attached to the condition of man.—The term ὑπηρέτης, which we translate by *minister*, strictly denotes a man who acts as rower under the orders of some one (ὑπό and ἐρέσσω); he is a man labouring freely in the service of others: it here denotes the acting and laborious side of the Christian ministry. The term

---

[1] [Our English translation renders literally.—Tr.]

οἰκονόμος, *steward*, dispenser, denotes, among the ancients, a confidential slave to whom the master intrusts the direction of his house, and in particular the care of distributing to all the servants their tasks and provisions (Luke xii. 42). This second term designates preachers as administrators of a truth which is not theirs, but their master's. It relates to the inward and spiritual side of the work of the ministry.—The trust administered by them is *the mysteries of God*. This term *mystery*, in the singular, denotes the plan of salvation in general (see on ii. 7). In the plural, it relates to the different designs included in this plan. The plural is here connected with the idea of distribution associated with that of steward. Perhaps Paul makes allusion to the choice which Apollos and he required to make among the manifold materials of Christian teaching, in order to use in every case only those which were appropriate to the state of the Corinthians (iii. 2).—The genitives *of Christ* and *of God*, which are certainly related to those of iii. 23, remind us that preachers, as labouring in the active service *of Christ*, the Head of the Church, and charged with distributing to it the truths *of God*, have to give account before these supreme authorities and not before the members of the Church. They go where Christ sends them, and deliver what God has given them. They are not to be judged *in this respect*. The only thing that can be asked of them, is to be faithful in the way in which they fulfil the missions confided to them, and in which they conform their teaching to the measure of light which they have received.

Ver. 2. "Now what¹ remains² to require³ of stewards is, that a man be found faithful."—The meaning of the received reading (ὃ δὲ λοιπὸν ζητεῖται ... ἵνα) is this: "As to what may be required moreover (λοιπόν, *for the rest*) of stewards, it is that..." According to this reading, the apostle means: the ministry of teaching being once confided by God to a man, the question is no longer if he is more or less eloquent, more or less profound, more or less captivating,—God, who chose and sent him, has alone to do with all these questions,—but only if he is *faithful*, that is to say, if he gives out conscientiously what is committed to him, if he puts all the gifts and powers with which he is endowed into the service of this task; if, as a devoted servant, he has only one interest, the cause of his Master. He can only be called to account for the conscientious use of what he has received.—This clear and natural meaning suits the context and leaves nothing to be desired. But several Mjj. of the *three* families present different readings. Some (A C D F G P) read ὧδε λοιπὸν ζητεῖτε, which would signify: "For the rest in these circumstances seek in stewards that each be found faithful ..." This meaning is inadmissible. In such a sentence two things, it is plain, are mixed up: an exhortation addressed to particular persons, the Corinthian readers (*seek*), and a general principle (*in stewards; each*, τίς). The *Sinaït.* attempts to remedy this awkwardness

---

[1] T. R. reads ὁ δέ (*now that which*) with E L and the most of the Mnn., while ℵ A B C D F G P It. Syr. read ὧδε (*in these circumstances*).

[2] After λοιπόν, ℵ reads τι (*something* or *what is it which?*).

[3] T. R. with B L Mnn. It. Syr. reads ζητεῖται (*it is sought*), while ℵ A C D E F G P read ζητεῖτε (*seek*).

by introducing after λοιπόν a τι, which can only be taken in an interrogative sense: "In these circumstances, moreover, *what* else seek ye in stewards, than that each . . . ?" The meaning is good in itself; only, instead of *in stewards*, there would need to be *in us*. For if this question expresses a consequence to be drawn from ver. 1, as the word ὧδε would demand *in this state of things*, it would require to be *in us* (*these* particular *stewards*), and not *in stewards* in general. The τις following is likewise suitable only to a maxim.—There remains the reading of B: ὧδε λοιπὸν ζητεῖται ἵνα: "In this state of things, the only thing sought (λοιπόν, the only thing which remains) in stewards is that . . ." This reading, though admitted by most commentators of our day, is no more admissible than the preceding, and for the same reason. The ὧδε, *in this state of things*, can relate only to the case of ver. 1, and consequently to the ministers denoted by the ἡμᾶς, *us* (Paul and Apollos), while the words: *in stewards*, give to this saying the character of an entirely general rule of conduct. We must therefore return to the reading and sense of the T. R. This is one of those cases in which all the presumptions of external criticism are of no avail, whatever may be said against exegetical reasons. It is easy enough to explain what has given rise to the corruption of the text in part of the documents of the three families, and so early as in the old versions. The beginning was made by substituting for ζητεῖται, *is sought*, the imperative ζητεῖτε, *seek*, either to continue the series of the preceding imperatives (καυχάσθω, λογιζέσθω), and to give to the sentence a hortative turn (the same error as in most of the Mjj., Rom. v. 1 : ἔχωμεν, and 1 Cor. xv. 49 : φορέσωμεν), or as a mistake arising from the pronunciation of αι (in ζητεῖται) as ε. The imperative once admitted, led to the change of ὃ δέ into ὧδε to make this verse an application of the idea of the preceding verse.—Λοιπόν, *moreover*, that is to say : beyond what God and Christ give to their agents ; comp. the expressions : "the grace given unto me," iii. 10, and the ὡς ἔδωκεν, iii. 5.—The relation between the two ideas of *seeking* and *finding* is evident. It is this relation which justifies the use of the conjunction ἵνα, *that*. Men seek with the view of finding.—The idea of the verse therefore is : that the only thing for which the steward is responsible, is his fidelity. Now this is the very point on which man's judgment is incompetent, vers. 3-5.

Vers. 3, 4. "But with me it is a very small thing that I should be judged, of you or of a human tribunal ; yea, I judge not mine own self. 4. For I know nothing against myself ; yet am I not hereby justified ; but[1] he that judgeth me is the Lord."—The two previous verses related to preachers in general, especially to Apollos and Paul. From this verse, the application becomes wholly personal to Paul. For in what he proceeds to declare, the apostle can evidently make no affirmation except in so far as concerns himself.—Ἐμοί : "*with me* (at least)." Paul cannot know whether Apollos thought like him on this point.—The preposition εἰς, which indicates motion, or tendency to a point, is slightly incorrect, with the verb of rest, ἔστι. It indicates the progressive reduction to a minimum of

---

[1] Instead of ὁ δέ, ℵ reads ὁ γάρ (*for* He).

value, in proportion as the apostle weighs the judgments which are passed on him at Corinth. These unfavourable judgments become more and more with him the last thing which disquiets him.—The *that* (ἵνα) does not entirely lose the notion of aim: Paul has no interest whatever *with a view to the fact that* these judgments exist or do not exist.—The term ἀνθρωπίνη ἡμέρα, which we render by *a human tribunal*, literally signifies *a human day*, a day of human assizes. The word *day* is used in the same way in the Latin phrase *diem dicere.*—These last words contain a softening of what Paul had just said of the small value which he attaches to the judgments of certain Corinthians. The same indifference he feels in regard to all human judgment in general.—The term ἀνακρίνειν denotes rather the examination than the judgment; but as the examination issues in a sentence, and as we have no verb to render the strict sense, we must translate by the word *judge.*—Once on this way, the apostle goes to the very end. He does not himself feel adequate to judge himself with certainty. The ἀλλά indicates the gradation: "I refuse not only the judgment of others, *but also* that of myself;" comp. 2 Cor. vii. 11. He feels that in his inner man there are unexplored recesses which do not allow him to discover thoroughly the real state of things, the full integrity of his own fidelity, and consequently to pronounce a valid sentence on himself.

Ver. 4. His inmost conscience does not upbraid him with any unfaithfulness; but for all that (ἐν τούτῳ), he is not yet justified, that is to say, found irreproachable, by Him who searches the hearts and reins (ver. 5). It is usually objected that in this so simple sense, held by Chrysostom, Calvin, de Wette, Osiander, Edwards, the term δικαιοῦσθαι, *to be justified*, is taken in a purely moral sense, quite different from the ordinary dogmatic sense which it has in Paul's writings. That is not exact. The meaning of the word *to be justified* remains at bottom always the same : to be declared just. Only this declarative act is applied to another period, and given forth under other conditions than in the use which the apostle ordinarily makes of it. The time in question here is the day of judgment, not the hour of conversion ; and consequently the condition of justification is not faith only, but holiness and fidelity, fruits of faith. At the time of conversion a man is declared just without yet being so; in the day of judgment, to be declared such he must be so in reality. The declarative sense of the word justify remains therefore as the basis of the use which the apostle here makes of the term; it is exactly the same in the passage Rom. ii. 13. — Melanchthon, Calvin, Rückert, Meyer, Beet maintain the application of the term to justification by faith in the ordinary sense of the word. The following is the wholly different explanation which they give of the verse : "It is to no purpose that I feel myself guilty of nothing ; it is not thereupon that my justification rests, but on Christ alone." Rückert and Meyer allege in particular the position of the words ἐν τούτῳ, *in this*, after the negative οὐκ, a position which makes the negative, instead of bearing on the verb, bear on ἐν τούτῳ; it is not therefore the *being justified* which is denied, but the *being justified on this* (ground), that is to say, through the fidelity of which Paul is conscious. He means: "I am justified not by this, but by something else." His system was well enough known, Rückert thinks, to make every one comprehend what was the other understood way. But Osiander rightly answers, that in this case, what Paul affirms so energetically is a thing which is understood of itself. Who could imagine that the apostle thought of founding on his present apostolical fidelity the absolution of all the sins of his past life? Then it would be strange if in opposition to the means of justification, which he so expressly excludes, he purely and simply should understand that which he maintains. Finally, vers. 3 and 5 manifestly transporting us to the day of judgment, we are obliged to refer ver. 4 also to that time. As to the position of the ἐν τούτῳ (*for this*) after the negative, it is intended to emphasize the idea of *for this* in the sense of "*even* for this," without there necessarily being a contrast to any other way of justification.—According to an explanation not infrequent in Catholic writers, the apostle is supposed here to express the uncertainty in which he is plunged as to his state of grace, and to teach thereby even the impossibility of the Christian's attaining the assurance of salvation here below, unless by an exceptional revelation. Calvin has already set aside this misunderstanding. Paul denies the competency of any human judge whatever, even himself. But if he did not obtain from God the full approbation after which he aspires, and to which he hopes he has a right, it would not follow in his view that his salvation was thereby compromised. Has he not just affirmed that the workman who has built with bad materials, but on the true foundation, shall not perish, but lose only the reward of his work ? How, then, should he put his own state of grace in doubt for some unfaithfulness which remained unperceived even by his conscience ? Though blameable in one point, he would not therefore be rejected.

If the meaning which we reject had been the one Paul had in view, he must have gone on to say : "*For it is the Lord who justifieth me.*" He says on the contrary, thinking of the judgment : "*Now it is the Lord who maketh the examination.*" — The *Sinaït*. reads γάρ instead of δέ, which gives an excellent meaning : " I am not justified by the fact of my good conscience ; *for* He who maketh the only valid examination, is the Lord." But the δέ, however, better emphasizes the distinction between this Judge, whose examination alone is competent, and the fallible man who claims to pose as judge. — The pres. participle ἀνακρίνων indicates the permanent function, the office. " He is the investigator of my life."

Ver. 5. " Therefore judge nothing before the time, until the Lord come, who even [1] will bring to light the hidden things of darkness, and will make manifest the counsels of the hearts : and then shall every man have praise of God."—This verse is, as it were, the full period put to the personal application which Paul has just made in vers. 1–4. The ὥστε, *so that*, therefore corresponds to that of iii. 21. There the meaning was : *therefore* no infatuation !—Here : *therefore* no

---

[1] D E F G It. omit καί (*even*).

judgment!—The τι is rather a qualifying pronoun than the indication of the object of κρίνετε: "Do not pass any judgment!"—The words, *before the time*, are explained by what follows: *till the Lord come*, the true Judge. This character which belongs to Him exclusively is explained by the two following relative propositions. In fact, the infallible judgment of a human life supposes two things: the revelation of the acts of that life in their totality, even the most unknown, and the manifestation of the inner springs of the will, in the acts known or unknown. This is what Paul means by the two phrases: "*the things of darkness*" and "*the counsels of the hearts.*" The hidden acts, which will be brought to light, are not only the bad, but also the good (Matt. vi. 3, 4, 6; 1 Tim. v. 23-25). It is the more necessary to have regard to the last here as there is no question afterwards except that of *praise*.—The inner springs and feelings are what determine the true quality of actions in the eyes of God; it is therefore on the complete knowledge of them that the just appreciation of a human life rests.—The καί before φωτίσει, which we have translated by *even*, which others render by *also*, has been variously understood. Osiander, Rückert: "He will come not only to judge, but *also* to set in light." This sense is inadmissible; for the second of these deeds should not follow but precede the first. Meyer: "Among other things, at His coming, He will *also* do this (set in light)." But why allude to other things, and what are those things? Hofmann establishes a correlation between the two καί in the sense of: *both . . . and . . .*; or of: *not only . . ., but also*. But why emphasize so strongly the hardly appreciable shade between the two almost synonymous verbs? It seems to me that the first καί, rendered by *even*, bears on the two following verbs, and contrasts the whole portion of the life *known* by other men with that which the Lord only knows and which He will then manifest. The second καί, *and*, serves only to connect the two parallel and equivalent verbs.—The *and then* brings out the gravity of this time of complete revelation; it contrasts it with the premature judgments of the Corinthians (*before the time*).—*Praise*: the true praise, that which will run no risk of being changed into a sentence of condemnation by a higher tribunal, like the premature praises which the Corinthians decreed to their favourite teachers. What a sting lay in this last word addressed both to the frivolous admirers and to the self-sufficient orators who had excited this profane enthusiasm! From the passage about to follow, iv. 18-21, we shall be able to gather to what point things were already going at Corinth in this painful direction.

4. *Pride the first cause of the evil* (iv. 6-21).

Here is the final and general application of the whole first part, relating to the divisions which had arisen in the Church. The apostle, after reminding the Corinthians of the true nature of the gospel, and deducing as a consequence that of the Christian ministry, makes palpable the vice which is eating into them: spiritual pride. He passes here from the defensive to the offensive; he has justified himself against the frivolous and rash criticisms of the

Corinthians; he proceeds now to their judgment.—
Ver. 6 is the transition from the foregoing exposition
to the practical conclusion.

Ver. 6. "Now these things, brethren, I have presented, by way of applying them to myself and to Apollos for your sakes; that ye might learn in us not[1] to go beyond this limit:[2] that which is written; that no one of you be puffed up for one against another."—
By the address, *brethren*, Paul puts himself by the side of his readers. The verb μετασχηματίζειν properly signifies: to present a thing or person in a form different from its natural figure, to transform, disguise. It is in this sense that it is applied to Saul in the LXX., 1 Sam. xxviii. 8 (Heinrici); comp. also 2 Cor. xi. 13, 14. St. Paul means that in the preceding passage (from iii. 5) he has presented, while applying them to himself and Apollos, the principles regarding the ministry which he was concerned to remind them of, in view of certain preachers and of the Church, which misunderstood them. He did not wish to designate those preachers by name, lest he should shock susceptibilities already awakened. He explains this method, which he thought himself called to use in the delicate circumstances, by the words δι' ὑμᾶς, *for your sakes*, which here signify: "the more easily to gain your acceptance of the truth thus presented."
Expressions like these: "Paul is nothing, Apollos is nothing" (iii. 7), applied to other leading persons at Corinth, would have seemed injurious, while in the

---

[1] T. R. reads φρονειν after γεγραπται with L P Syr.; all the rest omit it.

[2] T. R. reads υπερ ο with D E F G L Syr^sch; א A B C read υπερ α.

form used by Paul the truth declared lost all character of personal hostility. Hence it follows that the word ταῦτα, *these things*, applies solely to the last passage concerning the ministry, and not at all to the previous passages regarding the nature of the gospel. It is therefore a mistake to find here a proof in favour of applying to Apollos or his partisans the polemic against human wisdom in the first two chapters. The passage rather shows how thoroughly Paul felt himself one with Apollos, seeing he could treat him as a second self, and distinguish him so pointedly from the teachers who opposed him at Corinth.

After explaining the method used by him in the previous statement of doctrine, he points out the object of this teaching. In speaking thus of himself and his friend, he meant to indicate a limit they should never cross in estimating preachers whom the Lord gives them. All glory is to be refused to man in the spiritual work of which he is the agent. The T. R. gives as the object of μάθητε, *that ye may learn*, the infinitive φρονεῖν, to think of, aspire: "that ye may learn not to go in your thinking beyond . . ." But, according to the authority of the MSS., this word is probably a gloss; Hofmann thinks it borrowed from Rom. xii. 3. Rejecting it, the meaning remains the same; but the turn of expression is briefer and more pointed: that ye may learn the: not going beyond *what is written* (Greco-Lat. and Byz.), or *the things which are written* (Alex.). But of what is the apostle thinking in this ὅ or ἅ γέγραπται? The words might relate to what Paul himself has just written in the foregoing passage. In this case we must adopt the

Alex. reading, ἅ, *the things which*; for the form, *what* (ὅ) *is written*, would naturally apply to the Old Testament. But even with the Alexandrine form the application of the words to the preceding passage is far from probable. Would not Paul rather have said: ἃ προέγραψα or ἃ προεγράφη, *what I have*, or *what has been written before?* comp. Eph. iii. 3.—Or it has been thought that Paul was here referring to the words of Scripture which he had quoted above (iii. 19, 20; i. 31). But those quotations were too remote to lead the readers to understand such an allusion. Bengel, Meyer, Kling, Edwards refer the words, *what is written*, to the Old Testament in general, that supreme law of human thought, which takes all glory from man and ascribes all success to God. But a quotation so vague and general is far from probable. It seems to me, as to several modern commentators, that we must here see a proverbial maxim, in use perhaps in the Rabbinical schools: "Not beyond what is written!" The article τό, *the*, which precedes the words, seems in fact to give them this quasi-technical character; comp. the article τό, Rom. xiii. 9 and Gal. v. 14, thus used before well-known formulas. The meaning would then be: that ye may all retrace your steps in connection with what I have just told you of ourselves (Apollos and me), within the limit of a healthy appreciation: "Not beyond what Scripture says (Scripture which everywhere teaches the nothingness of man)!" This meaning thus amounts to the same as the previous explanation.

This first *that*, which is the explanation of *for your sakes*, must be a means in relation to a second more remote end. The meaning of the last proposition seems to me to come out clearly from the contrast between the two prepositions, ὑπέρ, *in favour of*, and κατά, *against*. The apostle has in view those members of the Church who were captivated by one teacher to the disparagement of another. The apostle calls this infatuation a *being puffed up*, because in exalting another man, one takes credit to himself for the admiration which he feels; one glories in being able to appreciate a superiority which others fail to know; the pride of the head of the party thus becomes the pride of the whole. The last words, *against another*, may refer either to this or that other teacher who is despised, or this or that other member of the Church who does not share the same infatuation, or who feels a quite different one. The contrast between the two adjuncts, *for the one* and *against the other*, seems to me to decide in favour of the first meaning. The pronoun εἷς, *one*, is used instead of τίς, *anyone*, with the view of isolating more completely the individual who poses as judge, and thereby breaks the unity of the body. And when this *one* is *each one*, what becomes of the Church ?—It is difficult to explain the form of the word φυσιοῦσθε. If it is the indicative, this mood does not agree with the conjunction ἵνα, *that;* and if it is the subjunctive, the regular contraction would be φυσιῶσθε. This dilemma has driven Fritzsche and Meyer to give to ἵνα the meaning of *where;* which would signify, "a state of things in which." But this meaning would be superfluous, and the word ἵνα is nowhere used in this way in the New Testament; even in classic Greek this use is found only in poetry. It must therefore be held either that in this case the apostle used an incorrect contraction, but one which might be common in later Greek or in the spoken language, or that he used the indicative mood with the conjunction ἵνα. This takes place often enough with verbs in the future, when it is wished to emphasize the reality of the action dependent on the *that*. By applying this construction here in the present, Paul would remind them forcibly that the fact, which ought not to be, is *really* passing at the time at Corinth. The same form reappears, Gal. iv. 17 (ζηλοῦτε for ζηλῶτε), and again in the case of a verb in οω; this circumstance might incline us to the first explanation.—The following verse proceeds to show all there is to be condemned in such a puffing up.

Ver. 7. "For who maketh thee to differ? And what hast thou that thou didst not receive? And if thou didst receive it, why dost thou glory as if thou hadst not received it?"—Here is the standard indicated by the *It is written*. For one of the fundamental truths of Scripture is that the creature possesses nothing which is not a gift of the Creator.—Sometimes the three questions of this verse have been applied solely to the party chiefs and not to the members of the Church. But the apostle does not distinguish so strictly between the admirers and the admired; for the line of demarcation between teachers and taught was not so exactly drawn then as it was afterwards.— The first question refers to the superiority claimed by each eminent member of a party relatively to those of the other parties. The apostle asks this man, who thinks himself superior to others, to whom he ascribes the honour of the privileged position he has gained. For this meaning of διακρίνειν, *to distinguish*, comp. xi. 29; Acts xv. 9. What is the answer expected? Some think it is: *nobody*. They rely on the fact that the answer to the second question is certainly: *nothing*. The apostle's object, on this view, is to deny even the superiority of which this individual boasts. But in this sense should not the apostle have written τί (*what is it that?*) rather than τίς (*who is he that?*)? Others think that the answer understood is *God:* "He that maketh thee differ from others by superiority of gifts, is not thyself, but God." This sense is certainly better. But thereby the question becomes almost identical with the following one. Is it not better to state the answer thus: "*not thyself.*" There is thus in the following question a gradation indicated by the δέ. Indeed, this second question bears on the qualities which are matters of pride to the individual, his gifts, lights, eloquence, and the answer is: "absolutely *nothing.*" The third question implies the conclusion to be drawn from the other two. The καί may be regarded as independent of εἰ: "If *really*" (Hofmann, Holsten). But it may also form with εἰ a single conjunction in the sense of *though:* "How, *though* having received, dost thou boast as if thou hadst not received?" This is the most natural meaning; comp. Edwards.—In this interrogative form thrice repeated, and in the individual apostrophe, *thou,* the emotion, the indignation even, which fills the apostle, shows itself strongly. He is revolted at the thought of those empty pretensions, so contrary to the humility which faith should inspire. At this point the spectacle of the sin of the Church passes before his view with such liveliness that his discourse all at once takes the form of a long sarcasm. He thinks he sees before him the old Pharisaism raised again in the forms of the Christian life. His burning irony does not take end till ver. 13, where it is extinguished in grief.

Ver. 8. "Now ye are full; now ye are rich; ye have reigned as kings without us; and I would to God[1] ye did reign, that we also might reign with you!"—The asyndeton is a new evidence of emotion. The ἤδη, *now*, placed foremost, repeated, and that in the same place in the second proposition, well expresses the movement of this whole passage: "Now already!" Paul and the other apostles are still in a world of suffering; but at Corinth the Church already lives in full triumph.—The *fulness* denotes the imperturbable self-satisfaction which characterized the Corinthians. It is all over among them with that poverty of spirit, that hungering and thirsting after righteousness, those tears of repentance, which Jesus had made the permanent condition of life in Him (Matt. v. 1–4). They are people who have nothing more to ask, all whose spiritual wants are satisfied; they have reached the perfect life!—The expression, *riches*, no doubt, alludes to the abundance of spiritual gifts which distinguished this Church above all others, and which Paul himself had recognised in the outset (i. 5, 7). The rebuke applies, not to the fact of their possession of gifts, but to the feeling of pride which accompanied it.—The aorist is substituted for the perfect, because the fulness is a state which remains, while the acquisition of riches is the initial

---

[1] D F G omit γε.

and momentary fact.—The ἐβασιλεύσατε signifies, *ye have become kings*. The advent to royalty is expressed by the aorist; for the aorist of verbs in ευω denotes, not the state, but entrance into the state. This royalty is, of course, that of the Messianic epoch, when the faithful are to reign with Christ. This condition of things glorious seems to have already begun at Corinth. No more obscurity, no more infirmity! The Church swims in full celestial state. Unspeakable delights, sublime illuminations, miraculous powers, captivating sermons : it lacks nothing.—The words χωρὶς ἡμῶν, *without us*, have been understood in the sense of "in our absence," or "without our co-operation;" as if Paul would say : " Grand things have passed at Corinth since we left you !" But in this explanation it is forgotten that the regimen *without us* takes the place, in this third proposition, of the ἤδη, *already*, which began the first two, and this leads to a meaning still more telling : " Without our having part in the elevation which is granted to you. Ye are rich, ye are kings ; we others are not so happy. . . . We still drag out the miserable existence of this nether world !" The *without us* paves the way for ver. 9.—The last words are thus easily explained : "And would to God this grand news were true, that ye were really on the throne ! For in that case, it is to be hoped that we should soon be seated with you." This σύν, *with*, corresponds precisely to the χωρίς, *without us*, in the preceding proposition.—The γε, as always, is restrictive : " If *this one* wish were realized, all the others would be satisfied." The restriction might also be understood in this sense : " If at least it were enough to desire it to secure that it should be!" This meaning seems to me less natural.—The second aorist ὄφελον (for ὤφελον), *I owed*, and hence *it would need*, is often used as a conjunction with the ellipsis of the following εἰ (*if*) to express *utinam;* the following verb is in the indicative, as dependent on the understood εἰ.

Ver. 9. "For I think that[1] God hath set forth us apostles, as the last, as appointed to death, for we are made a spectacle unto the world, both to angels and to men."—Most modern commentators make the irony stop here; they take the verb δοκῶ seriously: "*I deem that our position is full of sufferings.*" But the *for* rather leads us to suppose that the irony continues. There was in the thought of being associated *later* in the kingship, which the Corinthians already enjoyed, something very strange when it was applied to the apostles, the founders and guides of the Church; for was it not they who seemed entitled to enter on possession of kingship before all other Christians? Hence the words, *for I think*. "Ye outstrip us in the kingdom of God; for I think that God has assigned us the last place, us the apostles!" To justify this ironical supposition, the apostle in what follows draws a picture of the reproaches and sufferings of the apostolic life, contrasting them with the royal airs which certain of the Corinthians assume. Some understand the words τοὺς ἀποστόλους ἐσχάτους in the sense of "the last of the apostles," as if Paul alone were spoken of; comp. xv. 9: "I am the least of the apostles," and Eph. iii. 8: "To me who am the least of all saints." Paul thus designates himself, it is said, either as the last called to the apostle-

---

[1] T. R. with E L P reads ὅτι after γαρ.

ship, or as formerly a persecutor. But why should Paul put the plural here if he was speaking of himself personally? comp. vers. 3 and 4. Besides, to express this idea he must have used one or other of these forms: τοὺς ἐσχάτους ἀποστόλους, or τοὺς ἀποστόλους τοὺς ἐσχάτους, or τοὺς ἐσχάτους τῶν ἀποστόλων. Finally, the idea thus expressed would be opposed to the spirit of the context; for the peculiarity of being last of the apostles would be the very thing to justify God's supposed way of acting towards him, whereas Paul wishes to bring out the absurd character of such a supposition. We must therefore take τοὺς ἀποστόλους, *the apostles*, as in apposition to ἡμᾶς, *us*, and ἐσχάτους, *the last*, as the attribute of ἀπέδειξεν, *He hath set forth*: " He hath set us forth, us the apostles, as the last." By the words *us the apostles*, Paul understands, not only himself, or himself and his fellow-labourers, but himself and the Twelve who still share with him both the labours and the reproaches of the testimony borne to Christ. May there not be in this extension of the thought to the Twelve (as in the analogous passage, xv. 11), an evidence of the contempt with which *those of Christ* treated the Twelve no less than Paul? (See pp. 71, 79.)—The word ἀπέδειξεν (Beza: *spectandos proposuit*) indicates public exposure either to honour or reproach. The following words, *as condemned to death*, are explanatory of the attribute, *the last*. Down to the end of the verse the apostle is alluding to the gladiators who were presented as a spectacle in the games of the amphitheatre, and whose blood and last agonies formed the joy of a whole population of spectators. The passage xv. 32 seems to prove that the figure was once at least a reality in apostolic life.—The term θέατρον, *spectacle*, is in keeping with this public exhibition. The κόσμος, *world*, here denotes the whole intelligent universe which plays the part of spectator. It is subdivided (comp. the two καί, *both* . . . *and* . . .) into *men* and *angels*. By the former we need not understand merely unbelievers, persecutors, but all mankind, hostile or in sympathy. And by angels should not be understood, with some, only bad angels, with others, only the good. The bad are not excluded, that of course; the good are naturally embraced in the term, as appears to follow from Eph. iii. 10.—Instead of the past ἐγενήθημεν, *we were*, or *we became*, it seems as if the present ἔσμεν, *we are*, were required. But the aorist serves to designate this mode of existence as the lot which *was assigned* them once for all. "It seems truly that it was *God* who arranged things thus: the Church on the throne, and the apostles under the sword!"

Ver. 10. "We are fools for Christ's sake, ye are wise in Christ; we weak, ye strong; ye honourable, we despised." —The contrast between the two situations enunciated in vers. 8 and 9 is expressed in ver. 10 in three antitheses, which are, as it were, so many blows for the proud Corinthians. These words are addressed especially to the principal men of the Church, but at the same time to all its members who share in the pretensions of these proud party leaders. And, first, as to *teaching*, the apostles had to face the reputation of foolishness which the gospel brings on them, while at Corinth there is found a way of preaching Christ so as to procure a name for wisdom, the reputation of pro-

P

found philosophers and of men of most reliable judgment ($\phi\rho\acute{o}\nu\iota\mu\sigma$).—$\varDelta\iota\acute{a}$, *on account of* (for Christ's sake). As a Rabbin he might have become as eminent a savant as Hillel, as celebrated as Gamaliel; for Christ he has consented to pass as a fool. The Corinthians know better how to manage; they make the teaching even of the gospel ($\dot{\epsilon}\nu$ $X\rho\iota\sigma\tau\hat{\omega}$, *in Christ*) a means of gaining celebrity for their lofty wisdom.

The second contrast relates to *conduct* in general. They come before their public with the feeling of their strength; there is in them neither hesitation nor timidity. The apostles do not know these grand lordly airs. Witness the picture, chap. ii. 1–5, where Paul describes his state of trembling at Corinth. Finally, the third antithesis relates to the *welcome received* from the world by the one and the other. The Corinthians are honoured, fêted, regarded as the ornament of cultivated circles; there is a rivalry to do them honour. The apostles are scarcely judged worthy of attention; nay, rather reviled and calumniated. In this last contrast the apostle reverses the order of the two terms, and puts the apostles in the second place. This is by way of transition to one or two traits of detail in the apostolic life which he is about to draw. Indeed the word ἄτιμοι, *despised*, is the theme of the following verses.

Vers. 11–13. " Even unto this present **hour** we both hunger and thirst, are naked,[1] buffeted, without certain dwelling-place; 12. labour, working with our own hands. Being reviled, we bless; being persecuted, we

---

[1] א B C D E F G P read γυμνιτευομεν, instead of γυμνητευομεν which T. R. reads with L.

suffer it; 13. being defamed,[1] we intreat; we are made as the filth of the world, the offscouring of all, even until now."—The first words, *even to this present hour*, reproduce the thought of the whole passage: "As for us, up to this hour, we are little aware that the dispensation of triumph has already begun." The following enumeration bears, in the first place, on the privations and sufferings of all kinds endured by the apostles (vers. 11, 12ᵃ). To the want of suitable food and clothing there is sometimes added bad treatment; the word κολαφίζεσθαι may denote either blows with the fist or with the palm of the hand. Besides, as the rule, want of a fixed dwelling-place, of a home. Finally (ver. 12ᵃ), the manual labour imposed on Paul, especially the voluntary obligation to gain his livelihood by his own work (ix. 6).

The enumeration goes on by indicating the humble and patient conduct of the apostles in the midst of these sufferings (vers. 12ᵇ–13ᵃ). Three particulars form a double gradation: insults with sneering (λοιδορεῖσθαι), persecutions in a judicial form (διώκεσθαι), calumnies which assail honour (δυσφημεῖσθαι). The T. R. reads βλασφημούμενοι; but as the verb δυσφημεῖσθαι is much more rarely used in the New Testament, and as it is found in almost all the Mjj., it deserves the preference. —To sneering the apostles reply with *blessing*. The word εὐλογεῖν in the New Testament signifies *to wish well*, and that in the form which alone can render the wish efficacious, that of prayer.—To ill-treatment they reply by *suffering* (ἀνέχεσθαι, *to exercise self-control*);

---

[1] א A C G read δυσφημούμενοι instead of βλασφημούμενοι, which T. R. reads with all the rest.

they do not even complain. Finally, they oppose to calumnies kindly *intreating*; they beseech men not to be so wicked, to return to better feelings, to be converted to Christ.

But with this way of acting what do they get from the world? They become the object of its more complete disdain. This is what is expressed by ver. 13^b. The term περικάθαρμα, *filth*, denotes literally what is collected by sweeping all round the chamber (περί); and περίψημα the dirt which is detached from an object by sweeping or scraping it all round. These two figures therefore represent what is most abject. It has been sought to give to these two terms a tragical meaning, that of an *expiatory victim*, a sense in which they were sometimes taken among the Greeks. At times of public calamity, a criminal was chosen who was devoted to the angry gods to appease their wrath. This man, who was, as it were, the defilement of the people incarnate, bore the curse of all and perished for all. He was designated by the terms κάθαρμα or περίψημα. The formula with which the priest hurled him into the sea was this (according to Suidas): περίψημα ἡμῶν γενοῦ, ἤτοι σωτηρία καὶ ἀπολύτρωσις ("be our expiatory victim, and so our salvation and deliverance"). Did Paul mean to allude to the religious sense of the two terms which he uses? I do not think so; the saying thus understood would take an emphasis which hardly suits the sorrowful humility of the whole passage.—The plural of the first substantive relates to the different apostles, while the second substantive in the singular makes them one mass, an object of contempt, which is still more forcible. The adjuncts *of the world* and *of all* both indicate the totality to which the apostles naturally belong, but from which they are distinguished as being the most contemptible it contains. To the plural, *sweepings* (filth), there corresponds the singular, *of the world;* and to the singular, *the offscouring*, the plural, *of all:* They are what Paul says: each for all, and all for each. — The last words, *even until now*, betray yet once more before closing the feeling of sorrowful irony which inspired the whole passage. They are the counterpart of the ἤδη, *now*, with which he had begun, and they sum it up likewise as a whole. Rückert cannot approve of the sarcastic tone of this passage. He says, frankly (pp. 124, 125): "This passage of Paul's has always produced on me a repulsive impression. . . . There are found in it undeniable traces of wounded personal feeling, of irritation caused him by the loss of the consideration which he enjoyed at Corinth . . . everywhere there reigns concern about his own personality. I am pained to have to pass such a judgment on this great man; but he too was human . . ." This eminent commentator has not considered, — 1. that as against proud infatuation, the weapon of ridicule is often the only efficacious one; 2. that the indignation which inspired this passage bore on a state of things which was not only an attack on the apostle's person, but a mortal danger to the spiritual life and the whole future of the Church; 3. that the following words, expressive of incomparable fatherly tenderness and solicitude, do not well agree with those wholly personal feelings, which he ascribes so daringly to the apostle.

Vers. 14-21 are the conclusion of all the apostle has written from i. 12. He first makes an explanation about the severe manner in which he has just spoken to them. It is not resentment or enmity which has inspired his words, it is the painful solicitude he feels for them (vers. 14-16).

Ver. 14. "I write not these things to shame you, but as my beloved sons I admonish [1] you."—Ἐντρέπειν, *to turn one back upon himself*, and hence: to cause shame. The apostle no doubt spoke to them in a humiliating way; but his object was quite different from that of causing them shame; he wished to lead them with a firm hand into another way. It is somewhat different in vi. 5 and xv. 34; here he has positively the intention of making them ashamed.— We need not read with some Mjj., νουθετῶν, *admonishing you*. This form is imitated from the preceding participle. It is a new proposition: "This is what I really do when speaking to you thus." Νουθετεῖν, in a manner: to bring back the mind to its place; to lead one back to a calm and settled frame.—Paul has the right and it is his duty to act thus, for he is their spiritual father. He is himself the only one of their preachers who merits the name; this is what is brought out by the pronoun μου: "*my children.*" The following verse justifies the pronoun with its exclusive bearing.

Vers. 15, 16. "For though ye should have ten thousand tutors in Christ, yet have ye not many fathers; for in Christ Jesus I have begotten you through the gospel. 16. I beseech you therefore:

[1] ℵ A D P read νουθετων (*admonishing*), instead of νουθετω (*I admonish*).

be ye imitators of me."—In ver. 15, Paul presents the almost ridiculous figure of a flock of pupils placed under the rod of several thousands of tutors. There is an allusion to that host of teachers who had risen up at Corinth after the departure of Paul and Apollos, and to whom was addressed the warning in iii. 12-15, regarding those who continued a building once founded. The pedagogue (tutor) among the Greeks was the slave to whom a child's education was committed till he reached his majority; literally: he who guides the child to school.—'Ἀλλά: here, like the *at* of the Latins. It was Paul to whom God had given to *beget* the Corinthians to that new life which the others only promoted; comp. a similar figure, Gal. iv. 19. This term γεννᾶν, *to beget*, applies not only to the ministry of preaching, but to the intense labour of the whole man which is carried out in his personal relations and in the act of prayer. — It should be remarked that Paul prefixes to the idea of his labour the two qualifications: *in Christ Jesus* and *by the gospel*. It was in virtue of the communion and power of Christ, and by means of the gospel which he received from Him, that he was able to produce this spiritual creation. He thus excludes beforehand every appearance of boasting in what he says of himself in the last words: ἐγὼ ἐγέννησα.—But if it was Christ who acted with His power and word, it was nevertheless through him, Paul (ἐγώ, *I*), that He produced this creation. Hence Paul's right and duty to exhort them, and even to admonish them as he does.

Ver. 16. A father has a right to expect that well-born children follow his steps; hence the *therefore*.

The apostle is thinking particularly of the absence of all self-seeking and self-satisfaction, of the abnegation and humility of which they had an example in him. The νουθετεῖν (ver. 14) referred especially to their past, and to all that was blameworthy in it; the παρακαλεῖν applies to the future, and to the good which ought to appear among them. The word γίνεσθε, *become* (be), reminds them how far they have gone astray. — To help them on the way of return to a new course, Paul sends them one of his most faithful fellow-labourers, whom he hopes soon to follow himself (vers. 17-21).

Ver. 17. "For this[1] cause have I sent unto you Timothy, who is my beloved son and faithful in the Lord; he shall bring you into remembrance of my ways which be in Christ,[2] even as I teach everywhere in every Church."—We need not take the aorist ἔπεμψα in the sense of the Greek epistolary past, when the author, transporting himself to the time when his letter shall be read, speaks in the past of a present fact. The passage xvi. 10, 11, proves that the apostle means, *I have sent*, for Timothy had really started when Paul was writing, though he was not to arrive till after the letter; comp. Acts xix. 21, 22. How do such coincidences prove the accuracy of the narrative of the Acts!—In calling Timothy *his son*, he alludes to his conversion of which he had been the instrument, no doubt during his first visit to Lystra; comp. 2 Tim. i. 2. By this title he gives him, as it were, the position of an elder son relatively to the Corinthians, who, as younger children, should take rule from him.

---

[1] ℵ A P add to τουτο (*this*) αυτο (*this very*).
[2] ℵ C Mnn.: εν Χριστω Ιησου.

He characterizes him as *beloved*, which recommends him to their affection, and as *faithful in the Lord*, which is his title to their confidence. The term πιστός is used, like our word *faithful*, in the active sense: one who believes, or in the passive sense: one who may be believed, who should be trusted. It is the second sense which at least prevails here; he will be to them a sure counsellor in the things of the Lord. —His mission is *to bring them into remembrance*. This phrase, designedly chosen, distinguishes the part of Timothy from that of the apostle, and insinuates at the same time that the Corinthians are not ignorant, but that they have only forgotten.—What does the apostle understand by *his ways which be in Christ?* Is it the way in which he regulates his own conduct? But the words, "As *I teach* everywhere," do not suit this meaning. Meyer thinks that the words, *as I teach*, may be applied to the way in which he acted when carrying out his office as a preacher. This is an inadmissible makeshift. Or should we, on the contrary, apply the phrase, *my ways in Christ*, to the contents of the apostolic preaching? This meaning is no less forced. It only remains, as it seems to me, to apply the καθὼς διδάσκω, *as I teach*, to the apostle's practical teaching (as it is summed up Rom. xii.–xiv.), to the true method of Christian life: the humility, abnegation, self-forgetfulness, consecration to the Lord, which ought to characterize a true believer. This is the course which Paul himself has followed since he was in Christ (my ways in Christ); and it was this mode of acting pursued by the apostle which he inculcated in all the Churches. The word καθώς, *even as*, brings out the harmony between his life and this teaching.—The words *everywhere* and *in every Church* seem to be tautological. But the first signifies: *in* every sort of country, in Asia as in Greece. Timothy, who had followed him in all his journeys, could bear witness to this. *In every Church* signifies: *in each Church* which I found. He seeks to impress the same direction on these new communities; there is always the call to come down by humility, not to be exalted by boasting. No doubt there was the disposition to believe that Paul was imposing exceptional demands on the Corinthians. But no; they are the same as are accepted and practised by each of his Churches; comp. i. 2, xiv. 33, 35, 36. Timothy, who has himself witnessed all these foundations, will be able to certify them of the fact.—But this sending of Timothy might lead them to suppose that the disciple was a substitute for the apostle, and that after this visit the latter would not think of coming himself. This conclusion had already been expressly drawn, some had even made a triumph of it at the expense of the apostle. He had doubtless been informed of this by the three deputies, and it is to this insulting supposition that the final passage refers, vers. 18–21.

Ver. 18. "But some are puffed up, as though I would not come to you."—The δέ is adversative: "*But* do not proceed to conclude therefrom that . . ." The present participle ὡς μὴ ἐρχομένου, "as if I were not *coming*," has been explained by supposing that Paul here is quoting verbally the saying of his adversaries: "He is not *coming!*" This is far-fetched; the present is simply that of the idea; comp. xvi. 5.—Who are those *some*, so ready to interpret the steps taken by the apostle in a sense unfavourable to his character? The partisans of Apollo, answer many. There is nothing to lead us to this idea. On the contrary, we find, 2 Cor. x. 9, 10, a statement which is manifestly related to this: Paul's adversaries charged him with seeking to terrify the Church by threatening letters of excessive severity, but not daring to appear himself to bear out the energy of his language by his presence, because he was well aware of his personal weakness and insufficiency. It cannot be doubted that the people of this stamp were already at Corinth at the date of the First Epistle to the Corinthians and were passing such judgments. Now these people, as we know from Second Corinthians, were *those of Christ* (x. 7 and xi. 23). Such then were the men who, even at the date of the first letter, were allowing themselves to accuse the apostle so gravely. Perhaps, however, by the word *some* should rather be understood those of the Corinthians who had been led away, than those strangers themselves; in his First Epistle, Paul seems not yet inclined to come to close quarters with the latter.—The word *are puffed up* refers to the air of triumph with which this party hasted to proclaim the grand news in the Church : "Timothy is coming instead of Paul ; Paul is not coming."

Vers. 19, 20. "But I will come to you shortly, if the Lord will ; and will know, not the speech of them which are puffed up, but the power. 20. For the kingdom of God is not in word, but in power."—The δέ is again adversative : "But this malicious forecast will be falsified." The γνώσομαι, *I will know*, is the language of a judge proceeding to make an examination. This term has already a threatening solemnity; it gives a forewarning of the judgment about to follow (ver. 21). —Paul contrasts *the word*, here the fine discourses, the eloquent tirades, the profound deductions, which called forth the plaudits of the hearers, with *the power;* by which he designates the effectual virtue of the Divine Spirit which brings back souls to themselves, makes them contrite, leads them to Christ, and begets them to a new life. Paul will find out whether, with this abundance of talk which makes itself heard in the assemblies (chap. xiv.), there is found or there is lacking the creative breath of the Spirit. He is at home in this field; he will not be deceived like those poor dupes who have been misled at Corinth.—*Them that are puffed up:* all those self-inflated creatures, under whose eyes scandals are passing which they cannot or will not repress, who have only an insipid Christianity, and to whom applies the figure of salt without savour. Chap. v., ver. 2 in particular will show clearly what was already in the apostle's mind.

Ver. 20. The maximum of ver. 20 explains the necessity of such a judgment. It is impossible to refer the notion of the *kingdom of God*, as Meyer would have us, to the Messianic future. Paul is certainly speaking of the kingdom of God in the spiritual sense in which it already exists in the souls of believers. There, where the will of God has become the ruling principle, and where man's will is only the organ of the former, God reigns from the present onwards; comp. Rom. xiv. 17. This spiritual presence of the kingdom of God in the

heart is what paves the way for its future appearing.—
The most eloquent words do not guarantee the possession of this spiritual state, and cannot produce or advance it in others. What manifests its existence, is power to make hearts fertile in fruits of submission to the will of God.—Paul's work at Corinth will not be confined to taking knowledge of the evil; acts will follow as may be needed.

Ver. 21. " What will ye ? That I come unto you with a rod, or in love, and with a spirit of meekness ? "[1] —It is as if Paul said to them : " Peace or war : choose!" The emotion caused by this challenge, so boldly thrown out, explains the asyndeton. The preposition ἐν, *in*, is applied in classic Greek, as here, to denote the use of a weapon.—The figure ῥάβδος, *rod*, is connected with that of father, used above. It is the emblem of the disciplinary power with which the apostle feels himself armed.—There is something startling in the antithesis : *or with love*. Supposing he required to use the rod, would he not do so in love ? Certainly ; but if there is love in the act of striking, there is also something else : hatred of evil. And this will have no occasion to show itself, except in so far as there shall be something to correct. Let us add that the Greek term ἀγάπη denotes the love of complacency which is expressed by approving manifestations. — Some have understood the phrase, *spirit of meekness*, as if it were, with a *disposition* of meekness. But it is impossible wholly to make abstraction of the Divine breath in the use of the word πνεῦμα, *spirit*. Paul knows well that the meekness he will use, if it is in

---

[1] The MSS. write πραυτης or πραοτης.

his power, will not be natural good-naturedness, but the fruit of the Spirit, of which he himself speaks Gal. v. 23.

Already in these last verses we can discern the idea of *discipline* rising, which will be ·the subject of the following chapter. One is struck also at the degree of audacious hostility to which his adversaries in the Church had gone, in daring to express themselves in regard to him as they were doing (ver. 18), and in giving occasion to the use of so menacing a tone. But, as has been well observed by Weizsäcker, Paul does not wish for the present to open hostilities. He throws out a word in passing, then he resumes the course of his letter.

The first part of the Epistle is closed. The divisions which had arisen revealed to Paul the deep corruption which the gospel had undergone in this Church. He understood it : teachers are not changed into heads of schools, except because the gospel has been changed into a system. To ascend then to the true notion of Christianity, in order to deduce from it that of the Christian ministry, and to restore the normal relation between this office and the whole Church, such was his first task. The flock once gathered under the shepherd's crook, he may with hope of success attack the particular vices which had crept into it. These first four chapters are thus the foundation of the whole Epistle.

II.
DISCIPLINE (CHAP. V.).

A large number of commentators think that Paul here passes to the vice of impurity. But it is not till vi. 12 that he really attacks this vice. As to chap. v., they confound the occasion with the subject. The occasion is an act of impurity; but the subject treated, and that in consequence of the laxity which the Church had shown in regard to this scandal, is the duty of every living Church to take action against sin when it manifests itself openly within its pale.

It is impossible with the large number of the unconverted who become members of the Church, and with the sin which the converted themselves still bear in them, that evil should not sometimes break out in the Christian community. But the difference which should ever remain between the Church and the world is, that in the former sin should not manifest itself without falling under the stroke of rebuke and judgment. "There is a Holy One in the midst of thee," said the prophet Hosea to Israel. A Holy One lives also in the Church, and from Him there go forth, in every true Church which has life and not merely the name to live, a protest and reaction against all notorious wickedness. This reaction, the work of the Holy Spirit who proceeds from Christ, is discipline. Where it is weakened, the Church is in the same measure confounded with the world.

The chapter which we proceed to study is the classical passage of the New Testament on the subject; if the apostle has put it here, it is because the subject belongs, on the one side, to the ecclesiastical questions treated in chaps. i.–iv., and on the other to the moral questions which will be treated, chaps. vi.–x. It is therefore the natural transition between the two domains of ecclesiastical or collective life and the moral life of each member.—In vers. 1–5, Paul speaks of discipline in special connection with the particular case which obliges him to treat the subject, to pass thereafter to the condition of discipline in general (vers. 6–8); the passage, vers. 9–13, is an appendix.

Chap. V. 1–5.

Ver. 1. "In general, it is reported that there is fornication among you, and such fornication as is not found even among the Gentiles,[1] that one hath his father's wife."—The first word, ὅλως, has been variously explained. It signifies *totally*, and hence *in general* or *summarily*, but never *certainly*, as some have sought to understand it here. If this adverb qualifies ἀκούεται, *it is reported*, we may explain, "it is reported *everywhere*." But Paul would have found a clearer term to express this idea. Or we might understand it, "People talk generally of fornication among you;" but the sequel, καὶ τοιαύτη, *and such fornication*, . . . does not at all suit this meaning. The adjunct ἐν ὑμῖν, *among you*, cannot, of course, depend on ἀκούεται, *it is reported*; it must necessarily be referred to an οὖσα, *being*, understood: "It is reported *that there is* fornication among you." If it is so, the meaning of ὅλως is determined by the gradation following: καὶ τοιαύτη, *and even such*: "The vice of fornication exists *in general* among you,

[1] T. R. with L P Syr. reads ὀνομάζεται (*is named*) after ἔθνεσιν.

and it is even such a case as would scandalize the Gentiles themselves." The word ὅλως is used, vi. 7, exactly in the same way.—The verb ὀνομάζεται, *is named*, in T. R., is a gloss taken from Eph. v. 3. The word is wanting in most of the Mjj. We have simply to understand ἐστί.—Instead of saying, *his father's wife*, Paul might have used the word μητρυιά, *step-mother;* but the former expression brought out more strongly the enormity of the act. This is also expressed forcibly by the position of the pronoun τινά between the two terms *wife* and *father*. Was the father still living? We can hardly think so; the act would be too odious.[1] The marriage of a son with his step-mother was forbidden among the Jews under pain of death (Lev. xviii. 8). The Roman law equally forbade it. It is therefore probable that this union had not been legally sanctioned. Of the impression produced by such acts, even among the heathen, when they did exceptionally take place, we may judge from the words of Cicero in his defence of Cluentius: " O incredible crime for a woman, and such as has never been heard of in this world in any other than her solitary case!"—It appears from the whole chapter that the man only was a Christian; for if the woman had not been still a heathen, would not Paul have judged her as severely as the man? And what has been the conduct of the Corinthians in view of such a scandal?

Ver. 2. "And ye are puffed up, and have not rather mourned, that he that hath done[2] this deed might be

---

[1] The passage 2 Cor. vii. 12 ought not to be quoted in proof, as is often done. The term ἀδικηθείς can only refer to Paul himself.

[2] ℵ A C read πραξας, instead of ποιησας, which all the rest read.

taken away¹ from among you."— Even this fact has not sufficed to disturb the proud self-satisfaction which he has already rebuked in the Corinthians in the previous chapter, or to make them come down from the celestial heights on which they are now walking to the real state of things.—The word πεφυσιωμένοι, *puffed up*, goes back on the words, iv. 6 (φυσιοῦσθε), and especially ver. 19 (τῶν πεφυσιωμένων). What have they done, those grand talkers, in view of this monstrous scandal? This is what the apostle called " having speech but not power." Should not this moral catastrophe have opened their eyes to the fallen state in which their Church lay? Calvin admirably says: " *Ubi luctus est, ibi cessat gloriatio.*"— A living Church, which had in it the δύναμις of its Head, would have risen as one man, and gone into a common act of humiliation and mourning, like a family for the death of one of its members. This is what is expressed by the verb πενθεῖν, *to conduct a mourning.*—The aorist ἐπενθήσατε cannot merely designate a feeling of inward grief. It shows that Paul is thinking of a positive, solemn deed, of something like a day of repentance and fasting, on which the whole Church before the Lord deplored the scandal committed, and cried to Him to bring it to an end.

The words, *that might be taken away*, are referred by most commentators to the excommunication which the Church would not have failed to pronounce upon the guilty one as the result of such an act of humiliation. Calvin says without hesitation, " The power of excommunication is established by this passage." But

¹ T. R. with L reads ἐξαρθῇ, instead of αρθῇ.

it seems to me that neither the conjunction *that* nor the passive *might be taken away* is suitable to an act which the Corinthians should have done themselves. The *that* rather indicates a result which would be produced, independently of them, in consequence of the mourning called for by the apostle. It is the same with the passive form *might be taken away*. If Paul had thought of an exclusion pronounced by the Church itself, he would have said: "That ye might take away;" or, better still, "Ye have not mourned, and then taken away the offender." At the most he would have said, "Ye have not mourned, *so that* (ὥστε) he might be taken away." Whether we refer the ἵνα to the intention which would have dictated the mourning (Meyer, Edwards), or to that of the apostle who calls for it (de Wette), we do not sufficiently account for it, any more than for the passive form *might be taken away*. It must be confessed, it seems to me, that in Paul's view he who does the act of taking away is different from him who mourns, though the mourning is the condition of his intervening to strike. This is what the Corinthians should have known well, and this is precisely the reason why they should have mourned that he whose part it was to take away might act. The mysterious arm, which, if the Church had felt its shame, would have removed it by striking the guilty one, can only be the arm of God Himself. To the grief and prayer of the Church He would have responded in a way similar to that in which He had acted, on the words of Peter, toward Ananias and Sapphira, or as He was acting at that very time at Corinth, by visiting with sickness, and even with death, the profaners of the Supper (xi. 30-32).—Hofmann sees that in the ordinary construction these expressions cannot apply to an act done by the Church. And, as he does not suppose that the term can designate anything else than excommunication, he begins a new sentence with ἵνα, regarding this conjunction, with Pott, as the periphrasis of an imperative: "Let such a man be taken away from among you (by a sentence of excommunication)!" No doubt the ἵνα, *that*, is sometimes used thus. But it is hard to see how such an order would harmonize with what follows, where Paul relates what he has done to make up for what the Corinthians had not done. Besides, this construction would here be entirely unexpected and far from natural. The ἐξαρθῇ of the T. R. is taken from ver. 13. The reading should be ἀρθῇ, with most of the Mjj.—The verb αἴρειν, or ἐξαίρειν, is ordinarily used in Leviticus and Deuteronomy to denote the capital punishment inflicted on malefactors in Israel; comp. also the ἀπαρθῇ, Matt. ix. 15, and parallel, applied to the Messiah's violent death.—In saying *from among you*, Paul is certainly thinking of the way in which he had characterized his readers at the beginning of his letter: "Sanctified in Christ Jesus, saints by call." How could one guilty of adultery and incest have a place in such an assembly!—The term τὸ ἔργον τοῦτο has a certain emphasis: "An act such as this." The reading πράξας, in three Alex., might be preferred, because the verb πράσσειν is pretty often used in an unfavourable sense, in opposition to ποιεῖν (see John iii. 20, 21; v. 29, etc.). But ποιεῖν better expresses than πράσσειν the accomplishment of the deed.—After characterizing both the guilty pride and softness of the

Church, the apostle contrasts with them his own mode of acting.

Ver. 3. " For I verily, as¹ absent in body, but present in spirit, have decided already, as though I were present, [to deliver over] him that hath so done this deed..."—The *for* is thus explained: " Such is what you ought to have done; *for*, as for me, this is what I have done. The μέν, to which there is no corresponding δέ, serves to isolate Paul, putting him in contrast to the Church, and so strengthens the force of the ἐγώ, *I:* " I, for my part, while you . . . ! "—The first ὡς, *as*, is rejected by the majority of the Mjj., perhaps wrongly; it has been thought incompatible with the following ὡς before the second παρών. But these two ὡς may have their distinct value. The first bears strictly on the second participle : *present in spirit.* It signifies : " So far as absent in body, no doubt, but really present spiritually." It is the *as* which serves to express the *real* character in which the person acts; the second signifies, on the contrary, *as if.* Paul would bring out this contrast: " As for you who were present, you did nothing; and as for me, distant from you though I am, yet living spiritually among you, this is how I acted ! " The word *already* has great force here, whether it signifies, " while you remained inactive, you wise and eloquent preachers ; " or whether Paul rather means, " before even arriving among you."—The verb κέκρικα may be rendered by *I have judged*, or *I have decided.* Not being able to say [in French] *judged to deliver*, we have used the second term ; but in a passage of a judicial character like this the verb ought to express

¹ א A B C D P omit the ὡς (*as*), read by T. R. with E F G L It.

rather the idea of a sentence pronounced than of a simple resolution taken. This is undoubtedly what has led Hofmann and Edwards to give this verb for its direct object the following accusative: τὸν κατεργασάμενον, *him who has thus acted.* Now, as the verb παραδοῦναι (ver. 5) can be nothing else than the object of κέκρικα, we must hold in this case a mixture of two constructions, "I have judged this man," and "I have judged to deliver him over to Satan." This rather forced interpretation seems to me unnecessary. It is simpler to make τὸν κατεργασάμενον the object of παραδοῦναι, and τὸν τοιοῦτον (ver. 5) the grammatical repetition of the object, a repetition occasioned by the interposition of ver. 4. — But the important question is, whether the παραδοῦναι, *the act of delivering over*, the object of *I have judged*, or *decided*, should be regarded as the result of a future decision which Paul proposes to be taken by the Corinthians themselves, or whether he thinks of it as a decision already taken and decreed between God and him. Commentators agree in holding the first sense. Paul waits, they say, till, in consequence of the decision which he has taken by himself, the Church of Corinth shall assemble and pronounce a sentence in keeping, if one may so speak, with his premonition. This meaning is open to certain doubts. Would not Paul say in that case: "I have decided that the man *should be delivered over*," and not: "I have judged *to deliver him over*"? It might therefore be supposed that the judicial assembly of which the apostle speaks has already taken place at the time of his writing, and that the three deputies represented the Church in his presence. Thus the three acts would be naturally explained: κέκρικα, συναχθέντων, παραδοῦναι. But the participle συναχθέντων would in this sense require rather to be placed before κέκρικα, and the idea of a purely *spiritual* presence would rather apply to the Church than to Paul. We must therefore return to the ordinary explanation. Only there is not the faintest hint of making the pronouncing of the sentence dependent on the vote of the assembly which is to be held at Corinth, as if the apostle's decision could be annulled by the contrary opinion of a majority. For his part (μέν), everything is decided, and with his apostolical competency he has judged to deliver over [the offender]; there will be joined to him, in the assembly which he convokes to take part in this terrible act, whoever wishes and dares.—The apparent pleonasm, οὕτω τοῦτο, "who has *so* done *this*," has been variously explained. The word *so* is said to signify, "as a Christian," or "with the aggravating circumstances which you know," etc. It seems to me that we have here one of those circumlocutions in which judicial sentences delight. The protocol of a tribunal would be precisely expressed in this way. The object is to exactly define the deed, with all the circumstances known or unknown which make it what it is: its publicity, the shamelessness of its author, etc. In fact, these last words of ver. 3 contain, as it were, the *preamble* to the sentence delivered; and, in what immediately follows, everything bears a very pronounced judicial character.—But the essential thing with the apostle is not that the sentence be delivered, it is that it be so with the assent of the Church. For his aim, besides the saving of the guilty one, is to awaken the conscience of the whole community, its energetic protest against the scandal which it has witnessed till now in silence. And such is the intent of ver. 4, which indicates three things: 1. the assembly which is to take place; 2. its competency; 3. its power of execution. We are thus reminded of a tribunal prepared for the sentences delivered by it.

Vers. 4, 5. "Ye and my spirit being gathered together in the name of the[1] Lord Jesus Christ,[2] 5. to deliver with the power of our[3] Lord Jesus[4] such an one unto Satan for the destruction of the flesh, that the spirit may be saved in the day of the Lord Jesus."[5] —The tribunal is formed of the Christians of Corinth assembled in Paul's spiritual presence; his competency is the *name* of Jesus Christ, under whose authority the sentence is given; his ability to execute is the *power* of Jesus Christ.—There are four ways of connecting the two subordinate clauses, *in the name of* . . . and *with the power of*, with the two verbs, *being gathered together* and *delivering*. The first two make the two clauses bear on the same verb, either on *being gathered together* (Chrysostom, Theodoret, Calvin, Rückert, Holsten), or on *delivering* (Mosheim, etc.). According to the last two, they are distributed between the two verbs; some ascribing the first clause, *in the name of*, to the last verb *deliver*, and the second clause, *with*

---

[1] ℵ A here omit ημων (*our*), which is read by T. R. with all the rest, It. Syr.
[2] A B D reject the word Χριστου (*Christ*).
[3] All the Mjj., except P, here read ημων (*our*).
[4] ℵ A B D P omit Χριστου (*Christ*), which is read by T. R. with E F G L.
[5] So T. R. with ℵ L; B omits Ιησου (*Jesus*); P Or. read ημων after κυριου (*our Lord*).

the power of, to the first verb, *being gathered together* (Luther, Bengel, de Wette, Meyer, Kling, Edwards); the others making each clause bear on the verb which immediately follows it: *in the name of* on *being gathered together*, and *with the power of* on *delivering* (Beza, Olshausen, Ewald, Hofmann, Heinrici). I have no hesitation in preferring this last construction. Independently of the position of the words, which suits this meaning better than it does any of the others, the decisive reason seems to me to be the conformity of the notion of each clause with that of the verb it qualifies. Is it a judicial assembly which is in question, the important thing is its competency; and this is what is indicated by the ἐν ὀνόματι . . ., *in the name of* . . ., as qualifying *being gathered together*. Is it, on the contrary, the execution of the sentence which is in question, what is important is force, power *de facto;* and this is exactly what is expressed by the ἐν δυνάμει, *with the power of* . . ., as qualifying *to deliver.* This construction seems to me also to be confirmed by the striking parallel Matt. xviii. 18-20, a saying which must have been present to Paul's mind in this case: "Verily I say unto you, whatsoever ye shall bind on earth shall be bound in heaven. . . . Again I say unto you, that whatever two or three of you shall agree to ask on the earth, it shall be done for them of My Father. For where two or three *are gathered together in My name* (συνηγμένοι εἰς τὸ ἐμὸν ὄνομα), there am I in the midst of them." This promise certainly served as a ground for the actual conduct of the apostle. The moment has come for the Church to do what Jesus called *binding;* it has to judge. This judgment is to be pronounced by the faithful *gathered together in His name*, as many of them as will be found *to agree* in view of an interest of this kind, should there be only *two or three*.—The *name* denotes the person of the Lord in so far as it is revealed to the hearts of believers, recognised and adored by them.—Perhaps we should, with the documents, reject the word *Christ*, and preserve only the name *Jesus*, which calls up the historical personality of Him who has promised to be invisibly present at such an act. It is on this promised presence that the authority of the assembly which does it rests. The pronoun *ye* does not necessarily embrace the whole of the Church, for the matter in question here is not a vote by a majority of voices; it is a spiritual act in which, from the very nature of things, only the man takes part who feels impelled to it, and each in the measure in which he is capable of it. Two or three suffice for this, in case of need, Jesus Himself says; for the means of action in such discipline is agreement in prayer. How could all this apply to a decree of excommunication, pronounced after contradictory debating, and by a majority of voices, perhaps a majority of one? The things of God do not admit of being thus treated.

The most mysterious expression in this so mysterious passage is the following: καὶ τοῦ ἐμοῦ πνεύματος, *and my spirit*. At this assembly, which is to take place at Corinth, Paul will be present by his spirit (ver. 3). It would seem that what Paul here affirms of himself ought to be applied to Jesus. But it must not be forgotten that if Jesus is the Head of the Church in general, Paul is the founder and father of the Church of Corinth, and that in virtue of his personal union to Jesus, the spiritual presence of the Lord (Matt. xviii. 20) may become also that of His servant. In chapter xii. of the Second Epistle to the Corinthians, Paul does not himself know whether it was with or without his body that he was present at a scene in paradise.

The words σὺν τῇ δυνάμει, *with power*, cannot be connected with the participle συναχθέντων, *being gathered together*, whether we make Christ's power a sort of third member of the assembly, or whether we regard this power of Christ as sharing in the judgment in so far as it must carry it into execution. The first meaning needs no refutation; the second is an over-refinement. This regimen, on the contrary, is quite naturally connected with παραδοῦναι: "to deliver with the power of Christ Himself." There is nothing here opposed, as Edwards thinks, to the natural meaning of σύν. Certainly this preposition does not denote the means *by* which (διά, ἐν); but it can perfectly denote a co-operating circumstance, as in the phrases σὺν θεῷ or σὺν θεοῖς πράττειν, to do with the help of God; comp. Heinrici, ad h. l. Human action does not become efficacious except in union with Divine power.—The *repetition* of the words, *of our Lord Jesus* (or *Jesus Christ*), at the end of the verse, belongs to the forms of language used by the ancients in their formulas of condemnation or consecration (*devotio*). The object of *deliver* is briefly repeated by the τὸν τοιοῦτον, *such an one*, a form which brings out once more the odious character of his conduct.

The obscure expression παραδοῦναι τῷ Σατανᾷ, *to deliver to Satan*, is found only elsewhere in 1 Tim. i. 20: "Hymenæus and Alexander, whom I have delivered unto Satan, that they may learn not to blaspheme."—It has been understood in three ways. Some have found in it the idea of *excommunication* pure and simple (Calvin, Beza, Olshausen, Bonnet, Heinrici, etc.). Calvin thus briefly justifies this sense · "As Christ reigns in the Church, so Satan outside the Church. . . He then, who is cast out of the Church, is thereby in a manner delivered to the power of Satan, in so far as he becomes a stranger to the kingdom of God." But the insufficiency of this sense has been generally felt. Why use an expression so extraordinary to designate a fact so simple as that of exclusion from the Church, especially if, as those commentators hold, Paul had just designated the same act by a wholly different term (ver. 3)? Still, if the use of the term had a precedent in the forms of the synagogue! But Lightfoot has proved that this formula was never in use to denote Jewish excommunication. We have besides already called attention to the fact that the δύναμις, *the power*, of the Lord was not necessary to the execution of a sentence of excommunication. And how could this punishment have prevented Hymenæus and Alexander from blaspheming? Is it not possible to blaspheme, and that more freely, outside than within the Church? Finally, it remains to explain the following words: *for the destruction of the flesh;* we do not think it is possible on this explanation to give them a natural meaning.—Moreover, from the earliest times of exegesis down to our own day, the need has been felt of adding another idea to that of excommunication, viz. *bodily punishment*, regarded either as the proper consequence of excommunication (Calov), or as a chastisement over and above, added to excommunication by the Apostle Paul. To the Church it belongs to exclude from its membership; to the apostle to let loose on the excommunicated one the disciplinary power of Satan to punish him in his body (so nearly Chrysostom, Theodoret, Rückert, Olshausen, Osiander, Meyer). This sense certainly is an approach to the truth; but why seek to combine the idea of excommunication with that of bodily punishment? The former is taken from ver. 3, from the αἴρειν ἐκ μεσοῦ; we have seen that it is not really there. But what is graver still is, that it would follow from this explanation that the second chastisement, bodily punishment, would be inflicted on the incestuous person in consequence of the Church's neglecting to inflict on him the first. In fact, it follows from ver. 3 that the apostle's intervention in this matter was rendered necessary by the lax toleration of the Christians of Corinth. In these circumstances the apostle could no doubt inflict the penalty which the Church should have pronounced, but he could not decree an aggravation of punishment; for the fault of the Church added nothing to that of the culprit. In this respect the first explanation would still be preferable to this second. The latter nevertheless contains an element of truth which we should preserve, and which will constitute the third (Lightfoot, Hofmann, Holsten): the idea of a *bodily chastisement*, of which Satan is to be the instrument. Such is the punishment which Paul inflicts at his own hand,

and in virtue of his apostolic power, and which corresponds to the αἴρειν ἐκ μέσου, *taking away from among*, to the cutting off which the Church had not sought to obtain from God. Satan is often represented as having the power to inflict physical evils. It is he who is God's instrument to try Job when he was stricken with leprosy. It is he, says Jesus, who for eighteen years holds bound the poor woman who was bent double, and whom He cured on the Sabbath day (Luke xiii. 6). Paul himself ascribes to a messenger of Satan the thorn in the flesh, of which God makes use to keep him in humility (2 Cor. xii. 7). It is Satan who is the murderer of man in consequence of the first sin (John viii. 44), and he has the dominion of death (Heb. ii. 14). It is not hard to understand how a painful, perhaps mortal, punishment of this kind might bring the blasphemy on the lips of a heretic to an end. It is obvious how it might bring back to himself and to God a man who was led away by the seduction of the senses. Suffering in the flesh is needed to check the dominion of fleshly inclinations. The only difference between this chastisement decreed by the apostle, and that which the Corinthians should have asked from above, is, that the Church would have referred the mode of execution to God, while Paul, in virtue of his spiritual position superior to that of the Church, feels at liberty to determine the means of which the Lord will make use. For "he knows the mind of the Lord" (ii. 16). It will perhaps be asked how Satan can lend himself to an office contrary to the interests of his own kingdom. But we know not the mysteries of that being, in which the greatest possible amount of blindness is united to the most penetrating intelligence. "Malignity," says M. de Bonald, "sharpens the mind and kills sound sense." Was it not the messenger of Satan whom God used to preserve Paul from pride, and who kept him in that consciousness of his weakness by means of which the Divine power could always anew manifest itself in him?

The apostle adds: εἰς ὄλεθρον τῆς σαρκός, *for the destruction of the flesh*. Those who apply the foregoing expression to excommunication are embarrassed by these words. Calvin takes them as a softening introduced into the punishment, a carnal condemnation importing simply a temporal and temporary condemnation, in opposition to eternal damnation. This interpretation of the genitive σαρκός is its own refutation. Others think of the ruin of the worldly affairs of the excommunicated person, in consequence of his rupture with his former customers, the other members of the Church. How is it possible to ascribe such a thought to the apostle! The only tenable explanation is that which is found already in Augustine, then in Grotius, Gerlach, Bonnet: the destruction of the flesh, in the *moral* sense of the word, that is to say, of the sinful tendencies, in consequence of the pain and repentance which will be produced in the man by his expulsion from the Church. But,—1. Might not this measure quite as well produce the opposite effect? Thrown back into the world, the man might easily become utterly corrupt. 2. The term ὄλεθρος, *destruction, perdition*, would here require to denote a beneficent work of the Holy Spirit; that is impossible; see the threatening sense in which the word is always taken in the other passages of the

New Testament: 1 Thess. v. 3 and 2 Thess. i. 9 (ὄλεθρος αἰφνίδιος, αἰώνιος, *destruction sudden, eternal*); 1 Tim. vi. 9 (ὄλεθρος καὶ ἀπώλεια, *destruction and perdition*). Paul means here to speak of a real *loss* for the man, according to the uniform meaning of the word ὄλεθρος. The matter in question is the destruction of one of the elements of his being with a view to the salvation of the other, which is the more precious. When Paul wishes to express the moral idea of the destruction of sin, he uses quite other terms: *to reduce to impotence*, καταργεῖν (Rom. vi. 6); *to cause to die, kill*, νεκροῦν, θανατοῦν (Col. iii. 3; Rom. viii. 13); *to crucify*, σταυροῦν (Gal. v. 24); terms which have a different shade from ὄλεθρος. 3. The opposite of σάρξ, *the flesh*, in the following words, is πνεῦμα, *the spirit*. Now this second term cannot simply denote spiritual life, to which the expression *being saved* would not apply; it can only denote the substratum of that life, the spirit itself, as an element of human existence. Hence it follows that neither does *the flesh* denote fleshly life, but the flesh itself, the substratum of the natural life. —The flesh must therefore be taken in the sense of the earthly man, or, as Hofmann observes, of the *outward man*, in Paul's phrase (2 Cor. iv. 16: "If our outward man perish . . ."). It is in this sense that the word *flesh* itself is taken a few verses before (ver. 11), in the saying: "That the life of Jesus may be manifested *in our mortal flesh;*" so Phil. i. 22 (τὸ ζῆν ἐν σαρκί) and Gal. ii. 20 (ὃ νῦν ζῶ ἐν σαρκί). The apostle might have two reasons for using the term *flesh* here rather than *body;* in the first place, σάρξ expresses the natural life in its totality, physical and psychical; and next, the body in itself is not to be destroyed (chap. xv.). It is therefore the destruction of the earthly existence of the man which Paul meant to designate by the words ὄλεθρος τῆς σαρκός; and M. Renan is not wrong in saying: "There can be no doubt of it; it is a condemnation to death that Paul pronounces." The sudden death of Ananias and Sapphira offers an analogy to the present case, not that Paul is thinking of so sudden a visitation; the expression he uses rather indicates a slow wasting, leaving to the sinner time for repentance.

This destruction of the flesh has in view *the saving of the spirit, in the day of Christ.* Some versions translate: "that *the soul* may be saved . . .," as if the soul and spirit were in Paul's eyes one and the same thing. The passage 1 Thess. v. 23 proves the contrary. "The *soul* is, in man as in the lower animals, the breath of life which animates his organism; but the *spirit* is the sense with which the human soul is exclusively endowed to experience the contact of the Divine and apprehend it." This higher sense in the soul once destroyed by the power of the flesh, connection is no longer possible between the soul and God. This is undoubtedly what Scripture calls the second death. As the first is the body's privation of the soul, the second is the soul's privation of the spirit. This is why the apostle wishes at any cost to save the *spirit* in this man, in which there resides the faculty of contact with God and of life in Him throughout eternity. It need not be said that the spirit, thus understood as an element of human life, can only discharge its part fully when it is open to the working of the Divine Spirit.—The words, *in the day of the Lord*

R

Jesus, transport us to the time when Jesus glorified will appear again on the earth to take to Him His own (xv. 23); then will be pronounced on each Christian the sentence of his acceptance or rejection. These last words appear to me to confirm the explanation given of the phrase, *destruction of the flesh*. For if this denoted the destruction of the fleshly inclinations in the incestuous person, the awaking of spiritual life which would follow would not take place only at Christ's coming, it would make itself felt in him in this present life.—Rückert has very severely judged the apostle's conduct on this occasion. He is disposed, indeed, to make good as an excuse in his favour the impetuosity of his zeal, the purity of his intention, and a remnant of Judaic prejudice. But he charges him with having given way to his natural violence; with having compromised the salvation of the guilty person by depriving him, perhaps, if his sentence came to be realized, of time for repentance; and finally, with having acted imprudently towards a Church in which his credit was shaken, by putting it in circumstances to disobey him. We do not accept either these excuses or these charges for the apostle. The phrase *deliver to Satan*, being foreign to the formulas of the synagogue, was consequently, also, foreign to the apostle's Jewish past. The alleged violence of his temperament does not betray itself in the slightest in the severity of his conduct. The apostle here rather resembles a mother crying to God for her prodigal son and saying to Him: My God, strike him, strike him even to the death, if need be, if only he be saved! As to the Church, Paul no doubt knew better than the critic of our day how

far he could and ought to go in his conduct toward it.
—Another critic, Baur,[1] has taken up and developed
the observations of Rückert, confirming them by the
Second Epistle. In the passage 2 Cor. ii. 5-11, he
sees the proof that the apostle's injunctions had not
been executed, that the sentence pronounced by him
against the incestuous person had not been followed
with any effect, and that the apostolical power which
he claimed was consequently nothing but an illusion;
that after all, in short, nothing remained to the apostle
but piteously to beat a retreat, "presenting as his
desire what was done without his will," and putting on
the appearance of pardoning and asking favour for the
guilty one from the Corinthians, who pardoned the
delinquent in spite of him. — This entire deduction
assumes one thing: to wit, that the passage 2 Cor. ii.
5-11 refers to the affair of the incestuous person. But
the close relation between this passage and that of
vii. 12 demonstrates that it is nothing of the kind, and
that all that Paul writes in chap. ii. refers to an entirely
different fact, to a personal insult to which he had been
subjected at Corinth, and which had taken place posterior to the sending of the first letter.[2] And supposing
even that the passage of chap. ii. related to the incestuous person, what would it tell us? That the majority
of the Church (οἱ πλείονες, *the larger number*) had
entered into the apostle's views as to the punishment

[1] *Der ap. Paulus*, i. pp. 234, 235.
[2] In any attempt to maintain the reference of 2 Cor. vii. 7 seq. to the affair of the incestuous person, the word ἀδικηθείς, *he to whom a wrong has been done* (ver. 12), must be referred to the guilty man's father, as if such an act could be ranked in the category of injustices! Besides, does not the very fact of the incest necessarily suppose the father's death? See Hilgenfeld, *Einleitung*, pp. 284, 285.

of the culprit; and that the latter had fallen into such a disheartened state that his danger now was of allowing himself to be driven by Satan from carnal security to despair. If such was the meaning of the passage, what would it contain that was fitted to justify the conclusions of Baur, and the awkward light in which they would place the conduct and character of the apostle?

The apostle has terminated what concerns the particular case of the incestuous person. From this point onwards the subject broadens; he shows in the general state of the Church the reason why it has so badly fulfilled its obligations in this particular case (vers. 6–8).

Vers. 6–8.

Ver. 6. "Your glorying is not good; know ye not that a little leaven leaveneth [1] the whole lump?"—There are two ways of understanding the connection between the following passage and that which precedes: either the apostle continues to dwell on the disciplinary obligation of the Church,—and we must then regard the *leaven* to be taken away as either the incestuous person, or rather the vicious in general,—or it may be held that Paul, after upbraiding the Church with its negligence, seeks to guide its finger to the true cause of the mischief: the want of moral sincerity and firmness. This is the state which must be remedied without delay. Then reaction against the presence of the vicious will take place of itself. The first words are better explained in the second sense, for they relate to

[1] D reads δολοι (It. *corrumpit*).

the present state of the Church in general. I have translated καύχημα by *vanterie* (boasting), as if it had been καύχησις (the act of boasting), because we have no word in French to denote the *object* of boasting.[1] Chrysostom thought the word should be applied to the incestuous person himself, assuming that he was one of the eminent men in whom the Church gloried. Grotius and Heinrici have reproduced this explanation. It seems to us untenable : the Church was satisfied with its state in general, and in particular with the wealth of its spiritual gifts, on which Paul himself had congratulated it (i. 5–7), and of which chaps. xii.–xiv. will furnish proof. But this abundance of knowledge and speech was no real good except in so far as it effected the increase of spiritual life in the Church, and the sanctification of its members. As this was not the case, the apostle declares to them that their ground of self-satisfaction is of bad quality; a being vainly puffed up (iv. 19) : "Ye are proud of the state of your Church ; there is no reason for it!" He thus returns to the idea of ver. 2.—This judgment is called forth by the softness of their conduct in regard to the evil which shows itself among them. Should they who are so rich in knowledge fail to know the influence exercised on a whole mass by the least particle of corruption which is tolerated in it?—Paul clothes his thought in a proverbial form (Gal. v. 9). *Leaven* is here, as in many other passages (Matt. xiii. 33 ; Luke xii. 1), the emblem of a principle apparently insignificant in quantity, but possessing a real penetrating force, and that either for good (Matt. xiii. 33) or for evil (Matt. xvi. 6 ; Gal.

[1] [Our English *boast* is used in both senses.—Tr.]

v. 9). Does Paul understand by this *little leaven* (the literal sense), the incestuous person or any other vicious member of the same kind, whose tolerated presence is a principle of corruption for the whole community? This is the meaning generally held. Or is he rather thinking of evil in general, which, when tolerated even in a limited and slightly scandalous form, gradually lowers the standard of the Christian conscience in all? It does not seem to me likely that Paul would designate as a *little* leaven a sinner guilty of so revolting an act as that in question (ver. 1), or other not less scandalous offenders. It is therefore better to apply this figure to all sin, even the least, voluntarily tolerated by the individual or the Church. This meaning, held by Meyer, de Wette, Hofmann, Gerlach, is confirmed by vers. 7 and 8.

Vers. 7, 8. "Purge out[1] the old leaven, that ye may be a new lump, as ye are unleavened. For even Christ, our Paschal lamb, hath been sacrificed.[2] 8. Therefore let us keep the feast, not with old leaven, neither[3] with the leaven of malice and wickedness; but with the unleavened bread of purity and truth."—If the figure applied to the incestuous man or to the vicious, the word ἐκκαθάρειν, *to purify by removing*, would apply to an act such as the: *taking away from among* (ver. 2), and the: *delivering to Satan* (ver. 5); and the words: *that ye may be a new lump*, would signify: that ye may present the spectacle of a Church renewed by the absence of every vicious member. But the

---

[1] T. R. with C L P here add οὖν (*therefore*).
[2] T. R. with L P Syr. reads ὑπὲρ ἡμῶν (*for us*).
[3] C Or. read μη instead of μηδε.

epithet *old*, given to leaven, and ver. 8 show that leaven is here taken in an abstract sense: "the leaven which consists of natural malignity and perversity." The exhortation to *purging* applies therefore to the action of each on himself, and of all on all, in order to leave in the Church not a *single* manifestation of the old man, of the corrupt nature, undiscovered and unchecked.

The οὖν, *therefore*, of T. R. ought, according to most of the Mjj., to be suppressed. It only goes to weaken the vivacity of the imperative. It is well known that among the Jews, on the 14th Nisan, the eve of the first and great day of the feast of Passover, there was removed with great care all the leaven (*pain levé*, raised bread) which could be found in their houses; and in the evening, along with the celebration of the Paschal feast, the sacred week began, during which nothing was eaten but cakes of unleavened bread. Leaven represented, according to the particular ceremonial of this feast, the pollutions of the idolatry and vices of Egypt with which Israel had broken in coming forth from it. As Israel had providentially carried to the desert that night only unleavened bread, the permanent rite had been borrowed from the historical circumstance (Ex. xii. 39, xiii. 6-9). The apostle spiritualizes the ceremony. As the Israelites at every Passover feast were bound to leave behind them the pollutions of their Egyptian life, in order to become a new people of God, so the Church is bound to break with all the evil dispositions of the natural heart, or that which is elsewhere called *the old man*.—The desired result of this breaking on the part of each one with his own known sin, will be the renewing of the whole Church: *that ye may be a new lump.* Another allusion to Jewish customs. On the eve of the feast, a fresh piece of dough was kneaded with pure water, and from it were prepared the cakes of unleavened bread which were eaten during the feast. The word νέον, *new*, does not signify: new as to quality (as καινόν would do), but *recent*, as to time. The whole community, by this work of purification wrought on itself, should become like a piece of dough newly kneaded. Has not the awakening of a whole Church been seen more than once to begin with submission to an old censure which weighed on the conscience of *one* sinner? This confession drew forth others, and the holy breath passed over the whole community.

The phrase which follows, *as ye are unleavened*, has greatly embarrassed commentators, who have explained it as if it were, " ye should be," which grammatically is inadmissible. Chrysostom thinks of final sanctification, others of baptismal regeneration,—meanings equally impossible. In saying, *ye are*, the apostle thinks of what they are, not in point of fact, but of right; the idea is the same as in Rom. vi. 11 : death to sin and life to God, virtually contained in faith in the dead and risen Christ. For the believer nothing more is needed than to become what he is already (in Christ). He must become holy in fact, as he is in idea.— Grotius has proposed to give to ἄζυμος, *unleavened*, the active meaning belonging to the adjectives ἄσιτος, ἄοινος (abstaining from bread, from wine); according to him, Paul characterizes the

Corinthians as persons who no longer feed on leavened bread (in the spiritual sense). But this term cannot be twisted from the definite meaning which it has in the Jewish ritual, and which is perfectly appropriate. They ought to become individually the organs of a new nature, which is in accordance with their true character as beings unleavened so far as they are believers.—The proof that this is what they are in point of right is given in the sequel.

From the time when the Paschal lamb was sacrificed in the temple, no leaven bread was allowed to appear on an Israelitish table; and this continued during the whole feast. Similarly the expiatory death of Christ, containing the principle of death to sin, there begins with His death in the case of the Church and of each believer the great spiritual Passover, from which all sin is banished, as leaven was from the Jewish feast. Every Christian is an *azyme* (unleavened one).—The particle καὶ γάρ, *for also*, has for its characteristic the connecting of two facts of an analogous nature (*also*), the second of which is the ground of the first (*for*): this is exactly the case here.—The work πάσχα, strictly speaking, *passing*, denoted God's passing over Egypt, on the night when He smote the first-born and spared the houses of the Israelites sprinkled with the blood of the lamb. The word was afterwards applied to the lamb itself; in this sense it is taken here.—The words *for us*, read by T. R., are omitted in the majority of the Mjj.—By the complement ἡμῶν, *our*, Paul contrasts the Christian Passover with that of the Jews. As the latter began with the slaying of the lamb, ours began with the bloody death of Christ; Χριστός is in apposition to πάσχα. The practical consequence of His death thus understood, and of the new state in which it places believers, is drawn in the following verse.

Ver. 8. The Christian's Paschal feast does not last a week, but all his life. In an admirable discourse Chrysostom has developed this idea: "For the true Christian, it is always Easter, always Pentecost, always Christmas." Such is the sense in which the apostle exhorts the Corinthians to keep the feast.—The words, *not with old leaven*, signify, in accordance with what precedes : not by persisting in the corrupt dispositions of the old man.—The particle μηδέ, *nor any more*, according to Edwards, does not introduce an additional thought, but only the explanation of the preceding allegorical phrase. I do not think this meaning possible. The μηδέ seems to me intended to bring out a special feature in the general idea in direct connection with present circumstances; so, or nearly so, de Wette, Rückert, Meyer, etc. The word κακία denotes rather corruption of the nature or state, and the word πονηρία, deliberate malice of the will. In the context, the first of these terms relates to a corrupt state of the soul, which does not allow it to be indignant against evil, but leaves it to act toward it with lax toleration; the second goes further: it denotes active connivance and protection. These two vices, both proceeding from the leaven of the old nature, had been prominently manifested in the Church's conduct towards the incestuous person. With these dispositions Paul contrasts those which should characterize the renewing of the purified mass.

The two complements εἰλικρινείας and ἀληθείας are, like the two preceding, genitives of apposition: " unleavened bread consisting of . . ." The word εἰλικρίνεια, according to the most probable etymology, πρὸς εἴλην κρίνειν, to judge by the light of the sun, denotes proved transparency, and so the purity of a heart perfectly sincere before God, to which all sympathy with evil is completely foreign. This pure crystal is the opposite of κακία, the corrupted nature.—The second term, *truth*, ἀλήθεια, denotes righteousness in its active form, inflexible firmness, constancy in maintaining all that is revealed to the conscience as good, and consequently in struggling against evil without making the smallest compromise; it is the opposite of πονηρία. Hofmann has taken up the unfortunate idea—and he has been followed by Heinrici — of explaining the charge of malice contained in this verse by the misunderstanding, to some extent voluntary, on the part of the Corinthians, which Paul now proceeds to rectify. The apostle does not condescend to such petty recriminations.

Must it be concluded from these verses that the apostle wrote this letter at the time of the Passover? The figures used do not, as we have seen, contain anything which does not admit of explanation independently of all connection with the actual celebration of the Passover. Yet it is certain, that if we hold this feast and the composition of our letter to have been simultaneous, the choice of the figures, which come on us somewhat abruptly, is more naturally explained. This induction is confirmed by xvi. 8: " I will tarry at Ephesus until Pentecost." And as Acts xx. 6 shows that St. Paul, as well as the Churches founded by him, observed the Passover and celebrated it at the same time as the Jews, we shall not assuredly be going beyond his thought if we find in the words, "Let us keep the feast," an *allusion* to that which was being celebrated at the time in the Churches.

A second question often discussed is the following: May the words, "Christ, our Passover, has been sacrificed," be regarded as a testimony in favour of John's narrative, according to which Jesus died on the day (14th Nisan) when the Paschal lamb was sacrificed, and not, as it has been thought necessary to conclude from the synoptics, on the afternoon of the 15th Nisan? It seems to me that the name Paschal lamb, given to Jesus by St. Paul, does not depend in the least on the day or hour when He died. His relation to the Paschal lamb lies in the essence of things, and does not depend on a chronological coincidence. But there is one aspect in which Paul's words cannot be well understood, as it appears to me, except from that point of view which the narrative of John brings into light. The feast of unleavened bread began on the 14th in the evening, after the slaying of the lamb. Now this relation, which forms the basis of our passage, would be disturbed if Jesus, in Paul's view, did not die till the afternoon of the 15th, after the feast of unleavened bread had already lasted for a whole day.—After pointing out to the Church what it should have done, the apostle gives it to understand the reason why it has not done so: it is because the old leaven has regained the upper hand in its moral life, and that it requires to undergo a complete renovation. This said, the subject of discipline is finished; if Pauls adds a few more observations, it is to dissipate a misunderstanding arising from a passage of his on the subject in a letter which he had previously addressed to them.

Vers. 9–13.

Vers. 9, 10. " I wrote unto you in my epistle not to company with fornicators ; 10.¹ not altogether with the fornicators of this world, or with the covetous and ² extortioners or with idolaters ; for then must ye needs ³ go out of the world."—Paul begins with recalling the terms of which he made use (ver. 9); then he sets aside the false sense which had been attached to them (ver. 10), and states his real judgment (ver. 11); finally, he justifies his judgment in vers. 12, 13. — Ἐν τῇ ἐπιστολῇ, literally, *in the Epistle*, the one you know. It is vain for Chrysostom, Erasmus, Lange, to allege that Paul alludes to vers. 2, 6, and 7 of this same chapter, or for Lardner to attempt to find here the announcement of what is about to follow, vers. 10–13. It is easy to see that nothing in what precedes contained the direction given here, and that the ἔγραψα, *I wrote*, can only refer to the rectification of an idea which had been fathered on Paul, and which had been reported to him. A correspondence between Paul and the Church had certainly preceded our Epistle ; comp. vii. 1 : " Now concerning the things whereof ye wrote unto me." In 2 Cor. vii. 8, Paul refers, using the same expression, to

---

[1] T. R. with L P reads καί (*and*) ου πάντως.
[2] T. R. with E L Syr. reads η (*or*), instead of καί (*and*).
[3] T. R. with P: οφειλετε (*ye need*), instead of ωφειλετε (*ye would need*).

a previous letter. Had there not been dogmatic reasons for denying the possibility of the loss of an apostolic document, this meaning would not have been contested.—The term *to company* (mingle) *with*, συναναμίγνυσθαι, strictly denotes living in an intimate and continuous relation with one,—σύν emphasizing the intimacy, and ἀνά the repetition of the acts. Does the rupture demanded by the apostle refer to the conduct of Christians in private life, or to ecclesiastical communion? In any case, the Corinthians could not have thought of an ecclesiastical rupture with people with whom no ecclesiastical bond existed. Did they not apply Paul's regulation to sinners who were yet outside of the Church? We may see in 2 Thess. iii. 14 how the expression " not to company with " is synonymous with στέλλεσθαι ἀπό, *to hold aloof from*, of ver. 6; and in that context the term certainly refers to private life. Finally, if the matter in question here were the ecclesiastical relation, the apostle would not have to say to believers, " Do not company with the vicious," but, " Do not allow the vicious to company with you." This precept of Paul's is parallel to that of John, Second Epistle, ver. 10 : " If any one bringeth not this teaching, receive him not into your house, and give him no greeting."

Ver. 10. The καί, *and*, which begins this verse in the T. R., is too little supported to be authentic.—The words οὐ πάντως τοῖς πόρνοις naturally have the effect of an explanatory apposition added to the πόρνοις at the end of ver. 9, in this sense : " When I spoke of fornicators in my letter, I did not thereby mean all the fornicators of this world in general." After all attempts to explain this οὐ πάντως differently, it seems to me that this is the interpretation which holds good. Only, it logically implies that by the phrase, *the fornicators of this world*, Paul denotes, not only those who are without the Church, but those also who profess the gospel. It is the only way of explaining the οὐ πάντως, which is not the absolute negative, like πάντως οὐ, *absolutely not*, but, on the contrary, a restricted negative (*not absolutely, not entirely*) : I wrote to you to break with fornicators, not with fornicators in general, which would oblige you to go out of the world, but with those only who profess the gospel. This is the meaning adopted by Neander, Hofmann, and others. It is objected that the phrase, the fornicators *of this world*, must be exclusive of those *of the Church.* Why so ? The idea is simply, "not generally with all the fornicators living with you in this world." Such is evidently the meaning of the word *world* in the following sentence. Meyer has thought that it is to mark the difference between these two meanings given to the word *world* that Paul rejects the τούτου, *this*, in the following sentence. But it may also be to avoid an awkward and useless repetition. As to those who, like Meyer, de Wette, Edwards, hold that *the fornicators of this world* must here be necessarily contrasted with those of the Church, they are thrown into embarrassment by the οὐ πάντως, and they apply it solely to the *limitation* of relations with these fornicators : " I meant you not to have relations too complete (πάντως) with non-Christian fornicators," which would authorize restricted relations, without which life in the world would be impossible. But this meaning is not natural ; for what Paul here distinguishes is not the greater or less degree of intimacy in relations to impure heathen; he is contrasting with the relation to impure heathen, which he authorizes, the relation to impure Christians, which he forbids.—We do not take account here of the interpretations which separate οὐ from πάντως, connecting the former with the verb ἔγραψα, and the latter with the verb συναναμίγνυσθαι,—a separation far from natural,—nor of that of Rückert, who understands οὐ πάντως almost as if it were πάντως οὐ, *absolutely not*, though Paul knows perfectly the use and meaning of this form; comp. xvi. 12. However this may be, the view of the apostle remains substantially the same : the rupture which he demands is not applicable to the vicious in general, but only to those who lay claim to the name of Christians.—To libertinism Paul adds *covetousness* as to earthly goods, and that in the two forms of πλεονεξία, which, to have more, uses fraudulent and indelicate processes, like usury, and that of ἁρπαγή, injustice by violent means. These two words are connected, not by ἤ, *or*, but by καί, *and*, as two species of one and the same genus.— *Idolaters*, as such, would seem to be an impossibility in the Church; but there might be Corinthians who, after believing, had kept up habits of idolatry; and chap. viii. will show us that many of them could not bring themselves to give up the banquets to which they were invited in idol temples. These three vices, fornication, covetousness, idolatry, are related, as Estius and Edwards observe, the first to the individual himself, the second to his neighbours, the third to God.

It is evident that in a city like Corinth, to break off all connection with persons of these three categories would have been for a man to condemn himself to live as a hermit. This is probably what the Corinthians had retorted with a measure of irony; and so the apostle, no less than they, rejects an idea so absurd. The majority of the Mjj. read ὠφείλετε, *ye would need*, which gives a simple sense. T. R. with P and Chrysostom reads ὀφείλετε, *ye need*, a form which is also, though less easily, intelligible: " Since, if it is so, ye need . . ." Calvin, starting from this reading, has given the sentence a quite different meaning: "For ye need really to separate yourselves from the world (morally)." But the particle ἄρα, *then*, indicates, on the contrary, a consequence from what precedes.—And now Paul establishes his true thought.

Ver. 11. "But now I have written unto you not to keep company, if any man that is called a brother be a fornicator, or covetous, or an idolater, or a railer, or a drunkard, or an extortioner; with such an one, no, not to eat."—The words *but now* can only express a logical contrast. The νῦν contrasts Paul's true thought, which remains, with his thought as it was disfigured by the Corinthians, which is relegated to the past. — The emphasis is on the words, *who is called a brother;* as Paul goes on to say in ver. 12, he has not to exercise discipline on those who do not profess the faith. But when a man, who parades the title of Christian, exhibits this profession side by side with vice, the Church is bound to protest against this lying union, and with this view, so far as depends on it, to break off all relations with such a man. This is the way to tear from him the mask with which he covers himself to the shame of the Church and of Christ Himself.—The six following terms have been grouped, either in threes (Meyer) or in

s

three pairs (Hofmann), with more or less ingenuity. It seems to me that, as in the enumeration Rom. i. 29 seq., we have here rather an unstudied accumulation than a classification, strictly so called. It may be said that in such cases disgust excludes order. To the four terms of ver. 10 Paul adds two new ones: λοίδορος, a man who speaks rudely, who calumniates, and μέθυσος, *the intemperate man.*—We have already shown that the *not to company with* indicates the rupture of private relations. But should not the last words, *with such a man, no, not to eat,* be applied to the rupture of the ecclesiastical relation by his exclusion from worship and from the Holy Supper? The word μηδέ, *nay, no more, not even,* does not allow this explanation of συνεσθίειν, *to eat with.* For this act is thus characterized as a matter of less gravity, and Paul could never so speak of the Holy Supper. Among the ancients, for a man to receive any at his table was much more a sign of intimacy than in our day; and the apostle is unwilling that by the sign of so close a personal relation the idea should be authorized that the vicious man is acknowledged by other Christians as worthy of the name. Meyer, indeed, admits that the phrase, *no, not to eat with . . .,* can only refer to the believer's private table. But by an argument *à fortiori,* he concludes that it applies with still more certainty to the Holy Supper. Theodoret had already argued in the same way: "Not to eat, with stronger reason not to hold communion with him." In such a matter it is dangerous to proceed by way of logical deduction. In arguing thus, account is not taken of this difference, that the table prepared in my house is my own, while the Holy Supper is the Lord's Table.

I am therefore responsible for those whom I admit to the former, but not for those who appear at the latter. It appears from xi. 28, 29, that the Lord thinks good to leave each one liberty to eat and drink his condemnation at the holy table, and will not prevent him from doing so by external means. The parable of the tares already suggested such a course, the only one in keeping with God's regard for human liberty. The apostle justifies the distinction which he has just made between believers and unbelievers.

Vers. 12, 13. "For what have I to do to judge them also [1] that are without? do ye not judge them that are within? 13. But them that are without, God judgeth. And [2] put away [3] from among yourselves that wicked person."—The first question is the justification (*for*) of ver. 10: "We have not to judge unbelievers." The second is the justification of ver. 11: "But we have to judge believers."—Our competency to exercise discipline does not extend further than the solidarity established by confession of the common faith. This general truth the apostle expresses in his own person (μοί, *mine*), as is often done in stating moral maxims (vi. 12, for example); this form does not therefore assume, as has been sometimes thought, that the word κρίνειν, *to judge*, has here a particular meaning, applicable exclusively to the apostle; for example, that of laying down disciplinary rules: "The rules which I prescribe to you on this subject are not to be applied

---

[1] T. R. with D E L here adds καί (*also*).
[2] T. R. with E L Syr. reads καί (*and*), while this word is omitted in the other 8 Mjj.
[3] T. R. with E L reads ἐξαρεῖτε (*ye will take away*), instead of ἐξάρατε (*take away*), read by the 8 other Mjj.

to those who are without." This sense of κρίνειν is inadmissible. In any case, had it been the part which he had to take personally on which Paul wished to lay stress, he would not have used the enclitic form (μοι), but the full form (ἐμοί). He speaks of himself, not as an apostle, but as a Christian; and what he says applies consequently to every Christian. Every Christian has individually the mission to exercise the judgment of which he speaks in ver. 11. We have already pointed out the profound analogy which prevails between this chapter and the disciplinary direction given to the apostles by the Lord (Matt. xviii. 15-20). We find in the latter (in ver. 17) the same use of the singular pronoun, which strikes us here in the language of the apostle; only the pronoun is in the second person, because it is Jesus who is addressing the believer: "Let him be to *thee* as a heathen and publican." It is therefore every believer who is bound freely at his own hand to pronounce this rupture of relations with the unbelieving brother which Paul prescribes to the Church in general. For if it is in itself the duty of all, it cannot be other in point of fact than a completely individual act.—T. R. with 3 Mjj. reads: "What have I to do to judge those *also* (καί) that are without?" This καί may, after all, be authentic: "The competency which I have in regard to my brethren, should I not *also* extend to others?" The Jews called the heathen *chitsonim, those without* (Lightfoot, *Hor. hebr.*, p. 6). The apostle borrows the name from them to designate, not only the heathen, but the Jews themselves; comp. the analogous term used by Jesus, Mark iv. 11. In all the synagogues dispersed throughout heathen countries careful watch was kept over the respectability of the members of the community. Should the Church in this point remain behind the synagogue?—The term *judge* can only be explained in the context by what precedes. It can only therefore refer to the means which have just been indicated, viz. private rupture.

The second question (ver. 12^b) is in the same relation to ver. 11 as the first (ver. 12^a) to ver. 10. " I have not the task of judging them that are without; but have not you that of judging them that are within, the vicious among believers, and that in name of the faith which they profess along with you?" We are called to remark the emphasis put on the word ὑμεῖς, *ye*, in opposition to θεός, *God*, the subject of the following proposition.

Ver. 13 justifies by a remark, and moreover by a Scriptural quotation, the distinction laid down in ver. 12. There are two domains, each subject to a different jurisdiction: the Christian judges the Christian; the man of the world is judged by God. It is needless to say that this contrast is only relative. The unfaithful Christian is also judged by God (xi. 30-32); but he has at the same time to do with another judge, the Christian community to which he belongs; while the non-Christian can sin without being subjected to any judgment of the latter kind. It seems at the first glance as if this saying were in contradiction to that of our Lord: "Judge not. . . . Why seest thou the mote in thy brother's eye?" (Matt. vii. 1-3). But when Jesus speaks thus, the judgment which He would exclude is that of secret malevolence, which condemns precipitately, on simple presumptions, or putting a malignant construction on motives. St. Paul is equally averse to such judging, xiii. 7. The judgment he lays on the Christian as a duty is that of charity, which, in view of notorious facts, seeks the best means to bring a brother back to himself who is self-deceived as to his spiritual state, and to save him (ver. 5). The former of these judgments is accompanied with a haughty joy, the other is an act of self-humiliation and mourning (ver. 2). The first proposition of ver. 13 might be made the continuation of the second question of ver. 12 : "Do not ye judge . . . and does not God judge?" But the affirmative meaning seems simpler.—The verb κρινει might be a future (κρινεῖ): "God *shall judge;*" the words would then refer to the last judgment. But, after the presents κρίνειν, κρίνετε, the verb is rather a present (κρίνει), the present of the idea and competency: ". It is God who is their Judge."—The final proposition, containing a Scripture quotation, is usually separated from what immediately precedes, to form, as it were, a last peremptory order summing up the whole chapter. It is clear that in this sense the καί, *and* (before the imperative ἐξάρατε or the future ἐξαρεῖτε), is out of place. It is omitted therefore in the Alex. and Greco-Latin readings, which evidently proceed on this interpretation. But what is overlooked in adopting this sense is the close connection established by the last words: ἐξ ὑμῶν αὐτῶν, *from among yourselves*, with what *immediately* precedes (vers. 12, 13ª): "Thou shalt take away the wicked, not from human society, as if thou hadst to judge also them that are without, but *from the midst of thyself*, from those that are within." Such then is the *Scriptural justification* of the distinction laid down by Paul, vers. 10-13ᵃ, between the judgment of *those without* and of *those within*. As Israel was bound to cut off the malefactor, not from heathen nations, but *from its own midst*, so with the Church. From this point of view we cannot but adopt the καί, *and*, of the T. R. and of the Byzantines, to which must be added the support of the Peschito, a support by no means to be despised, notwithstanding all that Westcott and Hort say: "*And finally*, you remember the Bible rule . . . !" This is the final proof.—The same reason which led to the suppression of the καί, *and*, no doubt led also to the change of the future ἐξαρεῖτε, *ye shall take away*, into the aor. imperative ἐξάρατε, *take away!* Once this last word was held to be the summary of the chapter, it is evident the imperative alone was suitable. If, on the contrary, the explanation here proposed is the true one, the future ought to be preserved, as giving more literally the formula quoted; comp. Deut. xvii. 7-12, xxii. 21, xxiv. 7. It has been suspected that the reading ἐξαρεῖτε, *ye shall take away*, was borrowed from these passages; but the text of the LXX. has in all these sentences the sing. ἐξαρεῖς, *thou shalt take away*. Why should the Byzantine copyists have transformed it into a plural? —The term *take away*, like that of *judge* (ver. 12), should be determined by what precedes. The means of execution, of which the apostle is thinking, can only be the two indicated by himself, that of mourning, ver. 2, which appeals to the intervention of God (with or without the παραδιδόναι), and that of the personal rupture, indicated ver. 11, which plunges the sinner into isolation. Such are the weapons of Christian discipline, which correspond to Israelitish stoning; Paul knows no others, when once the first warnings have failed. The very act of *delivering to Satan*, which he does as an apostle, not without the co-operation of the Church, is not essentially different from the judgment which it should itself have carried out according to ver. 2.—Rückert, who always takes a very close grip of questions, does not think that the term τὸν πονηρόν, *the wicked*, can possibly designate any other than the incestuous person. These last words would thus be the summary of chap. v. : "Exclude that guilty one!" But then, how explain the two passages, vers. 6-8 and 9-13ª, which seem to deviate from the subject properly so called? The first, according to him, is intended to prove the *necessity* of the exclusion; the second, its *possibility*; then, lastly, would come the final order, as an abrupt conclusion. This is able, but inadmissible. The passage vers. 6-8 has a wholly different meaning, as we have seen. The passage vers. 9-13 is introduced, not by a logical connection, but by an accidental circumstance, the misunderstanding on the part of the Corinthians. The τὸν πονηρόν, *the wicked*, does not therefore refer in the least to the incestuous man personally, but, as in the precepts of Deuteronomy, to the whole category of the vicious who are within. Paul does not return to the case of the incestuous man, but continues to treat the general subject of discipline to which he had passed from ver. 6.

Ecclesiastical Discipline.

Let us briefly study the few passages of the New Testament which bear on this subject.

Matt. v. 22.—Jesus here distinguishes three judicial stages: the judgment (κρίσις), the Sanhedrim, and the Gehenna of fire. These phrases are borrowed from the Israelitish order of things, in which they denote the district tribunal, the superior court, and, finally, the immediate judgment of God. If we apply these terms to the new surroundings which are formed about Jesus, and regard the first as brotherly admonition, the second as that of the heads of the future community of which the little existing flock is the germ, the third as God's judgment falling on the incorrigible sinner, we shall have a gradation of punishments corresponding, on the one hand, to the received Israelitish forms, and, on the other, to the passages of the New Testament, including that which we are explaining.

Matt. xviii. 15–20.—Here is the fullest passage. Jesus begins with *admonition;* there are three degrees of it: 1. *personal,*—as it is a private offence which is in question, the offended man takes the initiative; then 2. it takes a graver character by the addition of *two witnesses;* 3. it is the whole assembly together which admonishes the culprit. In the second place, admonition is followed by *judgment;* the dealing of the Church having failed, the offended person and every member of the congregation regard the brother, now recognised to be guilty, as a heathen or publican, which, in Jewish language, signifies that they break off all personal connection with him. Finally, the Church does not yet abandon the guilty man; it prays that he may repent, or, if not, that God may punish him visibly. Two or three brethren are sufficient to carry out this appeal to God effectually. The last stage, final perdition, is not here mentioned by Jesus; but it had been indicated by Him in the saying Matt. v.

2 Thess. iii. 6, 14, 15.—The first stage, that of warning, is here satisfied by the apostle's own letters; comp. 1st Ep. iv. 11, and 2nd Ep. iii. 6–12. The second stage, that of judgment, begins at ver. 14. It is the σημείωσις, the *public declaration*, probably a communication from the rulers of the flock regarding what has taken place, and the invitation to the congregation to break off private relations with the culprit, without however ceasing to love him, and to act accordingly by praying for him and seeking to bring him back. The

apostle stops here, like Jesus, in the second passage of Matthew.

Rev. ii. 19-22.—A false prophetess, whom the bishop has not checked, is to be punished by a disease sent by the Lord. This threat corresponds to the judgment whereby Paul gives over the incestuous person to Satan; and John's position in delivering this message is not without analogy to Paul's in our chapter. With this punishment coming directly from the Lord might be compared the punishment drawn down by profane communions, of which mention is made in chap. xi. of our Epistle. But we would not anticipate the explanation of the passage.

It is clear that the means of excommunication cannot be supported by any passage of the New Testament, but that the Church is not for all that defenceless against the scandals which arise within it. After admonitions, if they are useless, it has two arms: 1st. humiliation, with prayer to God to act; and 2nd. private rupture. The use of these means depends on individual believers, and may dispense with all decision by way of a numerical majority. And how much ought we to admire the Lord's wisdom, who took care not to confide the exercise of discipline to such uncertain hands as those of the half plus one of the members of the Church. To be convinced of this, it is enough to cast our eyes on the use which the Church has made of excommunication. There is not on the earth at this hour a Christian who is not excommunicated: Protestants are so by the Roman Church; the Roman Church by the Greek Church, and *vice versa;* the Reformed by the Lutherans, who refuse to admit them to their Holy Supper; the Darbyites by one another. Is there not then enough here to cure the Church of the use of this means? "The weapons of our warfare," says St. Paul, 2 Cor. x. 4, "are not carnal, but are powerful by God." It is certainly probable that the incestuous member of the Corinthian Church, visited with judgment from above, and abandoned for the time by all his brethren, did not present himself at the love-feast and the Holy Supper. And even at this hour it is hard to believe that a scandalous sinner, with whom the most of his brethren have broken, and for whom they besiege the throne of God, would have the audacity to present himself with them at the holy table; but if he chooses, he should have it in his power as Judas had. If the Church lives, the Lord will show that He also is living. Excommunication may have been a measure pedagogically useful at a time when the whole Church was under a system of legality. Now the Church has recovered consciousness of its spirituality; ought not its mode of discipline to follow this impulse, and return to the order of primitive spiritual discipline?

III.

Lawsuits (VI. 1-11).

The subject of discipline, though connected with the domain of ecclesiastical life, trenched on the sphere of moral questions. We come now to the subjects which belong exclusively to the latter sphere.

As the apostle had dealt with discipline, first from the standpoint of the special case which had raised the question, then, more generally, he acts in a similar way in regard to the subject which is now to follow. He treats of lawsuits between Christians,—1. in vers. 1-6, from the special standpoint of recourse had to heathen tribunals; and 2. in vers. 7-11, from the more general viewpoint of the lack of righteousness and charity which such conflicts between brethren imply.

Meyer alleges that there is no logical relation between this subject and the preceding; he founds on the asyndeton between the last verse of chap. v. and our ver. 1. But the absence of any particle fitted to connect these two verses is much rather the evidence of a very profound bond of feeling between the two passages. For by this form the second becomes, as it were, a reaffirmation of the ideas expounded in the first. And, in point of fact, does not Paul here, as in the former passage, combat in this proud Church the total lack of care for its own dignity before God and men? "Not only do ye not judge those whom you have a mission to judge (*them that are within*); but, moreover, ye go to have yourselves judged by those who are beneath you (*them that are without*)!" The basis of these two passages is therefore the same: it is the idea of the judicial competency of the Church in relation to its own members, but applied to two wholly different sins. Edwards understands the thing nearly in the same way. "He has just expounded the greatness and power of the Church; and now he asks if one could be found among them who would dare to do violence to the majesty of Christ who dwells in it."

Vers. 1–6.

Ver. 1. "Dare any of you, having a matter against another, go to law before the unjust, and not before the saints?"—The word τολμᾷ, *dares he*, heads this passage, exactly because it appeals vigorously to Christian dignity: "What! there is one who has this miserable courage!" One needs courage to degrade himself. The pronoun τὶς, *some one*, does not mean that there are many who are in this case; but there are too many if there is one. A single such case casts reproach on the whole Church. The Jews, who had the feeling of their theocratic nobility, had not recourse in their litigations to heathen tribunals; a system of arbitration established among them decided such questions; and the Corinthians had not Christian honour enough to rise to the same level!—For the moment the apostle leaves out of account the fact of the κρίνεσθαι, *getting judged, having a suit;* he will return to it, ver. 6. Here he fixes solely on the *way* in which these affairs are treated at Corinth.—The article τόν, *the,* before ἕτερον, *other,* serves strongly to individualize the adverse party in every case.—The heathen, of whom the official judges form part, are designated, not as usual by the term ἄπιστοι (*those who do not believe*), but by the term ἄδικοι, *unjust.* The apostle would make palpable the contradiction there is in going to ask justice of those who are themselves devoid of justice. The prep. ἐπί here signifies *in presence of;* as in the phrases ἐπὶ δικαστῶν, τοῦ δικαστηρίου (Plato, Demosthenes). Christians receive the title of honour οἱ ἅγιοι, *the saints.* They are people whom a Divine consecration has profoundly separated from the unjust and sinful world, and who ought therefore to possess within them the standard of justice. Had not Daniel seen the judgment given *to the saints* of the Most High? (vii. 22).

Vers. 2, 3. "Or[1] do ye not know that the saints shall judge the world? And if the world shall be judged by you, are ye unworthy to judge the smallest matters? 3. Know ye not that we shall judge angels? much more things that pertain to this life."—The T. R. is mistaken in omitting the *or* at the beginning of the question. Its meaning is: "Or if you affect to justify this mode of action, are you then ignorant that . . . ?" By the formula, *do ye not know,* which occurs no less than ten times in our Epistle, the apostle alludes to the doctrines he had delivered to the Church at the time of its foundation. Here it applies to a very special point of Christian eschatology, and from the

[1] T. R. omits η (*or*) with E L.

example it may be concluded how detailed was the instruction which the Churches received from the apostle. The verb κρινοῦσι should evidently be taken as a future, *shall judge*, as well as the κρινοῦμεν, *we shall judge*, of the following verse. *The world*, which is to be judged by the saints, can only designate those who have rejected the appeal which had been addressed to them by the gospel.—The Greek Fathers have sought to spiritualize this notion of judgment by reducing it to the moral contrast, which will burst into view at the day of judgment, between Christian holiness and the pollution of other men (Matt. xii. 41); or there has been found in it the general notion of the kingdom and glory of believers yet to come (Flatt). But the idea of a real judicial act is demanded by the context. Lightfoot, Vitringa have thought that this was the announcement of a time when, the gospel having become supreme, courts of law would be composed of Christians; as if *the world* of which the apostle speaks in this passage could be Christendom! We have already quoted the saying of Daniel, according to which the world is to be judged by the saints. Jesus seems to apply this notion in a special way to the apostles (Matt. xix. 28): "In the regeneration which is to come, then ye shall be seated on twelve thrones, judging the twelve tribes of Israel." The Apocalypse extends this privilege to all believers (ii. 26, 27, and xx. 4).—Billroth has proposed to make the whole second part of the verse also dependent on: *Do ye not know . . . ?* "Do ye not know that . . . and that it is unworthy of you to appear before the lowest tribunals (those of the heathen)?" But this construction is complicated, and the word ἐλάχιστα, *the least*, does not lend itself well to this meaning; comp. the parallel expression, βιωτικά, *the things of this life*, in the following verse. The second proposition of ver. 2 is therefore also a question: "Are not ye, the future judges of the world, worthy to pronounce on things which have only the slightest value?" The present κρίνεται, *is judged*, expresses not an actual fact, but a principle.—The adjunct ἐν ὑμῖν, literally *in you*, may be explained by the idea of the accused's presence in the circle formed by the tribunal. But this meaning is far from natural, especially when the accused is such as *the world!* It is better to understand: "in your person, which has become (by Christian sanctification) the rule of absolute justice;" which amounts to saying: *by you;* comp. the ἐν, Acts xvii. 31. The complement κριτηρίων ἐλαχίστων is often translated by *the least things to be judged*. Meyer is perhaps right in saying that usage does not admit of this meaning; but it is not exact to allege that the word κριτήριον can signify nothing except "a tribunal." It has many and varied meanings besides (see Passow: means of judgment; court of justice; place of judgment). Consequently we are entitled to give it here an analogous sense such as the context naturally demands, viz. a *sentence delivered:* "How should ye, who are invested with so high a competency, be unworthy to deliver sentences of a greatly inferior order?"

Ver. 3 does not present a new argument; it is the previous one raised to its culminating point. For the angels also, according to Paul, form part of the κόσμος, the *world* (see on iv. 9). Again we have the phrase:

Do ye not know? but without the particle ἤ, *or*, precisely because here is the continuation of ver. 2. The more striking the fact indicated in this verse,—the judgment of angels by the saints,—the more entitled is the apostle to express his wonder that his readers can be ignorant of it or can act as if they were in ignorance.—Meyer maintains that the word *angels*, used simply, denotes in the New Testament only *good* angels. It is one of those statutes which this excellent commentator loves to set up as a barrier against the caprice of exegetes, but the yoke of which need not be taken up without check. I think that the explanation of the idea contained in the first part of this verse is found in our Epistle itself, xv. 24. If it is so, Paul can only be speaking here of higher powers of *wickedness*. This meaning is also that which best accords with the meaning of the word *the world* (ver. 2). According to Meyer and Hofmann (who applies the word at once to good and bad angels), the judgment to which good angels shall be subjected will bear on the degree of fidelity with which they have discharged their office as *ministering spirits* to believers (Heb. i. 14); but nowhere in Scripture is there mention of a judgment of the elect angels. And in any case, we must not overlook the absence of the article before the word *angels:* "beings belonging to the category angel." Paul does not mean to designate these or those angels; he wishes to awake within the Church the feeling of its competency and dignity by reminding it that beings of so exalted a nature shall one day be subjected to its jurisdiction.

It is remarkable that in the parables of the tares and

of the drag-net, it is the angels who effect the division between men (wheat and tares, good and bad fishes); while in our passage, it is sanctified believers who judge angels. It seems as if God would glorify Himself in each of these orders of His creatures by means of the other.—Let it also be borne in mind that in Daniel's description (chap. vii.) there is not a word said of the judgment of the angels by the saints; this is a detail absolutely peculiar to Paul, and which, like that mentioned 1 Thess. iv. 15, rests no doubt on a personal revelation.

The last words, *much more things of this life*, need not be regarded as the continuation of the previous question, as is done by Tischendorf; it is the conclusion in the form of an exclamation. The form μήτι γε is found nowhere else in the New Testament. The simplest way of explaining it is to understand the verb λέγωμεν; *né (μή) ullo quidem (γε) modo (τι) de rebus ad vitam pertinentibus (βιωτικά) loquamur;* "Not to speak even of earthly things; they follow *as a matter of course*, after what has been said of angels!" So far as sense is concerned, this is very much the same as our rendering: "much more." The γέ has here, as usually, the effect of emphasizing the preceding word (μήτι), so as to set aside every other supposition.

Ver. 4. "If then ye have judgments of things pertaining to this life, set them *to judge* who are least esteemed in the Church!"—Here is the practical conclusion from the foregoing argument; in its form there is a touch of irony. The μέν already suggests that after what Paul is about to say, he will have something more to add of a graver character: the unsuitableness

T

of law processes in themselves (ver. 6 seq.). It appears to me that the καθίζετε ought to be taken as imperative: "Set up!" as it has been by the old Greek commentators, the *Vulgate*, Calvin, Beza, Bengel, Hofmann, Edwards. "If it is needed to have judgments on earthly things, set up the least of you, those who pass for the least intelligent: they will be good enough for this want." Luther and most moderns (Olshausen, de Wette, Rückert, Meyer, Heinrici) have rejected this sense and taken the verb καθίζετε as interrogative or exclamatory, applying the words, "those who are least esteemed in the Church," to the heathen tribunals before which the Christians of Corinth went to crave justice: "Do you then choose as your judges those who . . . ?" or: "You set up as your judges those who . . . !" This meaning seems to me inadmissible: 1. because of the οὖν, *then*, the natural meaning of which cannot in this case be preserved; 2. the term *set up* cannot, without doing violence to the meaning of the word, signify: to take as judges men already constituted such by others; 3. the phrase, *them who are nothing esteemed in the Church*, cannot in the apostle's view apply to heathen. But Paul may well apply the term with a touch of irony to designate those of whom small account is made in their assemblies: "Do not go and seek your first orators to make them arbiters in such cases, but take the least among you." Ver. 5 very naturally connects itself with this meaning.

Vers. 5, 6. "I speak to your shame: is it so that there is [1] not a wise man among you, no not

---

[1] Instead of ἐστί, which T. R. reads with D E F G, the reading ἔνι is found in א B C L P.

one,¹ that shall be able to judge between his brethren!
6. But brother goeth to law with brother, and that
before the unbelievers."—The first words of ver. 5 may
bear on what precedes; in that case they signify:
"I am certainly not opposed to your choosing capable
men as arbiters; I have only spoken as I have done
(ver. 4) to make you ashamed, by showing how little
importance I attach to those wretched interests for
which you do not scruple to compromise the honour
of the Church." But the following οὕτως takes a
more serious and definite meaning, if the first proposition is connected with what follows, ver. 5:
"*Thus then* — I say this to your shame — in your
Church of wise men, not a wise man capable of
pronouncing on such affairs!" The proper reading
is οὐκ ἔνι (abbreviation of ἔνεστι), *there is not there*.
—The Alex. read: *not a wise man;* the Greco-Lat.:
not a single wise man; the T. R.: *no wise man, not
even one;* the last reading is preferable, at least in
point of sense.—The aorist διακρῖναι here signifies: to
decide summarily, settling the question with a stroke
of the pen. It is a case of arbitration, not a law
process. — The expression ἀνὰ μέσον τοῦ ἀδελφοῦ is
evidently incomplete; the ἀνὰ μέσον, *between*, supposes
a regimen formed of two terms: between a brother
(the plaintiff) and his brother (the accused); comp.
Gen. xvi. 5; Ex. xi. 7 and xxvi. 33 (in the LXX.).
Either the second term was understood, or it might
be supposed that by an elliptical form of the word
his brother was put for: "*the claim* of his brother."

¹ T. R. with L reads σοφος ουδε τις; א B C Or.: ουδεις σοφος; F G P:
ενδι τις σοφος.

The word διακρῖναι, to *distinguish, decide,* would then signify: to separate between the true and the false in this claim. In any case the meaning is: "No law pleading! The word of an arbiter, let that be final!" In this mode of expression there is a sort of disdain for the object of contention.

Ver. 6 is the exclamatory conclusion of the foregoing development. The ἀλλά is not a particle of gradation; it is simply the *but* adversative. To understand the contrast which it marks, we must take exact account of the difference in meaning and tense between the two verbs of ver. 5 and ver. 6, διακρῖναι and κρίνεσθαι. The former denotes the summary verdict of an arbiter: hence the aorist; the latter puts us face to face with all the lengthy processes and windings of a lawsuit: hence the present. — And that with a brother and before a heathen tribunal! What a scandal! what a shame to the Church!

Vers. 7–11.

Provisionally the apostle had passed over in silence the fact itself of the discussion of selfish interests between Christians, to condemn only their having recourse to the judicial intervention of heathen. In the first words of ver. 6, only, he had touched the deeper evil, that of such disputes at all between brethren. He now comes to this sin, the first occasion and cause of the other.

Vers. 7, 8. "Nay, already [1] it is altogether a defect

---

[1] T. R. reads οὖν (*therefore*) after ἤδη μέν, with A B C E L P Syr^{sch}; this word is omitted by ℵ D.

in you¹ that ye have lawsuits one with another. Why not rather take wrong? why not rather be defrauded? 8. Nay but ye yourselves do wrong and defraud, and that² your brethren!"—Here is the second charge which he brings against them, the fact of lawsuits in themselves. This charge essentially includes two. The ἤδη μέν, *already*, indicates the one; the ἀλλά of ver. 8 the other. And first, ver. 7, it is bad to have a lawsuit about a wrong which one considers to have been done to him by a brother. Why not bear a wrong? The *therefore* of the T. R. has no meaning; it ought to be suppressed.—The term ἥττημα, from ἡττᾶσθαι, *to remain beneath*, denotes a defeat when it is used in reference to a fight, and a deterioration or deficiency when applied to a state of things. The latter is the only meaning which is suitable here. There is a moral deficiency among them on this point compared with what they should be as Christians; ὅλως, *in general;* that is to say: "without dwelling longer on the particular fact which I have condemned above." We must certainly reject ἐν, *among*, before ὑμῖν, *you*: "It is a deficiency *on your part*, pertaining to you." —The reflex pronoun ἑαυτῶν is used here as it often is instead of the reciprocal pronoun ἀλλήλων; this form brings out the close solidarity in consequence of which a brother pleading against a brother pleads in a sense against himself.—The two questions which close the verse justify the idea expressed by the word ἥττημα. There is a defect in acting thus; for there is something better to be done: viz. to bear. There is there-

---

[1] The ἐν of T. R. is found only in the Mnn.
[2] T. R. reads ταυτα (*these things*), with L; all the rest: τουτο (*this*).

fore a lack of charity. Paul himself says, xiii. 4: "Charity suffereth long." Μᾶλλον, *rather;* that is to say, rather than enter into a lawsuit. Paul does not say that a Christian should do nothing to secure himself against injustice. But if it must come to a lawsuit, he advises *rather* to bear the wrong. Is he alluding to the precepts of Jesus in His Sermon on the Mount, Matt. v. 39-42? It seems very probable. The thought which Jesus undoubtedly meant to express in these paradoxical forms is this: Love, infinite as God, is ready, so far as itself is concerned, to bear everything. If therefore in practice it sets limits to this absolute patience, it is not from regard to itself, as if its endurance were at an end; but it is for the good of that very being with whom it has to do, so that it is in this case its own limit, in other words, it has no limit outside of itself.—The two verbs ἀδικεῖσθαι and ἀποστερεῖσθαι are in the Middle: to let oneself be wronged; to let oneself be robbed. The former refers to injustices in general, the latter to wrongs in regard to property.

Ver. 8. But there is more: to account for a lawsuit, there is needed something else than the lack of charity on the one hand; there must be a graver want still on the other, the want of justice. To speak of maltreated, robbed, is to speak of maltreating, robbing. Hence the gradation expressed by ἀλλά: *But much more!* The ὑμεῖς, *ye,* coming first, expresses indignation: "It is ye, Christians, who . . . !" The, *and that,* indicates a new gradation: the want of justice betrays a more odious character when it assails one nearer our heart, a brother!—It is easy to see why certain copyists have substituted ταῦτα (the two acts mentioned) for τοῦτο.—It really seemed that the Corinthians, since they had received grace, thought themselves freed from all moral responsibility; it is this dangerous security which the apostle attacks in what follows.

Vers. 9, 10. "Or know ye not that the unrighteous shall not inherit the kingdom of God? Be not deceived: neither fornicators, nor idolaters, nor adulterers, nor effeminate, nor abusers of themselves with mankind, 10. nor thieves, nor covetous, nor [1] drunkards, nor revilers, nor extortioners shall [2] inherit the kingdom of God." — The particle ἤ, *or*, signifies, as it usually does in this formula: "Or, if you think you can act thus without danger . . . ." The Corinthians seemed to imagine that their religious knowledge and Christian talk would suffice to open heaven to them, whatever their conduct otherwise might be. But how do they fail to understand that by falling back into sin, from which faith had rescued them, they themselves destroy the effect of their transition from heathenism to the gospel?—The *unrighteous* are placed first and separately named; for righteousness is the matter now in question (ver. 8).— The notion of the *kingdom of God* is here taken in the eschatological sense, that is to say, from the standpoint of the final consummation of this Divine state of things; and the verb κληρονομεῖν, *to inherit*, is an allusion to the inheritance of Canaan given to Israel as

---

[1] א A C P read ον, instead of ούτε (*nor*), which is the reading of T. R. with B D E L Syr.

[2] T. R. with L P here reads ων, which is rejected by all the rest.

a type of the blessedness to come.—The μὴ πλανᾶσθε, *do not deceive yourselves*, shows clearly that seductive arguments were in circulation by which the vicious succeeded in quieting their consciences.—The warning is generalized, as in chap. v. 9–11. The first five terms in the following enumeration relate more or less directly to the vice of impurity; the following five to the spoliation of another's goods.—Idolatry was closely connected with licentiousness in morals (see on chap. v. 11).—The effeminate, μαλακοί, are either those who give themselves up to some unnatural vice, or all in general who pamper their body; *abusers of themselves*, ἀρσενοκοῖται, are those who give themselves over to monstrous vices (Rom. i. 27). There is in the latter term the idea of activity; in μαλακοί rather that of passivity.

Ver. 10. The apostle closes the enumeration with ἅρπαγες, *extortioners;* this last term leads back to the principal subject of the whole passage, the ἀδικεῖν and the ἀποστερεῖν. — In one of the last terms, for οὔτε, *nor*, the apostle substitutes οὐ, *not*, as if the feeling of repulsion rose in him with the accumulation of terms: "No, in spite of all your reasonings, it will be of no avail! The drunkard shall not enter . . ."—The kingdom of God is a holy state of things, it receives none but sanctified members.

Ver. 11. "And such were some of you, but ye are washed, but ye are sanctified, but ye are justified in the name of the [1] Lord Jesus Christ,[2] and by the Spirit of our God."—Paul has been addressing the feeling of fear; he now appeals to the higher motive, that of

---

[1] B C P add ἡμῶν (*our*). [2] T. R. omits Χριστοῦ (*Christ*), with A L.

Christian honour. He thus returns to the feeling which had dictated the first word of the passage, τολμᾷ τις, *has any one the courage?*—The vices he has just enumerated belong to a past from which a series of Divine facts have separated them for ever. These facts are, first, baptism, then the consecration and reconciliation to God of which baptism is the symbol. Such a fathomless depth of grace is not to be recrossed!—Καί, *and* it is true.—There is in the verb ἦτε, *ye were*, more than the recalling of polluting acts; the term identifies their person with the pollutions to which they gave themselves up.—But, by the τινές, *some*, the apostle restricts the application of his saying, not only in the sense which Reuss ascribes to the words (one who was guilty of *one* of those vices, another of *another*), but so as to bring out that there was, after all, among them a goodly number of men who before their conversion had lived exempt from all those external pollutions. Billroth has made τινές an attribute, and connected it as such with ταῦτα in the contemptuous sense, "such a set of men!" This would have needed ταῦτά τινα, or τοῖοί τινες (Meyer).

The following verbs denote the three acts which constituted the entrance of believers into their new state. They are joined together by the ἀλλά of gradation: *but moreover* (2 Cor. vii. 11); from which it does not follow that the order in which these acts are placed is necessarily one of chronological succession, it may equally be one of moral gradation. For the apostle's intention is to bring out by each stroke, with more and more marked emphasis, the contrast between the former state of believers and the new state into which these acts had brought them.

All are at one in applying the first of the three verbs to *baptism*. In fact, outwardly speaking, it was the act which had transferred them from the state of heathens to that of Christians, from the condition of beings polluted and condemned to that of beings pardoned and purified. The Middle form of the verb ἀπελούσασθε, *ye washed yourselves*, expresses the freedom and spontaneity with which they had done the deed; comp. the ἐβαπτίσαντο, x. 2 (in the reading of the *Vatic.*); Edwards also compares Acts xxii. 16.— The term *bathe, wash*, is explained by the two following terms. Baptism, when it is done in faith, is not a pure symbol; two purifying graces are connected with it, *sanctification* and *justification*. The verbs which express these two facts are in the passive; for they signify two Divine acts, of which the baptized are the subjects. The two verbs in the aorist can only refer both of them to a deed done once for all, and not to a continuous state. This is what prevents us from applying the term *sanctify* to the growing work of Christian sanctification. This word here can only designate the initial act whereby the believer passed from his previous state of corruption to that of holiness, that is to say, the believer's consecration to God in consequence of the gift of the Spirit bestowed on him in baptism; comp. Acts ii. 38; 2 Cor. i. 21, 22; Eph. i. 13. They entered thereby into the community of saints which is presided over by Jesus Christ, the Holy One of God.—The verb *sanctify* is placed before *justify*, because, as Edwards says: " Paul, wishing to contrast the present moral condition of believers with their former state, lays special emphasis on the characteristic of sanctification." This is also the feature which most directly applies to the passage vers. 7–10.—From the fact that the term *justify* is placed second, many, even Meyer, have concluded that it could not here have its ordinary Pauline meaning, and that instead of imputed righteousness it must denote exceptionally the internal righteousness which God infuses into the hearts of believers during the course of their life. But this meaning is, whatever Meyer may say, incompatible with the use of the aorist (ye *were* justified), a tense which necessarily denotes the initial moment of the new state of righteousness, the transition from the state of corruption to that of regeneration. Besides, it would be impossible to distinguish from this point of view the meaning of the two acts sanctifying and justifying, and to understand how they could be joined, or rather contrasted, with one another by an ἀλλά of gradation: *but moreover.* It is therefore, also, wholly mistaken when Catholic theologians, and even Protestants, like Beck, make use of this passage to deny the notion of justification as the imputation of righteousness in Paul's writings. When an entire dogmatic view is thus made to rest on the succession of two terms, it should be remembered that the inverse order is given in i. 30. We have already indicated the reason why Paul emphasizes sanctification in the first place: it is to point out clearly the contrast between the normal state of the Christian and the degrading vices which were invading the Church; comp. i. 2. But thereafter he feels the need of ascending to the hidden foundation of this sanctifying action of the gospel, to the state of justification in which the believer is put by it. The question at the outset of the passage was whether Christians did not possess in themselves the standard of righteousness, by means of which they might regulate their mutual differences. From this point of view Paul had called the heathen οἱ ἄδικοι, *the unrighteous*. By closing with the idea of the justification bestowed on believers, he points to them as the true possessors of righteousness, first in their relation to God, and thereby in all the relations of life.

But what is it that gives to baptism such efficacy, that, when it is celebrated with faith, it is accompanied with such graces, and draws a line of demarcation so profound between two states in the believer's life? The apostle indicates the answer in the last words of the verse: *in the name of the Lord Jesus and by the Spirit of our God*. It seems to me that there is an unmistakable allusion in these words to the formula of baptism: " In the name of the Father, of the Son, and of the Holy Spirit." In the two passages we find the three names whose invocation constitutes the peculiar characteristic of this institution.—The construction of the sentence does not allow us to apply the first of these clauses exclusively to the one of the last two verbs, the other to the other (Flatt). It seems to me equally impossible to connect them both with the last verb, as Rückert and Meyer propose. I think that both together apply to the first verb, ἀπελούσασθε, *ye were washed*, and therefore to the two following verbs, which, as we have seen, are merely epexegetical of the first. As this verb expressly points to the ceremony of baptism, these two subordinate clauses reproduce the formula of invocation which was pronounced when the rite was celebrated. The *name of Jesus* denotes the revelation of His person and work, which has been granted to the Church. It is because of this knowledge that the Church carries out this act of spiritual purification on those whom it receives as its members.—The *Spirit* of God is the creative breath which accomplishes the new birth in the heart of the man baptized, and thus separates him from the pollutions of his past life. I cannot possibly understand why Meyer alleges that this second clause cannot apply to the verb ἀπελούσασθε as well as the first. Is not the action of the Spirit in the heart of the baptized, whereby he deposits in it the principle of consecration, the purifying act by way of excellence? (Titus iii. 5). By adding *of our God*, the apostle expresses the idea of the fatherly and filial relation formed by Christ between God and the Church, and in virtue of which He communicates to it His Spirit. The apostle never fails, while paying homage to the two Divine agents, Christ and the Spirit, to ascend to the supreme source of all this salvation, even God, who reveals Himself in Jesus, and gives Himself by the Spirit.—Hofmann has taken the strange fancy to connect these two clauses with ver. 12: "In the name of Christ, and by the Holy Spirit, all things are lawful to me." But if the maxim, *All things are lawful to me*, had been qualified from the first in this way, Paul would not have needed to limit its application afterwards, as he does on two successive occasions, and by two different restrictions in ver. 12 (see Meyer).

The formula of baptism in the Apostolic Church.

The idea has often been expressed, that the formula of baptism in the Apostolic Church was not yet that which is mentioned Matt. xxviii. 19 : " In the name of the Father, of the Son, and of the Holy Spirit," and that it was limited to the invocation of the *name of Jesus* (Acts ii. 38, viii. 16, x. 48, xix. 5). The passage which we have been studying does not appear to me to favour this view. For, as we have pointed out, the mention of the three Divine names contained in the formula Matt. xxviii. 19, is supposed by the terms used by the Apostle Paul. The idea even of God as Father seems implied in the pronoun ἡμῶν, *our* God.—There is another fact which seems to me to confirm this result; that which is related Acts xix. 1–6. Paul asks some disciples who have not yet heard speak of the Holy Spirit: "in what (εἰς τί) then (οὖν) they have been baptized?" The logical relation, expressed by *then*, between the ignorance of those persons in regard to the Holy Spirit and the apostle's question regarding the baptism which they have received, would not be intelligible if the mention of the Holy Spirit had not been *usual* in baptism as it was celebrated by the Apostolic Church. Now if the name of Jesus and that of the Holy Spirit were solemnly pronounced in baptism, that of God could not be wanting. Hence I conclude that the phrase : *to baptize in the name of Jesus*, frequently used in the Acts, is an abridged form to denote Christian baptism in general. This conclusion is confirmed by the fact that in the *Teaching of the Twelve Apostles* the Trinitarian formula found in Matthew is used side by side with the abridged form of the Acts; comp. vii. 1 and ix. 5.

IV.

Impurity (VI. 12–20).

It has sometimes been imagined that the apostle was here resuming the subject of chap. v., from which he had allowed himself to be diverted by the question of lawsuits. But we have seen that the subject of chap. v.

was not impurity at all, but discipline, treated in connection with a case of impurity. Lawsuits followed, by a transition which we have explained (vi. 1). And now Paul continues to treat of the moral disorders which he knows to exist in the Church. If the manner in which he enters on the subject in ver. 12 has been thought somewhat abrupt, it is because account has not been taken of the connection between the maxim: *All things are lawful to me*, and the warning of ver. 9 : *Be not deceived.* It is perfectly obvious that some at Corinth were indulging in strange illusions as to the consequences of salvation by grace, and even went the length of putting the practice of vice under the patronage of the principle of Christian liberty.—Neander has thought that in beginning as he does in ver. 12, the apostle proposed immediately to treat the subject of meats consecrated to idols, a subject in connection with which he repeats (x. 23) the same maxim, and that he was led away from the second part of ver. 13 to deal with impurity, to resume the subject of offered meats later (chaps. viii.-x.). The truth involved in this view is, that from this point the idea of Christian liberty is that which prevails to the close of chap. x. ; comp. Holsten, *Ev. des Paulus*, p. 293. But the order in which the subjects are linked to one another in this Epistle is the fruit of too serious reflection to allow us to hold such an interruption. And the relation which we have just pointed out between ver. 12 and vers. 9 and 10, where impurity holds the first rank in the enumeration of the vices mentioned, shows clearly that the apostle knew the goal at which he was aiming.

Ver. 12. " All things are lawful unto me, but all

things are not expedient ; all things are lawful for me, but I will not be brought under the power of any."— Paul himself had no doubt uttered this maxim at Corinth more than once : " All things are lawful to me," applying it to acts indifferent in themselves, but which the Mosaic law had forbidden, on account of its pedagogic nature. When the question was as to the use of certain meats, or observance of certain days, or any other external prescription, the apostle said without scruple in such a case : " All is lawful to me." This saying had not been forgotten ; it suited only too well the free disposition of the Greek mind. And perhaps the perverted application which certain members of the Church made of it was ascribed even to the apostle himself. Did this maxim figure in the letter which the Corinthians had addressed to him ? In any case, there is something striking in the repetition of the words in our verse ; it is intended to stigmatize the abuse of the dictum stupidly employed to justify evil. —Paul therefore means : "All things are lawful undoubtedly, and I have no thought of retracting what I have said." Then follow two restrictions which have a touch of irony : " All is lawful to me . . ., unless indeed it be doing evil to myself or my neighbour by the use of my liberty." The term συμφέρειν, *to contribute to the good*, is completed (x. 23) by οἰκοδομεῖν, *to edify ;* there accordingly it applies to good in general, while οἰκοδομεῖν applies specially to the good of our neighbour. Here the good of our neighbour is not in question, but that of the acting subject himself; the following proposition brings out another and more special trait. Then the apostle repeats the same dictum, as if to ridicule the unintelligent and mechanical use of it; and he limits its application by the second restriction, which applies, like the first, to the individual himself: "All is lawful to me, unless it be using my liberty to the extent of alienating it." There is an evident connection between the word ἔξεστι, *is lawful*, and the term ἐξουσιασθήσομαι, *I will let myself be brought under the power*. The regimen ὑπό τινος is certainly neuter: "by *anything;*" not, "by *any one.*" The reference is to everything which is included in the πάντα, *all things*, which precedes.—The pronoun μοι, *to me*, is used as in v. 12, to give the proposition the force of an axiom: *Vim habet gnomes*, says Bengel. Similarly the ἐγώ, *I*, used in the following proposition: I no longer really possess that which possesses me. This saying of the apostle reminds us of the adage of the Stoics: *Mihi res, non me rebus submittere conor*. Paul here puts himself at the standpoint of simple common sense. The reasonable use of my liberty cannot go the length of involving my own loss of it, or of rendering me a slave by reducing me to a thing. Thus Paul has beaten the adversary on his own ground. He has brought him to contradict himself by showing him that his principle, applied without discernment, is self-destructive. The second restriction: "I will not make myself the slave of anything," is developed in vers. 13–16.

Vers. 13, 14. "Meats are for the belly, and the belly for meats, and God shall destroy both it and them. But the body is not for fornication; but for the Lord, and the Lord for the body. 14. Now God hath raised up the Lord, and will also raise up[1] us[2] by His power."—Several commentators have thought that the contrast set up by Paul in these two verses, between the act of eating and the impure use of the body, was called forth by certain statements in the letter of the Corinthians, in which they justified this vice by assimilating it to the other bodily wants, such as that of eating and drinking. Rückert has combated this opinion, for the reason that the Church could not have gone the length of systematically justifying vice; and besides, would not Paul have repelled such an assertion with the liveliest indignation? But without any allusion to the letter of the Corinthians, he might say: "All is lawful; for, according to the principle laid down by Jesus, it is not what enters into a man that defiles him; this domain of food-taking has nothing in common with moral obligation and our eternal future; but it is wholly otherwise with impurity."—The apostle distinguishes two opposite elements in our bodily organism: the organs of nutrition, which serve for the support of the body, and to which, by a Divinely established correlation, there correspond the external objects which serve as meats. The morally indifferent character of this domain appears from the fact of its approaching destruction: God will abolish those functions in the day of the redemption of our bodies. But it is not so with our bodies strictly so called, with the body for which Paul exclusively reserves the name, and which he identifies with our very personality. This is the

---

[1] The T. R. with ℵ C E K L reads ἐξεγερεῖ (*will raise up*); A D P Q: ἐξεγείρει (*raises up*); B: ἐξήγειρεν (*raised up*).

[2] The ὑμᾶς (*you*) of the T. R. is a simple error.

permanent element in our earthly organism, that which forms the link between our present and our future body. Now this element, the essential form of our personality, is that which is involved in the vice of impurity. And hence the profound difference between impurity and the natural functions of physical life. There exists between our body and the Lord Jesus Christ a moral relation analogous to the material and temporary relation which exists between the stomach and meats. The body is *for Christ*, to belong to Him and serve Him, and Christ is *for the body*, to inhabit and glorify it.

Ver. 14. In consequence of this sublime relation, the body will not perish. As God raised up Christ, He will also raise the body which has become here below the property and sanctified organ of Christ. The apostle says, "will raise *us* also;" he thus expressly identifies our personality with the body which is to be its eternal organ.—The readings *raises* and *raised* are evidently erroneous. The former would be the present of the idea, which does not suit here; the latter would refer to the spiritual resurrection (Eph. ii. 5, 6), which is stranger still to the context. The idea of the future resurrection of this earthly body, like to that in which Christ lived, is fitted to impress us with the reverence due to the future organ of our glorified personality.— The last words, *by His power*, perhaps allude to some doubts in regard to the possibility of the fact.—It is remarkable that Paul here places himself in the number of those who *shall rise again*, as elsewhere he ranks himself with those who shall be *changed* at Christ's coming again. He had no fixed idea on this point, and he could have none, the day of Christ's coming being to him unknown.

Ver. 15. "Know ye not that your[1] bodies are the members of Christ? Shall I then take the members of Christ, and make them the members of an harlot? Let it not be so!"—Paul had just said that the body is not for fornication, but for the Lord. In the first proposition of this verse he justifies the *for the Lord*, to deduce from it as a conclusion in the second the *not for fornication*. Baur and Scherer see here a *petitio principii*, inasmuch as the term *harlot* already implies the guiltiness of fornication, which is precisely the point to be proved. But the apostle is not treating the question from the standpoint of rational morality; he starts from Christian premises: *Know ye not . . . ?* Now the relation between Christ and the believer, implied in faith, gives him logically the right to reason as he does.—As the Church in its totality is the body of Christ, that is to say, the organism which He animates with His Spirit, and by which He carries out His wishes on the earth, so every Christian is a member of this body, and consequently an organ of Christ Himself. By means of the Spirit of Christ which dwells in his spirit, and by means of his spirit which directs his soul and thereby his body, this body becomes as it were the body of Christ, the executor of His thought; hence the practical conclusion: This organ of Christ must not be taken from Him to be given to a harlot. Therein is a double crime: on the one hand, a revolt, an odious abduction ($ἄρας$); on the other, an act of ignoble self-debasement and the ac-

---

[1] א A read $ἡμῶν$ (*our* bodies).

ceptance of a shameful dependence. And hence the apostle's cry of indignation : *Let it not be so !*—Ποιήσω, perhaps the deliberative subjunctive aorist: "Shall I choose to make . . . ?" or simply the future indicative : "Shall I make?" The second meaning is better: one does not deliberate in regard to such an act.—But do not the expressions, "members of Christ" and "members of an harlot," contain something of exaggeration? This is what the light-minded Corinthians might ask, and it is to this objection that vers. 16 and 17 give answer.

Vers. 16, 17. "Or[1] know ye not that he which is joined to an harlot is one body [with her]; for the two, it is said, shall be one flesh. 17. And he that is joined unto the Lord is one spirit [with Him]."—The ἤ, *or*, is certainly authentic; as always it signifies, "Or indeed, if you deny what I have just said, are you then ignorant that . . . ?" The proof of the truth of the expression used (*members of an harlot*) is given by means of the Biblical words, Gen. ii. 24. Are these words in the narrative of Genesis the continuation of Adam's discourse, or a remark added by the author himself, as happens in several other cases (Gen. x. 9, xv. 6, xxxii. 32; see Hofmann)? It matters little; for the declaration can have value in the eyes of the sacred historian only in so far as it is the expression of a Divine truth.—The reg. *with her* is omitted in Greek after the word *one body*. This ellipsis arises from the fact that the nominative ὁ κολλώμενος and the dative τῇ πόρνῃ are morally regarded as forming one and the same logical subject of the proposition. The words

---

[1] D E K L 50 Mnn. omit the η (*or*) before ουκ.

οἱ δύο, *the two*, were added to the original text by the LXX., whom St. Paul here follows.—The subject of the verb φησίν, *says he*, may be either Adam, or Moses, or Scripture, or God Himself; or finally, as is shown by Heinrici, the verb may be a simple formula of quotation like our: *It is said.* This form is frequently found in Philo.—The expression *one flesh* finds its confirmation in the extraordinary fact that from this union there may proceed a new personality. Therein is contained, for the reflecting mind, the undeniable proof of the profoundly mysterious character of such a union; it appears like the continuation of the creative act.

Ver. 17 is not, as has sometimes been thought, foreign to the argument as a whole. As ver. 16 justifies by a Biblical quotation the strong expression of ver. 15: "Shall I make them the members of an harlot?" so ver. 17, framed as it were on the words of Genesis, justifies the equally strong expression of ver. 15: "Taking the members of Christ;" comp. xv. 45.—We again find here the ellipsis of ver. 16; the "with Him" is understood after the words *one spirit*, as if to say that the believer's union with Christ culminates in the existence of one and the same spirit, and consequently in the possession and direction by Christ of the believer's whole person, soul and body.— According to Holsten (p. 466 seq.), the assimilation of these two unions is so untenable logically, that vers. 15–17 can only be an ancient gloss intended to remove the obscurity of ver. 13. I think it is better to seek to penetrate the depth of the apostolic thought than arbitrarily to recompose the text according to our own ideas.

Under the sway of this holy view (ver. 17), the apostle, at the thought of the crime of fornication, utters, as it were, a cry of horror (ver. 18ᵃ); then he finishes his demonstration.

Ver. 18. "Flee fornication! Every sin that a man doeth is without his body; but he that committeth fornication sinneth against his body."—Anselm has well expressed the meaning of the first sentence of the verse: "If we must *fight against* other sins, we must *flee from* fornication;" witness Joseph's example.—The asyndeton betrays the apostle's emotion.

Thus far (vers. 13-17) the thought developed by Paul had been that of the *dependence* arising from impure intercourse: "I shall not make myself the *slave* of anything" (ver. 12^b). For a man to give to a degraded person a right over him by such a union, is not this to place himself in the most ignoble kind of dependence? From this point Paul passes to the development of the first thought of ver. 12: "All things are not *expedient*," and he shows the injury which the fornicator inflicts on his own body.—He here enunciates a distinction between fornication and other sins, which it is difficult to understand. How are passion, falsehood, intemperance, suicide, sins committed *without the body*, while fornication is one in the body? Rückert and de Wette acknowledge their inability to find a meaning for this contrast; Calvin and Neander see in it no other idea than that of the greater guiltiness which attaches to the sin of fornication. According to Meyer, Paul means that in other sins some external matter is necessary, while fornication proceeds entirely from within. Hofmann, after criticising those different explanations, gives one which is stranger still, and almost unintelligible: The man who commits any other sin does not keep in his body the matter of his sin (the drunkard, the suicide); while the impure person makes his very body the subject of his sin, and continues in his bodily life identified with the being to which he has given himself.—It seems to me that the contrast stated by Paul is to be explained only from the point of view at which ver. 13 placed us. The apostle means to speak of the body strictly so called, of the body in the body; he contrasts this living and life-giving organism with the external and purely physical organism. We possess a material body, the matter of which is being perpetually renewed; but under this changing body there exists a permanent type, which constitutes its identity. In chap. xv. 50, where Paul is teaching the resurrection of the body, he declares that "flesh and blood cannot inherit the kingdom of God." He therefore distinguishes between the organism composed of flesh and blood, which forms the outward wrapping of the man, and the body strictly so called, one with the person which animates this wrapping. It is the same distinction as we have found in vers. 13, 14 of our chapter. Now it is to this inner body that the sin of the fornicator penetrates; it is by and against this inner organism that he sins, while other sins only reach its wrapping, the external body. The εἰς, in so far as it is contrasted with the prep. ἐκτός, *outside of*, ought to signify *in*; but it differs nevertheless from the simple ἐν, *in*, in that it also denotes the *injury* which the body receives from it; hence the meaning of *against* which is added to that of *in.* Thus we understand the οὐ συμφέρει of ver. 1. Yet bodily injury is not the thing of which Paul is thinking. The sequel shows in what the punishment consists. The body thus profaned had a sublime destiny, and of this it is deprived by the violence done to it.

Vers. 19, 20. "Or know ye not that your body[1] is the temple of the Holy Spirit which is in you, and which ye have of God? And ye are not your own; 20. for ye are bought with a price; therefore glorify God in your body."[2]—The ἤ, *or*, signifies, "Or if you deny the fatal violence done to your body by fornication, you are ignorant of the holy dignity to which it is destined, and of which it is deprived by this sin. The fornicator sins and robs his body of the honour of being the temple of God."—According to Rom. viii. 11, the presence of the Holy Spirit in the believer is the pledge of a glorious resurrection for his body. To renounce this dignity of being a temple and organ of the Holy Spirit by the fact of fornication, is therefore to expose himself to lose this resurrection.—The phrase, *which ye have*, or, *which ye hold from God*, is intended to emphasize strongly the superhuman origin of that Spirit whom the believer receives, and the dignity of the body in which this Divine Guest comes to dwell. We must not translate: which ye have *by* God, as if ὑπό were used; ἀπό denotes the origin and essence.— It would not be unnatural to make the last proposition, *And ye are not your own*, also dependent on the inter-

---

[1] L Cop. and several Fathers read τα σωματα υμων (*your bodies*).

[2] T. R. with K L P Syr. here adds: και εν τω πνευματι υμων ατινα εστι του θεου (*and in your spirit, which are God's*).

rogative verb, *Know ye not that* . . . *?* But Hofmann rightly objects that the ὅτι would require to be repeated. It must therefore be regarded as a forcible affirmation: "And (because of the communication of the Spirit) ye do not any more belong to yourselves, and have consequently no longer right to dispose of your body at will." And this taking possession of the believer by the Holy Spirit is not only an act of power on God's part, it is founded on right. This is what is explained by the first proposition of the following verse.

Ver. 20. The taking possession is legitimate; for there was the payment of a purchase price. We must not therefore translate: "bought at a *great* price." The greatness of the price does not matter here. It is the fact of payment only which Paul would emphasize.—The particle δή is untranslateable; it implies the perfect evidence, and consequently urgency, of the fulfilment of the duty mentioned.— The phrase *glorify God* does not signify merely: not to dishonour Him; it means to display positively in the use of our body the glory and especially the holiness of the heavenly Master who has taken possession of our person. Man has lost, in whole or part, since his fall, the feeling which was so to speak the guardian of his body, that of natural modesty. Faith restores to it a more elevated guardian: self-respect as being bought by Christ the organ of the Spirit and temple of God. This is modesty raised henceforth to the height of holiness. — The words which follow in the T. R., *and in your spirit* . . ., are an interpolation added with a liturgical and hortatory aim.

The three essential ideas of the passage are therefore :—

1. That the use of Christian liberty as respects the body is naturally restricted by the danger of using that liberty so as to alienate it and destroy ourselves.

2. That fornication involves the Christian in a degrading physical solidarity, incompatible with the believer's spiritual solidarity with Christ.

3. That it renders the body unfit for its Christian dignity as a temple of God, and so for its glorious destination.

It appears from this entire development that contempt of the body goes side by side with abuse of the body, while respect for the body will always be the best means of ruling it. And so the whole of Scripture, from the first page of Genesis to the last of Revelation, pays homage to the dignity of the human body.

V.

MARRIAGE AND CELIBACY (CHAP. VII.).

Some commentators begin the second part of the Epistle here. According to them, the apostle up to this point answered the reports which had been made to him *viva voce* (i. 11 and v. 1); now he takes up the letter of the Corinthians to answer the questions it contains. It is certain that in ver. 1 the subject which he proceeds to treat is presented in reply to a question which had been addressed to him. A similar formula occurs viii. 1, xii. 1, xvi. 1, 12; and it is natural to hold that in each of these cases it introduces a subject raised by the letter of the Corinthians. Nevertheless the difference between verbal reports and epistolary communications would be too external to have determined the general arrangement of our Epistle. It is impossible to overlook a moral relation between the matter about to be treated in this chap. vii. and that of fornication, treated in the second half of chap. vi. It is easy to establish a still closer connection with what precedes. In ver. 12 of chap. vi. there had been put the question of Christian liberty and its limits. It was from this point of view that the apostle had treated the subject of fornication. Now the question of marriage (chap. vii.), as well as that of sacrificed meats (chaps. viii.–x.), and even, up to a certain point, that of the behaviour of women in meetings for worship (chap. xi.), all belong to this same domain. If then it is true that the apostle here passes to the questions put to him by the Corinthians, it must be acknowledged, on the other hand, that he does not do so without establishing a logical and moral connection between the different subjects which he treats in succession.

The questions examined in this chapter, the preference to be accorded to celibacy or marriage, as well as others subordinate to it, must have been discussed at Corinth, since the apostle's advice was asked about them. There were therefore in the Church partisans of celibacy and defenders of marriage. Did this division coincide in any way with that of the different parties? The attempt has been made to prove this. Schwegler regards the admirers of celibacy as Judeo-Christians of Essenian tendency, and identifies them with the party of Peter. But Peter himself was married (ix. 5; Mark i. 30). Others — Ewald, Hausrath, for example — have supposed that they were members of the party which designated itself *those of Christ*, and that they alleged against marriage the example of Jesus. But this example was too exceptional; and in any case Paul would have required to rebut this argument. The general current of the Jewish mind recommended and glorified marriage. We might therefore take them to be members of the Pauline party, who rested their argument on the apostle's example, and on some mistaken saying which he had uttered during his stay at Corinth. But there is nothing in chap. vii. leading to this supposition.—Grotius thought that the opponents of marriage at Corinth were men of culture, who, influenced by certain sayings of the Greek philosophers, regarded marriage as a vulgar state and one contrary to man's independence. But the apostle in his answer makes no allusion to such an idea, and the sayings of the Greek sages, which might be quoted, have rather the effect of whimsical utterances called forth by the troubles of family life, than of a serious theory. It seems simpler to hold that the opposition to marriage at Corinth proceeded from a reaction against the licentious manners which reigned in that city. New converts often go beyond the just limit of opposition to the life of nature, and easily lose sight of the Divine basis of human relations. The history of the Christian Church is full of examples of such extreme tendencies. It is easy therefore to understand how among the most serious Christians, especially among Paul's converts, men should be found, who, disgusted with all that belonged to the relations between the two sexes, proclaimed the superiority of the celibate life.

It was certainly one of the most delicate tasks for him whom God had called, not only to create the Church among the Gentiles, but also to direct its first steps in the new way which opened before it, to show the young Churches what they ought to reject and what they might preserve of their former life. So we shall see in this very chapter the apostle enlarging the question, and applying the solution which he gives in regard to marriage to other social relations in connection with which analogous difficulties were raised. The apostle needed all the wisdom which God had bestowed on him when entrusting him with his mission (Rom. xii. 3), and all the natural subtlety of his understanding, to resolve the questions proposed to him, without compromising the future of individuals and of the Church. Thus, as to marriage, he could not forget that the conjugal bond was a Divine institution; he had himself just quoted vi. 16, the saying on which the sacred and exclusive character of this relation rests. But, on the other hand, he contemplated the ideal of a Christian life freed from every bond and wholly consecrated to the service of Christ, and every day he felt from his own experience the value of such a state. The question must therefore have presented itself to his mind in two aspects equally grave, neither of which could be sacrificed to the other, and yet aspects apparently contradictory. The task was thus at once important and difficult.—He begins by treating of the *formation* of the marriage bond, vers. 1-9; then he takes up questions relative to the *loosing* of the bond, vers. 10-24; finally, he deals with the preference to be given to celibacy or marriage in the case of *virgins* and *widows*, vers. 25-40.

VERS. 1-9.

Notwithstanding the intrinsic excellence of celibacy, marriage should be the rule in practice. Such is the general meaning of this first passage.

Vers. 1, 2. "Now concerning the things whereof ye wrote unto me,[1] it is good for a man not to touch a woman; 2. but, to avoid fornication, let every man have his own wife, and let every woman have her own husband."—The form περὶ δέ, *now concerning*, is common in the classics (see Heinrici, p. 60). Paul thereby intimates that he is passing to a new subject, but one which has already been raised. The περὶ ὧν ought certainly to be grammatically expanded in this way: περὶ ἐκείνων περὶ ὧν ἐγράψατέ μοι λέγω τάδε —The δέ, *now*, lightly marks the contrast between the questions which Paul had treated at his own hand and those which were put to him by the letter of the Corinthians.—The pronoun μοί has been added rather than omitted by the copyists; there was no reason for rejecting it.—In what sense are we to take the word καλόν, *it is good?* Jerome, the great partisan of celibacy, took it in the moral sense: "it is *holy* . . .;" and he did not fear to draw from it the conclusion: "If it is good not to touch, then it is bad to touch."

[1] ℵ B C omit μοι (*to me*).

The logic of this argument is by no means unassailable. Anyhow, this consequence does not agree with the true notion of marriage according to St. Paul. To evade it, some have given the word καλόν, *good*, a purely utilitarian sense: " It is *expedient* . . ." And the possibility of this sense seems clearly to result from the comparison of Matt. v. 29 with xviii. 8, where in the same saying of Jesus the term συμφέρειν is used the first time, and καλόν the second. But the question is whether the word συμφέρειν itself has in the mouth of Paul and Jesus a purely utilitarian sense. In any case, it is not so in our Epistle, where, in the passages vi. 12 and x. 23, and in ver. 35 of our chapter, the word συμφέρειν certainly contains the notion of *moral* utility. With stronger reason ought it to be so with the word καλόν. In the well-known epithet καλὸς κἀγαθός, by which the Greeks designated the man every way honourable, man *as he should be* in all respects, the first adjective expressed the idea of beauty linked to that of goodness, the high propriety which distinguishes moral worth. Such, it seems to me, is the notion which the apostle would here express by the word καλόν. He proclaims aloud that the state of celibacy in a man is absolutely becoming and worthy, has nothing in it contrary to the moral ideal. There were assuredly at Corinth persons who maintained the contrary. This first verse has often been taken as a concession: " *No doubt* it is well to . . . *but* " (ver. 2). In this case, Paul must have said: καλὸν μέν. It becomes then a positive declaration, independent of what follows. Thereafter will come the restriction indicated by δέ.—In speaking thus, Paul felt himself supported by a decisive example, that of Jesus Christ, the realization of supreme moral beauty in human form, and moreover by the saying of Jesus, Luke xx. 34, 35: "The children of this world marry and are given in marriage; but they which shall be accounted worthy to obtain that world, and the resurrection from the dead, neither marry nor are given in marriage," a saying from which it followed that the splendour of the ideal shines still more perfectly in the person of the celibate than of the married Christian. No doubt there might have been quoted in objection to the apostle the words of God Himself: "It is not good that man should be alone," οὐ καλὸν εἶναι τὸν ἄνθρωπον μόνον (Gen. ii. 18). But the answer would not have been difficult. The believer who lives in union with Christ is no longer in the same position as the natural man. He has in the Lord that complement of his personal life, which the latter seeks in marriage. — No doubt that does not prove—and St. Paul, we shall see, does not seek to affirm—that celibacy in itself is *holier* than married life. The point in question is one of dignity, propriety. The apostle means simply to assert that there is nothing unbecoming in a man's living in celibacy.— The expression μὴ ἅπτεσθαι, *not to touch*, does not refer, as Rückert has thought, to the conduct of those united in marriage; it is at a later stage (vers. 3–5) that Paul treats this point. He wishes to tranquillize unmarried persons who are uncertain about the line of conduct they have to follow. The expression used is probably borrowed from the letter of the Corinthians. Holsten thinks that the expression also applies to illicit relations. But in chap. vi. Paul had completely exhausted this subject.

After clearly reserving the honourableness of celibacy, Paul passes to the practical truth which he is concerned to establish, the general necessity of marriage. For, as Reuss says, "his object is rather to protest against ascetic exaggerations than to favour them.'

Ver. 2. The δέ is adversative: "*but*, honourable as celibacy is, it should not be the rule." — The plural *fornications* refers to the numerous acts and varied temptations which abounded at Corinth. — When he says, *every man, every woman*, Paul of course understands the exception pointed out in ver. 7, and the case which he will treat specially vers. 25–38 (virgins). — Baur, Rothe, Scherer, Holsten, and even Reuss[1] accuse the apostle of proceeding on a view of marriage much inferior to the moral ideal of the relation. It would seem that he regards it only as a makeshift intended to remove a greater evil. But it is forgotten that the apostle is not here framing a theory of marriage in general; he is answering precise questions which had been put to him, and of whose tendency and tenor we are ignorant. In our very chapter, ver. 14 proves clearly that he knows the moral side of the relation perfectly; the same is true of the words xi. 3, which make marriage the analogue of the most exalted of all things: the relation between Christ and the human soul; nay,

---

[1] "It must be granted that this argument, dictated no doubt by a very laudable prudence, does not reveal a very elevated conception of marriage and of its moral aim."

even of the relation between God and Christ. Reuss acknowledges "that in other Epistles, marriage is spoken of from a less contemptuous point of view;" comp. Eph. v. 25-27. Now, as it is improbable that Paul modified his conception of marriage, and as the passages of our Epistle quoted above show that in fact there is nothing of the kind, it must be concluded that in this exposition the apostle desired to keep strictly within the limits traced out for him by the questions of the Corinthians on the subject. — But still, that marriage may correspond to the end pointed out, the life in this state must be in accordance with its nature. This is the meaning of the vers. 3-5, which are a short digression; after which the apostle follows up in ver. 6 the idea of ver. 2.

Vers. 3-5. "Let the husband render unto the wife her due,[1] and likewise also the wife unto the husband. 4. The wife hath not power of her own body, but the husband; and likewise also the husband hath not power of his own body, but the wife. 5. Defraud ye not one the other, except it be with consent, for a time, that ye may give[2] yourselves to prayer,[3] and come together[4] again, that Satan tempt you not for your incontinency." —The reading of the T. R., *due benevolence,* is a paraphrase substituted for Paul's real words, *the debt,*

---

[1] T. R. with K L Syr. reads την οφειλομενην ευνοιαν (*the due benevolence*); all the other Mjj. It. : την οφειλην (*the debt*).

[2] T. R. with A L : σχολαζητε, instead of σχολασητε, which is the reading of the other Mjj.

[3] Before τη προσευχη (*to prayer*), T. R. with K L Syr. reads : τη νηστεια και (*to fasting and*), which is omitted by the other Mjj. It. Or. and other Fathers.

[4] T. R. with some Mnn. only reads συνερχεσθε ; K L P Syr. : συνερχησθε ; the eight other Mjj. It. Or. : ητε.

with the view of avoiding what might be offensive in the latter in public reading. This verse confirms us in the idea that among some of the Corinthians there existed an exaggerated spiritualistic tendency, which threatened to injure conjugal relations, and thereby holiness of life.

Ver. 4. This verse justifies the direction given in the preceding. By the conjugal bond, each spouse acquires a right over the person of the other. Consequently each alienates a portion of personal independence. Hence precisely the καλόν of celibacy.

Ver. 5. In this verse there is reproduced the direction given in ver. 3, but in a negative form: *Defraud not*, to exclude expressly the contrary opinion, and at the same time to *limit* this prohibition, nevertheless under certain conditions fitted to remove the danger of the restriction. The interruption of the conjugal relations authorized by the apostle may take place on three conditions: 1. mutual consent; 2. temporary duration; 3. the aim of securing spiritual meditation; and the particle εἰ μή τι ἄν, *unless it is*, by which Paul authorizes the exception, is immediately determined by two restrictions, one of which gives it a purely contingent or *doubtful* (ἄν) character, the other a limited (τι) character. — To *prayer* T. R. adds *fasting;* but this is an interpolation arising from later ecclesiastical usages.—The reading συνέρχεσθε or συνέρχησθε, in the Byz. documents, instead of ἦτε, is due to the same cause as the variant of ver. 3.—Among the Jews, also, it was customary to prepare by temporary separation for acts of particular solemnity (Ex. xix. 15; 1 Sam. xxi. 4; comp. Josh. vii. 13, etc.). The spirit, by asserting its dominion over the senses, becomes more conscious of its own proper life, and by this concentration on itself, opens more profoundly to the communications of the higher world.—All these restrictions are suggested to the apostle by a double fear; on the one hand, the natural incontinence of his readers (ἀκρασία from ἀκρατής, one who is not master of himself), and on the other, the working of Satan, who fans carnal desires with his breath, and thus brings about from the smallest occasion the cause of a fall. These occasions were frequent at Corinth; there was one especially, of which the apostle will afterwards speak, participation in idolatrous banquets.

Vers. 6, 7. "Now I speak this by permission, not of commandment. 7. But[1] I wish that all men were even as I myself; yet every man hath his proper gift of God, one[2] after this manner, and another[2] after that."—The remark which the apostle makes in ver. 6 might be applied to the foregoing prohibition: "Defraud not . . . ;" or, as is done by Tertullian, Origen, Jerome, Calvin, to the precept: "that ye come together again." But this precept had been given only accidentally, and the ground for it had been too strongly stated to admit of its being afterwards presented as a simple counsel, and not as a positive rule. Meyer and Beet make this remark bear on the restriction: "Except it be for a time." Meyer paraphrases thus: "If I recommend you to keep apart only for a time, it is not an absolute command I give on the subject, it is

[1] T. R. with B K L P Syr. reads γαρ (*for*), while ℵ A C D F G It. read δε (*now* or *but*).
[2] T. R. reads ος μεν and ος δε with K L, while the rest read ο μεν and ο δε.

a simple counsel. But you may, if you think good, remain in this state of separation, provided it be with common consent." But, in the first place, this meaning is overturned by the same reasons as the preceding, from which it is not essentially different. Then what right have we to separate one of the three conditions (*common consent*) from the other two? Are they not put on exactly the same footing in ver. 5? Far from wishing by ver. 6 to attenuate the importance of the limits traced in ver. 5, the apostle aims, on the contrary, throughout this whole passage to combat a too pronounced ascetic tendency which threatened to prevent marriage, or to turn it aside from the end for which the apostle claims it as a general rule. If it is so, the remark of ver. 6 can only refer, as has been clearly seen by Beza, Grotius, de Wette, Hofmann, to the essential idea of the passage, as stated in ver. 2, and as it is to be restated in a new form in ver. 7: the general duty of marriage. Vers. 3–5 have only been a digression intended to maintain in the normal state the practice of marriage. The apostle now returns to the principal idea (ver. 2): "In speaking as I do, I do not for a moment mean to give you an apostolical command to marry. I give you a simple counsel, founded on the knowledge I have of your weakness."—The verb συγγινώσκειν, *to know with*, denotes the sympathetic feeling with which one appropriates the thought or state of another, condescension, accommodation, and even pardon. The substantive συγγνώμη consequently expresses an advice in which one takes account of circumstances. It was precisely in this sense that the apostle had laid down as a rule the married state.

Ver. 7. The received reading γάρ, *for*, rests on the *Vatic.*, the Peschito, etc. Its meaning is easy: "I certainly did not mean to enjoin you to marry; for my desire is rather . . ." But all the other Mjj., the *Itala*, and several Fathers read δέ, *but*, which is more difficult, and for that very reason more probable, and which can also be justified: "I commit you in general to marriage, *but* that is not my wish, absolutely speaking; on the contrary . . ." It seems as if instead of the indic. θέλω, *I wish*, the optative would have been required. But this would only have expressed a contingent wish, whereas the indicative expresses a real wish of the apostle, though he gives up its fulfilment for reasons independent of his wish. As Osiander observes, the form θέλω has in it something subjective. —Is the phrase, *all men*, which does not signify merely all Christians, as Osiander still thinks, determined by the near prospect of the end of the world? This is unnecessary. Absolutely speaking, Paul can only desire for every man what he has found best for himself; but no doubt on the condition that there be no essential difference between him and others.—From the words, *as I myself*, it may be inferred with certainty that Paul was not married, and quite as certainly that he was not a widower. For how could he have expressed the desire that all men were widowers! See on ver. 8.—The καί, *also*, after *as*, strengthens the idea of the resemblance which he would like to see existing between him and other men (Rom. i. 13; Acts xxvi. 29).

But the preference which Paul gives to celibacy meets with an obstacle in practice. There is a difference among men of which account must be taken.

Jesus had already pointed it out (Matt. xix. 10–12), and He had Himself drawn from the fact the practical consequences relating to the subject before us. There are men whom their natural temperament, in the first place, and then a spiritual grace which takes possession of this particular disposition, render capable of living in the state of celibacy without struggle and without inward pollution. Agreeably to this saying of Jesus, Paul desires that when one has the privilege of possessing the glorious faculty of consecrating himself without encumbrances to the service of God and men, he should not sacrifice it.—The expressions, *one after this manner, and another after that*, denote respectively, aptitude for life in celibacy, and aptitude for married life. It should be observed that these two aptitudes bear, both alike, the name of *gift*, $\chi\acute{a}\rho\iota\sigma\mu a$. And we can thus put our finger on the error into which Reuss falls, when he says: "If abstention, life in celibacy, is a particular gift of God's grace, it is evident that something is wanting to the man who does not possess it." The apostle is innocent of this erroneous conclusion. For he declares that there is not *one* single gift, but *two* different gifts. If the one is the gift of celibacy for the kingdom of God, the other is that of marriage, also for the kingdom of God. Meyer, it is true, alleges that the apostle is here expressing an abstract maxim, and that the two οὕτως, *thus*, do not properly apply either to celibacy or marriage specially. But what matters? If it is a general maxim, it is in any case stated here only with a view to its application to the two positions compared in the passage. Hence it follows that there is no less need of a gift of grace to use marriage Christianly than to live Christianly in celibacy.

In vers. 1–7 Paul laid down two principles: the intrinsic honourableness of celibacy (vers. 1 and 7^a), and the preference which must as a rule be given to marriage (vers. 2 and 7^b). He now draws, vers. 8 and 9, the consequences of these two principles; and first, ver. 8, the consequence from the first; then, ver. 9, that from the second.

Vers. 8, 9. "I say then to the unmarried and widows, it is^1 good for them if they abide even as I. 9. But if they cannot contain, let them marry; for it is better to marry^2 than to burn."—The δέ, *then*, indicates the transition from the grounds to the final sentence.—On καλόν, *good*, see on ver. 1. The αὐτοῖς, *for them*, is remarkable; used without regimen, the word καλόν would have been too absolute; it might have seemed to ascribe a moral superiority to celibacy.—The contrast between ταῖς χήραις, *widows*, and τοῖς ἀγάμοις, *the unmarried*, has led Erasmus, Beza, etc., to regard the latter as embracing only widowers. But there is no ground for thus restricting the meaning of ἄγαμοι; the word naturally comprehends also young unmarried men. On the other hand, Meyer extends the meaning of the word too far when he brings under it also virgins. The latter will have their chapter for themselves (ver. 25 seq.). It would even be altogether unsuitable to apply to them what is said in ver. 9. Why, finally, would the apostle have joined them with unmarried men

---

[1] T. R. with E K L reads ἐστιν (*is*), which is omitted by all the rest.
[2] א A C read γαμεῖν instead of γαμῆσαι, which T. R. reads with all the rest.

and widowers, instead of joining them with widows?
—The reason why widows are mentioned separately, while widowers are confounded with bachelors, is this, widowhood creates, in the case of the woman, a more special position than in that of a man; a widow differs much more socially from a virgin than a widower from a young man. Besides, the masculine χῆρος, *widower*, is in Greek an adjective rather than a substantive, while the opposite is the case with the feminine χήρα, *widow*.—From these last words, *if they abide even as I*, Luther, Grotius, etc., have concluded that Paul must have been a widower, but erroneously. The idea of *abiding* as Paul, according to the true meaning of ἀγάμοι, may embrace perseverance in celibacy, as well as perseverance in the state of widowhood (see on ver. 7). Clement of Alexandria also alleged that Paul was a widower; but it was neither on the ground of a tradition nor on account of this verse. Eusebius cites this Father's opinion (*H. E.*, iii. 24); he justified it by the passage Phil. iv. 3, where he erroneously ascribed to the word σύζυγος the meaning of spouse.[1]

Ver. 9. It is a good thing (καλόν) to remain free from every bond, if one can do so without sinning; but if sin is to be the result, it is better to marry; for sin is an evil, while marriage is not. — The compound word ἐγκρατεύεσθαι includes three ideas: *to possess in oneself* (ἐν) *the power of* (κρατεῖν) *controlling oneself* (the middle form). It is the opposite of the ἀκρασία of ver. 5.— The aor. imper. γαμησάτωσαν, *let them marry*, has something about it abrupt and dry: " Let them marry and

[1] "Paul does not fear, in one of his letters, to address his own wife" (σύζυγον).

have done with it!" The aor. ἐγάμησα in later Greek sometimes takes the place of the primitive aor. ἔγημα, which is found Luke xiv. 20.—The term πυροῦσθαι, *to burn*, does not at all apply to the torments of hell, as Tertullian and Pelagius thought. Paul by this word denotes every painful exercise of soul; comp. 2 Cor. xi. 29; here: the fire of inward lusts in conflict with conscience. Comp. the ἐξεκαύθησαν of Rom. i. 27, notwithstanding the difference of situation.

The fundamental question regarding the formation of the marriage bond is resolved. The apostle now examines the questions relating to the *maintenance* or *breach* of this bond. He here encounters two different positions. The first is that of the married who both belong to the Church (vers. 10, 11); the second, that of the married of whom one only is a Christian (vers. 12-16). There follows an appendix relating to some analogous questions (vers. 17-24).

Vers. 10-24.

Vers. 10-16.

The rules to be followed in the case of two Christian spouses (vers. 10, 11).

Vers. 10, 11. "But unto the already married I command, not I, but the Lord, that the wife depart[1] not from the husband, 11. that if she is parted, she ought to remain unmarried, or be reconciled to her husband, and that the husband do not put away his wife."— The γεγαμηκότες, *married*, are contrasted, on the one hand, with those who are widowers or bachelors (vers. 8, 9), and on the other, with the τοῖς λοιποῖς, *the others*,

[1] T. R. with ℵ B C K L P: χωρισθῆναι; A D E F G: χωρίζεσθαι.

or *the rest* (ver. 12); as these are also married, those of ver. 10 can only be regarded as spouses living in Christian marriage on both sides, and *the others*, of ver. 12, as living in mixed marriage (a Christian spouse with a Jewish or heathen spouse). To understand the apostle's mode of expressing himself, we need only call to mind that this letter was intended to be read in the assembly of the Church; consequently, when the apostle said: "Those who are in the state of marriage" (γεγαμηκότες, the perfect), he could only thereby designate two spouses who were both Christians.—The verb παραγγέλλω, *I command*, sometimes includes, along with the idea of commanding, that of transmitting; perhaps it is so in this passage: "As to this command, I do not give it to you myself; I transmit it to you."—What are the meaning and bearing of the distinction which Paul establishes in the words, *not I, but the Lord?* The simplest supposition is that he means to speak here of a command given by Jesus Himself during His earthly sojourn. And what confirms this meaning is, that we really find this precept in our Gospels proceeding from the mouth of Jesus, just as we read it here; comp. Matt. v. 32, xix. 9; Mark x. 11; Luke xvi. 18. Not that I hold that the three first Gospels were already composed and circulated in the Churches at the time when Paul wrote; rather he derives his knowledge of this saying from the oral tradition which proceeded from the apostles. Baur has objected that if Paul had meant to cite a positive command of the Lord, he must have used the past παρήγγειλεν (*He commanded*), and not the present. But the command of Jesus is regarded as abiding for the Church throughout all time. No doubt it might also be that the apostle meant to say he had received this command by way of revelation. But the fact that we find it expressly given in our Gospels by the Lord proves that this is the saying to which he alludes.—And what is the effect of the distinction which Paul establishes between what the Lord commands and what he himself prescribes (ver. 12)? Does he mean that his apostolical commands are less infallible than those of the Lord? But this would be to sap apostolical authority with his own hands, and the words, xiv. 37, where he calls certain prescriptions in regard to worship a commandment of the Lord, would certainly not confirm this distinction. He means rather to establish the difference between the commands given expressly by the Lord, which have consequently indisputable force for the whole Church, and those which emanate from himself, and which, as such, are law only for the Churches founded by him and subject to his apostleship. So the former required only to be cited; they had no need of being demonstrated to any one who professed faith in Christ. The latter, on the contrary, assumed the acknowledgment of Paul as an apostle of the Lord; the apostle therefore felt himself called to expound the reasons which justified them; comp. vers. 14 and 16.

In quoting the words of Jesus, Paul omits the limitation put by the Lord on the command not to separate : " unless it be for adultery." Luke and Mark likewise omit it in the account of this discourse. The reason is that it was taken for granted; for in this relation adultery is equivalent to death ; and such a crime was not to be thought possible in the Christian community.

—The wife is placed first, because it is from her, as the weaker party, that the inclinations for separation oftenest come. The apostle says, in speaking of her, χωρισθῆναι, *to be separated*, while in the end of the following verse, in speaking of the man, he says ἀφιέναι, *to send away*, or *let go*. The reason perhaps is because the man is in his own home, and remains there, whereas the woman leaves the domicile.

Ver. 11. The first part of the verse is a parenthesis; for the proposition begun in ver. 10 finishes with the last words of ver. 11. The apostle anticipates the case in which, notwithstanding his, or rather the Lord's, prohibition, a Christian woman has left her husband: ἐὰν δὲ καί, *but if even* (with and in spite of this prohibition). Such a violation of the Lord's words have been regarded as inadmissible. Hofmann therefore supposes that it is solely deeds already consummated at the time when Paul wrote his letter that are in question; and Holsten concludes from this same alleged impossibility that the parenthesis, ἐὰν δὲ . . . καταλλαγήτω, is only a later interpolation. All this is unnecessary. Paul could perfectly anticipate the case in which, notwithstanding this prohibition, a wife, outraged by the bad treatment of which she was the victim, would go off abruptly in a moment of lively irritation. Fearing to do more harm than good by doing violence to the state of things, Paul accepts the situation. But first he seeks to prevent a second and still graver evil from being added to the first, and that by a new marriage of the separated wife, a marriage which Jesus called adultery; then he recommends a reconciliation as soon as possible. It has been asked whether the interdict against a new marriage applied also to the case in which one of the spouses had been guilty of adultery; and next, whether in this case the prohibition applied to the injured party as well as to the criminal spouse. Catholic law absolutely forbids divorce, even in the case of adultery, while Protestant law in these circumstances allows it. And, as to second marriage, Protestant law likewise permits it, but only to the innocent party. The refusal of divorce in the case of adultery seems to us to transgress the meaning of the Lord's words; for by these adultery is implicitly put on the same footing as death. And, as to the right of remarriage granted to the innocent party, it does not seem to me at all contrary to the text of Scripture. But what seems to me absolutely irreconcileable with the Lord's words, is the readiness with which Protestant pastors, becoming the agents of a purely civil legislation, consent to bless *in the name of the Lord* marriages contracted between persons whose first marriage had not been dissolved for the only reason authorized by the Lord, so that this new union, according to His positive declaration, is adultery. To bless on His part what He Himself characterizes so severely is a strange way of acting in His name. The State may have excellent reasons for not imposing on human society in general such rules as in their severity go beyond its moral level (Matt. xix. 8); but the Church has reasons not less valid for refusing to follow it in this region contrary to the will of its Master. Of course this faithful conduct of the Church demands, as a consequence, the distinction between State legislation and Church legislation. After this parenthesis, the apostle finishes the quotation of the Lord's words, by adding what concerns the husband. On the term ἀφιέναι, *to put away*, see on ver. 10. For the rest, the two sexes are put on the same footing. Among the Greeks, the wife could separate freely from her husband.

Vers. 12, 13. "But to the rest, speak I,[1] not the Lord : If any brother hath a wife that believeth not, and she be pleased to dwell with him, let him not put her away ; 13. and the woman which [2] hath an husband that believeth not, if he [3] be pleased to dwell with her, let her not put away her husband."[4]—Those whom the apostle calls *the rest*, in contrast to the spouses of ver. 11, can only be the married who do not both belong to the Church, and only one of whom was present at the reading of this letter. The sequel will leave no doubt of this interpretation. It is clear that neither the apostle nor the Church would have authorized a marriage between a member of the Church and a Jew or heathen ; but one of two spouses might have been converted after marriage ; hence the possibility of mixed marriages. Jesus could not have thought of giving a direction for such cases ; so the apostle declares that he has no command to transmit from the Lord on this subject. It is therefore himself, Paul, who must regulate the case, drawing its solution, by way of deduction, from the essence of the gospel. It seems to me even that the expression, *I, not the Lord*, excludes not only any positive ordinance uttered

---

[1] T. R. with D E F G K L puts ἐγω (*I*) before λεγω (*I speak*) ; A B C P Syr^sch put it after.
[2] T. R. with 6 Mjj. : ἡτις (*who*) ; ℵ D F G P : ει τις (*if a*).
[3] T. R. with E K L Syr. : αυτος ; all the rest : ουτος.
[4] T. R. with K L P : αυτον (*him*) ; all the rest : τον ανδρα (*the husband*).

by the Lord during His life, but even any special revelation proceeding from Him on the subject. It does not follow, however, that he puts himself in this respect on the same footing as any other Christian. How, if it were so, could he say with authority in ver. 17 : " So ordain I in all the Churches " ? He knew himself to be enlightened, as an apostle, with a wisdom superior to ordinary Christian wisdom, and that even in cases in which he had neither an external revelation (ver. 10), nor an inward revelation properly so called (xi. 23) to direct him.

Two cases might present themselves in mixed marriages : Either the heathen spouse consented to remain with the Christian spouse ; this is the case treated vers. 12–14. Or he refused ; this is the case treated vers. 15, 16.

On the first supposition, the Christian spouse, whether husband or wife, ought to remain united to the Jewish or heathen spouse ; for the consent of the latter implies that he will not annoy the Christian in the discharge of her religious obligations.—The term ἀφιέναι, *put away*, is here applied to the wife as well as to the husband, perhaps because, as Bengel finely observes, in the eyes of the Church the Christian wife is, despite her sex, the nobler of the two ; or, more simply, because, in case of the heathen desiring to remain with his wife, it is she who would *speak the leave-taking* (give the *congé*) if she refused. This direction given for the first case, the apostle is careful to justify it, precisely because this is his ordinance, and not the Lord's.

Ver. 14. " For the unbelieving husband is sanctified

in the wife,[1] and the unbelieving wife is sanctified in the brother;[2] since otherwise were your children unclean; but now are they holy."—The essential idea is that expressed by the word put at the head of the first and second proposition: ἡγίασται, *is sanctified*. The use of this term is no doubt occasioned by the fear which the Christian spouse might have of contracting defilement by remaining united to a heathen or Jewish spouse. So some interpreters have given the word a a purely negative, or, what amounts to nearly the same, a Levitical and ritual sense. Paul, it is said, means: marriage in this condition does not become an impure state, does not affect the Christian with defilement similar to that which was produced under the law by the touch of a dead body, for example. But this meaning, held by Rückert, as being purely negative, is too weak to correspond to the positive term ἡγίασται; and besides, resting on the theocratical idea of an external and ritual purity, it is not in keeping with the spirit of the New Testament. Others, with different shades, take this term as expressing the hope of sanctifying influence which the Christian spouse will in the end exercise over the heathen or Jewish spouse; so Olshausen: the Christian spirit will distil on him; de Wette, Neander: he will be placed under the beneficent influence of his spouse and of the Church. But the perfect ἡγίασται, *has been put in a state of holiness*, cannot designate a hoped-for result; and ver. 16 precisely contradicts the certainty of such a

---

[1] D E F G It. Syr^sch add τη πιστη (*believing*).
[2] T. R. with K L Syr. reads ανδρι (*the husband*); all the rest: αδελφω (*the brother*).

result. Meyer and Reuss seek to evade these difficulties by making ἡγίασται here signify: "He is associated, affiliated to the Church by the conjugal bond which unites him to his spouse." But do we not thus come back to the idea of a purely ceremonial holiness, a consecration wholly objective and external? Hofmann thinks that we must here abstract from all influence over the person of the non-Christian spouse, and apply the idea of holiness only to the *bond* between the two spouses, to their conjugal relation as such. This amounts to saying, as in the first interpretation, that such a union is pure for the two spouses. But if this idea had been that of Paul, he would have expressed it in a less involved way. To get at his thought in this verse, we must take account of the perfect passive and of the preposition ἐν, *in*. The latter indicates that the heathen or Jewish spouse has his holiness *in* the person of his spouse, and the perfect passive indicates that the communication of this holiness or consecration to God is regarded by Paul as already finished. As the believer is consecrated to God in the person of Christ, and as by faith in Him he gains his own consecration in His (see on i. 2), so the non-Christian spouse is sanctified in his Christian spouse by his consent to live with her. This consent is, in his relation to his Christian spouse, what faith is, in the believer's relation to Christ. By consenting to live still with his spouse, the Jewish or heathen spouse also accepts her holy consecration and participates in it. Thus it is so long as he persists in this consent. The apostle of course reckons on the sanctifying influence of such a situation; but the use of the perfect and of the preposition ἐν, *in*, show that the point before him here is not strictly and above all that sanctifying influence, but the position of consecration in which the non-Christian spouse is at once placed by his determination to remain united to his Christian spouse.

Is this consecration of the one in the person of the other really tenable? Certainly; and the apostle proves it by an analogous moral fact and one universally admitted in the Church. The conjunction ἐπεί, *since*, is frequently used to mean: "since, *if it were otherwise*, this is what would happen" (*da sonst*, Passow); comp. for this meaning in the New Testament Rom. xi. 22: "since otherwise (that is to say, if thou persevere not) thou also shalt be cut off;" and in our own Epistle, v. 10 and xv. 29: "since otherwise (if there be no resurrection), what shall they do . . . ?" It is the same in profane Greek; comp. the numerous examples quoted by Passow. The ἄρα, *then*, announces an explanatory inference: "since if you refuse to acknowledge as true what I have just affirmed . . ." M. L'Hardy, in his book, *Le baptême des enfants* (1882), has disputed this universally admitted meaning of *since otherwise*, and has attempted to substitute for it the meaning, *seeing that, considering that*. The idea, according to him, is this: "Ye ought not to separate (ver. 13), first, because the unbeliever is sanctified in the believer (ver. 14ᵃ); and next, *from the consideration that*, if separation takes place, your children, deprived of family life, will be impure; whereas, if you remain united, they will be holy." We should thus have here a second reason to justify the μὴ ἀφιέτω, *let her not put him away*, of ver. 13. But in this sense the connecting particle with what precedes would be not ἐπεί, but καὶ δέ, *and moreover;* then the ἐπεί, *since*, can in any case only bear on the verb which immediately precedes, ἡγίασται, *is sanctified*, twice repeated, and not on the remoter imperative of ver. 13. It is in this case an argument whereby the apostle demonstrates the truth of the affirmation enunciated in the first part of the verse: *he is sanctified*.

The expression, *your children*, may be understood in two ways. It may be applied—and it seems at first sight the most natural meaning—only to children born of mixed marriages. So Chrysostom, Flatt, Bonnet, L'Hardy, and others. But from ver. 12, Paul, in speaking of spouses placed in this condition, has used the third person. Why would he pass all at once to the second while addressing the same persons: τέκνα ὑμῶν, *your* children? Then would the argument have been conclusive? Would a mother, who doubted the consecration of her husband by means of her own faith, have admitted more easily the state of consecration belonging to her children by means of her maintaining that conjugal life of whose purity she was distrustful? It is therefore more probable that the expression, "*your* children," contains, as Beet says, "an appeal to all Christian parents." Paul addresses them all (ὑμῶν, *you*) as present at the time when his letter is read in the congregation. The argument is this: "If it is a thing admitted by you all, that notwithstanding their original pollution, your children, who are not yet believers, are nevertheless already consecrated and holy in the eyes of God, and that in virtue of the bond which unites them to you, their parents, why would you make a difficulty about recognising also that an unbelieving husband may be regarded as consecrated to God in virtue of his union with his believing wife, and that by the fact of his desire to remain united to her?" So de Wette, Rückert, Olshausen, Neander, Meyer, Osiander, Hofmann, Heinrici, Edwards. By the form, *since otherwise*, this reasoning becomes an argument *ad absurdum*: "If you deny this participation of the non-Christian spouse in the consecration of the Christian spouse, you ought, if you are to be consequent, to declare your own children impure, to regard them as polluted beings, heathen children, which your Christian instinct refuses to believe." To give more force to this reasoning, Paul changes the ἡγίασται, *is sanctified*, into ἅγιά ἐστιν, *are holy*. This second term is stronger than the first. The verb, in the perfect passive, indicated a position in which the subject is placed in the person of another, whereas the adjective ἅγια, *holy*, expresses a real quality inherent in the subject, though the latter has not yet any share in the act (faith) which seems to be its condition. Now if this characteristic is indisputable in the judgment of Christian feeling, with stronger reason ought the privilege designated above to be so.—The term ἀκάθαρτα, *impure*, here signifies: yet plunged, like children of heathen parents, in their natural impurity. — The νῦν δέ, *but now*, brings out the contrast between the true, only tenable idea, and the absurd supposition conditionally stated.

But what exactly are we to understand by this word ἅγια, *holy* ? If ἀκάθαρτα, *unclean*, cannot in this case designate either an external and ritual defilement, like those which were contracted under the Old Testament, or a personal moral defilement, since it is infants who are spoken of, and can only consequently apply to natural corruption ; in like manner the word *holy* cannot designate here either a simply Levitical purity, for we are no longer under the Old Testament, or free and personal holiness, like that of regenerated believers. Is it possible then to discover an intermediate between these two alternatives ? De Wette, Olshausen, Osiander, Neander, Edwards think that the reference is to the Christian influence of parents by means of their prayers, instructions, example (*practical power*, Edwards). But this explanation carries us to the future, and to a very uncertain future (see ver. 16) ; whereas the verb ἐστί, *are*, denotes a real and present fact. The Reformers, from their viewpoint of absolute predestination, did not shrink from giving the fullest meaning to the word ἡγίασται.[1] According to Calvin (*Instit.* iv. 16, pp. 310–312), the children of Christians are holy from their birth, in consequence of supernatural grace. For this idea of the inward sanctification of the children of Christians from their birth, Beza substitutes that of their assured regeneration in consequence of their election. But it is not by denying liberty that any one will come to understand the notion of holiness in St. Paul. Calvin thinks of a holiness bestowed by *supernatural grace* on the children of Christians from their entrance into life. But do the facts confirm this

---

[1] See in Edwards the development of this point.

theory? Others, like M. Ménégoz,[1] explain the idea of the apostle by that of the solidarity and organic unity of the family. But does this law hold also in the spiritual domain? Hofmann understands, holy *in the eyes of the parents*, "who do not see the sin with which the child is born, but only the gift of God which they have received in the child." But how can we discover here the meaning of the word *holy?* Bonnet and L'Hardy start from the use of this word, Rom. xi. 16: "If the root be holy, so are the branches;" and they think that as there remains in the family of Abraham, even when rejected, a predisposition to the service of God, so the blessed effects of the covenant of grace extend from Christian parents to their children, because these are "the fruits of a blessed union in God." Here, then, we have "a natural holiness, one of position."[2] Beet, in an analogous sense, adduces the words, Ex. xxix. 37 : " Whatsoever touches the altar of God shall be holy." Children laid by the prayer of the parents on the altar of God become a holy thing; and so it is with the husband whom his Christian wife presents to God.—In my opinion there can be no doubt that the matter in question here is a transmitted grace, a consecration of the child to God resulting from the Divine offer of salvation under which it is put from its birth, whether it afterwards accept or reject it. But even in this case the assertion, *are holy*, still seems extravagant. There is something so firm and precise about it, that one involuntarily seeks a positive fact on which to support it. Certainly, since it is

---

[1] *Revue chrétienne*, Avril 1884; *Le Baptême des enfants.*
[2] L'Hardy, pp. 495, 514.

children and non-believers who are in question, it is allowable to hold by a notion of holiness which approaches that of the Old Testament; but in this sense the need of an external objective fact, to account for such a declaration, makes itself the more felt. This fact can only be, as it seems to me, the baptism of the Corinthian children in regard to whom the apostle expresses himself so categorically. No doubt the gravest German commentators find in this very saying an indisputable proof against the practice of infant baptism in the Churches founded by Paul. " If," it is said, " Christian children had been already introduced into the Church by baptism, their position would no longer have any analogy to that of the heathen spouses of whom St. Paul speaks in the first part of this verse, and he could not logically conclude from the former to the latter. His argument is valid only in so far as both alike lie outside at once of faith and baptism." But this objection rests on the idea that baptism is here regarded by Paul as the *principle* of the holiness ascribed by him to the children of Christians. From this point of view it would indeed differ totally from that which Paul, by his *is sanctified* (ver. 14ᵃ), can allow to non-Christian spouses. But if Paul regards the baptism of those children, not as the source, but as the *proof of the fact*, the seal of their state of holiness, the whole thing is changed. He means, not that they are holy because of their baptism, but that their baptism was the sign and proof of the fact of their state of holiness. And whence, then, arises this holiness which rises superior in them from their birth over natural corruption, and which rendered them fit to receive baptism, though they had not yet personal faith? As Jewish children did not become children of Abraham by circumcision, but as it was descent from their parents, children of Abraham, which made them fit to receive circumcision, so it is with the children of Christians. Their consecration to God does not depend on their baptism; but their fitness for baptism arises from the solidarity of life which unites them to their parents, and through them to the covenant of grace founded in Christ, and in which these live. Until Christian children decide freely for or against the salvation which is offered to them, they enjoy the benefit of this provisional situation, and are placed with all belonging to the family in communication with the holy forces which animate the body of Christ. And this is a state superior, though analogous, to that of the non-Christian spouse, who, in virtue of keeping up his union with his Christian wife, is not himself received into the covenant (ἅγιος, *holy*), but yet regarded as destined to enter into it (ἡγιασμένος, *sanctified*, consecrated, in the person of his wife, a member of the Church). If this second result were impossible, the first would be still more so.

Infant Baptism, in relation to the passage, vii. 14.

German commentators are almost unanimous (except Hofmann, who here follows a way of his own) in regarding infant baptism as incompatible with these words of the apostle. The latest English critics (Edwards, Beet), though knowing the German works, do not adhere to the conclusion drawn in them, and do not believe the words to be incompatible with the ecclesiastical practice of baptizing infants. For my part, I do not find Paul's expressions intelligible except on the supposition that this practice existed.

In his interesting and able work already quoted, Professor Ménégoz has proposed an intermediate way. According to him, when Paul baptized whole families, Jewish or heathen (Acts xvi. 15, 33, xviii. 8 ; 1 Cor. i. 16), it is indisputable that the children were included. But 1 Cor. vii. 14 proves, he thinks, on the other hand, that in Christian families the children born after the baptism of the parents did not receive it themselves, which M. Ménégoz explains by supposing that their baptism was regarded as included in that of their parents. They were looked on " as baptized in the womb of their mother." It was not, according to him, till later and gradually that baptism was extended to the children of Christians themselves, because this rite being the mode of enlisting into the Church, it could not in course of time be refused to the descendants of Christians without effacing the line of demarcation between them and the world.

This hypothesis, intended to reconcile the two classes of passages, which M. Ménégoz thinks he finds in the New Testament, seems to me inadmissible. According to it, there were in Paul's Churches two classes of Christians : the one baptized, those who had passed from heathenism or Judaism to Christianity ; the other unbaptized (except in the person of their parents), those who were born of parents already Christian. But where in the New Testament is there a trace of such a difference ? Does not the apostle say : " We *all* (ὅσοι, as many as there are) who were baptized in Christ . . . ? " The same expression, Gal. iv. 27, and in our own Epistle, xii. 13 : " We all (ἡμεῖς πάντες) were baptized into one Spirit to form one body." These expressions show that baptism was regarded as the external bond of all the members of the body of which the Spirit was the soul. And why, if M. Ménégoz' supposition was well founded, was not the baptism of children born of parents not yet Christian regarded as involved in that of their parents, as well as that of the infants born after their conversion, unless we are prepared to ascribe to the Church, and to Paul himself, the most grossly materialistic ideas ? Has not M. Ménégoz himself very properly reminded us of the fact that, according to the notions of antiquity, the father's religion determined that of the family ? His personal baptism should therefore have sufficed for all in the one situation as well as in the other. Finally, I think I have shown that the passage, 1 Cor. vii. 14, in favour of which so strange a hypothesis is proposed, not only does not require, but excludes it.

But does not ecclesiastical history protest against our exegetical result as false ? With the exception of two passages, the one from Origen, the other from Tertullian, it is silent on the point before us. Now, of these two passages, that of Origen is positive in favour of the apostolic origin of infant baptism (*Comment. in epist. ad Rom.* t. v. 9): "The Church learned from the apostles that it ought to give baptism to infants." In the second, Tertullian, after his going over to Montanism (*De baptismo*, c. 18), dissuades parents from baptizing their children; which proves that the practice existed in his time, but that Tertullian himself did not regard it as apostolical. These facts are insufficient, from the historical point of view, to authorize a sure conclusion either on the one side or the other. It is therefore for exegesis to enlighten history rather than the reverse.

The apostle now passes to the opposite case, that of the Christian spouse whose heathen partner does not consent to live with her.

Vers. 15, 16. "But if the unbelieving depart, let him depart; a brother or a sister is not under bondage in such things; but God hath called us[1] in peace. 16. For what knowest thou, O wife, whether thou shalt save thy husband? and how knowest thou, O man, whether thou shalt save thy wife?"—The rule to be followed in this case is given in ver. 15; the reason follows in ver. 16. The Christian spouse should in this case consent to a separation which she could not refuse without going in the face of incessant conflicts. The word, *let him depart*, throws back the

---

[1] ℵ A C K read υμας (*you*) instead of ημας (*us*), which is the reading of T. R. and all the rest, It. Syr.

whole responsibility on the non-believer. The expression ἐν τοῖς τοιούτοις might signify, *in such circumstances* (the refusal of the heathen spouse). But the plural leads more naturally to the sense, *in such things, in this kind of matters*. The apostle is no doubt thinking of the transient element in earthly relations in general, when compared with the eternal interests which alone can bind the believer absolutely. He has probably already in view the other analogous relations with which he proceeds to deal in this connection from ver. 17. The words ἐν εἰρήνῃ, *in peace*, have often been understood as if they were εἰς εἰρήνην, "to peace." But if this had been Paul's idea, why not express himself so? He means rather that the call to faith which they accepted, bore from the first a pacific character, for it consisted in the offer of peace with God; and consequently the stamp of peace ought to be impressed on all their earthly conduct. Chrysostom regarded this last remark as intended to restrict the liberty of separation granted in the previous words; in this sense: "Nevertheless consider well that it is to peace thy Master has called thee, and see yet whether thou couldest not maintain the union." But as Edwards says, if the non-believer has left the Christian, how is it possible to exhort the latter to live in peace with the former? Is it not clear that by persisting to impose her presence, the Christian spouse would put herself directly in contradiction to the spirit of peace? For this conduct could not fail to issue in a state of perpetual war. The δέ is adversative: *but*. It contrasts with the subjection, which is denied, the duty of living in peace, which is affirmed. One might also, like Beet, translate the δέ in the sense of, *and moreover;* this would give a gradation: "And not only are ye not subject in this case . . ., but moreover there is a duty to . . ."—The difficult question in regard to this verse is to determine whether the *is not under bondage* includes, besides the right of separation, that of remarriage for the Christian spouse. Edwards cites the fact that this was the opinion of Ambrosiaster, whereas the Council of Arles (314) decided the question in the opposite sense. Among Protestants, *malicious desertion*—such is the judicial name for the χωρίζεσθαι on the part of one of the spouses—is regarded in general as equivalent to adultery, and consequently as authorizing a new marriage. I do not think that it is possible exegetically, as Edwards proposes, to decide the question in the latter sense, for, as Meyer observes, the οὐ δεδούλωται simply authorizes separation, without containing, either explicity or implicitly, the idea of a new union. In any case, in application to our present circumstances, it must not be forgotten that separation between a Christian and a heathen spouse is not subject to the same conditions as separation between two Christian spouses. For the latter, the rule has been given, and that by the Lord Himself, vers. 10, 11.

The two questions of ver. 16 have been frequently understood, from Chrysostom to Tholuck, in a sense opposed to liberty of separation: "What knowest thou whether thou shalt not save . . . ?" Edwards has proved by several examples, taken from classic Greek, the *grammatical* possibility of taking εἰ in the sense of *whether;* comp. moreover in the LXX. Joel ii. 14;

Jonah iii. 9. But, as he rightly says, the context is decidedly opposed to this interpretation. It would assume that meaning of the preceding proposition which we have been obliged to reject; and so understood, the saying would demand of the Christian, with a view to a result very problematical and rendered almost impossible by the refusal of cohabitation on the part of the heathen spouse, an altogether disproportionate sacrifice.

Vers. 17–24.

To illustrate the spirit of the prescriptions which he has just given, and to trace at the same time the line of conduct to be followed in certain analogous cases which occurred in the life of the Church, the apostle widens the question, and shows that the general viewpoint which he has taken, to solve the questions relating to marriage, commands all the relations of the Christian life. The following passage is therefore a digression, but one intended to elucidate more completely the subject treated. In ver. 17 the principle is laid down on which all such questions depend; in vers. 18 and 19 this principle is applied to a first example; it is repeated in ver. 20, then applied to a second example, vers. 21–23; finally, it is repeated anew by way of conclusion, ver. 24.

Ver. 17. "Save this,[1] that as the Lord[2] hath distributed[3] to every man, as God[4] hath called every one, so

---

[1] Some Mnn. and Fathers read η μη (or *not*), instead of ει μη (*if not*), which is the reading of all the Mjj.

[2] T. R. with K L here reads ο θεος (*God*), instead of ο κυριος (*the Lord*), which is the reading of the other eight Mjj.

[3] א B: μεμερικεν, instead of εμερισεν.

[4] T. R. with K L here reads ο κυριος (*the Lord*), instead of ο θεος (*God*).

let him walk; and so ordain I in all the Churches."—
The particle εἰ μή, *unless*, or, *if it is not so*, has been
explained in a multitude of ways. Some have connected it with the preceding verse, in this sense:
"What knowest thou whether thou shalt save thy
wife, *or not?*" But there would have been needed at
least ἢ εἰ μή, or better, ἢ μή; and it is certainly from
this that there has arisen the reading ἢ μή, *or not*,
which is followed by Chrysostom and others, but which
has no authorities in its favour. Besides, why not add
this *or not* also to the first question? (de Wette). This
addition, finally, would be most superfluous. Rückert
would be disposed to make εἰ μή (supplying σώσεις, *thou
shalt save*) a new proposition: "But if thou knowest
not whether thou shalt save thy wife, here in any case
is the rule to be followed." This meaning would be
admissible, but an adversative particle would have
been indispensable. Beza takes εἰ μή in the sense of
ἀλλά, *but*, which cannot be supported grammatically.—
Already by the words ἐν τοῖς τοιούτοις, *in such things*,
the apostle had betrayed his intention of extending
the treatment of the question proposed to other analogous subjects. This transition is indicated by the
particle εἰ μή, *unless that*, which marks his return to
the general rule from which he had been forced to
deviate in the exceptional case treated, vers. 15 and
16. The principle, on which rested the two directions
given to spouses, vers. 10, 11, and 12–14, was to
remain as Christians in the situation where marriage
had previously placed them. After the exception to
this rule which he authorized, vers. 15 and 16, the
apostle returns, by the particle, *unless that*, or, *saving*

the case that, to the line of conduct indicated in the outset, and which he now states in a perfectly general way in ver. 17 : every believer ought to remain in the earthly situation in which the call to salvation found him. This is the meaning held by most modern interpreters (de Wette, Osiander, Meyer, Hofmann, etc.).— The authority of the Mjj. hardly allows us to admit the received reading, according to which the subject of the first clause is ὁ θεός, *God,* and that of the second, ὁ κύριος, *the Lord,* evidently Jesus Christ ; comp. viii. 6. This reading is, however, the most natural, for in the first proposition the subject in question is external circumstances over which *God* presides, and in the second the calling to salvation which is undoubtedly often ascribed to God, but which may also be attributed to *Christ.* Hofmann, too, prefers this reading to that of the majority of the Mjj., which reverses the order of the two subjects. With this last reading it must be held that Christ is regarded here as directing from the midst of His glory the course of things on the earth. For it does not seem to me possible to apply, as Reiche and Heinrici do, the verb ἐμέρισεν, *has distributed* (μεμέρικεν, of א B, is probably a correction after κέκληκεν), to the share of *spiritual* graces bestowed on each believer. The *assigned portion* in which each should continue can only be, according to the context, the circumstances, analogous to the state of Christian or mixed marriage, in which the believer was providentially placed at the time of his conversion : "The position in which thou didst hear and receive the Divine call is also that in which thou shouldest continue to live" (περιπατεῖν, *to walk*). A situation which could not prevent salvation from being realized in us, will not be incompatible with life in salvation.—The two *everys* are, by a strong inversion, placed before the conjunction which begins the proposition to which they belong. Thereby the apostle would emphasize the idea that there are as many particular positions as individuals called, and that each of them is their Divinely distributed lot which they ought not to change at will.

But Paul would not have it thought at Corinth that the principle here laid down is invented by him with a view to some present and special application which he contemplates within that Church. As to the rule, he lays it down in all the Churches founded by him, whose conduct amid such delicate questions he is called to direct. The word διατάσσομαι, *I ordain*, contains two ideas: that of a summary decision (διά), and that of apostolical competency (the middle, τάσσομαι, *I regulate in my sphere*).—The word *all* must of course be limited to the Churches dependent on his apostleship; comp. xiv. 37. The rule laid down in this verse is therefore this: the calling to the gospel ought not to be a reason with the believer for changing his outward situation. This principle well shows with what a conviction of its victorious power the gospel made its entrance into the world. It did not fear to confront any earthly position, lawful in itself; but it faced them all with the certainty of being able to penetrate and sanctify them by its spirit. As Edwards says: "The gospel introduces the principle of order as limiting that of liberty in the present life. It does not make slaves of us, but it does not plunge us into anarchy. It is not despotic; but neither is it revolutionary."

The apostle cites and deals with two examples: the state of circumcision or uncircumcision, and that of slavery or freedom.

Vers. 18, 19. "Is any man called being circumcised, let him not become uncircumcised; is any called[1] in uncircumcision, let him not be circumcised. 19. Circumcision is nothing, and uncircumcision is nothing, but the keeping of the commandments of God is everything."—Whether we give to the two verbs in the indicative the interrogative or affirmative sense matters little; it is here the hypothetical indicative. —The apostle is alluding to a custom which was introduced among the Hellenistic Jews, of practising a surgical operation intended to disguise their state of circumcision. They wished thereby to escape either persecution, or ridicule, in the public baths or games. These renegades were called *meschoukim, recutiti*. Epiphanius ascribes the invention of the process to Isaiah. Mention is made of it in the Book of Maccabees (i. 11, 15) and in Josephus (*Antiq.* xii. 5. 1). This difference, circumcision or uncircumcision, which had played so decisive a part from the religious standpoint of the Jews, was reduced to nothing by the gospel, which absolutely subordinates the ritual to the moral side of things. The coming of Christ inaugurated a new era, in which holiness alone remains; comp. Rom. ii. 29. In the expression *commandments of God* there are embraced the moral contents of the Jewish law and of the example and teachings of Jesus,

[1] T. R. with E K L: εκληθη, instead of κεκληται.

as well as the directions of His Spirit. Paul in like manner elsewhere contrasts with circumcision and uncircumcision the *new creature* (Gal. vi. 15), or *faith acting by love* (Gal. v. 6); comp. Rom. xiii. 9, where the whole law is summed up in love. It is evident that Paul is here speaking of the end to be realized, not of the means indispensable to its attainment.

Ver. 20. " Let every man remain faithful to the calling wherewith he was called."—Literally: " Let every man abide in the calling wherewith he was called." The word κλῆσις, *call, vocation*, cannot denote the earthly state or profession; it is applied here, as elsewhere, to the call to salvation. The pronoun ᾗ with ἐκλήθη would suffice to prove this: " the call *with which* he was called." Only the idea of the call must be taken to embrace all the external circumstances which furnish the occasion and determine the manner of it. What a difference between the manner of calling in the case of one circumcised and of one uncircumcised! Now this earthly situation, appointed by God, must not be left at one's own will. What was the means of thy call will not fail to exercise thy fidelity.—This maxim, which closes the treatment of the first example, serves as a transition to that of the second.

Ver. 21. " Thou wast called being a slave, care not for it; but if therewith thou mayest be made free, use it rather."—Here in this domain is the extreme case which can be conceived. Few situations could appear so incompatible with Christian holiness, dignity, and freedom as that of a slave. But a multitude of evidences proves that Christianity had quite specially found access to persons of this class. But, abnormal as this position may appear, it will not remain beyond the victorious influence of the gospel. The spiritual elevation which faith communicates, places the believer above even this contrast: slave, free.—There is something heroic in the word of the apostle: *care not for it.* " Do not let this position weigh either on thy conscience or on thy heart ! " Hofmann applies these words, not to the state of slavery, but to the counsel which the apostle has just given, in this sense : " Do not torment thyself with the counsel I give thee ; it should not prevent thee from accepting thy liberty, if an opportunity of recovering it presents itself." This explanation is not natural. For it is evident that it was his enslaved condition which would above all fill a Christian in this position with concern. The anxiety which Paul's order could cause him was only an effect of that which the position itself caused.

The second part of this verse has been understood in two diametrically opposite senses. The ancient Greek exegetes, and, among the moderns, de Wette, Meyer, Osiander, Kling, Reuss, Renan, Heinrici, Holsten, Edwards, Jean Monod (in a pamphlet published in connection with the American War on the subject of slavery[1]), among translators, Rilliet, Oltramare, Segond, Weizsäcker, think that the apostle means : " But, though thou mayest become free, use rather (slavery)." Calvin, Neander, Hofmann, Bonnet, Beet give this meaning, on the contrary, to the apostle's words : " But nevertheless, if thou canst become free,

[1] *Saint Paul et l'esclavage*, par J. A. Monod. Toulouse, 1866.

profit by it (by accepting the advantage which is offered thee)."

The reasons ordinarily alleged in favour of the first interpretation are: 1. The conjunction εἰ καί, which signifies *even if, although*: "But *although* thou mightest become free, remain a slave." 2. Ver. 22, which more naturally justifies the idea of remaining a slave. 3. The whole context, which rather calls for encouragement to remain what one is than to change his state. Renan compares Paul's counsel thus understood with the words of the sages of the time: "The Stoics used to say like St. Paul to the slave: Remain what thou art; think not of freeing thyself." According to this interpretation, the Christian slave would be invited to refuse, should the case occur, the liberation which was offered him, and "to regard his state, to use Reuss' expression, as a means of education to salvation and as a special sphere of activity assigned to him." But these reasons are far from seeming to me decisive. The form εἰ καί has not always the sense of *even if* or *though*. The two elements of which it is composed may remain distinct, so that the εἰ continues an *if*, and the καί an *also*. This is established by Passow by many examples (ii. 1540).[1] We see this in our Epistle (iv. 7), and even in our chapter, in vers. 11, 28, where the meaning of *though* would be absolutely illogical, and where the εἰ καί evidently signifies: *If therewith*, if however. A new fact (καί) presents itself, which gives a new aspect to the case. It is precisely

---

[1] "In the form εἰ καί," says he, "καί may be separated from εἰ and no longer bear on the whole, but on a single term of the hypothetical proposition."

so in our passage: "But if *therewith* (besides the internal liberty which thou possessest, or thy tranquillity of soul, thy οὐ μέλεσθαι), thou canst also become outwardly free . . ." (καί applying to δύνασαι γένεσθαι). It might even be asked whether, in the other sense, Paul would not have required to say: καὶ εἰ, *and even if.* On the connection with ver. 22, see below. Finally, as to the context, it agrees perfectly with the second explanation, if this counsel be regarded as a *restriction* brought into the general rule. This is what is naturally indicated by the ἀλλά, *but,* for in the other sense it would require to be taken as an ἀλλά of gradation: *but moreover;* which is rather forced. We here find a restriction parallel to that of vers. 15 and 16, which was also introduced by an adversative particle (εἰ δέ, *but if*). As, in these verses, the Christian spouse was authorized to deviate from the general rule and to separate from the heathen spouse who refused to remain with her; so in our verse the Christian slave, after having been exhorted to bear without a murmur the state of slavery, is authorized to take advantage of any opportunity which occurs of exchanging it for freedom: "But if, therewith, thou mayest be made free . . ."

The reasons which appear to me to decide in favour of this meaning are the following: 1. The natural regimen of χρῆσαι, *make use of,* after the words which immediately precede, *If thou mayest be made free,* is certainly: "make use of the possibility." It is much less natural to go to the preceding sentence to borrow the idea of slavery. 2. The μᾶλλον, *rather,* which some oppose to this meaning, is on the contrary much

more naturally explained if the apostle has in view the acceptance of liberty. He was well aware that the slave's situation might be such that he could legitimately prefer to remain in it. Hence it is that to his counsel to accept he delicately adds the word *rather*, which takes away from his words everything of an imperative character: "I would have thee in this case to incline *rather* to liberty." From the rule so forcibly inculcated: to remain in his position, there might in fact arise this misunderstanding, that a slave should not think himself free to profit by an offer of emancipation; this is what the apostle wishes to avoid.
3. Could Paul reasonably give to the Christian slave the advice to remain a slave if he could lawfully regain his freedom? Is not liberty a boon? Is it not the state which accords with the dignity of man? one of the features, the fundamental feature perhaps, of God's image in man? No doubt the Christian slave possesses inward liberty; for the Lord has set him free, not only from condemnation and sin, but also from the yoke of external circumstances, which he can henceforth accept as a gift of God. Nevertheless it remains true, that enjoying liberty, he will be able as a rule to give himself more efficiently to the service of God. What would be said of a prisoner who should refuse liberation, alleging that in his prison he enjoys moral liberty? Or of a sufferer, who, being able to recover health, should refuse to do so for the reason that on his couch he possesses spiritual life? The apostle had too much wisdom from above, and also too much natural good sense, to give himself up to such exaggeration, which belongs to an unhealthy asceticism.

Heinrici points out, rightly no doubt, the much more gentle and humane form which slavery had taken at that period. This is true: the master had no longer the right of life and death over his slave; but nevertheless he had the disposal of his person. And if the Christian could find strength in communion with Christ to overcome the temptations attached to such dependence, what an exaggeration would it be to bind him to reject an opportunity providentially offered of becoming free, and escaping from the cause of such conflicts!
4. Moreover, the apostle has himself clearly enough expressed his judgment on this question in the Epistle to Philemon; and all the torture to which Meyer subjects his words (see in his *Commentary*) does not avail to show that the apostle did not really and positively claim from Philemon the emancipation of Onesimus, who had become his brother by the common faith: "Knowing that thou wilt do even beyond what I say" (Philem. ver. 21). This passage may certainly be called the first petition in favour of the abolition of slavery. It is not by violent means, like servile wars, it is by the spirit which breathes in such words that Christianity has made and still makes the chains of the slave to fall. And as St. Paul could not contradict himself on this point, we may be assured that his thought was no other than this: "But if therewith (while consenting to live in the state of slavery, enjoying moral liberty) thou mayest become free, take advantage of it."

Vers. 22, 23. "For he that was called in the Lord being a slave, is the Lord's freedman; likewise[1] he that

---

[1] T. R. with K L adds καὶ (*also*) after ὁμοίως.

was called being free is Christ's slave. 23. Ye were bought with a price: become not the slaves of men!"—According to most commentators, ver. 22 is intended to justify the counsel to prefer servitude. Edwards: "A reason why the Christian slave should continue a slave rather than accept liberty." The reasoning in itself would be admissible: "The slave being spiritually free, and the free believer morally a slave, the contrast is neutralized; why make a change of state?"—But this verse may quite as well justify the counsel of ver. 21, as we have understood it; not in the sense that the first proposition of ver. 22 would justify the first counsel of ver. 21, and the second proposition the second. For in this case the second proposition would not answer the purpose, for the Christian slave called to liberty is not in the position of the free Christian who becomes the slave of Christ. It must be borne in mind that the second part of ver. 21 was a restriction arising in connection with the first, a sort of parenthesis; after which Paul returns to the general idea. We must therefore disentangle the thought common to the two propositions of ver. 22, and apply it to the passage as a whole: If in Christ slaves become free, and the free slaves, then neither slavery nor liberty is to be dreaded for the believer! Slavery will not take away from him his inward liberty, for he is Christ's freedman; and liberty will not plunge him into licence, for he has become Christ's slave. The consequence is, that the Christian slave may either remain a slave, or become free, without harm. For, in the latter case, he enters the class of the free who become the Lord's slaves.

The expression ἐν κυρίῳ κληθείς does not signify: called to communion with the Lord, but: called by a call addressed in the Lord.—The gen. κυρίου here is at once that of cause and of possession. The sentence of emancipation was pronounced by the Lord; by it He delivered this spiritual slave from the power and condemnation of sin; thenceforth this freedman belongs to Him as His servant.

Ver. 23. The second person plural which comes in here shows that the apostle is addressing the entire Church without distinction. If some from being slaves have become free, and the others from being free have become slaves, it is because a purchase has been made; this purchase, so far as it is a ransom, has freed the slaves, and, as a purchase price, it has brought the free into servitude.—But how is the warning which follows connected with the mention of the great fact of redemption? Some have thought that Paul meant thereby to prevent the free men of Corinth from selling themselves as slaves for the service of Christ (Michaëlis, Heydenreich). But no trace is found of such conduct, and in any case the transition to so new an idea would be denoted by some particle or other.—Monod compares this saying with a passage of the letter of Ignatius to Polycarp (c. 4), where the former writes of male and female servants: "Let them not desire to be set free at the charge of the common treasury, lest they should be found the slaves of their lust." Paul, he thinks, is reminding Christians thus redeemed that they ought to take care to maintain their independence overagainst the Church, or those who have rendered them this service. But how can we bring ourselves to apply to such a purchase the solemn expression, *bought with a price?* comp. vi. 20. Besides, Paul addresses this recommendation, as we have seen, to the whole Church. This last reason equally forbids us to accept the opinion of Chrysostom (*De Virgin.*, c. 41), quoted by Edwards, according to which Paul recommends slaves not to serve *servilely*, but as exercising their spiritual liberty; comp. Col. iii. 23. — Rückert, Hofmann, compare this warning with iii. 21: "Let no man glory in men;" they think that Paul is inviting the Church to shake off the yoke of the party leaders spoken of in the first chapters. Nothing appears in the context which could call forth such a warning here, and how should Paul immediately return from this strange thought to the general rule, ver. 24? Meyer's solution seems to me the most natural. Paul, he thinks, wishes to combat the docility of the Church towards certain agitators who were urging believers, in consequence of their conversion, to change their external situation. Indeed, Meyer rightly observes that unless we assume such a tendency, this whole digression (vers. 17–24) lacks a basis. Perhaps it was above all in regard to questions about slavery and liberty that those men sought to impose their opinions on the other members of the Church. Let the severe saying, iv. 15, be remembered: "Though ye should have ten thousand tutors in Christ . . . !"—The apostle concludes by reproducing in a summary form the general principle already twice stated, vers. 17, 20.

Ver. 24. "Brethren, let every man wherein he was called, therein abide before God."—The principal idea is not that of abiding *before God* in that state; it is abiding *in that state,* and that *before God.* By these last words, Paul reminds his readers of the moral act which has the power of sanctifying and ennobling every external position : the eye fixed on God, *walking* in His presence. This is what preserves the believer from the temptations arising from the situation in which he is; this is what raises the humblest duties it can impose on him to the supreme dignity of acts of worship. — Hofmann seeks to give to ver. 24 a different meaning from that of vers. 17, 20, by referring the two pronouns ᾧ and τούτῳ to the person of the Lord. But the parallelism with vers. 17, 20 is obvious at a glance; and the repetition is easily justified by the importance of the principle enunciated.

In fact, this principle has been of incalculable importance in the development of the Church. It is by means of it that Christianity has been able to become a moral power at once sufficiently firm and sufficiently elastic to adapt itself to all human situations, personal, domestic, national, and social. Thereby it is that without revolution it has worked the greatest revolutions, accepting everything to transform everything, submitting to everything to rise above everything, renewing the world from top to bottom while condemning all violent subversion. Whence has the apostle derived this principle in which there meet the most unconquerable faith and the most consummate ability? "I say unto you by the grace given unto me;" so Paul expressed himself when opening a series of purely practical prescriptions, Rom. xii. 3. Wisdom from on high did not less direct Paul the pastor than Paul the teacher. And then it is probable that he was not unacquainted with the Master's homely saying: "And she put the leaven into the meal, until the whole was leavened." The Holy Spirit had given him the commentary on this short parable.[1]

VERS. 25–40.

In this third part of the chapter, the apostle discusses the question of marriage as it relates to virgins (25–38), adding at the end a word in regard to widows (39, 40). No doubt in the first part of the chapter (vers. 1–9) he was occupied with the formation of the marriage-bond, and it might appear that the question of the marriage of virgins comes under this head. But the grounds which he had made good in this passage, as to celibates, widowers, and widows, did not altogether apply to virgins; and then, according to ancient custom, it was the father who decided the lot of these last. Hence Paul reserved to himself the opportunity of addressing parents on this subject in a separate passage. The advice which he gives, and then develops, is this: Parents, if circumstances allow it, will be right in preferring celibacy for their daughters (vers. 25, 26), and that for these two reasons: the difficulties of the present situation (vers. 27–31); the advantage which will accrue from it to their Christian activity (vers. 32–38).

Vers. 25–31: The present state of things.

---

[1] Is there not room for surprise that a Christian society can exist, which, while regarding St. Paul as an apostle of the Lord and an organ of the Divine Spirit, has adopted the method of immediately snatching away new converts from the duties of their natural position to launch them upon the world as agents in a work of evangelization? Is not this the antipodes of the principle thrice stated by the apostle?

Ver. 25. "Now concerning virgins, I have no commandment of the Lord; but I give my judgment, as one that hath obtained mercy of the Lord to be faithful."—The form of transition used by the apostle would lead us to suppose that he is replying to a special article of the letter of the Corinthians (comp. ver. 1); questions had certainly been put to him on the subject which he proceeds to treat.—If we compare vers. 27, 28, 29, where the apostle addresses young men, a reason might be found for applying the word παρθένος, *virgin*, with Bengel, to bachelors as well as to spinsters. Rev. xiv. 4 has been quoted for this wide meaning. But the uniform use of the word in classic and sacred literature does not authorize this meaning. In the passage of the Apocalypse it is an adjective, and ought probably to be taken in a moral sense. The entire sequel, vers. 32-38, proves that it is of maidens Paul meant to speak, and that if he says a word about young men, it is only in passing and to show that radically he makes no difference, in what he says here, between the two sexes. The principle which guides him is and remains this: to abide in the position where the Divine call found us.—The expression *commandment of the Lord* cannot denote, as in ver. 10, an order that proceeded from the mouth of Jesus during His earthly life. The form οὐκ ἔχω, *I have not*, would not be suitable in this sense, a commandment of Jesus not being Paul's personal property, but belonging to the whole Church. Paul therefore does not possess, either by way of tradition or of revelation, an order emanating from Jesus on this point.—But, as the Corinthians may desire to know his personal opinion, he does not refuse to communicate it to them. He rests the value of his counsel on the mercy of which he has been the object, a mercy which has made him a man worthy to be believed. The word πιστός, *faithful*, has, as we have seen, iv. 17, two closely connected meanings : one *who believes* firmly, and one *who may be trusted*. The second meaning appears in the context the more natural : "I have no infallible direction, coming from the Lord, to give you. But through the grace shown to me, I find myself in a position to give you a good advice." Comp. ver. 40.

Hence it follows that Paul does not give the counsel immediately to be mentioned in virtue of his apostolic authority, but as a simple Christian. The words are very instructive, as showing with what precision he distinguished apostolical inspiration from Christian inspiration in general, making the former not only the highest degree, but something specifically different from the second. He thus, with a consciousness perfectly assured, traced the limit between what he had directly received by way of revelation, with a view to his *apostolic* teaching, and what he himself deduced from Christian premises by his own reflections, as any believer may do under the guidance of the Spirit. We thus see what is implied in his view by the title of *apostle*, under the guarantee of which he places the contents of his Epistles. He was not of the mind—as is sought to persuade the Church in our day—that his gospel was only the result of his meditations and researches.—After this preface, he states the advice he has to give.

Ver. 26. "I think therefore that this state is good

for the present distress, seeing that it is good for man so to be."—This verse has been translated in a multitude of ways. As Paul seems to say two things at the same time, Rückert, Meyer, Edwards hold some incorrectness. After dictating the words: "I think this, that it is good because of the present distress," Paul, they say, forgot that he had already expressed the idea: that this is good, and repeated it by mistake, saying, "that it is good for man so to be." This is to hold a strange idea of the way in which Paul composed; and besides, did he not read over his letters before despatching them? Nor would it be possible to understand why in the second proposition he added the word ἀνθρώπῳ, *for man*, and substituted the verb εἶναι for ὑπάρχειν. Reuss holds an explanatory repetition: "My advice is, that this is good because of the difficult times which are coming; that it is good for man so to live." But to what purpose this repetition? and why the two changes which we have indicated? Holsten sees in τοῦτο, *this*, a pronoun representing by anticipation the idea of the second part of the verse: "I think that *this* (τοῦτο), [to wit] that it is good for man so to be, is good on account of the present necessity." Heydenreich and Heinrici take the ὅτι as a pronoun (ὅ τι), which leads to this meaning: "I think this, that [for virgins], on account of the present necessity, *all that is good* for man [to wit] so to be (to remain virgin) is good." The construction proposed by Hofmann surpasses, if possible, even these violences: "I think this: that it is good—because on account of the present necessity, it is good for man—so to be (to remain virgin)." There is, in my view, only one construction admissible, that proposed by de Wette; it is as simple in form as suitable in sense: "I think therefore that this (the state of virginity) is good on account of the present difficulties, seeing that in itself it is good for man so to be." The idea is this: "If, in general, celibacy is a state good for man (ἄνθρωπος, man or woman), now is the time for applying this principle, especially in regard to virgins, on account of the difficulties of the present time."—The pronoun τοῦτο, *this*, is not the object of νομίζω, *I think*, but the subject of the infinitive ὑπάρχειν; it relates to the state of celibacy, the idea of which was contained in the term παρθένων, *virgins*, ver. 25.—The verb καλὸν ὑπάρχειν denotes a goodness in point of fact, while καλὸν εἶναι, in the following proposition, denotes goodness of essence. The difference of expression is explained by the regimen διὰ τὴν ἐνεστῶσαν ἀνάγκην, *on account of the necessity*, of the *present*, or *imminent*, distress; an expression which gives to the καλόν of celibacy the character of suitableness. Hofmann has carried this regimen to the following proposition, beginning with ὅτι, *because*. But the idea of distress belongs rather to the first proposition, which is intended to characterize the present time as particularly inviting to celibacy.—The word ἐνεστώς strictly signifies *imminent* (comp. 2 Thess. ii. 2), or *present* (iii. 22; Rom. viii. 38; Gal. i. 4). The *imminent* tribulation denotes, it is held, the time of distress which is to precede the end of the world (Luke xxi. 25-27), what Jewish theology called *dolores Messiæ*, the crisis of the painful birth-pangs of the Messianic kingdom, the reign of the man of sin (2 Thess. ii.). Such is the meaning held by Meyer, Osiander, Edwards, etc. Others give ἐνεστῶσα the meaning of *present;* so Calvin and Grotius, who apply present distress, — the former to the troubles inseparable from married life; the latter to the sufferings of this earthly life in general. But the phrase *the present distress* is too precise to admit of such vague explanations. While holding the sense of *present,* which is the most common, it seems to me that we must apply the term *necessity,* or *distress,* to the whole state of things between the first and second coming of Christ. In Paul's view the *last times* began with Pentecost. From that date the character of human existence is one of incessant and painful tension, of struggle between the new life, which sprang up with the appearing of Christ, and the life of the old world, which is departing, but which will not pass away till the Lord's return. On the painful character of this whole period, comp. Luke xii. 51: " I am come, not to give peace on earth, but war; " and so xvii. 22. And how much more acute will the crisis be when persecution will emerge on this ground of trouble and suffering! It seems to me that ver. 28 speaks in favour of this explanation. No doubt in using the expression *present distress* to characterize the earthly future of the Church, the apostle had no idea that there could be a time when the world would be outwardly Christianized and Christianity secularized. Like the author of the Apocalypse, he saw the struggle of the two hostile principles going on increasing in intensity till the final crisis. If history has followed another course, and if the war already kindled in the apostolic time has given place to a false peace, this is due in great measure to the weakening of the heavenly virtues of the Church.

As it always is in the human domain, which is that of liberty, the Divine plan has been realized in this respect only in an abnormal way.

Under those conditions which were already difficult at the time when the apostle wrote, and which were to become always more so, the unmarried maiden would have, according to him, a much easier path than the woman burdened with a family. The second proposition adds to the reason drawn from the *present* situation a more general reason, which is no other than the opinion already given on celibacy, vers. 1 and 7ª. The ὅτι, *because*, signifies, "celibacy is preferable at this time for virgins, *because* in general it is preferable for man." The *permanent* (εἶναι) and *general* (ἄνθρωπος) judgment forms the basis of the *present* (ὑπάρχειν) and *particular* (παρθένοι) counsel.—The *so to be* may denote either the state of virginity (τοῦτο) or the state in which man naturally finds himself. The second sense agrees better with the term ἄνθρωπος, which includes the two sexes.

Ver. 26 therefore embraces two propositions, the first of which contains the particular counsel called for by the circumstances, the second the indication of the general preference to be given to celibacy. It is these two propositions which are taken up again and developed in the sequel, the first in vers. 27–31, the second in vers. 32–38.

Vers. 27, 28. "Thou art bound to a wife, seek not to be loosed; thou art loosed from a wife, seek not a wife. 28. But and if thou marry,[1] thou hast not sinned; and if a virgin marry, she hath not sinned; nevertheless such shall have trouble in the flesh; but I

---

[1] T. R. with K L: γήμῃς; ℵ A: γαμῃσῃ; B P: γαμησῃς.

would spare you."—The apostle would not, however, have ver. 26ᵃ understood in the sense of a *moral* superiority granted to celibacy. He therefore expressly repeats what he had said in ver. 10 (from a somewhat different standpoint) : He who is bound, whether as affianced or as married, ought not, with a view to realizing a higher sanctity, to break the bond. I do not think that there is ground for restricting the application of these first words to the *affianced*, as Hofmann does. —If one were to take the term λέλυσαι, *art thou loosed*, in the strictness of the letter, it would apply only to widowers and those divorced. But the context proves that, as Origen had already understood it, the word here signifies in general : *If thou art free from bond*, and that it refers also to celibates.

Ver. 28 is meant to prevent a misunderstanding to which the second part of ver. 27 might give rise. What Paul says here is not a command ; if one act differently he will not sin.—The form ἐὰν καί evidently means, as in vers. 11 and 21, *if therewith*, if nevertheless, and not *though*.—On the two forms γήμῃς and γαμήσῃς, see on ver. 9. Edwards remarks that if we read γαμήσῃς, we have here the two forms in the same verse.—The *flesh* strictly denotes the organ of physical sensibility ; but the meaning of the word extends very often to moral sensibility.—The term *trouble*, literally, *tribulation*, must denote the same thing as *the present necessity*, ver. 26, so : the state of permanent conflict in which the Church is with the world till the perfect establishment of the kingdom of God. As long as this state of things shall last, Christian parents who are tender and faithful will have to suffer much for themselves and for their children in a community which is strange to God. The οἱ τοιοῦτοι denotes those who marry in spite of this counsel.—There is a sort of paternal solicitude in the words, *but I spare you*. The path of celibacy which he recommends will be that in which they shall have least to suffer. St. Augustine makes a singular mistake in giving these words the meaning : " I spare you the enumeration of the troubles of family life."

But, in all that precedes, Paul has not yet gone to the root of the matter. What is of importance is not : marrying or not marrying ; but a habit of soul in keeping with the situation indicated above. And as in vers. 17–24 he had extended his point of view and generalized the question, so as better to justify his counsel to remain in their present state, so in vers. 29–31 he explains, while applying it to various analogous cases, his true view in regard to celibacy and marriage in present circumstances.

Vers. 29–31. "But this I mean, brethren,[1] the time is henceforth limited,[2] that they even that have wives be as though they had none ; 30. and they that weep, as though they wept not ; and they that rejoice, as though they rejoiced not ; and they that buy, as though they possessed not ; 31. and they that use this

---

[1] T. R. here reads ὅτι (*that* or *because that*), with D E F G It. Syr.; the other six Mjj. omit it.

[2] The Mnn. present three principal readings :—
T. R. with E K L : συνεσταλμένος τὸ λοιπόν ἐστιν ἵνα . . . (*the time is limited, as to what remains, that* . . .).
א A B D P : συνεσταλμένος ἐστι τὸ λοιπόν ἵνα . . . (*the time is limited that, as to what remains,* . . .).
F G It. Vulg. Tert. : συνεσταλμένος ἐστι, λοιπόν ἐστιν ἵνα . . . (*the time is limited ; it remains that* . . .).

world,[1] as not abusing it : for the fashion of this world passeth away." — The formula τοῦτο δὲ φημί, which begins ver. 29, does not announce a simple explanation, as a τοῦτο λέγω would do. The term φημί has a certain solemnity : " Now here is my real view, the most essential thing which I have to declare to you." —By the address : *brethren*, he draws near to them as if to gain an entrance into their minds for this decisive thought, with the particular applications they are to draw from it, each for himself. If, with T. R., we should read ὅτι before ὁ καιρός, it would require to be translated by *because*, and τοῦτο referred to what precedes (ver. 28); but the following sentence would become extremely heavy, on account of the two conjunctions ὅτι and ἵνα, which follow one another. We must therefore reject ὅτι. The participle συνεσταλμένος (from συστέλλειν, to furl sails, to pack luggage, to reduce into small volume, to shorten a syllable, etc.) may be taken either in the moral sense (straitened, pressed with trouble, 1 Macc. iii. 6 ; 2 Macc. vi. 12), or in the literal sense (reduced to small volume, concentrated, abridged). As the first meaning cannot well apply except to persons, the second is here preferable ; only it must be remarked that Paul does not use the word χρόνος, which denotes time in respect of its duration, but καιρός, time in respect of its character, season, opportunity. The apostle therefore means not that the present epoch will embrace a greater or less number of years, but that the character of the epoch is its being contained between precise limits which do

---

[1] T. R. reads, with E K L P, τω κοσμω τουτω ; D F G : τον κοσμον τουτον ; א A B : τον κοσμον.

not admit of its being extended indefinitely. These limits are, on the one side, the coming of Christ which took place recently, and on the other, His coming again, which may be expected any hour, and which will be the close of the καιρός. There is therefore no longer anything assured in the present existence of the world; it is profoundly compromised since the coming of Christ, who created thenceforth a higher sphere of existence; hence it follows that human life has no longer a future, except one limited and precarious; comp. Phil. iii. 20: "Our citizenship is in heaven." We are in *the last hour* (ἐσχάτη ὥρα ἐστί, 1 John ii. 18), of which no one knows how long it will last (Mark xiii. 32); for that depends on God, and also in part on the faithfulness of the Church, and on the conduct of the unbelieving world.—Of the three readings which we have given in the note, that of the T. R., supported by three Byz., signifies: "The time is limited as to what remains, that . . ." The reading of the four older Mjj. signifies: "The time is limited, that for the future (τὸ λοιπόν) . . ." That is to say, that the time for the future ought to be otherwise used than it has been in the past. The third, that of F G, signifies: "The time is limited; it remains (it follows therefrom) that . . ." This last ought to be rejected without hesitation; for the expression λοιπὸν ἵνα cannot signify: it follows that. In the Alex. reading we must accept the inversion of the τὸ λοιπόν, and bring it into the proposition of ἵνα. The emphasis put by this construction on τὸ λοιπόν is justified no doubt by the contrast between the remaining future and the past which has already elapsed. But the inversion is harsh, and the first reading, that of the Byz., seems to me preferable. Its meaning is very simple: "The time is limited as to what remains." The time which mankind have yet to pass is limited by the coming of Christ. And so, whereas unbelievers regard the world as sure to last indefinitely, the Christian has always before his eyes the great expected fact, the Parousia; hence there arises in him a wholly new attitude of soul, that which the apostle characterizes in the following words. The: *in order that*, shows that this new attitude of the heart is willed of God as the proper consequence of the character assigned to the present epoch. We must take care not to make the ἵνα depend on the verb φημί: "*I declare this to you in order that* . . ." This inward disposition of believers springs much more naturally from the character of the epoch in which they live, than from Paul's declaration, which is addressed only to some of them. The anticipation of Christ's coming is that which transforms the mode of regarding and treating all earthly positions.—The καί, which follows ἵνα, should be translated by *even:* Even the married ought in their attitude of soul to return to the state of celibates. By their detachment from the things of this earth, which are about to fail them, and their attachment to Christ, who is coming again, they recover that state of inward independence which they lost by marrying. Externally bound, they become free again as to their moral attitude; comp. the slave, ver. 22ª.

Ver. 30. Here is depicted the spiritual detachment in its application to the various situations of life. As nothing in this world has more than a waiting character, the afflicted believer will not be swayed by his pain; he will say to himself: It is no more worth the trouble! The man who is visited by joy will not be intoxicated by it; he will say to himself: It is but for a moment. He who buys, will not seize and hold the object he has got too keenly (κατέχειν, *to hold firmly*); for he will look upon himself as always ready to give it up. It is not meant that the believer will not rejoice or be afflicted or care for what he has. But, as Edwards well says: "Excess is prevented, not by the diminution of the joy or of the grief, but by the harmony of both. Joy and grief becoming more profound harmonize in a sadness full of joy and a joy full of sadness."

Ver. 31. The phrase *using this world* is a formula in which are embraced marriage, property, commerce, political, scientific, and artistic activity. The believer may use these things, provided it is constantly in a spirit which is master of itself, detached from everything, looking only to Christ.—It is a mistake here to translate the term καταχρῆσθαι in the sense of *abusing;* for there never is for any one a time of abusing. To the notion of the simple χρῆσθαι, *to make use of*, the preposition κατά adds, as in the preceding verb, a shade of tenacity, carnal security, false independence. He who uses the world, in these different domains, while keeping his eye constantly fixed on the future, ought to preserve the same inward calm as one might who had broken with the whole train of earthly affairs. The Alex. read the regimen in the accusative (τὸν κόσμον); this construction is found only in the later Greek, and that with the compound καταχρῆσθαι. —

The last words justify the disposition of detachment which the apostle recommends. They do not express merely the commonplace thought: that visible things are transitory in their nature. Undoubtedly Edwards is right in saying: "Every change proves that the end will come;" but we must not forget that this proposition is connected by γάρ, *for*, with the preceding: "The time is limited." This relation obliges us to apply the παράγει, *passeth away*, to the near coming of the Lord, who will transform the present fashion of the world, that is to say, of external nature and human society. The term τὸ σχῆμα, *the fashion*, the external state of a thing, proves that the world itself will not disappear, but that it will take on a new mode of existence and development; comp. Rom. viii. 19–22 and Matt. xix. 28.

The apostle has just developed the term *the present distress* (ver. 26ᵃ), and expounded the reason for the preference to be given to celibacy for virgins, taken from present circumstances. He passes to the more general reason stated in ver. 26ᵇ: "It is good *in itself* for man so to be."

Vers. 32–38 : The general suitableness of celibacy.

Vers. 32, 33. "But I would have you without carefulness. He that is unmarried careth for the things that belong to the Lord, [seeking] how he may please[1] the Lord. 33. But he that is married careth for the things that are of the world, [seeking] how he may please[1] his wife."—The subject is no longer merely the exceptional anxieties which the education and care of

---

[1] T. R. with K L P reads αρεσει (*will please*); all the rest: αρεσῃ (*may please*).

a family may cause parents, in a time dangerous for the Church. Paul has especially in view here the *moral* difficulties which the conjugal relation brings with it at all times. The δέ is the transition from the one of these ideas to the other. The term, ἄγαμος, *unmarried*, includes, as in ver. 8, bachelors and widowers. With the view of illustrating the general truth which he would apply to virgins, the apostle shows first that it applies also to men. The affirmation : *careth for the things of the Lord*, is not absolute. It is not always so, it is true ; but nothing prevents the Christian celibate from acting thus.

Ver. 33. The aorist γαμήσας signifies: *from the time he is married*. The step once taken, what follows is the necessary result. But it is no blame which Paul thereby throws on marriage ; it is a fact which he states to justify the greater *difficulty* a married man experiences in realizing in this state entire fidelity to the Lord. The unmarried man has only one question to put to Himself : how shall I act to please the Lord ? The married man is obliged to take into account another will than that of the Lord and his own, a will which he should consult and which must be gained for his plans. There are, besides, earthly interests to manage ; for they concern the future of her who shares with him the burden of the family. This care is not a sin, otherwise marriage would be a morally defective state; it is a sacred obligation, a duty at once of delicacy and justice, which the husband contracted by marriage. With the same measure of fidelity, the married man will therefore have a double difficulty to surmount, from which the celibate is exempt, that of getting his wife to accept the moral decisions which he feels bound to take, and that of not sacrificing his Christian walk to the earthly fortune of his family. — These reflections are true, practical, sensible, in accordance with the experience of life, and they do not in the least justify the charge brought against the apostle of degrading marriage. If the married believer comes out of these difficulties victorious, he will not be either more or less holy than the unmarried believer.—All this is only an introduction; in the following verses, the apostle reaches the subject strictly so called; for it is of virgins he is now speaking.

Ver. 34. "[1]The married[2] woman also is divided. The unmarried[3] virgin careth for the things of the Lord, that she may be holy both in body and in spirit; but she that is married careth for the things of the world, [seeking] how she may please[4] her husband."— The text, at the beginning of ver. 34, has been extraordinarily handled and re-handled. This arises, no doubt, from the uncertainty which copyists felt in regard to the verb μεμέρισται, *is divided*. Should it be made the end of ver. 33, or the beginning of ver. 34? On this there depended also in part the question of the καί (*and*) before the verb. The verb may certainly be

---

[1] The και (*and*) at the beginning of the verse is found in ℵ A B D P Syr^sch. T. R. omits it, with E F G K L It.
[2] The και (*and*) before η γυνη (*the woman*) is omitted by T. R. with D E.
[3] The words η αγαμος (*the unmarried*) are read twice in ℵ A, after η γυνη (*the woman*) and after η παρθενος (*the virgin*); and once only, after η γυνη (*the woman*), in B P, and after η παρθενος (*the virgin*) in D E F G K L It. Syr.
[4] T. R. with K L P: αρεσει; the rest: αρεση.

connected with the preceding sentence; in this case it ought to be preceded by καί: "He who is married cares for the things of the world, how he may please his wife; *and he is divided* (in himself)." It will be objected that such an addition destroys the parallelism with ver. 32; but there was no observation to be made on the result of the harmony between the will of the celibate and that of the Lord, whereas it is otherwise in the case of ver. 33. This meaning is that adopted by Neander, Hofmann, Edwards, Lachmann, Westcott, and Hort. Only one cannot help asking why the apostle did not likewise add an analogous reflection when concluding the case of the married woman in ver. 34. The parallelism between the two members of the sentence is rigorous, and seemed to demand it. It is better, therefore, to join the verb μεμέρισται (with or without the καί) to ver. 34. But in this case, what is the subject of the verb *is divided?* And how are we to read and punctuate the following words? One reading gives the epithet ἡ ἄγαμος, *unmarried, twice,* first after the word ἡ γυνή, *the woman,* and then after the word ἡ παρθένος, *the virgin;* another, only after the first of these words; a third, only after the second. Not only does the majority of the documents support this third reading; but its representatives are found in the three families of Mjj., and the two oldest versions testify in its favour, so that we ought to receive it as the most probable. The true text seems to us to be: Μεμέρισται καὶ ἡ γυνὴ [καὶ] ἡ παρθένος ἡ ἄγαμος μεριμνᾷ . . . But the question is, how far we are to extend the subject of μεμέρισται, *is divided.* Many think that the subject is double: *Both the wife and the virgin are divided.* Then the new sentence would begin with ἡ ἄγαμος, *the unmarried.* We should require to take the verb *is divided* in the sense of *is different* (so Chrysostom, Luther, Mosheim, etc.), or, what comes to nearly the same thing, in the sense of *going in opposite directions* (Theodoret, Meyer, Beet) : "There is a difference between the wife and the unmarried woman." But after the idea of a division of the same person by opposite cares had been so forcibly advanced in ver. 33, it is unnatural to give to the verb μερίζεσθαι, *to be divided*, the sense of *to differ*, all the more that the verb is in the singular, and that, notwithstanding all Meyer's subtle explanations, one would expect the plural (μερίζονται), as is shown by the paraphrase of Theodoret, who instinctively falls into the plural (μεμερισμέναι εἰσὶ ταῖς σπουδαῖς). This verb in the singular can only apply to one whole divided into several parts (comp. i. 13 ; Mark iii. 25, 26, etc.). Although, then, the Latin and Syriac versions, and almost all the Latin Fathers give this meaning, it appears to me difficult to accept it.—There remains, as it seems to me, only one possible explanation : that which assigns to μεμέρισται as its subject the following term only : *the woman*, ἡ γυνή, reading the καί : *The woman also is divided* (evidently *the married woman*). Ver. 33 had just shown the married man divided within himself by different anxieties. It is absolutely the same with the married woman, adds the apostle ; and he establishes it in the sequel of the verse, presenting first by way of contrast the description of the virgin who consents to remain so. The beginning of the following proposition is therefore ἡ παρθένος, *the virgin*. The καί before this word ought either to be understood in the sense of *also* (like the bachelor, ver. 17), or rejected. It may easily have been added under the influence of the widespread interpretation which made the following substantive a second subject of μεμέρισται.—The apostle forcibly brings out the contrast between the married woman who is inwardly divided, and the virgin whose happy inward harmony the apostle proceeds to point out. The apposition ἡ ἄγαμος, *the unmarried*, is not a pleonasm; it signifies: "the virgin *who remains* unmarried." She takes counsel only of the will of the Lord, without being obliged to put herself at one with the will of a human master; she has consequently only one perfectly simple aim to pursue, that which is indicated by the ἵνα, *in order that*, which follows. The word ἁγία, *holy*, is equivalent here to the term *consecrated*, that is to say, entirely devoted in her body and spirit to the service of the Lord. As to the words: *in her body*, we must compare ver. 4, where it is said of the married woman that she has not power over her own body. As to *the spirit*, compare what follows, where it is said of the married woman that she is under obligation to take account of her husband's will, as well as of earthly necessities. It is an ideal full of nobleness and purity which floats before the eyes of the apostle, when he thus describes the life of the Christian virgin being able to give herself up, without the least distraction, to the task which the Lord assigns her. He will give scope to this impression still more fully in ver. 35. In the last proposition of the verse, the apostle returns to the other alternative, that of marriage, and develops the first words of the verse: *The woman is divided.* The aor. γαμήσασα signifies: from the moment when she did the act of marrying. In English we should rather join these two propositions by a conjunction: "While the virgin cares for . . . the married woman cares for . . ."

Ver. 35. "And this I speak for your own profit, not that I may cast a snare upon you, but for that which is comely, and that ye may attend upon[1] the Lord without distraction."—Paul feels the need of defending himself from the charge which might be brought against him of giving scope to an individual preference, and of letting his private position influence his directions as an apostle. In all that he has just said, he has had in view nothing but the real advantage of those who have consulted him: the simplest and easiest possible consecration of their whole life to the Lord, without any concern to divert them from it.— The word βρόχος denotes the noose thrown in the chase to capture game. Some have thought that Paul meant that while thus recommending celibacy, he did not seek to make them fall into impurity. But would he have needed to set aside such a suspicion? The figure of *throwing a net over them* contains a wholly different idea: "I do not claim to make slaves of you, to hamper your liberty by forcing you to live to my taste, and according to my personal sympathies; but this is what I have in view." And he then expounds the ideal of Christian celibacy in the elevated and pure light in which he contemplates it, that is to say, as a state of supreme comeliness through the consecration

---

[1] T. R. with K reads: ευπροσεδρον; L: προσεδρον; the rest: ευπαρεδρον.

of body and spirit to the Lord.—Τὸ εὔσχημον denotes perfect fitness. Natural innocence raised to heavenly saintship through union with Christ, such, in the eyes of the apostle, is the incomparable adornment of the virgin. This first term refers to state; the second rather to action. The reading by far most widely spread is εὐπάρεδρον, a term compounded of three words: ἕζομαι, *I seat myself*; παρά, *by the side of*, and εὖ, *well, honourably*. The word therefore calls up the figure of a person nobly seated at the Lord's side. But two Byz. documents read,—the one εὐπρόσεδρον, the other πρόσεδρον, an expression if possible still more beautiful, the preposition πρός adding to the idea of παρά, *beside*, that of *being turned toward* (John i. 1): the state, that is, of a person seated beside the Lord, with his eye turned to Him. Of the two adjectives πάρεδρος and πρίσεδρος, the most frequently used is πάρεδρος; it is translated by assessor, colleague, disciple, etc. The word πρόσεδρος scarcely figures in Greek literature; a reason for giving it the preference, all the more that to the idea of assiduity it adds a notion of tenderness which is foreign to the other. Let us add that in Hellenistic Greek, which must have been especially familiar to the apostle, the use of the word προσεδρία is established to denote assiduity (3 Macc. iv. 15). These reasons will have some weight with those who think that in view of the different texts they ought to preserve their liberty of judgment.—The neuter of the two adjectives may be regarded as the equivalent of the verb in the infinitive (with the article); only by the form which the apostle chooses the act becomes in a sense a quality inherent in the subject.—The εὖ, *well*, in the two adjectives, expresses the propriety, the dignity, the moral beauty of this position, and of the activity of the Christian virgin ; here is the excellence, the καλόν, of celibacy, the utility, the συμφέρον of which has been described in vers. 34, 35. Finally, the adverb so full of gravity, ἀπερισπάστως, literally, without dragging in different directions, without distractions, closes this development with a last word which sums it up in its entirety; comp. the ἕως ἄρτι, iv. 13. The term reminds us of the double solicitude which divides the heart of the married woman : on the one side, concern for the will of the Lord ; on the other, concern about the will of her husband and the exigencies of the world.

It is difficult to think that Paul, in writing these exquisite lines on the position of the young Christian, had not in view the picture drawn, Luke x. 39–42, of Mary of Bethany seated at the Saviour's feet and hearing His words. As has been pointed out, the μεριμνᾷ of Paul (ver. 34) corresponds to the μεριμνᾷς of Luke, the εὐπρόσεδρον to the παρακαθίσασα, and the ἀπερισπάστως to the περιεσπᾶτο and the τυρβάζῃ.

The apostle has concluded the exposition of his reasons. The *present* excellence of celibacy for the virgin arises from the greater *facility* of life which it will procure for her; and to this advantage another is added, which belongs to the state of celibacy *in general:* the perfect *simplicity* of the task for which the unmarried Christian lives.

From these considerations Paul finally draws the practical conclusion. He puts two cases, as he had done in regard to married Christians, vers. 12, 15, and gives his decision as to the one (ver. 36), and as to the other (ver. 37); after which he sums up his judgment (ver. 38).

The first case:

Ver. 36. "But if any man think that he behaveth himself uncomely toward his virgin, if she pass the flower of her age, and need so require, let him do what he will; he sinneth not; let them marry."[1]—Paul introduces his advice by δέ, *but*, because this counsel is in contrast to the thought expressed, ver 35. The antithesis of ἀσχημονεῖν to τὸ εὔσχημον is manifest.—The verb ἀσχημονεῖν may have the active or passive sense: *to behave uncomely toward any one*, or: *to be the object of unsuitable treatment*. Of these two meanings the first only agrees with the preposition ἐπί which follows, and which indicates the object of the action; comp. also xiii. 5. But it might be a question whether the verb should not be taken here in an impersonal sense: "that there is no uncomeliness for his virgin." I know no example of this usage; but the *if she pass the age*, which has embarrassed Hofmann, would fall in better with this meaning than with the active sense. The proposition ἐὰν ᾖ would then be the logical subject of ἀσχημονεῖν. Several commentators (de Wette, Meyer, Edwards even) think that the dishonour of which Paul speaks is that which the virgin contracts by allowing herself to be drawn into evil. But the apostle's thought is far removed from such a supposition; and he would have expressed it by saying: "if any one *fears*," and not: "if any one *thinks*." He is speaking solely of that sort of shame which attached to the position of spinster, still more among the ancients than among us;

[1] D F G: γαμείτω (*let her marry*).

comp. Ps. lxxviii. 63, and a passage quoted by Heinrici (p. 213).[1]—With the words: "If she pass the flower of her age" (ὑπέρακμος), we must, of course, understand without marrying.[2]—The meaning of the word οὕτως, *thus, so*, is explained by the beginning of the verse and by the contrast to ver. 26; it is the state of marriage, whereas in ver. 26 the context would show that it was the state of celibacy. Hofmann, after Theophylact, makes the proposition καὶ οὕτως the principal one: "If any one ..., well! so it must be." But there would be a glaring tautology with the three following propositions, and there would be no ground for the καί. The καί here signifies, *and consequently*. The ὀφείλει, *it must be*, follows first from the father's judgment, determined by the general prejudice, and next from the circumstances (the desire of the daughter and mother) which press in favour of a consent, which nothing but the firmly opposed conviction of the father could prevent. Under these conditions, things *must* take their course.—In what follows the apostle means: "He might, no doubt, have done better for his child's happiness; but he has not made himself liable to any reproach." Holsten thinks that the subject of ἁμαρτάνει is the virgin; but it is the father who is regarded as acting throughout the whole passage.—The subject of γαμείτωσαν, *let them marry*, is, quite naturally, the virgin and the young man who asks her in marriage.

---

[1] *Phalaridis epist.*, p. 130: "For it is regarded by men as very shameful that a daughter remain at home beyond the time fixed by nature."

[2] Holsten gives this word a strange and unexampled meaning; he sees in it the idea of an over-excited sensibility (ὑπερ, in Paul's writings). Hence for the father the ὀφείλειν! This meaning is the less necessary because the father was already inclined to give his consent.

For there is no reason to suppose that the apostle is alluding, as Rückert has thought, to a definite couple, about whom the Corinthians had addressed a question to him.

The second case:

Ver. 37. "Nevertheless, he that standeth stedfast in his heart, having no necessity, but hath power over his own will, and hath so decreed in his own[1] heart that[2] he will keep his virgin, doeth[3] well."—This long sentence, loaded with incidental propositions, fully represents all the turnings which the father's original wish will have to take in order to reach at length a definite conclusion. This whole domestic drama has for its point of departure a *firm conviction*, already formed in the father's mind, that celibacy is preferable to marriage for his child; ἕστηκεν ἑδραῖος, *he has become and remains firm*. The participle μὴ ἔχων ἀνάγκην, *not underlying constraint*, qualifies the finite verb ἕστηκεν; it therefore signifies, the father has become and remains firm because there is nothing to hamper his liberty, neither the fear of opinion nor the character and indomitable will of the virgin, nor too ardent a wish on the part of the mother. The second finite verb ἔχει is not parallel to the μὴ ἔχειν; the construction, which has nothing irregular, gives it as its subject simply the ὅς, the subject of the first verb. After measuring himself with all the difficulties of the situation, and finding none of them insurmountable, the father remains *master of his own*

---

[1] ℵ B P: ιδια καρδια (*his own heart*); T. R. with the others: καρδια αυτου (*his heart*).

[2] ℵ A B P omit the του before τηρειν.

[3] ℵ A B: ποιησει (*will do*); T. R. with the other Mjj. It. Syr.: ποιει (*doeth*).

deliberate will, and may thus—here is the third verb—at length *take the* final *resolution* henceforth to refuse every offer for his daughter. These long circumlocutions do not at all suppose in him an arbitrary will which takes account of nothing but itself. On the contrary, they imply the fact that before taking the final decision, everything has been heard, examined, weighed.—The art. τοῦ before τηρεῖν is omitted in the Alex. reading. It presents a difficulty, which speaks in favour of its authenticity, as Meyer acknowledges. For the rest, if we take the word τηρεῖν, *to keep*, in its true sense, the difficulty vanishes, and the τοῦ, which expresses an *aim*, finds an explanation. In fact, the verb *to keep* does not signify, to maintain his daughter as a virgin (making παρθένον an attribute), but *to keep* her *for* the end to which she is consecrated (the service of Christ). Hence it follows that the act τηρεῖν is not an explanatory apposition to τοῦτο, *this*, which was clear enough of itself, but a definition of the end: "and who has decided *this* in his heart (not to marry his daughter), *with a view to* keeping her."—The words τὴν ἑαυτοῦ παρθένον, literally, "*the* virgin belonging to himself," *the object* of τηρεῖν (see ver. 36), express the feeling of solicitude which guides this father: "the cherished being who has been providentially confided to him."

The principal sentence, which consists of only two words, contrasts by its brevity with the whole series of parentheses which have preceded. It is the simple fact in which all the anterior deliberations issue.—Must we read with the Alex. ποιήσει, *will do*, or, with the other Mjj. and the two ancient versions, *Itala* and

Peschito, ποιεῖ, *doeth?* Meyer himself abandons the Alex. reading, and rightly. The present agrees better with the parallel term οὐχ ἁμαρτάνει, *sinneth not*, of ver. 36. The future has probably been imported here from the following verse, where it has rather fewer authorities against it and more internal probability.—The apostle closes this discussion by the brief and striking summing up of his view:

Ver. 38. "So then he that giveth in marriage[1] doeth[2] well, but[3] he that giveth not in marriage[4] will do[5] better."—We again find here one of those ὥστε, *so that*, with which Paul, in this Epistle, loves to formulate his final judgment on a question which he has finished treating.—There is in Greek, before the words *he that giveth in marriage*, καί, *both*, which serves to co-ordinate the subjects of the two parallel propositions: "both . . . and . . ." This particle was suggested to Paul, on beginning his sentence, by his feeling of the equality of the two subjects in their *doing well*, their καλῶς ποιεῖν. But as he proceeds in the expression of his thought, the idea of equality gives place to that of superiority in the second father, and he substitutes at the head of the second proposition, as we have it in the received reading, the δέ, *but*, which expresses a contrast or a gradation, for the καί, *and*, which was in his original intention. It is easy to see how the reading of the Byz., notwithstanding its apparent

---

[1] T. R. with L P: εκγαμιζων; all the rest: γαμιζων.—Besides, T. R. with K L omits την παρθενον εαυτου (*his virgin*).

[2] B: ποιησει (*will do*), instead of ποιει (*doeth*).

[3] T. R. with K L P: ο δε (*but he . . .*); all the rest: και ο (*and he . . .*).

[4] T. R. with K L P: εκγαμιζων; all the rest: γαμιζων.

[5] ℵ A B: ποιησει (*will do*); T. R. with the other Mjj. It.: ποιει (*doeth*).

incorrectness, corresponds better with the movement of the apostle's thought than the Alex. and Greco-Latin reading.—There is room for hesitation between the received reading, ἐκγαμίζων, and the Alex. reading, γαμίζων. But there can be little doubt that the words τὴν ἑαυτοῦ παρθένον (א A) or τὴν παρθένον ἑαυτοῦ (B D), *his virgin*, which are omitted by the T. R., are a gloss. It was easy to add them to fill in the ellipsis of the object, but there was not the slightest reason for rejecting them, if they had existed in the text. Meyer therefore rightly judges that here again the Alex. text is corrupt. There is thus room for supposing that ἐκγαμίζων is the true reading. In any case, it better expresses the feeling of self-deprivation on the part of the father.—The reading of the *Vatic.* alone, ποιήσει, *will do*, in the first proposition, is certainly a mistake. On the other hand, the future may well be held to be the true reading in the second proposition, since two other Alex. here agree with the *Vatic.* It was, no doubt, to complete the parallelism that the future was introduced into this MS. in the preceding member of the sentence, and even by some into ver. 37. The present was preferable in ver. 37, which contained a general maxim. But here there is something prophetic, and consequently encouraging, in the future: "This father will see that he has taken the better course."

This *well* and *better* sum up the whole chapter. The *well* proves that in the eyes of Paul there is neither defilement nor even inferiority of holiness in marriage, and that the *better* is uttered by him from the prudential point of view, either as to the sufferings avoided or as to the more complete personal liberty for the service of Christ. St. Paul could speak of this position from experience. What would have become of his ministry among the Gentiles on the day when he should have exchanged his independence as a celibate for the duties and troubles of family life? It may be objected, no doubt, that if Paul's principle became a generally observed maxim, the existence of the race would be compromised. But the apostle knew well that Christians will always be a minority in human society, and that among Christians themselves there will not be more than a minority possessing the special gift of which he spoke in ver. 7.

Vers. 39, 40: widows.

It has been asked why Paul returns to widows, after having already given in vers. 8 and 9 the direction which concerns them. Reuss supposes that Paul forgot what he had said in these verses, or that he judged it suitable to inculcate it anew. But in the verses quoted, Paul had only spoken of widows jointly with celibates and widowers. Now their social position was so far different from that of the latter, that he might judge it necessary to add a special explanation regarding them. According to ancient ideas, there was no doubt as to the legitimacy of a second marriage for widowers; but it was otherwise with widows. It is known how much perseverance in widowhood was honoured among the Jews; comp. Luke ii. 36 and 37; from this to the condemnation of a second marriage was not far. And we also know that among the heathen a sort of contempt was expressed for the *mulier multarum nuptiarum*, and that they went the length of inscribing this title of honour on the tombstone of a woman: *univira*.[1] In the second century of the Church we hear even Athenagoras call a second marriage, whether of man or woman, a decent adultery. Probably, therefore, among the questions put to the apostle in regard to marriage, there was one which bore on this particular point. The general answer given (vers. 8, 9) required, therefore, to be more specialized and confirmed; and this answer being only a particular application of all that he had just expounded in regard to virgins, could not be placed elsewhere than here. The only difference on this point between virgins and widows is, that in the case of widows everything is referred to their own wish, without any more question of the father's.

Vers. 39, 40. "A wife is bound[2] as long as her husband liveth; but if[3] her husband be dead, she is at liberty to be married to whom she will, only in the Lord. 40. But she is happier if she abide as she is, after my judgment. Now[4] I think that I also have the Spirit of God."—Γυνή, without article: a wife in opposition to a virgin,—*Is bound*: to her husband, as long as he liveth. The regimen νόμῳ, *by the law*, has no doubt been borrowed from Rom. vii. 2.—Paul limits the liberty which he concedes to the widow by the restriction, *only in the Lord*. In this context the meaning of the words can only be: on the basis of communion with Christ, consequently with a member of the Christian society. This is the meaning now

---

[1] See Heinrici, p. 214.
[2] T. R. reads, with E F G L P Syr.: νομω (*by the law*); this word is omitted in א A B D F*.
[3] F G L add και after εαν δε.
[4] Instead of δε (*now*), B reads γαρ (*for*).

generally held. The words would be superfluous, if we made them signify, with Chrysostom, Calvin, and others: honourably and piously. Reuss objects to the meaning, "with a Christian," that the same reservation should have been made also in the case of virgins. But in regard to the latter Paul had not said: *to whom she will.* For in that case there was the paternal will which watched over their lot.

Ver. 40. By the word *happier* the apostle sums up the two reasons, the one general, the other particular, whereby from ver. 25 he had justified his preference given to celibacy for the Christian virgin. There is therefore no question of a superior holiness in this world, or a more glorious position in the next, attributed to this state.—The apostle on this point does not arrogate more to himself than a *view*, an *advice*, the value of which every one can appraise at his pleasure. It is evident how far he was removed from that exaltation which makes fanatics take all their ideas for revelations. Nevertheless he certainly claims an inspiration, such as that which all Christians share, and consequently he traces to the direction of the Divine Spirit the advice which he has just expressed. But we must beware, as we have already said, ver. 10, of concluding from this, with several (comp. in particular Reuss, p. 197), that he did not claim, besides this, revelations of a wholly special kind, going beyond what was granted to the Church in general. In other cases he is careful to affirm, in regard to directions which he gives, that they proceed *from the Lord;* comp. xiv. 37, and also the expression vii. 17. If he thus expresses himself in connection with simple directions about public worship or Christian practice, how much more conscious was he of being the organ of a Divine revelation of a wholly personal kind when the matter in question was the very essence of his religious teaching, *his gospel!* We are led, therefore, to distinguish here three degrees of authority,—1. The direct commands *of the Lord*, which He gave during His sojourn on the earth, and which Paul merely quotes without discussing their grounds (ver. 10). 2. The *apostolic* commands of the apostle, which are imposed on Churches subject to his jurisdiction, and which he gives them as the organ of a higher illumination attached to his special mission. As to these he is careful to expound their reasons, being unwilling to ask his brethren to give a *blind* obedience (vers. 12–17); comp. x. 15. 3. The directions which he gives as a *simple Christian*, which he himself declares to be purely optional, and which he leaves to the judgment of every believer (ver. 25). Far from confounding these different degrees, and assimilating, for example, the second with the third, we should recognise and admire the precision with which the apostle distinguished them and could draw the practical consequences of the distinction.—The word δοκῶ, *I think*, is not in the least, as Chrysostom and others have thought, a modest way of affirming his inspiration. It is evidently, especially if account be taken of the κἀγώ, *I also*, an ironical expression: "Now I hope, however, even if my apostolical authority is disputed among you, that you will not deny to me the possession of the Divine Spirit, such as you recognise in all Christians, and specially in the numerous spiritual guides to whom you give your confidence" (iv. 15).

There are few chapters of the apostle which have drawn down on him such severe judgments.

In connection with the passage vers. 29–31, it has been asserted that his morality itself was "the plaything of a shortsighted Christology." What we have found in the passage are practical directions in which St. Paul takes account of the relation between the world and the Church on to the Parousia, a relation which may in the course of time be more or less strained, but which in any case renders it always difficult for Christian spouses to educate and guide a family. What pious parents have not had painful experience of the fact? In truth, the apostle did not foresee the armistice which would be established for a time between the two hostile societies; but the conflict between the opposing principles which animate them has never ceased, and, in proportion as the last times approach, it will again become more and more what it was in apostolic times. Paul's ethics do not therefore depend on a chronological error; they rest on the just appreciation of the Church's position in the world down to the coming of the Lord.

It is objected to this same passage that every believer is placed in it face to face with the Parousia, as if this event were to terminate his own life. But, in speaking thus, Paul only does what the Lord Himself did. Jesus very expressly set aside the idea of the nearness of His return (Matt. xxv. 5; Mark xiii. 35; Luke xii. 45, xiii. 18–21, xxi. 24; Matt. xxiv. 14; comp.

Mark xiii. 32); and yet this is how He speaks to His disciples (Luke xii. 36): "Be ye like men looking for their lord, when he shall return from the wedding, that when he cometh and knocketh, they may open to him immediately." This is because, in fact, death is to every believer a personal and anticipated Parousia. The saying of Jesus is therefore for all on to the last day a moral truth, but this truth is only relative, till the promise be accomplished in its strict sense to the last generation. So it is with the sayings of Paul.

Again, it has been alleged that Paul here taught the religious and moral superiority of celibacy, and while some have praised him for so doing, others have sharply reprimanded him.[1] His accusers charge him with nothing less than putting himself in manifest contradiction to the saying of Jesus, which he quotes himself, and to God;[2] and what is more astonishing is, that they claim to be thereby doing no violence to his apostolic infallibility. Indeed, does not Paul himself declare that he is here speaking as a simple Christian, not as an organ of Divine revelation?—But is it credible that Paul, an intelligent man, should not have noticed the contradictions between his advice and the declarations of God and of Jesus Christ, while the author of the writing quoted discerned them so easily? Or that Paul, having seen these contradictions, should

---

[1] In particular Mme de Gasparin in her work on *Les Corporations Monastiques*.

[2] The work quoted, ii. p. 422: "The Lord declares: It is not good for man to be alone! Paul declares: It is good for man not to marry! Paul says: I command them, yet not I, *but the Lord:* Let the woman not depart (ver. 10)! And scarcely has he traced these infallible sayings, when, of his own authority, he overturns them: Let her depart (ver. 15)!"

have audaciously faced them, and that without even attempting to say a word to resolve them? The fact is, that all that the author writes on this subject proceeds on the erroneous opinion, that Paul ascribes a superiority in *holiness* to celibacy. This is what he does not do for an instant, as we have seen, not even in the passage vers. 32–34.

Sabatier, in *l'Apôtre Paul*, p. 142, has reproduced, as Reuss and Scherer had done, the judgment of Baur, according to which Paul had formed at this period a gross idea of the conjugal bond. "In the Epistles of the captivity," says he, "we shall see St. Paul reaching a broader appreciation of marriage and of domestic life." We shall set over against this judgment the views of a very independent-minded German critic, Heinrici, who thus expresses himself (p. 136): "We have here (ver. 14) the proof that the apostle recognises the *moral character* of marriage and of its relation to the kingdom of God." If with this verse we join ver. 16 and xi. 3, it will be seen which of the two judgments is based on the facts. *To save, to sanctify*, such is certainly the higher end of the marriage union from the Christian point of view, according to the author of the Epistles to the Corinthians.

VI.

THE USE OF MEATS OFFERED TO IDOLS, AND PARTICIPATION IN THE SACRIFICIAL FEASTS (CHAPS. VIII.-X.).

The apostle passes to a new subject, which, like the preceding, seems to be suggested to him by the letter of the Corinthians, and belongs to the domain of Christian liberty. The believers of Corinth and the other Greek cities found themselves in a difficult position in regard to the heathen society around them. On the one hand, they could not absolutely give up their family and friendly relations; the interests of the gospel did not allow them to do so. On the other hand, these relations were full of temptations and might easily draw them into unfaithfulnesses, which would make them the scandal of the Church and the derision of the heathen. Among the most thorny points in this order of questions were invitations to take part in idolatrous banquets. The centre of ancient worships was the sacrifice; it was in this religious act that all the important events of domestic and social life culminated. As in Judaism (comp. Deut. xxvii. 7, the peace-offerings), these sacrifices were followed by a feast. All that remained of the victim's flesh, after the legs, enclosed in fat, and the entrails had been burned on the altar (see Edwards), and after the priest had received his portion, came back to the family which offered the sacrifice, and these consecrated meats were eaten either in the apartments or sacred wood belonging to the temple, or in the worshipper's house; sometimes, also, they were sold in the market. And as the sacrifice usually took place in connection with some joyful circumstance, relatives and friends were invited to the feast, among whom it might easily happen that there were Christians. So also, when those meats were sold in the market, a Christian might find himself exposed to the eating of them either at his own house or that of others.

Now various questions might be raised on this subject. And first of all, Is it allowable for a Christian to be present at a feast offered in the temple of an idol? Some, in the name of Christian liberty, answered: Yes! They boldly took advantage of the adage: All things are lawful for me (vi. 12, x. 23). Others said: No! for in such a region one subjects himself to the danger of malign and even diabolical influences. The scruples of the more timorous went further: Even in a private house, even in one's own house, is it not dangerous to eat of that meat which has figured on the idol's altar? Has it not contracted a defilement which may contaminate him who eats it? Not at all, answered others. For the gods of the heathen are only imaginary beings; meat offered on their altar is neither more nor less than ordinary meat.

The latter were certainly of the number of those who, at Corinth, called themselves Paul's disciples. Must we thence conclude, with Ewald and others, that the former were solely Christians of Jewish origin, who styled themselves Peter's disciples? There is nothing to prove this. It is even somewhat difficult to maintain, as we shall see, in view of certain passages of chap. viii., that these sticklers were mainly Christians of Jewish origin. Several commentators, last among them Holsten, rather regard those timid Christians, and rightly I think, as believers of Gentile origin, who could not free themselves all at once and completely from the idea in which they had lived from infancy, that of the reality and power of the divinities which they had worshipped. They might be confirmed in this view by the Jewish opinion, of which traces are found still later in the Church, that idols represented evil spirits. As to Jewish Christians, the passage Rom. xiv. shows that in any case we ought not to exclude them wholly. These were men whom the gospel had only as yet half freed from their national prejudices, particularly from that which held the heathen deities to be so many diabolical personalities.

The solution of these questions bristled with difficulties. The one party held strongly to their liberty, the other not less seriously to their scruples. The apostle must avoid favouring either superstition in the latter or libertinism in the former. He needed all his practical wisdom and all his love to trace a line of conduct on this subject which would be clear and fitted to unite hearts, instead of dividing them.

It has been asked why he did not here simply apply the decree of the Council of Jerusalem (Acts xv.), which called on the Gentile believers of Syria and Cilicia to give up the use of meats offered to idols, out of regard to the repugnance of Jewish Christians. And some have even gone the length of alleging the apostle's silence as an argument against the historical reality of the decree. But (1) this decree, from its very nature, could only have a temporary value, and it soon came out at Antioch, in connection with Peter's sojourn (Gal. ii.), what practical difficulties stood in the way of its application. (2) At the time and in the circumstances in which Paul had accepted it, this apostle did not yet hold his normal position in the Church. His apostolical authority had just been recognised with difficulty by the apostles. In Syria and Cilicia he was not yet on his own domain, for it was not he who had founded the Church there. But it was now entirely different in Greece; and it would have been to derogate from his apostolical position, as well as from his evangelical spirituality, to resolve a question of Christian life by means of an external decree like an article of law. It was from the spirit of the gospel that, in virtue of his apostolical authority and wisdom, he must derive the decision which the Church needed. (3) It was the more important for Paul to act thus because he had above all at heart to form the conscience of the Corinthians themselves, and to educe spontaneously from it the view of the course to be followed: "I speak unto you as unto wise men; judge yourselves what I say" (x. 15). It is precisely because of this method followed by the apostle that the discussion contained in these three chapters may still be so useful to us, though referring to wholly different circumstances. Paul on this occasion ascends to the first principles of Christian conduct, and we have only to gather them up to apply them to our own circumstances. (4) Finally, this subject presented a host of complications which could not be resolved by the summary decree of Acts xv., and which demanded a detailed examination.

The following is the order adopted by the apostle: He first treats the question by putting himself at the viewpoint of love. A Christian ought not to ask: What suits me best? but: What will most surely contribute to the salvation of my brethren? (viii. 1–ix. 22). Then the apostle passes to a second consideration: that of the salvation of the man himself who is called to act. He must take care while using his liberty not only not to destroy others, but also not to destroy himself (ix. 23–x. 22). Finally, he concludes by recapitulating the whole discussion, and laying down some practical rules in regard to the different particular cases which might present themselves (vers. 23-33).

I. THE QUESTION CONSIDERED FROM THE VIEWPOINT OF OUR NEIGHBOUR'S SALVATION (VIII. 1-IX. 22).

The apostle proves that if there is a knowledge which all equally possess (vers. 1-6), there remains a difference of degree which imposes duties on one class relatively to others (vers. 7-13); then he shows by his own example how such obligations ought to be discharged (ix. 1-22).

1. *The knowledge common to all* (vers. 1-6).

Vers. 1-4. "Now, as touching things offered to idols, we know that we all have knowledge,—knowledge puffeth up, but love edifieth. 2. If[1] any man think that he knoweth[2] anything, he knoweth[3] nothing

---

[1] ℵ A B P here omit the δε (*but* or *then*), which T. R. reads with all the rest.

[2] T. R. reads, with K L, ειδεναι (*savoir, to know* a fact), instead of εγνωκεναι (*connaître, to know* a person or thing), which is the reading of all the rest.

[3] T. R. with E K L: εγνωκε; all the rest: εγνω. The latter omit ουδεν (*nothing*), which is added by T. R. with the same three.

yet¹ as he ought to know. 3. But if any man love God, the same is known of Him — 4. as concerning therefore the eating of those things that are offered in sacrifice to idols, we know that an idol is nothing in the world, and that there is no God² but one."—We might take the preposition περί, *on the subject of*, with its regimen as a sort of title: "As to what concerns consecrated meats. . . ." In that case we must understand: "This is what I have to say to you;" comp. vii. 1. But we might also make this preposition depend on the verb οἴδαμεν, *we know*, or finally, on the expression γνῶσιν ἔχομεν, *we have knowledge;* in this sense: "We know that on the subject of meats offered in sacrifice we all have knowledge." In itself this last meaning might be suitable; but in ver. 4, where the sentence is taken up again (after an interruption), the words: *we have knowledge*, are omitted, and the περί, *on the subject of*, can only be explained there, and consequently also in ver. 1, in one of the two first meanings. The first construction is likewise set aside by ver. 4, where the περί can only depend on the verb which follows it, οἴδαμεν, *we know*. We are thus perforce brought to the second construction: "On the subject of meats . . . we know."—After such a verb as *we know*, it is more natural to give ὅτι the meaning of *that*, than the meaning of *because*. This sense is confirmed by ver. 4, where it is evidently the only one possible.—Several (Flatt, etc.) have supposed that these first words: *On the subject of . . . we know that . . .*,

---

¹ א A B P: ουπω (*not yet*), instead of ουδεπω (*not even yet*), the reading of T. R. with the rest.

² T. R. with K L Syr. here adds ετερος (*other* god).

were taken word for word by the apostle from the letter of the Corinthians. The most advanced members of the Church, they hold, expressed themselves thus: "We know that every one is sufficiently enlightened on this subject, and consequently we are perfectly free to use our liberty in the matter." Paul afterwards shows (ver. 7), they continue, that this affirmation is far from being exact. But, if it were so, we must also ascribe to the Corinthians vers. 4-6, which are a continuation of the sentence begun at ver. 1; now it is evident that it is Paul who speaks in these verses. The subject of *we know* is therefore, first of all, Paul and Sosthenes, who address the letter, but at the same time the Corinthians, whom the authors include with them in the same category. Perhaps the Corinthians had written something similar to these opening words; and Paul chooses to emphasize it as his own affirmation: "Yes, undoubtedly, we know, as you love to repeat that . . .;" comp. the similar maxim reproduced by Paul, vi. 11.—As this beginning of the sentence is taken up again, ver. 4, it must necessarily be held that a parenthesis begins in ver. 1 and continues to the end of ver. 3. The only question is where this parenthesis begins. Luther, Bengel, Olshausen, Heinrici, Edwards, etc., think that it opens with the conj. ὅτι, to which they give the meaning *because*. We have already set aside this meaning of ὅτι, and we add that the following asyndeton: "knowledge puffeth up . . .," would be far from natural so soon after the beginning of a parenthesis; two successive interruptions of the thought are inadmissible. The parenthesis therefore does not begin till the second proposition of the verse: "Knowledge puffeth up. . ."—*All* denotes in Paul's view all those who composed the Church. They had in baptism abjured the errors of polytheism, and accepted what the Church taught regarding the only true God. They had therefore all a certain measure of knowledge. How can Edwards go astray so far as to see in this πάντες, *all*, an allusion to the other apostles and to the decree of the Council of Jerusalem?

But, at this word knowledge, the apostle all at once stops short; and he gives himself up to a brief digression on the uselessness and nothingness of a certain kind of knowledge, as well as on the true nature of that for which this fair name should be reserved. "Knowledge, yes, every one has it; but when it is only in the head, and the heart is empty of love, knowledge produces only a vain *inflation*, presumption, vanity, lightness." With this idea of inflation the apostle contrasts that of *edification*, that is to say, of a solid and growing building; fulness, that is, reality, in opposition to emptiness and appearance. *Love* alone can produce in him who knows, and, through him, in his brethren, serious moral progress. Love alone draws from God the real knowledge of Divine things, and teaches him who receives it to adapt it to the wants of his brethren.

Ver. 2. The asyndeton of ver. 2 (the δέ of the T. R. should, it appears, be rejected) does not indicate a new interruption. It is that frequent asyndeton which announces the more emphatic reaffirmation of the previous thought: "Yes, that knowledge devoid of love and of power to edify, when we look at it more nearly, is not even a true knowledge." The expression εἰ τις δοκεῖ, *if any one thinketh he knoweth*, indicates an empty pretence; real knowing, on the contrary, is denoted by the words, *as he ought to know*. The reading should certainly be, with almost all the Mjj., ἐγνωκέναι, instead of the εἰδέναι of T. R.; as Edwards says, the second of these terms signifies: *to know* a fact, while the former signifies: *to be thoroughly acquainted with*, to have penetrated the thing. Now this second meaning is the only one which is suitable here.

It matters little whether we read with the Alex. οὔπω, *not yet*, or with the Greco-Lat. and the Byz. οὐδέπω, *not at all yet*. As to the pron. οὐδέν, *nothing*, of the T. R., it ought certainly to be suppressed (with the majority of the Mjj.). It weakens the idea instead of strengthening it. It is not the knowledge of this or that which the apostle denies to the man who is full of self and empty of love; it is the very possibility of knowledge. One can only know by assimilating the being to be known, and one can only assimilate him by renouncing self to give himself to him. Love, therefore, is the condition of all true knowledge, and that above all, when, as here, it is God and His thought and will which are in question; comp. 1 John iv. 8: "He who loveth not, knoweth not God; for God is love."

Ver. 3 is the antithesis of ver. 2: Without love, no knowledge (ver. 2); with love, true knowledge (ver. 3). But why, instead of: "The same knoweth God," does the apostle say: *The same is known of God?* Does he mean to deny the first of these two ideas? Assuredly not. But he clears, as it were, this first stage, which is self-understood, to rise at a bound to the higher stage, which supposes and implies it. To be known of God is more than to know Him. This appears from Gal. iv. 9: "But now, having known God, or rather being known of Him." In a residence, every one knows the monarch; but every one is not known by him. This second stage of knowledge supposes personal *intimacy*, familiarity of a kind; a character which is foreign to the first. We need not therefore seek to give the expression, "to be known of God," an exceptional meaning, which was done by Erasmus: "he is *acknowledged* of God as His true disciple;" and by Grotius: "He is *approved* of Him." Beza went even the length of giving to the passive ἔγνωσται, *is known*, the sense of a Hebrew Hophal: "he *is* rendered knowing, put in possession of the knowledge of God." The word *know* is here taken in the same sense as in Ps. i. 6: "The Lord knoweth the way of the righteous," a passage which Heinrici rightly compares. The eye of God can penetrate into the heart that loves Him and His light, to illuminate it. In this light an intimate communion is formed between him and God; and this communion is the condition of all true knowledge,—of man's being known by God as of God's being known by man.—The pronoun οὗτος, *this same*, does not refer to God, but to man; it signifies: "This same truly," in opposition to those πάντες, *all*, to whom the privilege of knowledge was so freely ascribed at Corinth (ver. 1).

After this digression, for which there was only too much reason, the apostle returns to the thought which he had begun to enunciate, ver. 1.

Ver. 4. The οὖν, *therefore*, indicates, as it does so frequently, the resuming of the interrupted sentence; but with this difference, that for the *fact* of knowledge (the γνῶσιν ἔχειν) Paul substitutes as the object of the *we know* the *contents* of the knowledge.—The term βρῶσις, the *act of eating*, which he here introduces (it did not occur in ver. 1), has in it something disdainful; it emphasizes the lower and material character of the act in question.—The contents of the knowledge which Paul ascribes to all Christians, are the monotheistic creed, as it is summed up in the two following propositions. And first the nothingness of idols; οὐδέν might be an adjective: "*no* idol." In that case we must apply the term idol to the false deity itself. None of those *deities* worshipped by the heathen has any existence in the circle of real beings (*the world*). So Meyer, de Wette, etc. But, says Edwards, it is doubtful whether εἴδωλον, the *idol*, can denote the false God, without the image representing it; the examples quoted do not prove this. He explains thus: There is not in creation any visible image of God; the only real image of God is that which is in heaven: Christ (Col. i. 15; 2 Cor. iv. 4). But one feels at once how foreign this thought is to the context. The subject in question for the time is God; only afterwards will Paul come to Jesus Christ, as the only *Lord* (ver. 6). What has led some to make οὐδέν an adjective, is the following οὐδείς, which evidently signifies *no*. But why should the construction of the two propositions be the same? The οὐδέν ought to be taken as a predicate: "That an idol *is nothing* in the world." It must be remembered that the statue was judged by the heathen to be the dwelling and agent of the god himself, so that the apostle means: If in the world of beings you seek one corresponding to the statue and person of Jupiter, Apollo, etc., you will find *nothing*.—In the following proposition, the word ἕτερος, *other* (which is found in the T. R.), must be rejected.—There was certainly not a single Christian at Corinth who had not subscribed to these two propositions; and the apostle may have borrowed them from the Church's own letter. He himself confirms while explaining them, but at the same time completing and prudently limiting them in the two following verses.

Vers. 5, 6. "For though there be that are called gods, whether in heaven or in earth, as there be gods many, and lords many, 6. but to us there is but one God, the Father, of whom are all things, and we in Him, and one Lord, Jesus Christ, by[1] whom are all things, and we by Him."[2]— Καὶ γάρ, *and indeed*. Paul affirms, in harmony with the Corinthians, that whatever may be the multiplicity of gods worshipped by the heathen, the Christian recognises only one God, Him whose character he here defines, and but one Lord, the Mediator between God and men. "The imagination of the Greeks," says Beet, "filled with divinities the visible and invisible heavens, and on earth, mountains, forests, and rivers." These are the λεγόμενοι θεοί, the beings designated by the name of gods and worshipped as such, but who, as the epithet indicates, have only the *name* of deity. The two

---

[1] B only reads δι' ὃν (*on account of whom*), instead of δι' οὗ (*by whom*).
[2] In some Fathers and Mnn. there is found the addition: "And one Holy Spirit, in whom are all things."

propositions which begin, the one with εἴπερ, *even though*, the other with ὥσπερ, *as indeed*, have been very variously understood, according as the two verbs εἰσί, *are*, which stand at the head of both, have been taken to denote a logical or a real existence. In the view of Rückert, Olshausen, Meyer, Kling, Hofmann, real existence is to be understood in both cases in this sense : " Even if (εἴπερ) the gods of mythology really exist (a supposition which is not absurd), agreeably to the fact that (ὥσπερ) there really exist gods and lords in abundance (the angels in their different orders enumerated by Paul, Eph. i. 21 ; Col. i. 16 ; comp. Deut. x. 17 and Ps. cxxxvi. 2, 3), even if such gods really exist, yet there is for us, Christians, only one God and one Lord." But it is not easy to explain clearly the relation between these two real existences, the former of which on this understanding is put as hypothetical, and then the second as certain, and which nevertheless both relate to one and the same subject. Others, like Chrysostom, Calvin, Beza, Neander, de Wette, regard these two existences as imaginary. " Even though (εἴπερ) the heathen worship a multitude of fictitious gods, as one may see, indeed (ὥσπερ), that according to them, every place is full of gods and lords. . . ." But de Wette himself cannot help seeing the useless tautology of these two propositions of really identical meaning. Commentators of a third view, like Grotius, Billroth, understand the former of the two εἰσί, *are*, in the sense of a real existence, the latter in that of an imaginary existence : " Even though there really exists a host of beings, such as the sky, the sun, the moon, the earth, the ocean, which are made gods, as it may be seen in fact that among the heathen these are deities." But with what view would the apostle thus insist on the reality of the creatures which heathenism had deified? If, as is exact, one of the two verbs should denote a real, the other a fictitious existence, is it not much more natural to interpret in the latter sense that one of the two εἰσί (*are*), which is accompanied by the participle λεγόμενοι, *called?* For this apposition undoubtedly does not force us (comp. 2 Thess. ii. 4) to attribute an imaginary character to these gods, but it permits and leads to it. In this case the following would be the meaning of the verse: "Even though there are in abundance beings called gods, and worshipped as such, with whom the imagination of the heathen peoples both heaven and earth (Jupiter, Apollo, Mars, Ceres, Bacchus, Nymphs), as in fact (ὥσπερ) there really exist—we must not be deceived on the point—gods many and lords many. . . ." By these last words the apostle means, that if the particular mythological deities are only fictions, there is yet behind these fictions a reality of which we must take account. In x. 20 he expressly declares, that "what the Gentiles sacrifice they sacrifice to demons;" not, certainly, that he regards the god Jupiter as one demon and the god Apollo as another; but in heathenism in general he recognises the work of malignant spirits, who have turned man away from God, and filled the void thus formed in the soul with this vain and impure phantasmagoria. It is in the same sense that he describes demons, Eph. vi. 12, as "rulers of the present darkness;" that he calls Satan, 2 Cor. iv. 4, the *god of this world* who blinds the unbelieving; and that Jesus

Himself calls him the *Prince of this world* (John xii. 31, xiv. 30). The term, *gods many*, refers to the heads of this kingdom of darkness; the term, *lords many*, to the inferior spirits, the subordinate agents; comp. in our Epistle xv. 24.—If criticism, such as is practised in our day, had the least interest in setting our Epistle in opposition to that of the Romans, how easy would it be for it to maintain by means of this passage, either that they proceed from two different authors, or that the apostle's ideas had become changed in the interval between the one and the other! In point of fact, the explanation which the apostle gives of the origin of heathenism in the Epistle to the Romans (chap. i.) is purely psychological, and leaves wholly out of account all influence exercised by superior beings. But the two explanations hold true together and complete one another. The apostle emphasizes in each Epistle that which is of importance to the subject he is treating; in Romans, where he wishes to bring out the corruption of mankind, he shows the *moral* origin of idolatry: how this great collective sin proceeded from the heart of man; in our Epistle, where he has in view certain practical rules to be drawn for the conduct of the Corinthians, he emphasizes the diabolical influence which concurred to produce heathenism. Is there not a lesson of prudence and wise reserve to be drawn from this fact for so many other analogous cases? It will be seen afterwards with what view the apostle here presents simultaneously these two aspects of the truth: on the one side, the nothingness of heathen divinities; and, on the other, the diabolical reality which is hidden under this empty phantasmagoria.

The first point of view will justify the liberty allowed in regard to the eating of offered *meats;* the second, the absolute prohibition against taking part in the idol *feasts.*

Ver. 6. With these fictitious, and yet, in a certain sense, real gods and lords, Paul forcibly contrasts by the adverb ἀλλά, *but,* and the pronoun ἡμῖν, *for us,* put first, the only God and the only Lord recognised by the Christian conscience. The title *the Father,* added to the word *God,* is taken in the absolute sense in which it embraces His Fatherhood both in relation to Christ and to us. The apostle here adds two notions: the proceeding of all things from God alone (ἐξ οὗ, *of whom*), and the moral consecration of believers to Him alone (εἰς αὐτόν, *for Him*). In such a context he cannot be intending to describe thereby His greatness and perfection; but he means that nothing of all that forms part of the universe created by such a Being (offered meats in particular) can defile the believer (x. 25, 26). How could that which is made by God prevent him from being and remaining for God what he ought to be? (see Hofmann).

As God, the Father, is contrasted with the principal heathen deities, *Christ, the Lord,* is so with the secondary deities who served as mediators between the great gods and the world. What Paul means is, that as the world is *from* God, and the Church *for* God; so the world is *by* Christ, and the Church also *by* Him.

The former of the two propositions relative to Christ: *by whom are all things,* can only apply, as is recognised by all the critics of our time, de Wette, Heinrici, Reuss, Meyer, and even Pfleiderer and Holtzmann, to the work of creation. Baur thinks that the διά may be referred in the first proposition, as well as in the second, to the work of redemption. But the ἡμεῖς, *we*, of the second proposition evidently contrasts Christians, as objects of redemption, with τὰ πάντα, *all things*, as objects of another work, which, as is shown by the previous proposition, can only be creation. Holsten, alone, cannot bring himself to this avowal. In the words, *all things by Him*, he finds only the idea of the government of all things by the glorified Christ. But the *by Him* corresponds to the *of Him* (ἐξ αὐτοῦ) of the previous proposition, and can consequently apply only to the same work, that of creation, of which God is the author and Christ the agent. It is the same thought as in Col. i. 15-17, where the ἐν corresponds to our διά, and as in John i. 3, where the δι' αὐτοῦ expresses the creation of all things *by* the Logos. The idea which Holsten finds in this proposition would, besides, be out of all relation to Paul's object, which is to show that a meat divinely created cannot separate man from God. The *Vaticanus*, instead of δι' οὗ, reads δι' ὅν, *on account of whom;* evidently the mistake of a copyist.—In the second proposition the word ἡμεῖς, *we*, contrasted with *all things*, shows that the subject in question is the spiritual creation accomplished by Christ, the work of salvation. These words have their commentary in Col. i. 18-22, as the preceding in Col. i. 15-17. They form the counterpart of the second preceding proposition relating to God. In the physical order we are *of* God and *by* Christ; in the spiritual order we are *by* Christ and *for* God.

We have already pointed out more than once how,

notwithstanding the diversity of forms, the views of Paul coincide with those of John. We have just seen this in connection with the regimen δι' οὗ, which so vividly reminds us of the δι' αὐτοῦ of John i. 3. This connection is equally striking if we compare from the Christological viewpoint this saying of Paul with John xvii. 3. In the two passages, the personal distinction between God and Christ is strongly emphasized, though the community of nature between both appears from this very distinction, and from all the rest of the books where these sayings are contained. Reuss maintains that there are in the Gospel of John two opposite theories going side by side; but we must in that case say the same of the writings of the Apostle Paul, whose rigorous logic no one disputes. In point of fact there is no contradiction in either; for both emphasize with the full consciousness of what they affirm the subordination of the Son in the unity of the Divine life; see on iii. 23.

Here we have one of the passages which establish the complete unity of the apostle's Christology in his first letters, and in those of his imprisonment (Col., Eph., Phil.). "Let there be an end then," says Gess rightly (*Apost. Zeugn.*, ii. p. 295), " to the assertion that the Christology of the later Epistles is contrary to that of Paul; according to which Christ, it is held, is nothing more than the ideal or celestial man, and that though one is forced to allow that our passage makes Him the mediator of the creation of the universe!"

Thus far, St. Paul would say, we are all at one, but here now is the point where difference begins, and this difference impresses the Christian who loves, with regard and sacrifices toward those whose judgment differs from his.

2. *Difference in knowledge, with the practical obligations arising from it* (vers 7-13).

Ver. 7. "Howbeit there is not in every man that knowledge. Some, through the habit[1] which they have to this[2] hour of [believing in] the idol, eat the meats as offered to the idol, and their conscience being weak is defiled."—The strong contrast indicated by the ἀλλ' οὐκ, *but not*, and by the place given at the opening of the sentence to the ἐν πᾶσιν, *in all* (opposed to ἡμῖν, *to us*, ver. 6), may be paraphrased as follows: "But this monotheistic knowledge possessed by us all has not yet unfolded in the consciousness of all its full consequences." At the first glance the opening words of this verse seem to contradict the assertion of ver. 1 ("we know that we all have knowledge"), and it was this supposed contradiction which led several critics to refer the words of ver. 1 only to the enlightened Christians of Corinth (Beza, Flatt, etc.), or to these with the addition of the apostle (Meyer). Ver. 7 in this case would refer to the weak Christians only, and would agree without difficulty with ver. 1. But in thus escaping from one contradiction, we fall into another. How, on this view, can we explain the πάντες, *all*, of ver. 1, having regard to the οὐκ ἐν πᾶσιν, *not in all*, of ver. 7 ? The *all* of ver. 1 would necessarily require to have been qualified by some restriction.

[1] א A B P Cop. Cyr. read συνηθεια (*the habit*), while T. R. with D E F G 4 Mnn. It. Syr^sch Vg. reads συνειδησει (*the consciousness*).

[2] The two words εως αρτι (*to this hour*) are placed by T. R. with A L P after του ειδωλου, while א B D E F G It. Syr^sch Cop. put them before.

Besides this, as de Wette observes, the apostle has just unfolded in ver. 6 the contents of the knowledge, and he has done so as speaking not in the name of some, but of *all* Christians (*we*, in opposition to the heathen). The apparent contradiction between vers. 1 and 7 must therefore be resolved differently. Account must be taken of two differences of expression. In ver. 1: *we all have;* here: *in all there is not;* in ver. 1: [some] *knowledge,* a certain knowledge (γνῶσις without article); in ver. 7, [the] *knowledge* (γνῶσις with the article): "All have the monotheistic knowledge in general (a certain knowledge, ver. 1); but *the* precise knowledge which is in question here (to wit, that heathen deities do not exist, and consequently cannot contaminate either the meats offered to them or those who eat them), this knowledge is not *in all,* has not yet penetrated the conscience of all to the quick, so as to free them from every scruple." How many truths do we possess, from having learned our catechism, the practical conclusions of which we are yet far from having drawn! How many people ridicule belief in ghosts, whom the fear of spirits terrifies when they find themselves alone in the night! The idolatrous superstitions are numerous which still exercise their influence on our monotheistic Christendom.—The *strong* among the Corinthians did not make this distinction between theoretic knowledge and its practical application; and hence it was that they thought themselves entitled to set aside all consideration for the weak: "Freedom to eat meats offered to idols follows logically from the monotheistic principle common to all; so much the worse for those of us who want logic! We are not called to put ourselves about for a brother who reasons badly." This was strong in logic, but weak in ἀγάπη (*love*). And hence it was that the apostle had introduced at the beginning of this chapter the short digression on the emptiness of knowledge without love.

There is room for hesitating between the reading of the T. R. : τῇ συνειδήσει, *through conscience*, after the Byz. and Greco-Lat.'s, the *Itala* and the *Peschito*, and that of the Alex. and of a later Syriac translation : τῇ συνηθείᾳ, *through habit*. Meyer, Heinrici, Holsten have returned, contrary to Tischendorf's authority (8th edition), to the received reading. They allege its difficulty. But is it not very improbable that the word συνήθεια, so rare in the New Testament (it is found only twice), has been substituted for the term συνείδησις, which occurs in this same verse and twice besides in this chapter? (vers. 10 and 12). As to the sense, συνείδησις, *conscience*, would denote the inward conviction of the *reality* of the idol, which in such persons has survived their conversion. The term συνήθεια denotes the *habit* which they have of regarding the idol as a real being. The words ἕως ἄρτι, *till now*, especially placed, as they are in most Mjj., before τοῦ εἰδώλου, apply naturally, not to the verb, but to the substantive which precedes, and agree perfectly with the notion of habit : a habit (which lasts) till now even after the new faith should have put an end to it. If this is the true reading, the conclusion is almost necessary that the persons in question were of heathen origin. The old prejudice, under the dominion of which they had lived, resisted logic. They could not imagine that the powers they had so long revered under the names of Zeus, Mars, Minerva, etc., had not some reality. Hence the meats offered on their altar could no longer be simple meats; they must have taken something of the malignant character of those beings themselves. And therefore the Christian who eats them in this character (ὡς εἰδωλόθυτον, *as sacrificed*) is *ipso facto* polluted.—What does the apostle mean by the expression *weak conscience?* The term συνείδησις, *conscience*, strictly denotes the *knowledge* which the *Ego* has of itself, as willing and doing good or evil (the moral conscience), and of itself in what it thinks and knows (the theoretical conscience).[1] It is the moral conscience which is here in question. It is weak, because a religious scruple, from which the gospel should have set it free, still binds it to beings which have no existence and hinders it from acting normally. Probably those former heathen, while adhering to belief in one God, still regarded their deities of other days, if not as gods, at least as terrible powers. The apostle adds that this conscience will be *defiled*, if the person eats of those meats in this state. In fact, this act remains upon it as a stain which separates from the holy God the man who has committed it while himself disapproving of it.

Vers. 8, 9. "Now meat commendeth[2] us not to God: for[3] neither,[4] if we eat, are we the better; neither,[4]

---

[1] See the development of this subject in Holsten, *Evangelium des Paulus*, t. i. p. 311.

[2] T. R. with D E L P reads παριστησι (*commendeth*), while א A B Cop. read παραστησει (*will commend*).

[3] א A B omit γαρ (*for*).

[4] We have followed in the order of these two propositions the reading of א D E F G L P It. Syr. ; the inverse order is followed by A B.

if we eat not, are we the worse. 9. But take heed lest by any means this liberty of yours become a stumbling-block to them that are weak."[1] — The transition between this verse and the foregoing is as follows: By eating such meats thou mayest therefore lead the weak brother to defile himself (ver. 8); but as for thyself thou hast nothing to gain, any more than thou hast to lose, by not eating. The conclusion is obvious.—The verb παριστάναι, *to present*, is often used of the presenting of offerings to God; comp. Rom. xii. 1, vi. 13, etc.; and if we read the verb in the present with the T. R., it is the most natural sense: "It is not in the power of meats to add anything to or take anything from the value which our consecration to His service has in the sight of God." If we read the future with the Alex., we must, like Holsten and others, apply the verb to the day of judgment; comp. 2 Cor. iv. 14; Rom. xiv. 10: "Meats will not make us stand before God in that day." This meaning is much more foreign to the context; for the threat will not come till later (vers. 11, 12). The parallels quoted in its favour prove nothing, the verb *present* being used in a wholly different relation. Here we have a general maxim, with which the present is in keeping. — Bengel, Meyer, Hofmann, in order to explain more easily the connection of this proposition with the two following alternatives, give the verb a morally indifferent meaning: "Meats determine our relation to God neither for good nor evil (*neque ad placendum, neque ad displicendum*, Bengel)." This sense would be more natural in the philosophical style

[1] T. R. with L: ἀσθενοῦσιν; all the rest: ἀσθενέσιν.

than in biblical language. The meaning which we have given may be suitable in the two following propositions; the privation of that which has no relation, causes no loss.—The order of the two following propositions in A B (see critical note) is condemned by the other Mjj. and by the ancient versions.—Calvin, Mosheim, and others have seen in this verse an objection of the Corinthians: "Meats not being able to procure either approval or condemnation, we may consequently act at will." Paul, they say, answers in ver. 9. But this argument would rather be opposed than favourable to the conduct of the strong. For if those meats neither caused them gain nor loss, but may through them cause their brother to sin (ver. 7), it is evident that they ought to abstain in cases where this last result may be produced. The consequence of ver. 8 therefore is, that no importance whatever is to be attached to those meats in themselves. Hence ver. 9: But there is importance in not causing one's brother to sin by means of those meats.

Ver. 9. The δέ is adversative: *but*. The term βλέπετε, *consider well*, is opposed to the lightness with which the Corinthians used their right.—In the word, ἐξουσία, *power, right*, here *liberty*, there is an allusion to the favourite formula of the strong at Corinth: "All things are lawful for me." The connection must be observed between ἐξουσία and ἔξεστι. —The pronoun αὕτη, *this liberty*, strongly contrasts this power, which is in itself an advantage, with the evil effects which it may produce when imprudently exercised. — And now from these general considerations the apostle comes to their application.

Vers. 10, 11. "For if any man see thee,[1] which hast knowledge, sit at meat in the idol's temple, shall not the conscience of him which is weak be emboldened to eat those things which are offered to idols? 11. And[2] so through[3] thy[4] knowledge thy weak brother[5] perisheth,[6] for whom Christ died."—The *for* indicates that here is the danger Paul had in view when he said: *Take heed!* in ver. 9.—This *any man* is one of the *some* of ver. 7.—The reading σέ, *thee*, must evidently be preferred to that of the Mjj., which omit this pronoun.—The term εἰδωλεῖον, the situation in which the idol is set up, is not common in classic Greek; it is not even mentioned in Passow's large dictionary. It was formed by Jewish writers (1 Maccab. i. 47, x. 83) on the model of the words βακχεῖον, ποσειδωνεῖον, temple of Bacchus, Neptune, etc.; the apostle no doubt uses it to avoid the word ναός (Edwards).—It is far from probable that one formerly a Jew would be found within the enclosure of an idolatrous temple, and still less that the sight of a Christian partaking of such a banquet would have inspired him with the desire to eat meats offered to the idol; this spectacle, on the contrary, would have filled him with horror. The weak brother is therefore, as we have said, rather a former heathen.—The term οὐκ

[1] B F G omit σε (*thee*).
[2] T. R. with D E F G L Syr. reads και (*and*); ℵ B: γαρ (*for*); A P: ουν (*therefore*).
[3] T. R. with L reads επι (*upon*); the rest εν (*in, through*).
[4] B omits ση (*thy*).
[5] T. R. with L P places the word αδελφος (*brother*) after ασθενων (*weak*), while the rest read ο αδελφος (*the brother*) and place these words after γνωσει (*knowledge*).
[6] T. R. with E F G L Syr. reads απολειται (*will perish*); ℵ B D P: απολλυται (*perishes*).

οἰκοδομηθήσεται, *will be edified*, [emboldened], is used with evident irony. It suffices to call to mind that the more advanced believer should by his superior knowledge have edified the other by enlightening his conscience and emancipating him from his false scruples, whereas by his imprudence he leads him to trample upon his conscience, and thus substitutes false edification for the true: he enlightens and strengthens him to his loss! Fine edification! It may appear surprising that Paul here lets the conduct of the strong Christian pass without calling his attention to the evil which he may do himself by taking part in such a banquet in such a place. But the apostle never wanders from his subject. His subject here is the self-denial imposed by love to our neighbour. He will afterwards (x. 15–21) treat the other side of the question, that concerning the danger to which the strong believer exposes himself.

Ver. 11. If we read *for*, with the two oldest Mjj., this particle refers to the ironical term *will be edified* [emboldened]: "edified, *for* as the fruit of it he perishes!" But it seems to me more natural simply to read, with all the other Mjj. and the *Peschito*, καί, in the sense of: *and so*. As to the tense of the verb, the present, *perisheth*, in the Alex. should be preferred to the future, *shall perish*, of the T. R. The apostle is thinking of the immediate effect: "He is from that moment in the way of perdition." An unfaithfulness, however small it may appear, separates the believer from his Lord; by interposing between the branch and the stock, it interrupts the communication of life which ought to take place from the one to the other. From that moment spiritual death commences, and if this state continues and becomes aggravated, as is inevitable in such a case, eternal perdition is the end of it; comp. Rom. xiv. 15. Every word of this verse has a force of its own: *cause to perish;* what success! A *weak brother;* what magnanimity! Through *knowledge*, which ought to have been used for his advancement; what fidelity in the use of grace received! A *brother* over whom thou shouldest have watched as over the apple of thine eye; what love! A man for love of whom *Christ* gave Himself to die; what gratitude!— It is this last particular, the sin against Christ, which the apostle more especially emphasizes as the gravest of all, in the following verse.

Vers. 12, 13. "But when ye sin so against the brethren, and wound their weak conscience, ye sin against Christ. 13. Wherefore, if meat make my[1] brother to offend, I will eat no flesh while the world standeth, lest I make my brother to offend."—Every violence done to a brother's conscience, even though he should not thereby be drawn into a deed of unfaithfulness, is a sin committed against Christ, whose work so painfully accomplished we compromise. Here again there is a marked force in every term: τύπτειν, strictly speaking, *to strike;* συνείδησις, *conscience,* the most sacred of things; ἀσθενοῦσα, *weak,* tottering with weakness, and consequently claiming the greatest regard; εἰς Χριστόν, *against Christ,* the highest of crimes.

Ver. 13. This thought of ver. 12 tells so vividly on the apostle's heart, that it inspires him with a sort of vow whereby he is ready to devote his whole life.

---

[1] D F G It. omit μου (*my*).

The διόπερ, *wherefore*, sums up all the grounds previously indicated, in particular that of ver. 12 : *against Christ.*—Instead of, *a* [kind of] meat, we ought logically to read, *this* [kind of] meat, or a [kind of] *flesh*. But the apostle generalizes the idea; though in the second part of the verse, by the use of the expression : *flesh*, he returns to the particular case. He employs the first person, because the sacrifice in question is one which a man may impose on himself, but which he has no right to impose on others. He would rather abstain from flesh all his life than by using it cause one of his brethren to fall even once.—Holsten well sums up the idea of the chapter thus : The strong sought the solution of the question from the standpoint of knowledge and its rights; the apostle finds it from the standpoint of love and its obligations.

The last words of this chapter evidently form the transition to the following passage, in which Paul continues to present to the Corinthians his own example, by reminding them of the great and constant voluntary sacrifice with which he accompanies the exercise of his apostleship. As Calvin observes to perfection (and such is the real transition from chap. viii. to chap. ix.) : " *Quia in futurum pollicendo non omnibus fecisset fidem, quid jam fecerit, allegat.*" To the contingent sacrifice of ver. 13 he adds, as a still more convincing example, the sacrifice which he has already made, and which he renews daily, his renunciation of all recompense from the Churches founded by him.

END OF VOLUME I.

GRIMM'S LEXICON.

Just published, in demy 4to, price 36s.,

GREEK-ENGLISH LEXICON OF THE NEW TESTAMENT,

BEING

Grimm's Wilke's Clavis Novi Testamenti.

TRANSLATED, REVISED, AND ENLARGED

BY

JOSEPH HENRY THAYER, D.D.,

BUSSEY PROFESSOR OF NEW TESTAMENT CRITICISM AND INTERPRETATION IN THE DIVINITY SCHOOL OF HARVARD UNIVERSITY.

EXTRACT FROM PREFACE.

'TOWARDS the close of the year 1862, the "Arnoldische Buchhandlung" in Leipzig published the First Part of a Greek-Latin Lexicon of the New Testament, prepared, upon the basis of the "Clavis Novi Testamenti Philologica" of C. G. Wilke (second edition, 2 vols. 1851), by Professor C. L. WILIBALD GRIMM of Jena. In his Prospectus Professor Grimm announced it as his purpose not only (in accordance with the improvements in classical lexicography embodied in the Paris edition of Stephen's Thesaurus and in the fifth edition of Passow's Dictionary edited by Rost and his coadjutors) to exhibit the historical growth of a word's significations, and accordingly in selecting his vouchers for New Testament usage to show at what time and in what class of writers a given word became current, but also duly to notice the usage of the Septuagint and of the Old Testament Apocrypha, and especially to produce a Lexicon which should correspond to the present condition of textual criticism, of exegesis, and of biblical theology. He devoted more than seven years to his task. The successive Parts of his work received, as they appeared, the outspoken commendation of scholars diverging as widely in their views as Hupfeld and Hengstenberg; and since its completion in 1868 it has been generally acknowledged to be by far the best Lexicon of the New Testament extant.'

'I regard it as a work of the greatest importance. . . . It seems to me a work showing the most patient diligence, and the most carefully arranged collection of useful and helpful references.'—THE BISHOP OF GLOUCESTER AND BRISTOL.

'The use of Professor Grimm's book for years has convinced me that it is not only unquestionably the best among existing New Testament Lexicons, but that, apart from all comparisons, it is a work of the highest intrinsic merit, and one which is admirably adapted to initiate a learner into an acquaintance with the language of the New Testament. It ought to be regarded as one of the first and most necessary requisites for the study of the New Testament, and consequently for the study of theology in general.'— Professor EMIL SCHÜRER.

'This is indeed a noble volume, and satisfies in these days of advancing scholarship a very great want. It is certainly unequalled in its lexicography, and invaluable in its literary perfectness. . . . It should, will, must make for itself a place in the library of all those students who want to be thoroughly furnished for the work of understanding, expounding, and applying the Word of God.'—*Evangelical Magazine.*

'Undoubtedly the best of its kind. Beautifully printed and well translated, with some corrections and improvements of the original, it will be prized by students of the Christian Scriptures.'—*Athenæum.*

T. and T. Clark's Publications.

Recently published, in demy 8vo, price 16s.,

HISTORY OF THE CHRISTIAN PHILOSOPHY OF RELIGION,
FROM THE REFORMATION TO KANT.

By BERNHARD PÜNJER.

Translated from the German by W. HASTIE, B.D.
With a Preface by Professor FLINT, D.D., LL.D.

'The merits of Pünjer's history are not difficult to discover; on the contrary, they are of the kind which, as the French say, *sautent aux yeux*. The language is a most everywhere as plain and easy to apprehend as, considering the nature of the matter conveyed, it could be made. The style is simple, natural, and direct; the only sort of style appropriate to the subject. The amount of information imparted is most extensive, and strictly relevant. Nowhere else will a student get nearly so much knowledge as to what has been thought and written, within the area of Christendom, on the philosophy of religion. He must be an excessively learned man in that department who has nothing to learn from this book.'—*Extract from the Preface.*

'Pünjer's "History of the Philosophy of Religion" is fuller of information on its subject than any other book of the kind that I have either seen or heard of. The writing in it is, on the whole, clear, simple, and uninvolved. The Translation appears to me true to the German, and, at the same time, a piece of very satisfactory English. I should think the work would prove useful, or even indispensable, as well for clergymen as for professors and students.'—Dr. HUTCHISON STIRLING.

'A book of wide and most detailed research, showing true philosophic grasp.'—Professor H. CALDERWOOD.

'We consider Dr. Pünjer's work the most valuable contribution to this subject which has yet appeared.'—*Church Bells.*

'Remarkable for the extent of ground covered, for systematic arrangement, lucidity of expression, and judicial impartiality.'—*London Quarterly Review.*

Just published, in Two Vols., in demy 8vo, price 21s.,

HANDBOOK OF BIBLICAL ARCHÆOLOGY.

By CARL FRIEDRICH KEIL,
DOCTOR AND PROFESSOR OF THEOLOGY.

Third Improved and Corrected Edition.

NOTE.—This third edition is virtually a new book, for the learned Author has made large additions and corrections, bringing it up to the present state of knowledge.

'This work is the standard scientific treatise on Biblical Archæology. It is a very mine of learning.'—*John Bull.*

'No mere dreary mass of details, but a very luminous, philosophical, and suggestive treatise. Many chapters are not simply invaluable to the student, but have also very direct homiletic usefulness.'—*Literary World.*

'A mine of biblical information, out of which the diligent student may dig precious treasures.'—*The Rock.*

'Keil's Biblical Archæology will be a standard work from the day of its appearance.'—*Presbyterian Review.*

Just published, in demy 8vo, price 10s. 6d.,

THE FORM OF THE CHRISTIAN TEMPLE.
Being a Treatise on the Constitution of the New Testament Church.

By THOMAS WITHEROW, D.D., LL.D.,
PROFESSOR OF CHURCH HISTORY IN MAGEE COLLEGE, LONDONDERRY.

'We welcome the appearance of another work from the scholarly pen of Dr. Witherow. . . . No such able discussion of the constitution of the New Testament Church has appeared for a long time.'—*The Witness.*

T. and T. Clark's Publications.

In Two Vols., demy 8vo.—Vol. I. now ready, price 10s. 6d.,

A NEW COMMENTARY ON
THE BOOK OF GENESIS.
By Professor FRANZ DELITZSCH, D.D.

MESSRS. CLARK have pleasure in intimating, that by special arrangement with the author they are publishing a translation of the Fifth Edition, thoroughly revised, and in large part re-written, of this standard Commentary. The learned author, who has for a generation been one of the foremost biblical scholars of Germany, and who is revered alike for his learning and his piety, has here stated with evident care his latest and most matured opinions.

'Thirty-five years have elapsed since Prof. Delitzsch's Commentary on Genesis first appeared; fifteen years since the fourth edition was published in 1872. Ever in the van of historical and philological research, the venerable author now comes forward with another fresh edition in which he incorporates what fifteen years have achieved for illustration and criticism of the text of Genesis. . . . We congratulate Prof. Delitzsch on this new edition, and trust that it may appear before long in an English dress. By it, not less than by his other commentaries, he has earned the gratitude of every lover of biblical science, and we shall be surprised if, in the future, many do not acknowledge that they have found in it a welcome help and guide.'—Professor S. R. DRIVER, in *The Academy*.

'The work of a reverent mind and a sincere believer, and not seldom there are touches of great beauty and of deep spiritual insight in it. The learning, it is needless to say, is very wide and comprehensive.'—*Guardian*.

Just published, in post 8vo, price 9s.,

THE TEXT OF JEREMIAH;
OR,
A Critical Investigation of the Greek and Hebrew, with the Variations in the LXX. Retranslated into the Original and Explained.

By Professor G. C. WORKMAN, M.A.,
VICTORIA UNIVERSITY, COBURG, CANADA.

WITH AN INTRODUCTION BY PROFESSOR F. DELITZSCH, D.D.

Besides discussing the relation between the texts, this book solves the difficult problem of the variations, and reveals important matter for the history, the interpretations, the correction, and the reconstruction of the present Massoretic text.

'A work of valuable and lasting service.'—Professor DELITZSCH.

Just published, in demy 8vo, price 7s. 6d.,

THE BOOK OF PSALMS.
The Structural Connection of the Book of Psalms both in single Psalms and in the Psalter as an organic whole.

By JOHN FORBES, D.D.,
PROFESSOR OF ORIENTAL LANGUAGES, ABERDEEN.

'One cannot but admire the keenness of insight and deftness of handling with which thought is balanced against thought, line against line, stanza against stanza, poem against poem. Only long familiarity and loving research could have given such skill and ease of movement. . . . A more suggestive, able, and original biblical monograph has not appeared recently, the contents and purport of which commend themselves more powerfully to believers in the Christian revelation and the inspiration of the Scriptures.'—*British and Foreign Evangelical Review*.

T. and T. Clark's Publications.

Just published, in demy 8vo, price 10s. 6d.,

THE JEWISH
AND
THE CHRISTIAN MESSIAH.
A STUDY IN THE EARLIEST HISTORY OF CHRISTIANITY.

By VINCENT HENRY STANTON, M.A.,
FELLOW, TUTOR, AND DIVINITY LECTURER OF TRINITY COLLEGE, CAMBRIDGE;
LATE HULSEAN LECTURER.

'Mr. Stanton's book answers a real want, and will be indispensable to students of the origin of Christianity. We hope that Mr. Stanton will be able to continue his labours in that most obscure and most important period, of his competency to deal with which he has given such good proof in this book.'—*Guardian.*

'We welcome this book as a valuable addition to the literature of a most important subject. . . . The book is remarkable for the clearness of its style. Mr. Stanton is never obscure from beginning to end, and we think that no reader of average attainments will be able to put the book down without having learnt much from his lucid and scholarly exposition.'—*Ecclesiastical Gazette.*

Now ready, Second Division, in Three Vols., 8vo, price 10s. 6d. each,

HISTORY OF THE JEWISH PEOPLE IN THE TIME OF OUR LORD.

By Dr. EMIL SCHÜRER,
PROFESSOR OF THEOLOGY IN THE UNIVERSITY OF GIESSEN.

TRANSLATED FROM THE SECOND EDITION (REVISED THROUGHOUT, AND GREATLY ENLARGED) OF '*HISTORY OF THE NEW TESTAMENT TIME.*'

The First Division, which will probably be in a single volume, is undergoing revision by the Author. (The Second Division is complete in itself.)

'Under Professor Schürer's guidance, we are enabled to a large extent to construct a social and political framework for the Gospel History, and to set it in such a light as to see new evidences of the truthfulness of that history and of its contemporaneousness. . . . The length of our notice shows our estimate of the value of his work.'—*English Churchman.*

'We gladly welcome the publication of this most valuable work.'—*Dublin Review.*

'Most heartily do we commend this work as an invaluable aid in the intelligent study of the New Testament.'—*Nonconformist.*

'As a handbook for the study of the New Testament, the work is invaluable and unique.'—*British Quarterly Review.*

Just published, in demy 8vo, price 10s. 6d.,

AN EXPLANATORY COMMENTARY ON ESTHER.

With Four Appendices,
CONSISTING OF
THE SECOND TARGUM TRANSLATED FROM THE ARAMAIC WITH NOTES, MITHRA, THE WINGED BULLS OF PERSEPOLIS, AND ZOROASTER.

By Professor PAULUS CASSEL, D.D., Berlin.

'A specially remarkable exposition, which will secure for itself a commanding position in Biblical literature. It has great charms from a literary and historical point of view.'—*Sword and Trowel.*

'A perfect mine of information.'—*Record.*

'It is manifestly the ready expression of a full and richly stored mind, dispensing the treasures accumulated by years of labour and research. . . . No one whose fortune it is to secure this commentary will rise from its study without a new and lively realization of the life, trials, and triumphs of Esther and Mordecai.'—*Ecclesiastical Gazette.*

T. and T. Clark's Publications.

LOTZE'S MICROCOSMUS.

Just published, in Two Vols., 8vo (1450 pages), SECOND EDITION, *price 36s.,*

MICROCOSMUS:
Concerning Man and his relation to the World.
By HERMANN LOTZE.
Translated from the German
By ELIZABETH HAMILTON AND E. E. CONSTANCE JONES.

'The English public have now before them the greatest philosophic work produced in Germany by the generation just past. The translation comes at an opportune time, for the circumstances of English thought, just at the present moment, are peculiarly those with which Lotze attempted to deal when he wrote his "Microcosmus," a quarter of a century ago. . . . Few philosophic books of the century are so attractive both in style and matter.'—*Athenæum.*

'These are indeed two masterly volumes, vigorous in intellectual power, and translated with rare ability. . . . This work will doubtless find a place on the shelves of all the foremost thinkers and students of modern times.'—*Evangelical Magazine.*

'Lotze is the ablest, the most brilliant, and most renowned of the German philosophers of to-day. . . . He has rendered invaluable and splendid service to Christian thinkers, and has given them a work which cannot fail to equip them for the sturdiest intellectual conflicts and to ensure their victory.'—*Baptist Magazine.*

'The reputation of Lotze both as a scientist and a philosopher, no less than the merits of the work itself, will not fail to secure the attention of thoughtful readers.'—*Scotsman.*

'The translation of Lotze's Microcosmus is the most important of recent events in our philosophical literature. . . . The discussion is carried on on the basis of an almost encyclopædic knowledge, and with the profoundest and subtlest critical insight. We know of no other work containing so much of speculative suggestion, of keen criticism, and of sober judgment on these topics.'—*Andover Review.*

In Two Vols., 8vo, price 21s.,

NATURE AND THE BIBLE:
LECTURES ON THE MOSAIC HISTORY OF CREATION IN ITS RELATION TO NATURAL SCIENCE.
By Dr. FR. H. REUSCH.
REVISED AND CORRECTED BY THE AUTHOR.
TRANSLATED FROM THE FOURTH EDITION BY KATHLEEN LYTTELTON.

'Other champions much more competent and learned than myself might have been placed in the field; I will only name one of the most recent, Dr. Reusch, author of "Nature and the Bible."'—The Right Hon. W. E. GLADSTONE.

'The work, we need hardly say, is of profound and perennial interest, and it can scarcely be too highly commended as, in many respects, a very successful attempt to settle one of the most perplexing questions of the day. It is impossible to read it without obtaining larger views of theology, and more accurate opinions respecting its relations to science, and no one will rise from its perusal without feeling a deep sense of gratitude to its author.'—*Scottish Review.*

'This graceful and accurate translation of Dr. Reusch's well-known treatise on the identity of the doctrines of the Bible and the revelations of Nature is a valuable addition to English literature.'—*Whitehall Review.*

'We owe to Dr. Reusch, a Catholic theologian, one of the most valuable treatises on the relation of Religion and Natural Science that has appeared for many years. Its fine impartial tone, its absolute freedom from passion, its glow of sympathy with all sound science, and its liberality of religious views, are likely to surprise all readers who are unacquainted with the fact that, whatever may be the errors of the Romish Church, its more enlightened members are, as a rule, free from that idolatry of the letter of Scripture which is one of the most dangerous faults of ultra-Protestantism.'—*Literary World.*

T. and T. Clark's Publications.

Just published, in post 8vo, price 7s. 6d.,

THE PREACHERS OF SCOTLAND FROM THE SIXTH TO THE NINETEENTH CENTURY.

TWELFTH SERIES OF CUNNINGHAM LECTURES.

BY W. G. BLAIKIE, D.D.,

PROFESSOR OF APOLOGETICS AND PASTORAL THEOLOGY, THE NEW COLLEGE, EDINBURGH.

'Exceedingly interesting and well worth reading both for information and pleasure. . . . A better review of Scottish preaching from an evangelical standpoint could not be desired.'—*Scotsman.*

Just published, in crown 8vo, price 3s. 6d.,

SECOND EDITION, REVISED.

THE THEOLOGY

AND

THEOLOGIANS OF SCOTLAND,

CHIEFLY OF THE

Seventeenth and Eighteenth Centuries.

Being one of the 'Cunningham Lectures.'

BY JAMES WALKER, D.D., CARNWATH.

'These pages glow with fervent and eloquent rejoinder to the cheap scorn and scurrilous satire poured out upon evangelical theology as it has been developed north of the Tweed.'—*British Quarterly Review.*

'We do not wonder that in their delivery Dr. Walker's lectures excited great interest; we should have wondered far more if they had not done so.'—Mr. SPURGEON in *Sword and Trowel.*

In Two Vols., 8vo, price 21s.,

A SYSTEM OF BIBLICAL THEOLOGY.

BY THE LATE

W. LINDSAY ALEXANDER, D.D., LL.D.,

PRINCIPAL OF THE THEOLOGICAL HALL OF THE CONGREGATIONAL CHURCHES IN SCOTLAND.

'A work like this is of priceless advantage. It is the testimony of a powerful and accomplished mind to the supreme authority of the Scriptures, a lucid and orderly exhibition of their contents, and a vindication, at once logical, scholarly, and conclusive, of their absolute sufficiency and abiding truthfulness. It is a pleasure to read lectures so vigorous and comprehensive in their grasp, so subtle in their dialect, so reverent in spirit, and so severely chaste in their style. There are scores of men who would suffer no loss if for the next couple of years they read no other book than this. To master it thoroughly would be an incalculable gain.'—*Baptist Magazine.*

'This is probably the most interesting and scholarly system of theology on the lines of orthodoxy which has seen the light.'—*Literary World.*

'This has been characterised as probably the most valuable contribution which our country has made to theology during the present century, and we do not think this an exaggerated estimate.'—*Scottish Congregationalist.*

'Oh, that Scotland and Congregationalism had many worthies like Dr. Lindsay Alexander! . . . The ripe man, full of rich experience and heavenly knowledge, will prize each leaf, and give himself a glorious drilling as he masters chapter by chapter.'—Mr. SPURGEON in *The Sword and Trowel.*

T. and T. Clark's Publications.

WORKS BY PROFESSOR I. A. DORNER.

Just published, in demy 8vo, price 14s.,

SYSTEM OF CHRISTIAN ETHICS.

BY DR. I. A. DORNER,
PROFESSOR OF THEOLOGY, BERLIN.

EDITED BY DR. A. DORNER.

TRANSLATED BY
PROFESSOR C. M. MEAD, D.D., AND REV. R. T. CUNNINGHAM, M.A.

'This noble book is the crown of the Systematic Theology of the author. . . . It is a masterpiece. It is the fruit of a lifetime of profound investigation in the philosophical, biblical, and historical sources of theology. The system of Dorner is comprehensive, profound, evangelical, and catholic. It rises into the clear heaven of Christian thought above the strifes of Scholasticism, Rationalism, and Mysticism. It is, indeed, comprehensive of all that is valuable in these three types of human thought.'—Professor C. A. BRIGGS, D.D.

'There rested on his whole being a consecration such as is lent only by the nobility of a thorough sanctification of the inmost nature, and by the dignity of a matured wisdom.'—Professor WEISS.

'This is the last work we shall obtain from the able pen of the late Dr. Dorner, and it may be said that it fitly crowns the edifice of his manifold labours.'—*Spectator.*

In Four Volumes, 8vo, price £2, 2s.,

A SYSTEM OF CHRISTIAN DOCTRINE.

'In all investigations the author is fair, clear, and moderate; . . . he has shown that his work is one to be valued, for its real ability, as an important contribution to the literature of theology.'—*Scotsman.*

'Had it been the work of an entire lifetime, it would have been a monument of marvellous industry and rare scholarship. It is a tribute alike to the genius, the learning, and the untiring perseverance of its author.'—*Baptist Magazine.*

'The work has many and great excellences, and is really indispensable to all who would obtain a thorough acquaintance with the great problems of theology. It is a great benefit to English students that it should be made accessible to them in their own language, and in a form so elegant and convenient.'—*Literary Churchman.*

In Five Volumes, 8vo, price £2, 12s. 6d.,

HISTORY OF THE DEVELOPMENT OF THE DOCTRINE OF THE PERSON OF CHRIST.

'So great a mass of learning and thought so ably set forth has never before been presented to English readers, at least on this subject.'—*Journal of Sacred Literature.*

In crown 8vo, price 4s. 6d.,

THE BIBLE

AN OUTGROWTH OF THEOCRATIC LIFE.

BY D. W. SIMON,
PRINCIPAL OF THE CONGREGATIONAL COLLEGE, EDINBURGH.

'A more valuable and suggestive book has not recently come into our hands.'—*British Quarterly Review.*

'This book will well repay perusal. It contains a great deal of learning as well as ingenuity, and the style is clear.'—*Guardian.*

'A book of absorbing interest, and well worthy of study.'—*Methodist New Connexion Magazine.*

'Dr. Simon's little book is worthy of the most careful attention.'—*Baptist.*

'We have read the book with much appreciation, and heartily commend it to all interested in the subject with which it deals.'—*Scottish Congregationalist.*

T. and T. Clark's Publications.

In extra 8vo, price 12s.,

THE PHILOSOPHICAL BASIS OF THEISM.

An Examination of the Personality of Man, to ascertain his Capacity to Know and Serve God, and the Validity of the Principles underlying the Defence of Theism.

By REV. SAMUEL HARRIS, D.D., LL.D.,
PROFESSOR OF SYSTEMATIC THEOLOGY, YALE COLLEGE.

BY THE SAME AUTHOR.

Just published, in extra 8vo, price 12s.,

THE SELF-REVELATION OF GOD.

This work is a re-statement of the evidence of the existence of God and of the reality of His revelation of Himself, as modified by and in harmony with the legitimate results of recent thought, and meeting scepticism in its present positions.

'In "The Philosophical Basis of Theism" Dr. Harris laid the foundation, in the present work he raises the superstructure, and in both he has done good service to philosophy and theology. His is a mind full of knowledge, and rich in ripe reflection on the methods and results won in the past, and on the problems of the present hour. His argument is always conducted with the most direct reference to the state of the question now, and the difficulties he endeavours to meet are not those which were current a century ago, or half a century ago, but those which are raised by the writings of such men as Herbert Spencer, Matthew Arnold, Frederic Harrison, and other leaders of thought at the present time.'—*Spectator.*

'We admire this work alike for its solid learning, its broad philosophical insight, its firm grasp of details, its luminous style, and its apt illustrations gathered from all branches of our literature. No student, who wishes to be fully abreast of the times, should be without this really great book.'—*Baptist Magazine.*

'The student who accepts Dr. Harris as his teacher will find himself in most efficient hands; and by thoroughly mastering this volume will save himself the trouble of perusing many others. Certainly it is a volume which no one interested in philosophy or apologetics can afford to neglect.'—*Expositor.*

Just published, in Two Vols., crown 8vo, price 16s.,

THE APOSTOLIC AND POST-APOSTOLIC TIMES.

Their Diversity and Unity in Life and Doctrine.

By G. V. LECHLER, D.D.

Third Edition, thoroughly Revised and Re-Written.

TRANSLATED BY A. J. K. DAVIDSON.

'In the work before us, Lechler works out this conception with great skill, and with ample historical and critical knowledge. He has had the advantage of all the discussions of these forty years, and he has made good use of them. The book is up to date; so thoroughly is this the case, that he has been able to make room for the results which have been won for the early history of Christianity by the discovery of the "Didachè," and of the discussions to which it has given occasion. Nor is it too much to say that Dr. Lechler has neglected nothing fitted to throw light on his great theme. The work is of the highest value.'—*Spectator.*

'It contains a vast amount of historical information, and is replete with judicious remarks. . . . By bringing under the notice of English readers a work so favourably thought of in Germany, the translator has conferred a benefit on theology.'—*Athenæum.*

'Scholars of all kinds will welcome this new edition of Dr. Lechler's famous work. It has for long been a standard authority upon the subject which it treats. . . . The book has not only been "revised," but actually "re-written" from end to end.'—*Literary World.*

T. and T. Clark's Publications.

Just published, in Three Vols., demy 8vo, price 31s. 6d.,

APOLOGETICS;
OR,
THE SCIENTIFIC VINDICATION OF CHRISTIANITY.

By J. H. A. EBRARD, Ph.D., D.D.,
PROFESSOR OF THEOLOGY IN THE UNIVERSITY OF ERLANGEN.

'The author of this work has a reputation which renders it unnecessary to speak in words of general commendation of his "Apologetics." . . . Dr. Ebrard takes nothing for granted. He begins at the beginning, laying his foundations deep and strong, and building upon them patiently and laboriously, leaving no gaps, no loose work, but adjusting each stone to its place and use.'—*Church Bells.*

'A work of quite unusual grasp and force among treatises of its class; and it cannot fail, in our opinion, to become one of the most valued translations to be found even in so important a series as that of Messrs. T. & T. Clark has now grown to be.'—*Literary Churchman.*

In crown 8vo, price 5s.,

BIBLICAL ESSAYS;
OR,
EXEGETICAL STUDIES
ON THE
BOOKS OF JOB AND JONAH, EZEKIEL'S PROPHECY OF GOG AND MAGOG, ST. PETER'S 'SPIRITS IN PRISON,' and the KEY TO THE APOCALYPSE.

By CHARLES H. H. WRIGHT, D.D.
OF TRINITY COLLEGE, DUBLIN; M.A. OF EXETER COLLEGE, OXFORD.

'Dr. Wright is favourably known as the author of the Bampton Lectures on the Prophet Zechariah, and the Donnellan Lectures on Ecclesiastes. These Essays are marked by the same qualities—solid scholarship, careful and sober criticism, and a style which is pure and lucid.'—*Church Bells.*

'We are glad to receive "studies" so learned in the best sense of the word as these, so broad and philosophical in their grasp, so able in their treatment, and so lucid in their style.'—*Baptist Magazine.*

In demy 8vo, price 10s. 6d.,

SYSTEM OF THE CHRISTIAN CERTAINTY.

By Dr. FR. H. R. FRANK,
PROFESSOR OF THEOLOGY IN THE UNIVERSITY OF ERLANGEN.

Translated from the Second Edition, Revised and Improved throughout,
By REV. MAURICE J. EVANS, B.A.

'To study this volume as it deserves would be the task of months; but even a hasty perusal has convinced us that no weightier or more valuable theological work has come to us from Germany since the publication of Dr. Dorner's "Christian Doctrine."'—*Literary World.*

'Dr. Frank's work is valuable to theologians of every type of thought.'—*Scottish News.*

'Scarcely any praise could be excessive of the penetrativeness of the discussions in this book, and of the value which they have for the theological student.'—*United Presbyterian Magazine.*

T. and T. Clark's Publications.

WORKS BY PATON J. GLOAG, D.D.

Just published, in demy 8vo, price 10s. 6d.,

INTRODUCTION TO THE CATHOLIC EPISTLES.

'Dr. Gloag, whilst courteous to men of erudition who differ from him, is firm and fearless in his criticism, and meets the erudition of others with an equal erudition of his own. He has displayed all the attributes of a singularly accomplished divine in this volume, which ought to be eagerly welcomed as a solid contribution to theological literature; it is a work of masterly strength and uncommon merit.'—*Evangelical Magazine.*

'We have here a great mass of facts and arguments relevant in the strictest sense to the subject, presented with skill and sound judgment, and calculated to be of very great service to the student.'—*Literary Churchman.*

In crown 8vo, price 5s.,

EXEGETICAL STUDIES.

'Careful and valuable pieces of work.'—*Spectator.*
'A very interesting volume.'—*Literary Churchman.*
'Dr. Gloag handles his subjects very ably, displaying everywhere accurate and extensive scholarship, and a fine appreciation of the lines of thought in those passages with which he deals.'—*Baptist.*
'Candid, truth-loving, devout-minded men will be both instructed and pleased by studies so scholarly, frank, and practical.'—*Baptist Magazine.*

In crown 8vo, price 7s. 6d.,

THE MESSIANIC PROPHECIES,

BEING THE BAIRD LECTURE FOR 1879.

'It has seldom fallen to our lot to read a book which we think is entitled to such unqualified praise as the one now before us. Dr. Gloag has displayed consummate ability.'—*London Quarterly Review.*

'We regard Dr. Gloag's work as a valuable contribution to theological literature. We have not space to give the extended notice which its intrinsic excellence demands, and must content ourselves with cordially recommending it to our readers.'—*Spectator.*

In demy 8vo, price 12s.,

INTRODUCTION TO THE PAULINE EPISTLES.

'A work of uncommon merit. He must be a singularly accomplished divine to whose library this book is not a welcome and valuable addition.'—*Watchman.*

In Two Volumes, 8vo, price 21s.,

A CRITICAL AND EXEGETICAL COMMENTARY
ON
THE ACTS OF THE APOSTLES.

'This commentary of Dr. Gloag's I have examined with special care. For my purposes I have found it unsurpassed by any similar work in the English language. It shows a thorough mastery of the material, philology, history, and literature pertaining to this range of study, and a skill in the use of this knowledge which places it in the first class of modern expositions.'—*H. B. Hackett, D.D.*

T. and T. Clark's Publications.

PROFESSOR GODET'S WORKS.
(Copyright, by arrangement with the Author.)

Just published, in Two Volumes, demy 8vo, price 21s.,

A COMMENTARY ON
ST. PAUL'S FIRST EPISTLE TO THE CORINTHIANS.

By F. GODET, D.D.,
PROFESSOR OF THEOLOGY, NEUCHATEL.

'We do not know any better commentary to put into the hands of theological students.'—*Guardian.*

'We heartily commend this work to our readers as a valuable and substantial addition to the literature of this noble Epistle.'—*Homiletic Magazine.*

'A perfect masterpiece of theological toil and thought. . . . Scholarly, evangelical, exhaustive, and able.'—*Evangelical Review.*

In Three Volumes, 8vo, price 31s. 6d.
(A New Edition, revised throughout by the Author.)

A COMMENTARY ON
THE GOSPEL OF ST. JOHN.

'This work forms one of the battle-fields of modern inquiry, and is itself so rich in spiritual truth that it is impossible to examine it too closely; and we welcome this treatise from the pen of Dr. Godet. We have no more competent exegete, and this new volume shows all the learning and vivacity for which the author is distinguished.'—*Freeman.*

In Two Volumes, 8vo, price 21s.,

A COMMENTARY ON
THE GOSPEL OF ST. LUKE.

'Marked by clearness and good sense, it will be found to possess value and interest as one of the most recent and copious works specially designed to illustrate this Gospel.'—*Guardian.*

In Two Volumes, 8vo, price 21s.,

A COMMENTARY ON
ST. PAUL'S EPISTLE TO THE ROMANS.

'We prefer this commentary to any other we have seen on the subject. . . . We have great pleasure in recommending it as not only rendering invaluable aid in the critical study of the text, but affording practical and deeply suggestive assistance in the exposition of the doctrine.'—*British and Foreign Evangelical Review.*

In crown 8vo, Second Edition, price 6s.,

DEFENCE OF THE CHRISTIAN FAITH.
TRANSLATED BY THE
Hon. AND REV. CANON LYTTELTON, M.A.,
RECTOR OF HAGLEY.

'There is trenchant argument and resistless logic in these lectures; but withal, there is cultured imagination and felicitous eloquence, which carry home the appeals to the heart as well as the head.'—*Sword and Trowel.*

T. and T. Clark's Publications.

HISTORY OF THE CHRISTIAN CHURCH.
By PHILIP SCHAFF, D.D., LL.D.
New Edition, Re-written and Enlarged.

APOSTOLIC CHRISTIANITY, A.D. 1–100. Two Vols. Ex. demy 8vo, price 21s.

ANTE-NICENE CHRISTIANITY, A.D. 100–325. Two Vols. Ex. demy 8vo, price 21s.

NICENE and POST-NICENE CHRISTIANITY, A.D. 325–600. Two Vols. Ex. demy 8vo, price 21s.

MEDIÆVAL CHRISTIANITY, A.D. 590–1073. Two Vols. Ex. demy 8vo, price 21s. (Completion of this Period, 1073–1517, in preparation.)

MODERN CHRISTIANITY. The German Reformation, A.D. 1517–1530. Two Vols. Ex. demy 8vo, price 21s.

'Dr. Schaff's "History of the Christian Church" is the most valuable contribution to Ecclesiastical History that has ever been published in this country. When completed it will have no rival in point of comprehensiveness, and in presenting the results of the most advanced scholarship and the latest discoveries. Each division covers a separate and distinct epoch, and is complete in itself.'

'No student, and indeed no critic, can with fairness overlook a work like the present, written with such evident candour, and, at the same time, with so thorough a knowledge of the sources of early Christian history.'—*Scotsman.*

'In no other work of its kind with which I am acquainted will students and general readers find so much to instruct and interest them.'—Rev. Prof. HITCHCOCK, D.D.

'A work of the freshest and most conscientious research.'—Dr. JOSEPH COOK, in *Boston Monday Lectures.*

'Dr. Schaff presents a connected history of all the great movements of thought and action in a pleasant and memorable style. His discrimination is keen, his courage undaunted, his candour transparent, and for general readers he has produced what we have no hesitation in pronouncing *the* History of the Church.'—*Freeman.*

Just published in ex. 8vo, Second Edition, price 9s.,

THE OLDEST CHURCH MANUAL
CALLED THE
Teaching of the Twelve Apostles.

The Didachè and Kindred Documents in the Original, with Translations and Discussions of Post-Apostolic Teaching, Baptism, Worship, and Discipline, and with Illustrations and Fac-Similes of the Jerusalem Manuscript.

By PHILIP SCHAFF, D.D., LL.D.
PROFESSOR IN UNION THEOLOGICAL SEMINARY, NEW YORK.

'The best work on the Didachè which has yet appeared.'—*Churchman.*

'Dr. Schaff's "Oldest Church Manual" is by a long way the ablest, most complete, and in every way valuable edition of the recently-discovered "Teaching of the Apostles" which has been or is likely to be published. . . . Dr. Schaff's Prolegomena will henceforth be regarded as indispensable. . . . We have nothing but praise for this most scholarly and valuable edition of the Didachè. We ought to add that it is enriched by a striking portrait of Bryennios and many other useful illustrations.'—*Baptist Magazine.*

www.ingramcontent.com/pod-product-compliance
Lightning Source LLC
Chambersburg PA
CBHW022141300426
44115CB00006B/287